THE ZOO

'Barrie' Barrington-Johnson has been fascinated by animals and by London Zoo since he was a boy. He studied zoology to BSc level and has been a Fellow of ZSL (Zoological Society of London) since the age of 21. He is one of the original zoo volunteers, a member of the Society's Education Committee and was on the Society's Council for fourteen years. He also chaired the committee which proposed the way forward for London Zoo after the difficult financial period of 1990/1.

Sir Stamford Raffles, Founder and first President of the Zoological Society of London (© ZSL)

THE ZOO

The Story of London Zoo

J. Barrington-Johnson

Robert Hale · London

Typeset by e-type, Liverpool
Printed in Singapore by Kyodo

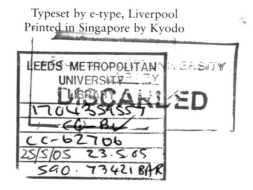

Contents

I dedicate this book to the memory of my mother who, many years ago, did so much to encourage my interest in animals and London Zoo

Acknowledgements

I acknowledge the advice and encouragement given by many of the staff of ZSL, but in particular by Claire Robinson, Head of Visitor Information and Education, Roger Tomlinson, Animal Activities Manager, and Paul Pearce-Kelly, Curator, Invertebrates. I am indebted to Clinton Keeling, past member of ZSL Council, for reading the draft of this book and correcting several errors, and to Sheila Anderson, Ken Sims and Harry Wilkinson, members of ZSL Council, and Dr Jo Gipps, former Director of London Zoo, for their encouragement.

Last, but by no means least, my wife for her tolerance of my many absences during fifty-five years of visits to the Zoo.

I also thank the following for allowing the inclusion of excerpts from their books:

The Lutterworth Press – *The Zoo Quest Expeditions* by Sir David Attenborough; HarperCollins – *Memories* by Sir Julian Huxley, published by George Allen & Unwin; ZSL – *Centenary History of the Zoological Society of London* by Sir Peter Chalmers Mitchell.

Picture Credits

In addition to the Zoological Society of London (ZSL), illustrations have also been made available by:

The National Monuments Record
The Natural History Museum, London
Roger Tomlinson, Animal Activities Manager, ZSL
Dave Clarke, Team Leader, Invertebrate Conservation Section, ZSL
Mike McQueen and Tony Dennett

and my especial thanks to Colin Whyman for his generosity in time and costs while taking many photographs for inclusion, at both London Zoo and Whipsnade Wild Animal Park

Foreword

London Zoo, and the Zoological Society of London (ZSL) of which it forms such an integral part, has had a chequered history – of this, there can be little doubt. But about which organization that has existed for 168 years could this not be said?

There have been some supremely high points, and some depressingly low ones. I joined London Zoo as Curator of Mammals in 1988, just a few years before the major financial crises of 1990 and 1991, and I became Director in March 1993, when things were better, but the future was by no means clear. So the author of this book and I have both lived through good times and bad at ZSL.

Perhaps, therefore, I am somewhat biased, but what this fascinating book shows so clearly is that organizations like London Zoo, as part of a larger zoological institution like ZSL, *can* bounce back from crisis and go on to thrive. In the case of ZSL, the unique combination of an urban zoo in the capital, an open, country zoo (at Whipsnade in Bedfordshire), a major zoological research institute devoted to conservation science, and an active field conservation programme, collectively impart great strength and resilience in depth – the whole is truly greater than the sum of the parts.

What matters is whether the accumulated sum of all the good and bad elements of an organization's history is positive or negative. I believe that, for ZSL, the answer to this question is undoubtedly the former – the world is surely a better place for its existence – both animals and humans have benefited greatly as a result of its long (and chequered) history.

In this comprehensive account of the history of arguably the world's most famous zoo (can anyone suggest a shorter address than 'London Zoo' that would guarantee delivery by any post office in the world?), Barrie has covered all the highs and lows, and the story is immensely rich. The world's first Reptile House (1849), first public Aquarium (1853), the only Quagga ever photographed, first Insect House (1881), first Children's Zoo (1938), first 'open' zoological park at Whipsnade, and many other landmark events in the history of the world zoo community, mean that ZSL has earned an undoubted leading place in the intellectual development of zoological institutions worldwide.

It continues to be a world leader, particularly with respect to scientific research for conservation and support for conservation activity in the wild.

The recently established collaborative relationship with the Wildlife Conservation Society (which owns and runs the Bronx and other zoos, and which has the most extensive field conservation programme of any zoo in the world) has created a truly powerful and effective conservation and science partnership, with the added commitment to public education and inspiration.

In 2005, the World Association of Zoos and Aquariums, whose Conservation Committee I am privileged to chair, will deliver the World Zoo and Aquarium Conservation Strategy, for the use of zoos worldwide. This document has been written and compiled by a large number of contributors from around the world, and will articulate the ways in which the world's zoos, working collaboratively, will make their contribution to saving biological diversity for future generations.

The task is huge and daunting – wildlife and wild places are under immense pressure wherever on the planet you care to look, and there are no grounds for great optimism – but we cannot give up and admit defeat; as Confucius said 'It is better to light one small candle than to curse the darkness.' As this fine book shows, London Zoo and ZSL have an excellent record in the candle-lighting department, and long may it continue.

Dr Jo Gipps
Director of Bristol Zoo Gardens

Preface

My earliest memories are of animals, in which I have had a keen interest all my life. My mother first took me to London Zoo at an early age, and by the time I went to school this had become an annual pilgrimage during the summer holidays; it was the thing I most looked forward to all year.

The Zoo was very different then from now. It did not concentrate on animal conservation, the need for which had not in the 1930s yet become apparent, and it was relatively easy to obtain animals for the Zoo although many of the cages would now be considered quite unsuitable, but the visitor was able to see a huge variety of animals and I was avid to see and learn about them; I was thrilled to see the many weird and wonderful animals that were visible in the Zoo. My family moved away from London at the start of the war and I was unable to visit London Zoo until our return when I was 17, but I then visited it every weekend (except for one week spent at Whipsnade Zoo) until I was called up for national service a year later.

It was after the end of the war, when I was serving in occupied Germany, that I spotted a book in the Salvation Army library, *The Zoo You Knew?* by L.R. Brightwell, and reading this I realized for the first time just how old London Zoo was and what an interesting, and at times amusing, history it had. At the age of 21 I became a Fellow of the Zoological Society of London, which owns London Zoo, and in the years that followed I not only came to love the Zoo as well as its inmates, but also was able to add to my knowledge of its story. However, it was not until my retirement years later (from work quite unrelated to the animal world in which I was so interested) that I had sufficient time to research this book, which I wanted to write in order to bring to other people the story that I found so fascinating.

To do so has required much research in books, the Society's Council Minutes, Committee notes et cetera, as well as discussions with keepers and other staff. There are many things I have omitted from the book, not only because to include them all would require a second volume, but also because I have decided to select only those occurrences which I feel to be of general interest or amusement, although I have diverged occasionally to include some interesting animal fact related to the main story. Nor have I kept everything in strict date order, although the story does progress from the Zoo's beginnings, through time to the present day. The illustrations, selected partly from the thousands kept in the Society's vast library, have been chosen to add some-thing to the text, and the addition of a selection of Zoo plans may also help to bring the written word to life.

I suppose a more correct title would be 'The History of London Zoo', but personally I found History a rather dull subject at school – and I trust you will not find this book dull! The study of zoos and their histories has become a hobby in itself for a select few enthusiasts, and I hope they will not frown on the popular presentation of this light work. But I hope that you, whether an occasional visitor to the Zoo or a youngster as keen to embark on the study of animals as I was all those years ago, will gain not only a new insight into the oldest Zoo in the world intended for the study of living animals, but also much pleasure as you turn these pages.

Let me not delay you any longer.

1 Raffles

With a fair wind blowing, the *Fame* was 50 miles out from land when the cry of 'Fire! Fire!' was shouted by the watch. That cry struck terror in the wooden ship and the lifeboats were hastily launched. All the crew and the passengers escaped from the burning ship but the fire had quickly spread.

Raffles was heartbroken. As he wrote of the disaster: 'Everything, absolutely everything, perished.' For five years he had been living in Sumatra, at Fort Marlborough, as Lieutenant-Governor. He was an enthusiastic naturalist and had, during those five years, amassed a large collection of mammals, reptiles and birds to add to his many documents, diaries and over two thousand drawings of animals. All this great collection was lost in the fire, but, having got back safely to Sumatra, at the age of 42 and in ill health he set about amassing a second collection, which was to form the basis of the first scientific zoo in the world and an internationally renowned institution.

Sir Thomas Stamford Raffles, best known as the colonial administrator who founded Singapore, was born at sea off Jamaica on 5 July 1781 on board a merchant ship commanded by his father. When he was ten years old his father died, and his mother brought him to England with his brothers and sisters. He became a clerk in the offices of the East India Company when he was only 14, and ten years later he was sent to Penang as Assistant Secretary to the first Governor. He also acted as a Malay interpreter, having learned the language during his long journey from England. Within two years he was promoted to Secretary.

His health began to suffer the following year so he was posted to Malacca in Malaya. Despite his many duties and his poor health, his interest in living things had been flourishing. One of his discoveries in Malaya was a family of fungi which were parasitic on the roots of vines. One of these fungi has the largest 'flower' known, measuring 18 inches across and weighing 15 pounds, but smelling of rotting meat. It was named the 'Rafflesia' after him. Another of his discoveries was the clouded leopard, one of the most strikingly marked of the big cats.

By carrying out his duties in a most efficient manner, Raffles impressed his employers and in 1812 he was appointed Lieutenant-Governor of Java, a post he held for four and a half years before coming to England on leave for the first time. Although he returned to the Far East for a further seven years (during which time he founded Singapore), it was on his year's leave in England that his great idea was born.

He had arrived in an England that had a growing interest in science. The Royal Society had been founded 150 years earlier to promote 'natural knowledge', but had by now become lethargic; other, more specialized, Societies had been or were being formed – the Linnæan Society, the Geological Society, and the Royal Astronomical Society. Amateur naturalists were numerous but there was at that time no such person as a 'professional' zoologist.

Small travelling menageries toured the countryside in those days, exhibiting such animals as a lion in a tiny cage, monkeys on leads and dancing bears; the latter were taught to 'dance' by being made to walk on hot coals while a violin played, after which training they would associate the sound of a violin with sore paws and 'dance'. Regrettably this practice has not yet died out in some Middle Eastern countries.

There were in England a few permanent collections of popular animals, kept under very poor conditions for the money they could earn from visitors. One of the largest collections was Exeter 'Change in London's Strand, a cramped, two-tier line of small cages around the walls containing a lion, tiger, leopard and bear, and, above them, a porcupine, monkeys and birds. At the end was a cage containing an elephant; the elephant eventually 'went berserk' and was shot – though it took 152 bullets to kill the poor animal. The proprietor was an animal dealer named Cross who at least deserves to be remembered as having allowed a certain young child to play with some of his animals. Thus began the animal education of Abraham Bartlett, one day to become famous as the Superintendent of London Zoo for many years; his story is told later.

Another menagerie was that owned by the King in the Tower of London, started as long ago as 1245. The polar bear there was later allowed into the Thames on the end of a rope to fish for its own food. At one time there was a 'Keeper of the Royal Lions'; these lions were kept near the (still so-named) Lion Gate of the Tower and when, later still, the public was allowed into the menagerie, a visitor could save the 1½ pence admission fee by giving a dog or cat to be fed to the lions! Bull-baiting and cock-fighting were still common, and one showman, George Wombwell, even tried to stage a fight between a lion (of which at one time he had twenty) and six mastiffs.

Such was the England to which Raffles returned for a year. As an ardent naturalist, he saw animals not as creatures to be kept only for amusement and profit, but as a source of wonder, and he discussed enthusiastically with friends his idea that a scientific study of them should be carried out by those interested in them and their varied ways of living.

While on leave, Raffles visited the Jardin des Plantes in Paris, first formed in 1626 as a herb garden, then extended to cover a great variety of plants and trees, and by the end of the eighteenth century including animals, thus making it probably the greatest living museum then in existence. He was impressed by this natural science collection, but, with his personal knowledge of exotic animals, realized how little even the Jardin des Plantes did to demonstrate the variety of animal life in the world as their animal collection at that time was little more than another menagerie of a few common animals. He was fired up by the thought of how wonderful it would be to set up a 'garden' devoted to animals, where natural historians could, for the first time, see and study animals from all corners of the world. As he later wrote to his cousin:

> I am much interested in establishing a Grand Zoological collection in the Metropolis, with a Society for the introduction of living animals, bearing the same relations to Zoology as a science as the Horticultural Society does for Botany.

Had he not been so enthusiastic, it is doubtful whether, when he lost his entire collection of notes, sketches and animals in the ship's fire, he would have continued with his plans, but for seven years after his leave he had nursed his idea and now, having no official duties to perform while awaiting another ship, he spent a year forming a second animal collection and eventually sailed with it to London in 1824.

He was to live only for another two years, but in that time he would found an institution which is still respected throughout the zoological world to this day.

By this time in his life, Raffles had been knighted and was a well-respected man with some influential friends. He was a Fellow of the Royal Society, and discussed his idea with its President, Sir Humphry Davy, now best remembered for his invention of the miners' safety lamp, but probably the greatest chemist of his day. Davy became equally enthusiastic and the two men set up a committee of twenty influential people, with Raffles as Chairman, who called themselves 'friends of a proposed Zoological Society'. Such was their influence that even the Prince Regent became interested.

A subscription list was opened and a prospectus issued which stated that the object was not only to

> … establish a Society bearing the same relation to Zoology and animal life that the Horticultural Society bears to Botany and the vegetable kingdom …

but also, astonishingly, to

... attempt the introduction of new races of quadrupeds, birds or fishes, etc., applicable to purposes of utility.

The latter statement seems to have been added at Davy's insistence and may have put off many potential subscribers. One correspondent to a journal popular at the time wrote: 'What the dickens does this assertion mean? Are we to have animals that never existed before?' Some 150 people each subscribed £3 to join and £2 for the annual subscription – quite a considerable sum in those days, as by 2001 £3 would have been equivalent to £140 – and although Raffles was disappointed at the response, it was sufficient to launch the new Society.

Raffles, elected the first President, was concerned that the Society be primarily for scientific purposes and the study of animals, but Davy was more insistent on its immediate practical uses. Although one of the purposes embodied in the Society's Royal Charter, granted three years later, was 'the introduction of new and curious subjects of the Animal Kingdom', nothing was achieved in this direction. However, with a fast-growing population, the possibility of increasing food production caught the imagination of the people who mattered, and it was possibly this aspect which resulted in the Crown leasing a tiny area of Regent's Park's 400 acres to the new Society. They were given about five acres altogether, although they had asked for twenty.

While the general public was shortly to become enthusiastic, as yet it knew little of the project, but the increasingly frequent comments in newspapers and journals of the day (often scathing) did much to give it publicity. Now that the prospect was becoming a reality, letters appeared in the press, calling the proposed collection of animals 'an Ark in London', and the Zoological Society the 'Noah's Ark Society'. Interest, or curiosity, was growing, and the stage was set for the first truly scientific zoo in the world.

But Raffles was never to see it materialize. He had presided over only two meetings when, in 1826, the very year in which his ten-year dream was taking shape and the Zoological Society of London was founded, he died of apoplexy (which we now call a stroke) on 5 July – his 45th birthday.

2 Beginnings

To spend a day at London Zoo is nowadays so easy that it is difficult for us to appreciate that in 1826 it was almost impossible for most people living more than 10 miles away. There were no buses or trams, even horse-drawn ones, and a railway network was still a thing of the future, the first passenger line (12 miles long) having opened only the previous year in the north of England. Most roads were still rutted dirt tracks as McAdam's development 30 years before was only gradually being introduced. Just six of the present 14 bridges spanned the Thames in Greater London, and it was still easier to travel from the City of London to Westminster by boat than to try to walk along the Strand! For those who could afford them, horses were the most usual form of transport, either by riding on them or by travelling in horse-drawn cabs. When travelling long distances, stagecoaches were most uncomfortable; only the newest ones had springs, and the cobblestones in towns and the ruts in country roads deterred people from making any journey but the most essential.

Greater London had a population less than a quarter of its present numbers, and for most of them travel after dark was difficult and even dangerous. Faraday was only now experimenting with electricity, so candles and oil lamps were used for lights in houses, and gas was the source of lighting for only a few of the principal streets, so lanterns had to be carried by pedestrians not wishing to walk in the dark. Sir Robert Peel was not to form a police force until three years later, and thieves, pickpockets and footpads were not uncommon, even in daylight, particularly in open spaces like Regent's Park.

The park had been called Marylebone Fields until a few years earlier. Camden Town was isolated from Central London by fields, and Primrose Hill really did have primroses in its hedgerows, which swept right down to the bank of the canal near the site of the proposed zoo. George IV had intended, in 1822, when he was Prince Regent, to build a palace in Marylebone Fields. He instructed John Nash to design some impressive houses at the entrance (the

Regency Terrace) and an equally impressive approach road (Regent Street), and to design the park with a lake. These were completed in 1823, but the palace was never built; instead the Queen's House, built for Queen Anne, was reconstructed, and it was renamed Buckingham Palace.

Against this background it is astonishing that, under the travel circumstances of the time, it was possible to transport animals from around the world to arrive, still alive, at the Gardens. A journey that can now be completed in one day, with the animals' correct food being provided, back then took many weeks, with no refrigeration to keep the food fresh. Unlike the few other animal collections, such as the private one at Schönbrunn in Austria, the Gardens of the new Zoological Society were conceived for the scientifically minded only and there was no thought of opening the Gardens to the public. So for almost twenty years the Zoo was open only to the Friends (or Fellows, as they later called themselves) and their acquaintances and, indeed, even after that first year, the Gardens were open to the public for only two days each week.

Enthusiasm, and perhaps a lack of appreciation of the many problems which lay ahead of them, propelled the Friends at their first meeting in April 1826. They elected a Council of 18 Fellows, plus the President, Secretary and Treasurer, as the controlling and organizing body, and to this day the Council of 21 still performs these functions, although their responsibilities have grown enormously over the intervening years. The Council held its first meeting in May, and found a house in which to set up offices in Bruton Street, near Bond Street, in the centre of London. As the Society was intended for zoological research, the Council planned to create:

1. a museum, to be the centre for classifying animals and maintaining a 'standard' specimen of each one;
2. a library, to build up and centralize zoological knowledge;
3. a collection of living animals for observation and study.

The museum was to thrive for only a few years, although from the start it grew fast with donations of dead animals from many people. But space to house the collection quickly became a major problem, with the dead museum specimens vastly outnumbering the living animals. By 1836 there were six hundred mounted fishes alone, and nearly a thousand specimens of all types of animal waiting to be mounted. The museum was housed in the Society's offices in Bruton Street, and originally some of the living animals had also to be kept here, both inside the building and in the small garden, while preparations were made for their proper housing in Regent's Park. The living animals sometimes created a problem with members of the public. Particularly guilty of this was a wanderoo monkey (now called a lion-tailed macaque) named Jack, who was tethered by a long lead to a pole in the garden. He made raids on passing pedestrians, grabbing hats and handbags, and, on one occasion, the wig of a very irate bishop, after which Jack's freedom had to be severely restricted!

The museum continued to grow until, after nearly thirty years, it had become an even more comprehensive collection than that in the country's national collection, formed seventy years earlier and housed with the nation's art treasures in Bloomsbury. This early natural history collection had always taken second place to the rest of the exhibits; its stuffed animals were by now in poor condition, and records were almost non-existent. To solve the overcrowding problem, in 1855 the Zoological Society presented to the nation most of its collection of museum specimens and classification records, and, together with the Bloomsbury collection, these became the nucleus of the Natural History Museum, for which the imposing building at Kensington was built. Duplicated specimens were given by the Society to provincial museums.

Although the Society's museum lasted only 29 years, its library, while also growing apace, has continued to the present day. It is now by far the greatest private collection in the world devoted entirely to animals, containing as it does over 200,000 books, journals and other publications, and now also including a collection of some 20,000 photographs. Open to members of the public on payment of an admission fee, the library is but one of many aspects of the Zoological Society not known about by the majority of visitors to London Zoo.

One of the first animals to be presented to the Zoo was a griffon vulture, named by the keepers 'Dr Brookes' after Joshua Brookes, who donated him. Joshua Brookes ran a school of anatomy near Oxford Street, and 'Dr Brookes' was one of several vultures he was thought to keep to dispose of the human remains from his anatomical demonstrations! 'Dr Brookes' had been in the Zoo for about 40 years when he died, and how old he was when originally presented is not known.

To house its collection of animals, one of the first acts of the Council was to appoint an architect to design gardens on their rented site in Regent's Park which, although only five acres in area to start with, after two further concessions was to grow to 25 acres within eight years. (To this day it is only 36 acres in size.) The architect they appointed was 27-year-old Decimus Burton, then little-known but destined to become famous for, among other structures, the Wellington Arch at Hyde Park Corner and the great Greenhouse at Kew. He was shortly to design the first buildings to be erected in the Zoo, but first had to design the layout of the Gardens. He put the entrance at the north-west corner of the small triangle of land, and today this is still the Entrance Gate, although now it is in the middle of the area covered by the present-day Zoo.

At this early stage the animals not kept in the Bruton Street offices were housed in mobile cages kept overnight in Camden Town and wheeled daily to the Gardens – in effect just another travelling menagerie! This state of affairs was highly undesirable, although unavoidable, and as soon as the early plans for the general layout had been implemented, work started on railing-in some areas as small enclosures, some with ponds, for such animals as the otters, beavers, storks and emus. The first permanent cage was built about a year after work had started, and was intended to house a pair of macaws, though it quickly proved unsuitable for these large birds, which were then replaced with ravens. The Raven's Cage was used for this purpose for nearly fifteen decades and is still to be seen (now disused, but retained for sentimental reasons) on the Fellows' Lawn – almost the exact spot upon which it was first erected.

In 1828 Decimus Burton built the first brick animal house in the Gardens – a small building, referred to as the Llama Hut, with only two rooms, each containing one llama, and a smaller room between them for the keeper. The animal rooms had wooden doors to let the animals out to their outdoor paddock each day. A Clock Tower was added to the 'Hut' the following year (at a cost 'not to exceed the sum of £100', as Council minutes show), and the llamas were later replaced with their larger relatives, camels. A bell, which can still be seen on one end wall, was sounded at closing time each day for almost a century and a half. This little building, the precursor of so many larger and finer ones much more suitable for animals, was in fact used for camels for nearly 150 years and is now also kept for sentimental reasons, although both the Clock Tower and the Raven's Cage are now listed buildings, so cannot be pulled down, even if this was desired.

The Clock Tower is the only original building of that early Zoo to survive to this day virtually unchanged, although Burton designed and built a number of others. Some early buildings remained until the 1930s, such as the grandiose Elephant House, while Burton's 1836 Giraffe House is still externally as he designed it, but now has a modernized interior and forms part of the Cotton Terraces; and Three Island Pond, attractive still with its flamingos and pelicans, he designed as long ago as 1832.

But in those early days Burton soon met a design problem which he had to overcome. The first grant of land by the Crown was bordered by the Outer Circle, a road which runs round the inside of Regent's Park. The first addition the following year was a strip of land on the other side of that road, between it and the Regent's Canal. Burton decided to excavate a tunnel beneath the road rather than build a footbridge, and this tunnel, built at an original cost of £1,005, is still in use today. Over the tunnel entrance at each end, though only one has survived, he designed an attractive classical portal, in the style of Nash's Regent's Park buildings, with a balustraded footpath in front of Doric columns. This is the tunnel through which Jumbo the elephant was destined to flee some years later, and which, many years later still, was to delay a renewal of the Zoological Society's lease from the Government because the Government wanted the Society to become responsible for the Outer Circle road above the tunnel in case lack of its maintenance should cause the road to subside. The lease, which had already been queried in detail for a long time, was eventually signed nearly three years after the previous one had expired, and in the meantime caused delays in obtaining over £1 million co-funding from the National Lottery for a new building in the Zoo, which could not be awarded until the Society again had formal entitlement to be on that land!

During 1828, much building work was being carried out. The minutes of a Council meeting held in July of that year recorded that buildings which had been ordered included a stable for zebras and a kangaroo shed, as well as another shed for Indian cows and sheep to replace the Goat House, accommodation for tortoises and another house for dogs, and an owls' aviary. By 1829, within three years of the first Council meeting, the Gardens had become very attractive. In addition to the buildings just mentioned, they contained several other permanent structures as well as a number of landscaped lawns and enclosures housing a surprising number of animals – though not necessarily in conditions we should consider ideal today. For example, there were the Monkey Poles – a row of poles all with a small shelter at the top. The monkeys, one to a pole, each had a thin leather belt around them with a lightweight chain attached to a ring which slid up and down the pole, enabling them to climb to their shelters or run around on the ground at the base of their poles. Close contact between visitors and monkeys was therefore possible – indeed inevitable – and so many hats, gloves and handbags were purloined, often ending up in the shelters at the tops of the poles, that the monkeys were soon confined to the Monkey House.

Another early structure which today would not be considered acceptable was the Bear Pit. This was a square, brick-sided pit in the ground, with access for the bears to their side-dens at night. In the centre of the pit was a pole up which the bears could climb to the level of the human visitors, who fed them with buns pushed on the ends of their walking-sticks. An early visitor to the Zoo once lost his hat in the Bear Pit and climbed down to collect it. Luckily a keeper was there to drive off the bears before they harmed the man, but he still did not have his hat and so the next day sent a bill to the Zoo for its cost! This was not a unique occasion, and several other visitors were in due course also to try to claim from the Zoo for losses incurred through their own stupidity. It was also here, in 1830, that the first injury to a keeper occurred, when Josiah Graver was injured by a polar bear. He died a month later, and the Council arranged to pay for his funeral as well as paying his father £10 to cover his expenses travelling down from Norfolk and for mourning clothes.

The first cage in the Zoo, originally built for macaws but now unused and relocated nearby on the Fellows' Lawn (© *Crown Copyright. NMR*)

The Council also offered to employ another of his sons the first time a labourer's job became available!

A straight path led from the Zoo entrance to the Bear Pit, later improved and named the 'Fellows' Terrace'. It became very popular with the ladies of the period, who used to stroll along it showing off their ornate dresses and parasols, displaying in much the same way as the peacocks were displaying their feathers nearby! From 1844, special Promenade days were held for the Fellows and their

The Clock Tower was the first animal house built, originally for llamas. It is one of the fifteen listed buildings in the Zoo (© *Crown Copyright. NMR*)

friends, with a brass band playing in the gardens, and even in the 1930s there were bands playing regularly in a bandstand near the Lion House. This band-stand was used as an enclosure for dingoes during the Second World War.

In 1831, one enterprising person started a horse-drawn omnibus service to the Zoo from Westminster, but it was the congestion caused by carriages in the Outer Circle near the Zoo entrance that required police assistance the next year, and by 1835 the Council had decided that an enclosure be provided 'for

This painting by Scharf is of the first Monkey House, with the East Tunnel entrance nearby (© ZSL)

the accommodation of servants in waiting on the visitors', though a decision on whether benches should be placed in it for them was delegated to the Garden Committee. By 1836 the traffic problem had become so great that advertisements were placed in three morning papers warning that police had been instructed to prevent any carriages from parking within 100 feet of the entrance or being 'double-parked'. The Fellows' Terrace survived for 130 years, leading past the later Monkey House until this was pulled down in 1972 to make way for the new Sobell Pavilions for Apes and Monkeys, which now covers the whole area.

The young Zoological Society, being the first of its kind, had slowly to learn the ideal way to keep each kind of animal and, while the Monkey Poles and Bear Pit were, by later standards, quite unsuitable for keeping animals, they at least enabled their occupants to enjoy the open air instead of always being cooped up inside a building. This was quite an innovation, which seems to have been put into practice for many of those early animals. Paddocks were built for zebras and elephants, and the first Monkey House had a number of outside enclosures, each as large as the ones outside the third Monkey House, which was demolished in 1972. But the benefits of the open air were not fully recognized then (possibly because of the damp and foggy winters experienced), and the second Monkey House, built in 1864 and used for the next sixty years, had

no outside enclosures at all. It was felt that animals such as monkeys and lions, that came from tropical countries, should be kept in heated houses, and this view prevailed until nearly the end of the century, by which time it had become apparent that it was indeed possible to keep such animals outdoors in the British climate; being warm-blooded they adjust to, and even thrive in, a colder climate, unlike reptiles and other cold-blooded animals.

While the welfare of the Zoo's animals was a prime consideration, even in those early days, this was largely the case in order to keep the animals alive and healthy for observation, whereas nowadays one of the objectives of all good zoos is to provide opportunities for a full range of natural behaviours, encouraging the animals to breed, not only so that we may continue to see them, but also to try to counteract, to some extent, the wholesale loss of so many species from their wild habitats. In this way zoos can maintain a 'pool' of animals that could hopefully be returned to their natural habitats if and when conditions are safe so to do.

The observation of living animals resulted in the discovery of many hitherto unknown facts about them, which were discussed at the Society's Scientific Meetings and written up in the many learned papers issued. Already the Society was beginning to try its hand at breeding animals in captivity and keeping them in more natural habitats where possible. In the very first months of its forma-

The entrances to the East Tunnel were designed by Burton to match Nash's impressive buildings around Regent's Park. Only the portal at the south end remains (© *Crown Copyright. NMR*)

tion, the Council entered into negotiations for some land with ponds at Carshalton, in Surrey, for the purpose of the 'preservation of Fish and Wild Fowl'. Negotiations for this lease fell through, but in 1829 the Society opened its Richmond Park Farm and tried to raise several species of fish in the ponds, including eels. The attempts were unsuccessful, however, and after three years the idea was dropped. In the Gardens themselves, an aquarium was not to be built until 20 years later, but this would be the first one in the world.

The general public was becoming more and more interested in the collection of animals being assembled in Regent's Park. Newspapers frequently gave information about new arrivals never before seen in the country, and magazines of the day often carried articles about the Gardens. The Scientific Meetings of the Society brought it fame throughout the scientific world, and other cities started planning similar collections of animals, the first being at Dublin, next at Clifton, near Bristol, and the third one at Belle Vue, Manchester.

Bennett, the Society's Vice-Secretary (a post later abolished), edited a book issued by instalments and called *The Gardens and Menagerie of the Zoological*

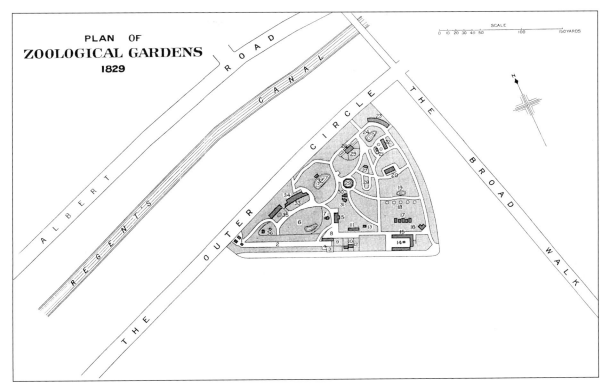

Society Delineated, which became the model for most later books published on natural history. Its title highlights the cumbersome name of what we now call 'London Zoo' that was increasingly being referred to in the newspapers and journals of the popular press. It was inevitable that a more acceptable name would replace 'The Gardens and Menagerie of the Zoological Society of London'.

It is not known who first coined the word, but about forty years after the Gardens were first opened to the public, they became known as the 'Zoo'. Vance, a famous London music hall artist at that time, sang a ditty about the Zoo, and it may have been he who first invented the word; certainly his use of it put the term on everyone's lips (except the Fellows, who were horrified!) and now 'zoo' is, of course, a recognized dictionary word in use all over the world. But originally it was applied to London Zoo, which can therefore justifiably call itself *the* Zoo!

1829. Within two years of opening, already the gardens had been laid out by Decimus Burton and the first cages and houses had been built – dog and fox cages (15), a Monkey House (20) and aviaries at 23, 26 (for owls), 29 and 33. The very first constructions were the cage for macaws and the Llama House (7 and 5). Monkey Poles are on a lawn and numbered 18. The Zoo entrance is in the top left-hand corner, entry being from the Outer Circle, as it still is today (© ZSL)

3 Progress

It was in 1827 that the Zoo first opened its gates – to Fellows only. Fellows were also issued with tickets to give to their friends who, on presenting a ticket at the gate, were allowed in on payment of one shilling (five pence), except on Sundays, which were reserved exclusively for Fellows.

In that year also, the Zoo employed its first (and, at that time, only) keeper, James Cops, for a salary of one guinea (£1.05) a week; but his tenure was short-lived – he was sacked after only eight months, after 'several acts of misconduct' were reported. In subsequent years, however, the Zoo has been very lucky with the many keepers it has employed, the vast majority being hard-working and highly conscientious, the care of their animals being their prime consideration. One exception was a reptile keeper who, many years ago, took some friends into the Zoo after closing time. He was drunk at the time and 'showed off' by handling a venomous cobra. He died of snake-bite!

A daily record of 'Occurrences at the Gardens' was started, and has continued in modified form ever since, now weekly, and originally showing births, deaths, arrivals and departures of animals, together with other matters of interest or concern. The very first record, dated Monday 25 February 1828, reads:

MENAGERIE – Received 11 Ducks from the lake caught for the purpose of being pinioned and then to be returned.

Received 6 Silver Hair'd rabbits from Mr Blake.

Otter died as a consequence of a diseased tail.

Emu laid her fourth egg on 24 inst.

All Animals and Birds well.

WORKS – Pit for Bears. House for Llamas in progress.

Boundary wall for supporting the bank next the Bears pit began.

SERVANTS – All on duty.

NO. OF VISITORS – Four.
PARTICULAR VISITOR – Lord Auckland.

(Lord Auckland was 'particular' because he was a member of Council!)

The collection of animals was intended for scientific study by the Fellows, but costs were rising and were barely covered by the subscriptions of Fellows. Even so it was nearly twenty years before the general public was allowed into the Zoo on a regular basis, to increase income, and even then not on Sundays, which remained a prerogative of the Fellows and their friends. The Sunday 'Fellows and ticket-holders' rule applied for nearly a hundred years, until 1940, and even after that time Sunday mornings were reserved exclusively for them for several years.

There were at first no official guides or plans of the Zoo for visitors, but popular journals of the day contained many sketches and articles. Some of these were general descriptions in the often rather pompous wording of the time, such as the following, from the *Mirror* (now defunct) of 6 September 1828:

> We are again in Regent's Park; but we must leave its architectural splendour for the present, and request our readers to accompany us towards the eastern verge of the Park, to the gardens of the Zoological Society … The grounds are daily filled with fashionable company, notwithstanding the great migrations which usually take place at this season of year, and almost depopulate the western hemisphere of fashion. The Gardens, independent of their zoological attractions, are a delightful promenade, being laid out with great taste …

From then on the Zoo gathered momentum, attendances increasing each year and the animal collection being added to continuously. As already noted, records show that when the Zoo first opened it already had many kinds of animal, including bears, zebras, llamas and kangaroos.

The year 1829 saw the arrival of the Zoo's first tiger and two polar bears, and in 1831 its first elephant arrived, an Asiatic bull elephant. Male elephants are notoriously difficult to keep in captivity because they are unpredictable and potentially bad-tempered, but this one was then a youngster, and was moved from London Docks to the Zoo simply by walking it there. During the journey it snatched a hat from one lady's head and a bag from another lady, both of which articles it ate! During the following hundred years new elephants were always walked from the Docks to the Zoo, the last recorded instance being in 1927, when a photograph was taken of the elephants as they walked past King's Cross station.

Because of the number of British colonials abroad, the Society had a category of Fellowship called 'Corresponding Members', intended for those

For the first 100 years almost every new elephant was walked from London Docks to the Zoo. These were the last to arrive this way, photographed passing King's Cross Station in 1927 (© ZSL)

who, unable to visit the Zoo, nevertheless assisted considerably by submitting 'papers' on their observations of animals for reading at the Scientific Meetings, and by collecting animals for exhibition at the Zoo. The Foreign Office instructed civil servants abroad to give every assistance to such members of the Society, and also to procure animals where these would be of value to the Zoo. Consequently, a steady stream of animals was appearing in the Gardens, and houses for them were being built apace.

One of the first animals that a child recognizes is a giraffe, and this animal is always one of the most popular in the Zoo. The Society had been trying hard to obtain one ever since the building of the Giraffe House in readiness (which had, in the meantime, been used to house their first orang-utan), but several years had gone by before they met with success. They had been offered at least one giraffe, but this animal, offered to them by a dealer for £2,000, was said to be 'guaranteed to do well on beans, barley, green stuff, bread and fruit' – a remarkable diet for an animal which in the wild lives almost entirely on leaves! Needless to say, the Society turned down the offer.

The central block with its 16-foot doors is the original Giraffe House, to which the right wing was later added to accommodate Obaysch. The surrounding water eventually replaced the enclosure railings (© *Crown Copyright. NMR*)

Eventually, they commissioned a Frenchman, a Monsieur Thibaut, to organize an expedition to Upper Egypt, and he obtained four giraffes, three males and one female, at a cost of £700. These were quarantined for nearly a month before being transported by ship to London Docks, where they arrived on 24 May 1838, and from where, like the elephant, they were walked to the Zoo.

Nothing quite like that event has since been seen in London. The procession was headed by the Society's Vice-President, Bennett, accompanied by M. Thibaut dressed as an Arab; then came the four giraffes led by Nubian and Maltese keepers, and the whole company was surrounded by a detachment of the Metropolitan Police. All traffic was stopped, and side turnings closed, and the public was asked to keep quiet so as not to frighten the animals; indeed, the only time the giraffes were scared was when they passed a field near Commercial Road and saw a cow for the first time. It was a little while before they could be coaxed past, but eventually the giraffes completed their eight-mile walk in little more than three hours.

They quickly settled down in the Zoo, and the breeding record of giraffes in that house over the following century and a half has been remarkable – seventeen were born during the first twenty years alone!

Animals that are now rare began to arrive, but in those days these animals were rarities only because they had never before been seen in England or, indeed, in many cases, by anyone outside of their native countries. The first Great Indian one-horned rhinoceros, with its huge body-plates of leather, arrived in 1834 (to be most unfortunately killed fifteen years later by an elephant). Zoologists were very excited when the first giant anteater arrived, and had earlier, in 1845, been even more astonished when the first echidna, or spiny anteater, was put on display.

This animal, looking like a dark, fat hedgehog, had been the subject of great debate since it had first been discovered in Australia. Scientists had only recently accepted the fact that marsupials, or pouched mammals, were an early form of mammal which had died out almost everywhere except Australia. The echidna was certainly like a mammal in being warm-blooded and having hair, some hardened into spines, but it was claimed that because it laid eggs, it was impossible for it to be a mammal! Scientists came to realize that the echidna is in fact an even more primitive mammal than the marsupials; it is a monotreme. It does lay eggs like its ancestors, the reptiles, and, also like them, has only a single orifice for the disposal of all body wastes and for breeding purposes, but it also suckles its young, although it has no teats, the milk just oozing from mammary glands under the skin inside a rather incomplete pouch. The arrival of the first living specimen in England was, therefore, an event of great scientific importance.

The Society was keen to find and exhibit other animals which were known only from skins or skeletons. The dodo was known to have become extinct many years earlier, but there was doubt about the moa, a flightless bird like the ostrich but very much larger, standing up to four metres in height – as tall as an elephant. Many bones of moas had been found in New Zealand, and in 1843 the Society entertained hopes that they might not be extinct and that one could be shown in London, but their hopes were to be dashed. According to a letter published in the Proceedings of the Society, two Englishmen and some native guides had set out into 'Moa country' and sat all night waiting for one of the giant birds. Suddenly they saw one in the moonlight, advancing towards them, and they all turned tail and fled! Who can blame them? But the incident, if true, made them the last people ever to see a living moa, which is therefore one animal the Zoo has never possessed.

It is ironic that, at the selfsame time, the Zoo was in possession of an animal that was about to become extinct, but they did not realize its future

Professor Owen standing beside this skeleton of one of the largest of the moas gives some idea of its size – far larger than an ostrich (© ZSL)

was in jeopardy. That they had zebras in the Zoo from the day it opened has been mentioned already, but in 1831 the Zoo purchased a quagga. This was a close relative of the zebra, but had stripes only on its shoulders and neck, the rest of its body being donkey-like. Quaggas had lived in vast herds in South Africa, but white settlers found they were easier to catch and kill than zebras and were good to eat. As a consequence they were hunted to extinction.

But their doom was not yet apparent in the 1830s and over the following

The quagga became extinct over 100 years ago. This was the last one of three to be seen in the Zoo, photographed in 1864 (© ZSL)

thirty years the Zoo exhibited three of them. The quagga became extinct in the wild while the third of these animals was still in the Zoo. This last one in the Zoo died in 1872.

The last quagga in the world died in Amsterdam Zoo on 12 August 1883.

4 Growth

The Society's Bruton Street building quickly became too small, housing as it did their offices, meeting room, library and rapidly growing museum, so in 1836 the property was given up and the Society moved to 28 Leicester Square. But still the collections grew, and in 1843 a further move was made, this time to 11 Hanover Square. At the same time the museum was transferred to the Zoo itself, into the converted Carnivore House, where it remained for 12 years until it was given to the State.

It was not until 1910 that custom-built offices were erected within the Gardens of the Zoo as, by then, travel across Regent's Park had become easier and safer, and thus evening Scientific Meetings no longer needed to be held in the centre of London.

The collection of living animals was also growing rapidly, and every year saw a number of animals arriving that were new to the collection. Many, such as the echidna, had never previously been seen in Europe, and amongst the most notable of the new arrivals were:

1831 – the first kiang (a wild horse)
1845 – the first sloth, taken out of its cage each morning and 'hung' in a nearby tree until evening
1848 – the first Tree kangaroo
1850 – the first hippopotamus
1856 – the first Arabian oryx – an antelope which, 100 years later, was saved from extinction with the help of London Zoo
1860 – the first shoebill (a bird almost as difficult to believe in as the dodo!)
1868 – the first black rhinoceros
1874 – the first Javan rhinoceros, now almost extinct.

All the time, the Society was understanding more about how to keep animals fit and healthy while in captivity. Some of the early buildings were most unsuitable for their proposed occupants and had therefore to be put to other uses

The Zoo was being laid out most attractively. This painting by James Bakewell shows a grass enclosure with a fountain, for various birds, and in the background large cages for more birds (© *ZSL*)

while improved buildings were designed for the animals in the light of experience gained. It was a learning curve and the Zoo was getting better all the time.

As late as 1883, for example, the building that is now the Bird House was originally built for reptiles; the later Reptile House, built in 1926, was a great improvement, but, again from experience, could still be improved upon. We now know that it is not only necessary to keep reptiles warm, but also to provide 'hot spots' for them so that there are temperature variations within each enclosure, and also to be able to vary the general temperature within some enclosures to provide seasonal changes and induce breeding conditions, as in nature.

Unsuitable though some of them were, buildings had nevertheless to be provided, and many were being designed for the first time anywhere. Indeed, the very first Reptile House (*not* the one just referred to) was erected in 1849, only 20 years after the Zoo first opened its gates. It was the first one in the world, and was at that time considered to be one of the wonders of the age. It included tortoises, crocodiles and over twenty different species of snake which, as the building was warmed only by stoves, were provided with woollen blankets for shelter and warmth!

Another, even more wonderful, creation would be unveiled in 1853 – the first aquarium ever to have been built. Today there are aquaria throughout the world, as well as many private fish-tanks in people's homes. Nowadays, electricity makes the heating and water circulation automatic, and the lighting, which is so necessary for the plants, can be provided without effort, but before the use of electricity things were very different. And yet, only two years later, the Zoo was able to keep not only a freshwater aquarium, but also a marine aquarium, a feat that even today compounds the difficulties of fish-keeping! In the Fish House, as it was called, the first recorded photograph of a living fish was taken in 1854.

Fish had for many years been kept in ponds, and in 1842 a Dr James Johnstone was using small jars to keep and observe seaweeds, starfish and small shellfish. Plate glass had first been made in Lancashire in 1773, and, because of its strength, it was possible to make it into larger containers suitable for observation. When used to house an animal these glass containers were called vivaria. At the suggestion of Philip Henry Gosse, the Council agreed to build an 'Aquatic Vivarium', later abbreviated to 'Aquarium'.

The Fish House, as it was originally called, was one of the 'firsts' for London Zoo – the world's first public aquarium (© *ZSL*)

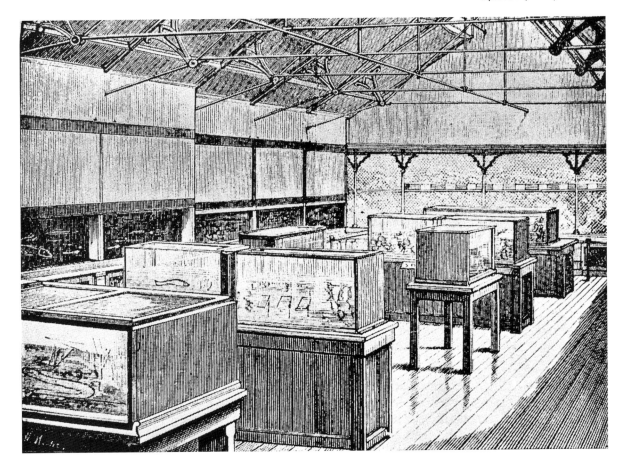

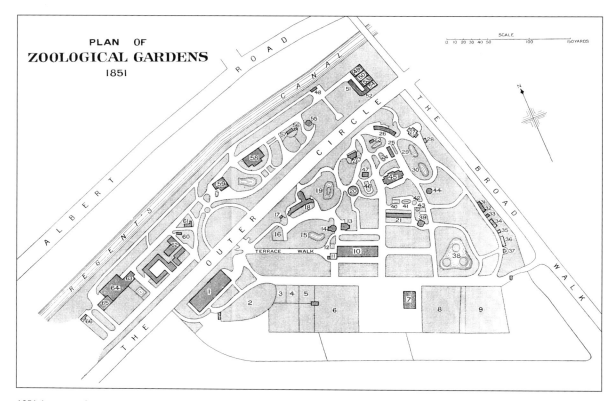

PLAN OF
ZOOLOGICAL GARDENS
1851

1851. In twenty-four years the Zoo had expanded greatly and a second entrance had been added. The Terrace Walk from the Main Entrance was the 'fashionable' walk and all the areas to the south of this (numbered 1–9) had been added from Regent's Park; number 7 is 'Mr. Gould's humming-birds', for which this house was built. The land between the Outer Circle and the canal had also been added and contained huts and sheds for deer, antelopes and zebras (50–58), as well as a small Elephant and Rhinoceros House (59), a Tapir House (60) and the first Reptile House in the world (49). The Giraffe House (64) had been built fifteen years earlier and is still occupied by giraffes today (© ZSL)

A number of stout boxes were made and waterproofed, with their sides having glass inserted, and these were stood on a series of solid wooden benches around the floor of the house. No individual tank heating was provided, but this was not needed anyway as at that time no tropical fish were kept. There must, however, have been serious problems in keeping the tanks sufficiently cool in summer, or light enough in dark, foggy winters since no individual lighting could be provided, either.

For the later marine exhibits, the Great Eastern Railway Company carried over barrels of seawater, and the simplest of pumps was used to circulate this unfiltered water through the tanks. That the system was successful is shown by the number of exhibits on display – over 60 kinds of sea fishes and over 200 invertebrates, such as crabs, sea anemones and shellfish. It was to be over twenty years before another public aquarium was opened, at Naples, with the help of the Zoological Society of London.

Several years before the aquarium, the Zoo held what could be called the first dog show. The first show of the kind we know today was not held until 1859, in Newcastle, and the Kennel Club, the organizers of Cruft's, was not formed until ten years later still. But the Zoo had started it all by putting on display, near Three Island Pond, some of the larger breeds of domestic dog from around the world – Tibetan watchdogs, Grecian greyhounds, Persian sheepdogs, Spanish bloodhounds, Newfoundlands, Chinese dogs (probably chows) and, the sensation of the day, St Bernards from Switzerland.

Then, in 1845, the Zoo held the first poultry show. Visitors were astonished at the varied collection of chickens, ducks, geese and turkeys gathered together. So many strange breeds were on display, which had not previously been seen in the country, that one writer declared it would have been 'quite in keeping if some of them had laid triangular eggs'! This first show opened in a terrific storm, and as a consequence was something of a failure, but the event was repeated several times during the rest of the century.

5 Zoo Personalities

Any story of the Zoo would have to include the names of many characters, both human and animal, who contributed to that story. Some were known for the books they wrote about animals and about the Zoo, such as E.G. Boulenger, the first Curator of Reptiles, or for the photographs they took in the Zoo, for example those of F.W. Bond, the Society's accountant, or F. Martin Duncan, librarian for 20 years. Some became radio or television personalities, such as George Cansdale, and Desmond Morris with Congo, the chimpanzee. Many others are remembered for the buildings they erected in the Zoo – Decimus Burton, J.J. Joass (the famous Mappin Terraces), Lubetkin (the Penguin Pond), and Lord Snowdon (the 1965 walk-through aviary) – or for the large donations they made towards buildings (John Newton Mappin, Charles Clore, Swraj Paul and many others). Some of these personalities had no name at first, for example the golden eagle that escaped from the Zoo for two weeks and lived in Regent's Park; when asked by the media for its name, the keeper hurriedly thought of 'Goldie', and by this name the Golden Eagle was famous for the rest of his days.

There are many Zoo characters in the pages that follow, but this chapter is devoted to two of them from the early days of the Zoo, one animal and one human – Obaysch and John Gould.

One of the very earliest animals about which the public became enthusiastic was Obaysch, the Zoo's first hippopotamus. Now long forgotten, Obaysch caused such a stir at the time that crowds came to the Zoo just to see him; the newspapers and journals were writing constantly about him, and there was even a dance composed in his memory. For some time prior to 1850, the Zoo had been anxious to obtain and exhibit a hippopotamus, and had already built an extension to the Giraffe House, complete with a pool, in order to accommodate one. Their keenness to obtain one is understandable for, whereas hippos inhabited the Thames in prehistoric times (their bones have been found at Charing Cross in London), none had been seen in England nor, indeed, anywhere else in Europe since the days of the Roman Colosseum, where they were among the featured animals in the arena for the 'Games'.

Britain's Consul-General in Cairo knew that Abbas Pasha, the ruler of

Egypt, had a great desire for English thoroughbred and sporting dogs. He made it known to Abbas Pasha that the Zoological Society was anxious to obtain a hippo and dropped a hint that an exchange might be possible, whereupon the Pasha summoned the Commander of his Nubian army and told him to obtain a young hippopotamus 'forthwith'. The Commander, appreciating that heads might roll if he was unsuccessful (including his own), consequently devoted the greater part of his army to the search, and eventually they managed to capture a baby hippo high up the White Nile near an island named Obaysch, after which the animal was named.

A boat was specially constructed to carry the young hippo down river, with a small herd of cows and goats to provide him with milk. He was said to have drunk between seven and eight gallons of milk every day while in Cairo, where he arrived in November to pass the winter before attempting the sea journey to England. The following spring, Obaysch was taken to Alexandria in a padded cart accompanied by his Arab keeper, Hamet Saafi Cannana, who had been enlisted to devote himself exclusively to the hippo and had even taken to sleeping alongside Obaysch, having grown very fond of him. The baby was at that time about eight months old and was seven feet long – about the same length as the circumference of his waist!

In Alexandria the P & O steamship *Ripon* awaited him, a special pool having been constructed on it. This ship brought him to Southampton, from where he was taken by special train to London, with crowds at every station, waiting to catch a glimpse of him, although all they might have seen was Hamet's head stuck out gasping for some fresh air. The newspapers had been writing about Obaysch for months, and the press artists (in those days long before press photographers) were eagerly awaiting his arrival at the Zoo; as this took place after dark, however, they had to make their sketches by lantern light. The next morning, Obaysch was so frightened by the size of his new pool that Hamet had to coax him in, by going in first, up to his waist.

During the long journey from Cairo, Hamet had been helped by two assistants, an old man and his nephew who were snake-charmers by profession, and after their arrival these two gave daily demonstrations of snake-charming in the public area of the Reptile House, with visitors standing around in a semicircle – though none of them came too close!

London talked of nothing but hippos for weeks after Obaysch's arrival. Cockney conductors of the London horse-drawn buses could be heard warning their driver when a fat man got on the bus 'Don't let the 'orses see the 'ippo!' *Punch* magazine published cartoons and articles about Obaysch a number of times, referring to him as HRH (His Rolling Hulk), and a new dance became the vogue, 'The Hippopotamus Polka'.

For a few years prior to Obaysch's arrival, the Zoo had been suffering financially, but the hippo's arrival worked wonders and visitor attendances doubled during his first year there. Caroline Owen who, with her husband, the scientist Richard Owen, had taken some friends to see the hippo, wrote in her diary:

> There was a dense mass of people waiting their turn to get inside [the Giraffe House] and the whole road leading to that part of the Gardens was full of a continuous stream of people.

Queen Victoria herself went to see Obaysch in July (the first of five visits she made to the Zoo), and wrote about him in her diary, as well as a description of a demonstration by the snake-charmers that had been put on in the Giraffe House for her benefit.

In 1860, long after he had become fully grown, Obaysch escaped from his enclosure by dislodging the wooden bar used to secure the door. Abraham Bartlett at that time had been Superintendent of the Zoo for only a year; he realized that to attempt to recapture a four-ton male animal of doubtful temper would be a dangerous undertaking with little guarantee of success. The hippo happily ate the hay given to him, but refused to follow a handful of hay back to his enclosure, so Bartlett sent for Matthew Scott, the elephant keeper, whom he knew Obaysch disliked intensely for some reason. Using himself as a decoy, Scott shouted at Obaysch from a distance and the hippo immediately charged. Despite their bulk, hippos can run faster than a man, but Scott probably broke the sprint record as he raced back to Obaysch's enclosure! Closely followed by the charging hippo, Scott ran across the enclosure and up the emergency stairs provided, while the door was firmly shut on the animal.

On another occasion, Hunt (who was then the hippo keeper) did a foolish thing. Returning from a public house one very hot August night, and knowing that he had securely locked Obaysch in his inner den for the night, Hunt decided to have a cool dip in the hippo pool. What he did *not* know was that a nightwatchman had reported to Bartlett that Obaysch seemed distressed by the heat, and so Bartlett had ordered the door to his inner den to be opened. Hunt dived into the pool – and came up under Obaysch! He did not waste any time in getting out of the pool again, which he probably did even more quickly than he had got in.

As for Abbas Pasha, he received a gift from the Zoo of greyhounds and deerhounds, under the care of an experienced trainer, as a 'thank you' for Obaysch, and in 1854 the Pasha supplied the Zoo with a young female hippo, although 17 years would elapse before a calf was born. In 1871, Adhela (nicknamed Dil) produced a calf which, unfortunately, died only two days later. She had a second one the following year which, because it would not feed, was taken away for hand rearing, but this one also died a few days after. Towards the end of the same year, however, Dil gave birth to a third baby, on 5 November, and this one survived.

Not surprisingly, in view of its date of birth, and despite some objections, the baby hippo was named Guy Fawkes – quite inappropriately, as it turned out, considering that it was later discovered to be female, but the name stuck. At birth, Guy Fawkes weighed about 100lb. (45 kg.). She and her mother did not rejoin Obaysch for eight months, and Bartlett later described how, when the family was first put together, Dil displayed so much protectiveness for her baby that she savagely fought Obaysch, and then pushed him into the pool, drove him into a corner and kept guard over him, with Guy Fawkes safely perched on her back! Obaysch, however, showed no animosity towards the baby, and within a short time they settled down as a happy family unit.

Obaysch died of old age in 1878, six years after the birth of Guy Fawkes, and an obituary for him appeared in *The Times*. His arrival at the Zoo 28 years earlier had provided sufficient additional income from the public for the Society to start making a pictorial record of the animals kept in the Gardens. By now their collection of animal prints must be amongst the finest in the world. This collection includes many beautiful plates of parrots, lithographed and hand-coloured by the man who, 150 years after he did them, is better known for his Nonsense Verse – Edward Lear. At 18 years of age Lear started going to the Zoo and making drawings there, and years later, when ill health forced him to live abroad, he wrote:

> Those Gardens are such a Milestone and Landmark in my life that I like to go there when in England.

Some of Lear's coloured plates were included by John Gould in his folio volume of birds, which includes 3,000 illustrations. In 1827, aged 23, Gould had been appointed by the Society as taxidermist to their museum. He died at the age of 77, but through all those years Gould had connections with the Society, and some of the books he produced are amongst the most prized possessions of their library.

After studying the zoological specimens brought back by Charles Darwin in 1836 from his voyage round the world in the *Beagle*, Gould decided to visit Australia for two years, and this resulted in two publications, one of which was *Birds of Australia*. In this book he describes a bird which, 18 years later, had this entry in the Zoo's first Visitor Guide:

> *The Zebra Grass Parakeet*, more generally known by the native name of 'BETCHERRYGAH'. The first living specimen was brought from Australia by Mr Gould, on his return to England in 1840.

No one at that time could have guessed that the little bird would prove to be such a popular household pet as to rank third favourite, after cats and dogs – the budgerigar.

Seventy-six other species of parrot are listed as being exhibited in the Zoo in that first Zoo Guide, together with some animals now extinct, such as the passenger pigeon and the thylacine, or Tasmanian wolf (or Tasmanian tiger, as it has more recently been called). It was a veritable book of 60 closely printed pages and cost 6d. (2½p). Referring to the Zoo's collection of carnivores, housed in one building, the Guide's entry reads:

> The collection of Carnivora contained in this building is limited to the larger forms, popularly known as the 'Wild Beasts'.

The huge number of carnivores listed in that first Guide in 1858 included cheetahs, clouded leopards (the animal first discovered by Raffles), hyenas, Indian lions, binturongs, Tasmanian devils and 'the Five-Striped Paradoxure', now called by a much shorter name – the civet. The plan of the Gardens, issued even earlier, in 1851, shows the remarkable diversity of animals then forming its collection little more than 20 years after the Zoo started.

The thylacine, or Tasmanian wolf, was one of Australia's marsupial animals, and was a natural predator. Now almost certainly extinct, this was the last one to be seen in the Zoo, photographed in 1913 (© ZSL)

One of the most strikingly coloured of all small birds, the gouldian finch of Australia, is named after John Gould. For many years this bird could not be bred in this country, because it refused to acknowledge the change of season, insisting on nesting in the depths of an English winter – the Australian summer.

After Gould had left the Zoo's staff he still maintained his interest in and connections with the Society. He amassed a huge collection of humming-birds, which he had stuffed and mounted and, in the year of the Great Exhibition, with its Crystal Palace erected in Hyde Park, he arranged with the Society for them to be displayed to the public in the Zoo. A special house was built, where there is now a lawn for bird displays, and this accommodated about thirty glass cases containing 1,500 specimens. During the first two years it was open, the display received 75,000 visitors at a charge of 6d. each (2½p), all of which money was given to Gould. Queen Victoria made another of her visits, in order to see the collection, with Prince Albert and their children. *The Times*,

This is perhaps the last surviving of John Gould's showcases of stuffed humming-birds and illustrates the Victorian way of displaying dead birds (© *The Natural History Museum, London*)

writing up the occasion, said in its rather pompous way that the exhibition 'supplied in the only possible manner a great desideratum in the ornithological part of the Society's Collection' – or, in other words, that it filled a large gap in the Zoo's bird collection!

After Gould's death 30 years later, the Society managed to obtain a grant of £3,000 from the Government to purchase the collection, together with another 3,800 humming-birds that were unmounted, and 7,000 other birds. Part of this collection was later presented to the Natural History Museum at Kensington, and one of Gould's original cases of humming-birds can, at the time of writing, still be seen in the Bird Hall there as an example of a Victorian museum exhibit. The remainder of the Gould collection was given to the Tring Museum.

6 Abraham Bartlett

The man who undoubtedly made the most impact on the development of the Zoo in the nineteenth century, and therefore on the keeping of animals in captivity throughout the world, was Abraham D. Bartlett, who was the Superintendent of London Zoo for nearly forty years.

He was 14 years old at the time the Zoological Society was founded, and lived with his parents near the Strand. As a boy he was a frequent visitor to Exeter 'Change – the Strand menagerie mentioned in Chapter 1. There, he got to know about animals, and, although there is no record of what his views were on how they were caged (if, indeed, he had any particular views at that age), his visits to the 'Change fostered his interest in animals and undoubtedly influenced him in later life. While still young he was given a number of birds that had died at the 'Change and these he stuffed and mounted. In time he became so proficient at taxidermy that at the Great Exhibition of 1851 he was awarded first prize 'for specimens of taxidermy and models'.

A physician of Parliament Street introduced Bartlett to the Zoological Society and he then became acquainted with a number of people connected with the Society, including John Gould. At the same time he was corresponding with a Mr D.W. Mitchell, who lived in Cornwall. This gentleman came to London and learned a lot about the Society from Bartlett, who later wrote:

> This resulted in his obtaining the Secretaryship, greatly to my astonishment. He did not fail, however, to consult me upon the subject of the future prosperity of the Society, and this led to the opening of the Gardens to the public on payment of sixpence [2½p] on Mondays.

In 1859, when he was 47 years old, Bartlett was appointed Superintendent, a position which roughly equates with the post of Director of London Zoo. He lived in a house within the Zoo and was concerned with virtually everything that occurred. He could handle both staff and animals well, and during the 38 years he was Superintendent he became a familiar sight to regular visitors as he went about whatever occupied him in the Zoo – always dressed in a top hat and a black coat with long tails. In the popular press he was invariably called 'Papa' Bartlett.

Bartlett was involved in many different aspects of the Zoo, and in this way played a part in many interesting incidents. He also operated on many animals as a 'Vet', breaking new ground in this field, carried out post-mortems on a number of animals that had died in the Zoo, learning much that could be applied for the benefit of future Zoo occupants, and kept notes on events that had occurred in the Gardens. Many of these notes and anecdotes were included in a book published by his son three years after Bartlett's death, *Life Among Wild Beasts in the Zoo*, although this book also mentions a number of things which occurred outside the Zoo.

One of these other stories involved two Frenchmen who were in London with a large bear. An old lady was so frightened by the animal that she called the police, who did not understand French. According to Bartlett, '... the consequence was an altercation with the gentlemen in blue ...', who tried to take the Frenchmen into custody, '... but were met with resistance'. The Frenchmen were sent to prison for one month by the magistrate. However, the bear scratched and fought anyone who went near, so for the first night the men and the bear were all bundled into a cell together, along with, for reasons unknown, a large dog.

The next day, the Zoo was asked to take the bear away. The first attempt failed, but, Bartlett says, the officials then 'obtained an omnibus and softly, as they thought, shut him in and started; but the bear preferred to ride outside'. It broke the windows of the horse-drawn bus, got out, and stopped the bus 'by hanging on the hind-wheel'. As the bear's chain was fastened to the inside of the bus it could not escape, but one can picture the scene with the annoyed bear outside, two probably very frightened horses, and Zoo keepers, policemen and, no doubt, members of the public, getting more frustrated as time went on. Eventually the police had to return to the prison and obtain the release of the two Frenchmen to help get things sorted out!

Another incident involved a bear that had been presented to the Zoo by the then Prince of Wales. The young bear quickly grew in size and strength until it could bend the bars of its cage and escape, which it did one night. A frightened nightwatchman in the Zoo roused Bartlett in his house. He hastily dressed and together they hurried round to the bear's cage, but the animal was nowhere to be found. According to Bartlett, their attention was attracted by the driver of a cab outside the Zoo, 'whose frightened horse was in a nervous state of excitement' having come face to face with the bear in the Outer Circle – the road within Regent's Park which runs through the Zoo. The man who had been in charge of the young bear on its voyage to England had described it as friendly, but it was far from being so now and Bartlett wrote that he had to give it 'two or three whacks on the nose' before it allowed a cord to be put around its neck so it could be led to a safer cage. As can be seen, Bartlett was no coward!

He recorded one occasion when two boa constrictors, one 11 feet long and the other 9 feet long, tried to swallow the same pigeon. The larger snake then proceeded to swallow the smaller one! Bartlett wrote:

This plaque and photograph, forming a memorial to Abraham Bartlett, were placed in the Giraffe House 100 years after he was Superintendent of the Zoo (*Colin Whyman*)

> It had no longer the power of curling itself round … and appeared to be at least three times its normal size in circumference. It was almost painful to see the distended skin, which had separated the scales all over the middle of its body.

He recalled a similar case, where the snake doing the swallowing had died, but this one did not die. In fact, just four weeks later it ate another pigeon.

Bartlett was always keen to keep animals in the Zoo that were unusual, and while some of them have now become familiar sights, others would be rarely seen today. During his early years as Superintendent, 'first arrivals' at the Zoo included an aardvark, or African anteater, a lesser bird of paradise, and a lyre-bird. The aye-aye, a strange kind of lemur from Madagascar, also made its first appearance in the Zoo. This is a tree-climbing animal, rather larger than a cat, that has a long, thin middle finger with which it winkles insect grubs out of tree crevices.

One of Bartlett's less successful attempts at keeping unusual animals followed reports of a white whale having lived for two years in Boston. Bartlett had a Whale Pond constructed in which to keep porpoises, which were regularly caught in fishermen's nets, and the first porpoise arrived in November 1863. It was in poor condition on arrival and died shortly after, despite Bartlett wading into the cold water to give it sal volatile and brandy. Several more arrived during the following year, but, despite a special corps of keepers who rushed to the coast whenever a message came, none survived. Some joker erected a large notice on the beach at Southsea which read:

Notice to Sick Porpoises

If visiting this beach their carriage to London will be paid. A Doctor will be in attendance and medicine, in the shape of no end of grog, will be found.
Please land early.

We now know how carefully dolphins (their near relatives) must be lifted and transported, how their delicate skins must be kept wet, and how (unlike sealions) they must be kept in salt water to maintain health. It is small wonder then that attempts to keep porpoises in the Zoo in those early days were quickly given up, and it was to be over a century before dolphins were successfully kept, at Whipsnade Zoo, and with a mass of expensive equipment to maintain the water conditions and circulation. Even these conditions, however, were not considered ideal, and no dolphins are now kept in British zoos.

The Zoo's first sealion made its appearance three years after the attempt to keep porpoises. It arrived with the French sailor who had caught it in the Falkland Islands, a Monsieur Lecomte. Since his arrival in England, Lecomte had taught the sealion to perform simple tricks, and Bartlett took him on to the staff at the same time as the animal. At feeding time each day Lecomte would put down a chair on to which the sealion would climb and, leaning over the back, give Lecomte a kiss for his food. That sealion died only a year later, after swallowing a fish hook from one of the fish fed to it, but Lecomte lived for another ten years, during which time he made two rather unsuccessful animal-collecting trips to the Falklands. On the second of these, a passenger on board died of yellow fever on the return journey. The ship's doctor ordered that all the fish be thrown away, and so Lecomte could then only feed his sealions on the flying fish which landed on the deck.

Despite being the most senior member of the Zoo staff, Bartlett was far from averse to taking part in any practical operations necessary to deal with the animals, sometimes even placing himself in the greatest danger. During autumn, some of the more delicate inhabitants of the Zoo needed to be moved to warmer quarters for the winter months, and in the autumn of 1865 Bartlett decided that two half-grown Great Indian one-horned rhinos (the species with the leather armour-plating) could be moved without necessitating all the time and trouble of crating them. A large collar was fitted round the neck of each animal, with a long rope attached to each side, and 24 keepers were called out to hold the four ropes – six men to each.

Then Bartlett and a Dr Corrigan from Dublin Zoo, who was visiting London Zoo at the time (and no doubt soon began to wish he wasn't), walked in front of the rhinos carrying half a loaf of bread in each hand as bait. The rhinos followed and behind them, holding the ropes, walked the keepers. The rhinos hurried to catch up with the bait, so Bartlett and Corrigan hurried as well. Still not reaching them, the rhinos started trotting, and then galloping, with the keepers all hanging on as best they could in four tumbling heaps. Bartlett raced into the rhinos' winter quarters, closely followed by both animals, and vaulted the safety barriers just in time, then gave the animals the loaves, which kept them occupied while their collars were removed. Where the good doctor had got to is not recorded, but he was not seen again that day and no doubt hastily returned to Dublin!

The rhinos continued to grow through the winter, of course, and the following spring a crate on rollers was made to move the male back again. The female was a more docile animal, so Bartlett moved her as he had done before, but this time he employed thirty keepers for the one animal – the entire staff of the Zoo!

There was a further incident involving a rhino the following winter, when 25 keepers had to be used to haul an adult rhino from his pond. He had walked on to the ice and, weighing almost four tonnes, had fallen through. As he clambered out, the keepers all dropped the ropes that they had been pulling and bolted for the narrow exit gate, in which one rather plump keeper became wedged. Luckily for him the rhino must have been suffering from shock, and it took no notice while he was being freed.

One new arrival from North America at this time was a prongbuck. This animal, called an 'antelope' by the Americans, had never been seen before in Europe and was not very well-known even in the USA, where it was some-times hunted. Little more than one metre high at the shoulders, it had a pair of narrow, upstanding horns which curved backwards at the top, each having a short prong projecting forward near the base, from which it gets its name. Antelopes' horns, unlike those of deer, are not shed each year but retained for life, so Bartlett was horrified when the prongbuck's keeper rushed into his

This Greater one-horned rhinoceros, largest of the rhinos, lives at Whipsnade and is a very elderly, 34-year-old female. This is the species moved by Bartlett, using keepers and a rope! (*Colin Whyman*)

office one morning to tell him that one of the animal's horns had dropped off! Bartlett hurried to the enclosure and arrived just in time to see the other horn drop, leaving the animal with two short spikes sticking up from its head.

Bartlett studied the prongbuck over a period and discovered that a new horn grows each year up the hollow centre at the base of the old one, finally pushing it off. Eventually he gave a talk on the subject at one of the Scientific Meetings of the Society, and the prongbuck became recognized as the only living member of a family of animals that is as distinct from antelopes as is the giraffe.

In 1876 the 'new' Lion House, which was to remain in use for a hundred years, was opened. It had been designed after studying the lion houses of some other European zoos, but was highly innovative in allowing some of the occupants access to outside cages. Until then it had been believed that big cats, being mostly tropical animals, needed to be kept in a warm, moist atmosphere, and many people at that time thought that the chilly, damp and foggy climate of Victorian London would bring an early death to these animals, but, instead of the average life of about six years' length in their previous quarters,

most of the occupants of the new house lived nearer their normal lifespan of something like twenty years. Indeed, so healthy did the lions become that by the beginning of the next century London Zoo was supplying lion cubs to zoos in South Africa since they were finer than ones that could be captured in the wild, although this was also partly due to changes in their diet.

Although feeding of the carnivores was not improved until after his death, it was Bartlett who had first pointed out that their diet of only 'muscle and bone' was incomplete in that it did not include the skin, intestines and blood eaten by their wild cousins, and that this could be the cause of Zoo-born lion cubs never having survived more than a few years. We now know that the components missing from their diet were vitamins and minerals, which are provided these days by a 'feline supplement' powder sprinkled on to their meat.

Bartlett had the problem of moving all the big cats from the old Terraces to their new house. The public readily joined in solving the problem by writing many letters of suggestions, including chloroforming all the animals (this was in days long before tranquillizer darts could be fired from guns) or building

A long row of cages containing roaring and snarling animals, for 100 years feeding time was one of the great attractions of the 1876 Lion House. It was replaced by the present Lion Terraces of only seven enclosures, covering twice the area (© ZSL)

an iron tunnel from the old premises across the Gardens to the new ones, but Bartlett managed to achieve the move quietly over several days while visitors were still in the Zoo. He had wooden crates put inside the cages with the animals' food placed inside, and as a cat entered its crate the sliding entrance door was dropped shut; then the bell on the clock tower was rung, calling selected keepers from their current duties to push the crate to the new house. In this way some twenty big cats were transferred without the visitors being aware of anything unusual.

Not only was Bartlett involved in the practicalities of running the Zoo, but also he was a keen observer of animals, being scientifically minded. A number of 'papers' that he read out at the Scientific Meetings were printed in their 'Proceedings and Transactions'. He wrote an appendix to one 'paper' presented by a Fellow on the arrival of some African lungfish encased in dried mud, describing their release, as the mud dissolved and the fish returned to an active life in water, and their subsequent behaviour and growth.

His correspondence must have been great as he always tried to provide answers to queries raised, particularly those of a scientific nature. Charles Darwin was a Fellow of the Society and wrote to him several times while writing his books, asking such questions as 'Do elephants carry their tails aloft like horses when turned out into a field?', 'Do certain monkeys when they cry wrinkle their faces as seen in the human child?', and 'Can the bower bird distinguish colours?' On one occasion Darwin sent him a copy of his book, *The Origin of Species*, as a gift and in his accompanying letter wrote:

> I was very glad to see a donkey with a wild ass in the Gardens, for I infer from this that you intend rearing a hybrid; If so I hope you will look carefully for stripes on the *shoulder and legs in the foal*: you will see why I am so anxious on this head, if you will read the little discussion in the *Origin* from pages 163 to 167.

Bartlett also carried out some veterinary work – almost unknown in the Zoo during its first sixty years. His lancing of an elephant's abscess is mentioned in the chapter about Jumbo, and he used a two-foot-long pair of forceps to remove an ulcerated tusk from a hippopotamus while two keepers held Bartlett round the waist to help pull. By 1889 he had used an anaesthetic for the first time in the Zoo when removing a decayed tooth from a baboon with the help of a private dentist. Despite the baboon actually drinking the chloroform neat instead of only breathing it, the operation was a success and the baboon was eating heartily only minutes after regaining consciousness!

Bartlett was often placed in danger, through no fault of his own, particularly when buying animals. On one occasion he visited an animal dealer who told him he had 'some nice snakes' for him, only to be horrified to find the dealer's wife unpacking, and putting by the fire 'to thaw out', a crate of deadly puff adders. Another time, a sailor walked into his office and tipped a cobra out of a sack on to his desk, having brought it by bus across London in that sack.

One new animal he obtained was the first aardwolf to come to the Zoo – a rare hyena-like animal from southern Africa. Nothing Bartlett suggested could induce the animal to eat until, in desperation, he had some tripe stewed in milk and poured it over the aardwolf, which then licked itself clean, finished up the tripe, and never lost its appetite again.

He was no fool, and when a Japanese dealer offered him 'some Yokohama fowls' with tails six metres long, his knowledge of taxidermy showed itself and he agreed to buy the birds provided he was first allowed to dip their tails in warm water; he could tell that the tail feathers were not attached naturally and would come unstuck. The dealer beat a hasty retreat.

But towards people other than rogues Bartlett displayed a kindly nature. Once, a woman dropped her purse while getting on the howdah to have a ride on an elephant; the elephant promptly picked it up with its trunk and ate it. Very upset, the woman searched out Bartlett and told him what had happened. He gave her a sovereign to get her home and tide her over for a few days (£1 had a reasonable value in those days), and promised to have a careful check kept to try to recover her money. He ensured that a careful examination of the elephant's droppings was made each day, and sure enough after nine days money began to appear, though it was rather dented from the crunching of the elephant's huge teeth. A little over half of the money was eventually recovered and returned to her.

On another occasion, an old cab driver brought his horse to Bartlett to ask if he would buy it for £2 and see that it was humanely killed. The lions were normally fed on horse meat and it was customary for people to bring their favourite horses to the Zoo to be humanely put down rather than take them to a horse-dealer. (On holiday, when the subject of his job came up, Bartlett used to mystify enquirers by saying that he bought hundreds of horses each year, seldom paid more than a few pounds for each one, and never parted with one of them for money!) The old cab driver was obviously attached to his horse, which had been well looked after and was in good condition, and Bartlett felt that the light work required of horses pulling the Zoo rubbish cart would not be too much for it. He therefore offered the man twice the asking price, provided he was allowed to use the horse for this purpose. This was agreed, and the horse did this work until it died of old age six years later, during which time the 'cabby' and his wife came every Sunday to see their old friend.

In May 1897, 'Papa' Bartlett died at the age of 85, still the Zoo's Superintendent after having held this post for 38 years. He was buried in

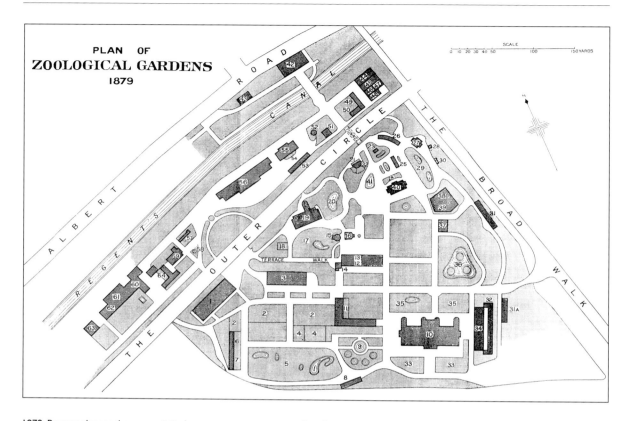

PLAN OF
ZOOLOGICAL GARDENS
1879

1879. By now the southern part of the Zoo had been developed to create a Rodent House (6), a seal pond (9) and two large buildings which were to stand for 100 years – the Deer and Cattle Sheds (32/34) and the Lion House (10) – as well as the first aquarium in the world, the Fish House opened in 1853 (37). A Monkey House (3) had been built near the Main Entrance. In the Middle Gardens the small Elephant House had grown in size (56) and houses had been provided for animals rarely seen in this country nowadays – wombats, Brush turkeys and markhors (50–52). North of the canal, added land now included a Tortoise House (43) (© ZSL)

Highgate cemetery, not far from a man whose name is today better known – Karl Marx. Exactly a hundred years later, the Society acknowledged what a remarkable man Abraham Bartlett had been, and how much London Zoo was indebted to him, and erected a brass plaque to his memory in the Giraffe House.

7 Jumbo

Just as London Zoo gave the word 'zoo' to the English and all other languages, so also the name of one of their most famous inhabitants has so completely entered the language that it, too, can be found in the dictionary:

jumbo: anything very big of its kind.

In Africa, several Bantu languages contain the word *Njamba* for 'elephant', and so it seems likely that this was the origin of the name 'Jumbo', given to a young, dirty and rather emaciated African elephant that arrived at the Zoo on 26 June 1865. Although elephants had already been seen in the Zoo for 34 years, they had all been of the Asiatic species, and Jumbo was the first African elephant the Zoo had possessed. He would grow to be a veritable giant, at 11 feet high (nearly 4 metres), but at the time he arrived he stood only four feet tall.

Bartlett was Superintendent of the Zoo at that time, and to ensure that his instructions regarding Jumbo's welfare were carried out, he appointed Matthew Scott to have sole charge of him. Scott was the antelope keeper and knew nothing whatever about elephants, so Bartlett quite rightly felt he would obey him implicitly. Bartlett wrote:

> The first thing was to endeavour to remove the accumulated filth and dirt from his skin. This was a task requiring a considerable amount of labour and patience, and was not to be done in the space of a moment.

He and Scott coaxed and fed him and gained his confidence, so that he quickly became healthy and settled down.

Under instruction from Scott, as he grew older Jumbo was trained to give visitors rides on his back as did the Asiatic elephants. African elephants are more temperamental than their Asiatic relatives, and male elephants are notoriously untrustworthy. While in recent years hand-reared African elephants have become tame enough to carry people on safaris, they are still considered too unreliable to give rides in zoos, and this is particularly the case for males.

The 1869 Elephant House demonstrates the Victorian way of building, considering appearance as well as practicality, and compares with the Casson building some 100 years later. It was demolished in 1938 (© *ZSL*)

Today, therefore, no one would take the double risk of allowing a male African elephant to mix with the public, but back then, experience had not yet been gained – and, in fact, Jumbo behaved very well for several years, giving rides to many hundreds of people. Eventually, however, disaster nearly struck. One day, while in the grounds giving rides, something frightened him and he panicked and hurried to his house with the howdah strapped to his back. The Elephant House of that time was situated in the Middle Gardens, necessitating going through the tunnel in order to reach the riding area in the Main Gardens. Elephants cannot run, but they can walk very fast indeed, and Jumbo hurried through the tunnel. No one was riding on him at the time, and this was most fortunate because there was no room above the seats, and they scored a groove along the top of the tunnel that could still be seen until the tunnel roof was re-cemented over a hundred years later.

After this incident Jumbo was no longer allowed to give rides, and shortly afterwards, as a now fully mature bull elephant, he began having periods of 'musth'. These are periods of 'madness', connected to their sexual cycle, to which all mature bull elephants are prone, when a tar-like substance trickles down their foreheads and they become quite violent and uncontrollable. Jumbo, weighing five tonnes and almost twice the height of a man, began charging the door of his enclosure, which had to be hastily reinforced with iron bars for his own and everyone else's safety. On one occasion such was his violence that he broke off both his tusks near their base.

Between these 'musth' periods he returned to normal and was perfectly good-tempered and obedient, although he would never accept instructions from anyone but Scott. Scott in turn, realizing he was indispensable in handling Jumbo, became a law unto himself and would answer to nobody but Bartlett, to whom, however, he always remained loyal. Scott probably derived a good supplementary income in tips from visitors because of Jumbo, who had become the darling of the public following all the publicity he had

Probably the most famous Zoo animal in the world, Jumbo giving rides. His huge size can be seen by a comparison with his keeper (© *ZSL*)

been given by the press from the time of his arrival at the Zoo. Animal rides were at that time free, visitors tipping the keepers as they saw fit, but although Jumbo no longer gave rides, he was still no doubt a source of many tips for Scott by obeying instructions such as picking up coins and giving them to his keeper.

Elephants have only four teeth other than their tusks, two molars on each side of their mouth to grind the colossal amount of food they eat – nearly 150 kilos each day. Each tooth is about the size and weight of a house brick, and is replaced as it is worn down about every eight or nine years. Seven replacements occur in an elephant's lifetime, and after the last one is lost an elephant would die of hunger if it had reached that age. But the tusks, which are the front, incisor teeth, continue to grow throughout an elephant's life, and when the broken stumps inside Jumbo's mouth had grown a little it became apparent that they were twisted, pushing his cheeks out on either side of his trunk.

The result was a painful abscess on each side of his face, which he would nevertheless allow Bartlett to touch and even rub. Eventually Bartlett decided that the thick skin would have to be cut in order to drain each abscess. He had a special scalpel made – a steel rod half a metre in length, with a sharp hook at the end flattened on the inner edge and made razor-sharp. Standing under the huge animal's lower jaw, Bartlett gave a sharp pull on his scalpel, cutting through the thick skin and, in his own words, 'causing a most frightful discharge of very offensive matter'. Jumbo uttered a loud shriek and rushed away, but then returned to have the wound bathed! The next day, with some trepidation, Bartlett returned to operate on the other cheek, but, to his surprise, Jumbo stood perfectly still and allowed the second cut to be made. The operations were successful and Jumbo's broken tusks grew once again without paining him further.

The Zoo had several elephants at that time, including Alice, a female African elephant purchased only a few months after Jumbo, and an Asiatic elephant presented by the Prince of Wales. This elephant had, in 1878, probably quite by accident, trampled on the elderly keeper of the Parrot House, Goss, who had been left in charge of it for only a few minutes. Goss (who, as a young man, had held the parrots that Edward Lear was drawing) died around three weeks later, and some adverse correspondence was written to *The Times* about the incident. You can read more about this in the next chapter.

Probably influenced by this accident, and knowing how unmanageable Jumbo was in the hands of anyone but Scott, Bartlett was understandably worried as to what would happen if the animal went berserk when Scott was not around. The Elephant House had already, in Bartlett's words, been 'propped up with massive timber beams', and because Jumbo could be very dangerous in Scott's absence, Bartlett asked the Society's Council for permission to obtain a sufficiently powerful rifle to kill the elephant should this become necessary; his request was granted. It must be borne in mind that male elephants are potentially highly dangerous animals, and, whereas nowadays zoos are very reluctant to keep a male elephant, precisely because of this danger, and take great care to provide suitably reinforced housing if one *is* kept for breeding purposes (as has now been provided at Whipsnade), London Zoo was breaking new ground in the captive treatment of male elephants and had little earlier experience to draw upon.

It is not surprising that the Council members were becoming alarmed at the idea of having a bull elephant on the rampage – the mind boggled at the damage he could do in the Zoo and, an even more frightening thought, in London itself! It must, therefore, have been with sighs of relief that they received a letter in 1882 from Phineas Barnum, the great American showman, offering to buy Jumbo (so far had his fame spread!) and asking them to name a price. Bartlett was instructed to dispose of the animal for £2,000, and he wrote to Barnum telling him he could have Jumbo for this price 'as he stands', thus avoiding the expense to the Zoo of crating and transporting him all the way to the USA. Barnum replied by telegram: 'I accept your offer; my agents will be with you in a few days.' (Two thousand pounds was a huge sum in those days, but Barnum later admitted that he would have paid three thousand.)

And then the storm broke!

For years Jumbo had been receiving much publicity in the press, and he was a great favourite with the public. A giant among animals, and gentle (most of the time), he had for a long time been the greatest 'draw' in the Zoo, and hundreds of visitors had ridden on his back. If the news that he might have to be shot one day had shocked the public, then the further news that he was to go to America caused an uproar! Most happenings are newsworthy for only a day or two, but this remained a top-line matter of concern for many weeks. Angry correspondents wrote to *The Times* and every other newspaper, while editorials and articles on the 'scandal' appeared daily.

The 'Great Macdermont', a music hall comic of the day, wrote and sang a ballad of six verses, with an eight-line chorus which ended:

> But, oh, Englishmen, can it be true?
> For a paltry two thousand they're going to part
> With old Jumbo, the pet of the Zoo.

Then Jumbo's name became linked with Alice, the female elephant, with whom he was said to be 'in love', and in the world of the newspapers Alice even became an expectant mother! In fact the two animals had never been together, and had hardly even caught sight of each other (illustrating very

Designed by Sir Hugh Casson in 1965 to house elephants and rhinos, this building gives the feel of the huge and heavy animals for which it was built. The 'periscopes' provide light to the internal enclosures while visitors remain in subdued light (© *Crown Copyright. NMR*)

clearly the newspaper maxim: 'Facts are the enemy of a good story'), but this was yet another aspect of the story that caught the public's imagination, and once again verses were written, the most popular song being:

> Jumbo said to Alice: I – love – you.
> Alice said to Jumbo: I don't believe you do,
> For if you really loved me as you say you do
> You wouldn't go to Yankeeland and leave me in the Zoo.

Children, and some of the adults, who visited him in the Zoo were in tears, and even Queen Victoria asked that Jumbo might remain in England – though this was one of the rare occasions that a Royal request was politely but firmly turned down. A fund was started to collect 'blood money' and 'save Jumbo for the Nation', and the editor of the *Daily Telegraph* (which, in its 27-year existence, had regularly attacked the Zoological Society) sent the following telegram to Barnum in New York:

Editor's compliments. All British children distressed at elephant's departure. Hundreds of correspondents beg us to enquire in what terms you
will kindly return Jumbo. Answer prepaid, unlimited.

Barnum replied:

My compliments to editor *Daily Telegraph* and British nation. Fifty
millions of American citizens anxiously awaiting Jumbo's arrival. My
forty years invariable practice of exhibiting the best that money can
procure makes Jumbo's presence here imperative. Hundred thousand
pounds would be no inducement to cancel purchase …

In hindsight, over a century later, it still seems that the Society's Council
made the right decision to dispose of a potentially dangerous animal, for
which they had neither the space nor the facilities to be able to restrain it
safely and yet at the same time allow it reasonable freedom while ensuring
complete safety for the public as well as the Zoo's own staff. To this day
London Zoo is considered unsuitable for male elephants, and it has taken the
space and facilities of Whipsnade Zoo to keep one safely. The same applies to
the majority of zoos, and few try to breed elephants because of the dangers
inherent in keeping males – in zoos, more keepers have been killed by
elephants than by any other animal.

But such reasoning (in those days unsupported by experience) had little
effect on the public, and even amongst the ranks of the Society's Fellows there
was dissent. A number of them thought the Council out of order in making
such a momentous decision without calling an Extraordinary General
Meeting, and they applied to the High Court to restrain the Council from
completing the sale, and were granted an interim injunction pending a hearing. Mr Justice Chitty then heard the case, which lasted a whole week,
although much of the evidence was quite irrelevant. The crux of the case was
a clause in the Society's Royal Charter by which disposal of its exhibits could
be regulated by the Crown Office, but the judge found in favour of the Society
(probably accompanied by sighs of relief from the Crown Office, who were
unlikely to welcome this added responsibility). One factor which swayed the
judge was the statement by Barnum's agent that, while Jumbo was undoubtedly a dangerous animal in England, he could quite safely be kept under the
conditions he would experience in America.

While all the furore continued, plans progressed for Jumbo's removal. The
public flocked to the Zoo in even greater numbers and queued for hours to
see 'their' beloved Jumbo, and a steady stream of gifts arrived for him –
mostly food and titbits for the long journey, but also less practical items such
as dolls, books and even a sewing machine.

The *Pall Mall Gazette* wrote an article:

> What Jumbo himself thinks of his change of prospects is only too pathetically certain. He won't go. To every attempt to inveigle or force him he opposes an intelligent, patient, resolute resistance ... Jumbo is evidently as unwilling to part with his London friends as they, if they have any sense or feelings, will be desolate at the thought of losing him.

A huge, strong, wooden crate had been prepared, weighing about eight tonnes, with open bars at one end to enable the elephant to see out; but getting him to enter it was quite another matter.

Council, anticipating problems and recognizing that they would have little control of the situation since they had left the crating and transporting to Barnum's agent, insisted that someone from the RSPCA be present, and in the event of the RSPCA interfering, Zoo staff were instructed to withdraw their assistance immediately. Thus they ensured that no cruelty would be involved if people's patience wore thin.

Not only is it extremely difficult to persuade an elephant to do something against his will (you can't just put a shoulder to him and push!), but also entering a dark box is never an attractive idea, and Scott, the only keeper Jumbo would obey, was undoubtedly not happy at the prospect of losing him (and his attendant additional income from 'tips'). Some people at the time suggested that Scott had secretly given Jumbo a sign not to co-operate, but even without this Jumbo would not have entered his crate without firm and correct instructions from Scott. The plan was then tried of walking him to Millwall Dock, from where he could be hoisted on to the ship by crane and lowered into his crate, but they only got as far as the Zoo gates before Jumbo refused to go any further.

It was a month later that, still having been unsuccessful, Barnum's agent eventually offered to take Scott also, and the keeper accepted. Whereupon – surprise, surprise – Jumbo promptly walked into his crate. It *might*, of course, have been a pure coincidence! Council must have heaved a collective sigh of relief at being rid of two troublemakers in one go.

Once in his crate, Jumbo was pulled by six horses to the dock, transferred to a barge and finally hoisted on board the steamship *Assyria Monarch*, bound for the USA. Once in America he again played up, and even the coaxing of Scott could not persuade him to enter the railway wagon which had been specially constructed for him. Eventually, three other elephants were necessary, one pulling and two pushing with their foreheads, before Jumbo was safely in and could be transported.

For three years he seems to have behaved himself; he was a huge draw for Barnum and Bailey's 'Greatest Show on Earth'. But then he died as spectacu-

larly as he had lived – being hit by a freight train while crossing the railway line at St Thomas in Canada. He was killed almost instantly, and so was the engine driver, while two of the rail trucks were derailed.

Scott was offered a job as keeper to other elephants, but he turned this down because he would have been expected to dress in oriental clothes. He spent some time showing Jumbo's stuffed skin around the United States, but then returned to England, where he was last heard of making a living by selling copies of a little booklet describing his twenty years with Jumbo.

As for Jumbo himself, his stuffed skin was still to be seen in Tufts University, Boston, until a fire destroyed it in the 1970s, and his skeleton was kept in the American Museum of Natural History in New York and, so far as I know, is there still. Another memento of Jumbo is the Bird House in London Zoo, which was originally built as a Reptile House using the £2,000 proceeds of Jumbo's sale to Barnum.

But his lasting memorial must surely be his name, 'Jumbo', now a word used daily throughout the English-speaking world over a hundred years after his death.

The Bird House was originally built as the Reptile House with the proceeds received from the sale of Jumbo (*Colin Whyman*)

8 The Turn of the Century

By 1890, poultry shows were occurring around the country and so the Zoo's encouragement was no longer necessary; their own poultry shows therefore ceased until, fifty years later, chickens were again kept in the Zoo, to demonstrate to wartime Londoners how to keep them (as well as to provide eggs for some of the Zoo animals).

Although it lost its poultry shows, the Zoological Society gained responsibility for the Zoological Record. This is a huge work of reference originally started by Van Voorst in 1864 and consisting of nothing less than the annual recording of all zoological papers published throughout the world, for reference by scientists in all countries. The task had become too much for one man and, as the years went by, was eventually to prove too much for the Society also, so in 1980, after ninety years, the Society co-operated with BIOSIS (the Biological Abstracts/BioSciences Information Service, in Philadelphia) to form a partnership that has, using computer technology, continued to produce the Zoological Record. An anniversary meeting was held in December 1989 to celebrate the publication of volume 125; there was by then a machine-readable version of the Record, which by that year contained over 800,000 entries. But at the close of the nineteenth century there was no thought of using typewriters, let alone computers, and the Zoo itself would hardly be recognized by the end of the twentieth century.

Horses were used in London by the thousand to pull carts containing all the goods to be sold in shops and, consequently, the smell was, to put it mildly, quite noticeable. Even so, the smells in some of the Zoo's animal houses were even more noticeable, and caused visiting ladies to hold scented handkerchiefs to their noses. These days it is difficult for children to appreciate how important is the sense of smell to many animals, and there are now few smells in the Zoo, but this was far from the case a hundred years ago.

Not only were the aromas of the animals themselves noticeable, but also the Zoo still had no proper drainage system. Some of the animals' waste matter was sold as manure, and more was taken in barges to a dump at West Drayton, but much was emptied directly into the Regent's Canal. London's sewage system had been completed only relatively recently, but the suggestion that the Zoo should use it caused some stormy meetings of the local council at first. However, the waters of the canal, which had been used by everyone as a dumping ground since it was built in 1820, were analysed with such frightening results that permission for the Zoo to use the sewage system was quickly granted.

During the first seventy years of its existence, the Zoo and its occupants had been represented by hundreds of drawings and sketches in daily newspapers and popular journals such as *Punch* and the *Illustrated London News*. Numerous also were the paintings and drawings made over the years by such artists as Josef Wolf, Edward Lear and Sir Edwin Landseer. Photography was of growing interest, and towards the end of the century a few photographers were trying their hand within the Gardens. Many more years were to pass before sensitized film would replace the chemically coated glass plates previously necessary, enabling everyone to record personally their day at the Zoo.

In the 1890s the first pioneer of serious animal photography was Gambier Bolton, who was the accepted Zoo photographer. With his heavy camera, glass plates and wooden tripod, he was denied the benefits of hundredths-of-a-second photographs, having to wait until the animal was quite still before making an exposure. He usually poked the lens of his ungainly camera through the bars, sometimes having it damaged by an unwilling subject and narrowly escaping personal injury on several occasions. When photographing lions he usually had three helpers: one man with a pole, to stop the lion attacking him; another with a pole, to keep the animal in sunlight; and a third man above the cage, dangling a piece of meat to hold the lion's attention. And remember, the exposure would last several seconds. As Bolton himself said during a lecture he gave, reported in the *Globe* in 1892:

> Did a puff of wind move mane or tail or feather, a slight sound cause a twitching of an ear, or even the movement necessary in breathing mar the perfect reproduction of every little detail, the plates were thrown away.

Despite all the problems, his results were remarkably good, and his photographs were still being used as book illustrations forty years later, in the 1930s.

Frank Buckland, an enthusiastic Victorian naturalist who visited the Zoo many times and was a friend of Bartlett, the Superintendent, delighted in sampling the unusual meats that resulted from the deaths of Zoo animals. He once made a huge pie from part of an old rhinoceros that had died, to be tried by the audience of a lecture he was giving in Brighton; the general opinion was that it tasted very much like tough beef!

Mention has already been made of the feline supplement sprinkled on the big cats' meat to replace missing minerals and vitamins. Buckland was a serious naturalist and wrote that the lions were fed alternately on beef and horsemeat, which, from time to time, was sprinkled with '... a proper allowance of common flower of brimstone, or sulphur, as this keeps the animals in good health and condition, upon the principle of giving our own youngsters a treat of brimstone-and-treacle by way of a change'. It is doubtful whether sulphur had the same effect as our feline supplement!

In his book, *Curiosities of Natural History*, published in 1891, Buckland wrote:

I hear there is just a possibility of a large space being enclosed at the Gardens, with a strong iron palisade, so as to form one gigantic cage in which rocks etc. will be placed; forming, in fact, a gigantic 'den' for the lions. What a treat it will be to see the noble creatures in comparative freedom ...

It was to be 85 years before such an enclosure materialized in London, although one was built at Whipsnade only 40 years after Buckland wrote of the idea.

The turn of the century saw the end of the reign of Dr P. L. Sclater as Secretary to the Society. Appointed in 1859, the same year Bartlett became Superintendent, Sclater, unlike Bartlett, was never an object of admiration, nor did he attract loyalty from the Zoo staff. He became involved in several arguments with the public, and appeared to them, and even to some of the Society's Fellows, to be stubborn and at times even arrogant. 'Reformer' wrote to the *Marylebone Mercury* in 1875:

The Council of the Society consists of 1st Mr Bartlett, 2nd Mr Sclater; and to appeal from Mr Sclater as Secretary to Mr Sclater as Council is to appeal from Lord Eldon, sitting as Chancellor, to Lord Eldon, sitting as Judicial Committee of the House of Lords. Lord Eldon used to boast that he never had a judgement reversed. Mr Sclater can similarly claim that the Council has never overruled his decision.

It must be borne in mind that, while Bartlett's job required his presence in the Zoo, and he even lived in it, Sclater was usually in the Society's offices in Hanover Square; he was not, therefore, 'on site' to be able to exercise adequate control over practical affairs. It must also be said that his scientific contributions to the Society were many, as can be seen from numerous entries in the 'Proceedings and Transactions' of the Society. After his first ten years as Secretary, the publication *Scientific Opinion* wrote of Sclater that he 'unites a wide practical zoological experience with a love of scientific research and a thorough appreciation of the commercial aspects of the Zoological Gardens'.

However, this was not of advantage to the Society when, in 1874, Council decided to instigate a weekly series of popular lectures, free of charge, for Zoo visitors. They were to be given by eminent zoologists throughout the summer, and the first, on the subject of the Zoo's occupants, was given by Sclater, about which one newspaper wrote that the animals were:

> ... constantly described as 'specimens' of their respective classes and species, without any attempt at those personal sketches of character and biography to which many of them might aspire. Even the lamented Joe was referred to as 'an Anthropoid Ape' of the 'Species Chimpanzee'.

Sclater gave several of the lectures, making them sound highly scientific and no doubt contributing to their poor attendance. One example, as reported in *Nature*, is typical; talking on the subject of waterfowl, he said:

> Of the whole number of 174 generally recognized species of Anatidae, 77 may, I think, be best set down as Arctic, although some of them, such as [giving a string of Latin names], cannot be strictly so termed as they inhabit only the temperate portion of the Palearctic region.

How is that for a 'popular' lecture?

In 1874 an item of news in the *Daily Telegraph* was to spark off a furore. The article described how an accident had occurred to two elephant and rhino keepers, Godfrey and Thompson, when a Great Indian rhinoceros was able to get in from its outside paddock while they were sweeping out its cage. The rhinoceros was reported to have 'knocked the men down, and tried to trample on them'. According to the article, Scott, an assistant keeper, entered the cage, drove off the rhino and dragged the two men behind the protective iron screen in the corner of the cage. The news item lost nothing in the telling, and apparently 'Godfrey at once fainted, and fell with his head in the cage', where the rhino again attacked him and was chased off by Scott. Godfrey was then said to have fallen a second time, when the rhino 'tore the flesh off the man's leg from the thigh down, laying bare the bone', according to the news item – which then went on to say that the rhino had no horn!

The leader article enlarged even further on the occurrence, to such an extent that Frank Buckland felt obliged to write to the paper's rival, *The Times*, and try to set the record straight: Godfrey's leg was only bruised, no bones were broken and the skin only grazed; Thompson was even less hurt; both men walked out of the den and were not carried by Scott, and both were expected to resume their duties shortly. This was, of course, the kind of rebuttal which should have been written by Sclater, but, as it was, Buckland's letter treated Scott rather shabbily, giving him no thanks for his part in the affair, and, indeed, claiming that he should have been checking the rhino in the outside paddock at the time. Consequently, the *Telegraph* then published a number of angry replies reiterating praise for Scott's 'heroism' and even launching an appeal for a collection on his behalf.

All then went quiet until some eight months later, when someone calling himself 'An Old FZS' wrote to the paper asking how it was that Godfrey had not resumed his duties for six months and Thompson never at all.

How does it happen that Thompson has been discharged altogether ... after thirty years spent in the service of the Society ... without even a pension? Why is it that Godfrey has been ... degraded to an inferior post?

More leading articles followed, and more letters, but still Sclater maintained a complete silence. Eventually Thompson wrote a letter protesting that upon his return he was sent to work in the cattle and deer sheds:

... the hardest work in the gardens. At that time I was suffering from the shock to the system, and had a rheumatic attack. I had even to be dressed and undressed by others and to go, therefore, to the new work would have been simply to send me back to bed.

This letter, and another from a Fellow, resulted in Sclater at last writing to the *Telegraph* himself, but only to suggest that the Fellow either visit him at the Society's offices or raise the matter at the next Monthly General Meeting. Another of the Fellows did visit him and was told that by refusing to work where directed, Thompson had discharged himself. The Fellow gained the impression that he would get nowhere in discussing the matter and 'asked, quite frankly, whether I was not wasting time? I received a courteous assurance that I had wasted a good deal of time already; and accordingly the interview came to an end.'

With the advantage of hindsight so long afterwards, it is apparent that the original accident was caused by unforgivable carelessness on the part of the two keepers by not first checking that the rhino's connecting door was securely shut before venturing in – the primary lesson to be learnt by all new keepers – and this must surely have been the reason for their transfer (not necessarily 'degrade') to another house where, perhaps, it was considered they could do less harm. This was, however, never explained in answer to newspaper correspondents, and it was possibly because of this that the resulting public support encouraged Thompson to be defiant over his transfer and later to exaggerate his medical condition. We shall never know, but Sclater was surely at fault for maintaining silence for so long and, later, for his brusque treatment of one of the Society's Fellows who, after all, was helping to keep him in office. It seems to be another case of taking the correct action, but not communicating effectively; such cases occur in the business world and, sadly, from time to time in the Zoo also.

As mentioned in the previous chapter, in 1878 there was another accident in the same house, when an elephant trampled on Goss, the elderly keeper of the Parrot House, who was looking after the animal for a few minutes. A letter to *The Times* expressed surprise that no news had appeared of the accident, particularly in view of Goss's severe injuries which had left him in 'a critical state' in hospital. On this occasion Sclater did reply, saying that Goss was *not* in 'a critical state' and 'was going on very favourably'. Goss died three weeks later, and Sclater did not then reply to a further letter from the same correspondent!

A much more pleasant story about a keeper concerned Benjamin Misselbrook, who had joined the Zoo in December 1828, aged seventeen, at a salary of three shillings (15p) a day, and retired in 1889 after sixty years' service, for the last twenty of which he had been a head keeper. There were, of course, no pension schemes in those days, but the Annual Report for that year says that the Council 'thought it right to allow this old and valued servant, who had attained an advanced age in the Society's service, to retire on full pay, and are certain that they will receive the full approbation of the Fellows in adopting this course'. Four years later, Misselbrook died at the age of eighty-two, and in view of his long and industrious life in the Society's service, 'the Council have thought it proper to confer on his widow a pension of £26 a year for the rest of her life'.

Yet another controversy involving Sclater was the matter of providing live food for the snakes. By 1881 there had been a growing, though still minority, objection to this practice for the past ten years, although feeding time in the Reptile House seems to have been a most popular event. In that year a magazine published extracts from forty letters attacking the Society in general and its Secretary, Sclater, in particular, for retaining live feeding and for allowing the public, including children, to be spectators. Sclater's response was, in effect, that no cruelty was involved, that live prey was necessary for snakes and that, while the Zoo made no attempt to attract visitors by advertising reptile feeding times, 'the spectacle … was a reasonable and desirable source of healthy amusement to children and young persons'. Once again Sclater's judgement was at fault, and at its very next meeting the Council decided that, in future, reptile feeding would be done after closing-time. It was to be another 25 years, after Chalmers Mitchell had replaced Sclater and had spent four years persuading the keepers and studying the practice, before live feeding was finally stopped. To this day, however, dead food has to be offered to many of the snakes by dangling it from long forceps to simulate movement, enabling the snake to recognize potential food and strike.

While on the subject of animal foods, a 'table of the provisions purchased' was drawn up for the Annual Report of 1895 from which it is interesting to see that included on it were 15 tonnes of biscuits, nearly 24,000 eggs, over 17 tonnes of fish, 16,900 oranges and 7,500 'Fowl-heads'!

Philip Lutley Sclater eventually resigned in 1902, and his son, William Lutley Sclater, whom he had hoped would succeed him and who was then Director of Cape Town Museum, was temporarily appointed until ratification by the Fellows at the next Annual General Meeting. However, at that meeting in April 1903, a second candidate was nominated by a group of Fellows. This other candidate was voted Secretary with a majority of 200 votes. He was 39-year-old Dr (later Sir) Peter Chalmers Mitchell, who was to have a very profound effect upon the popularity of London Zoo and on the Zoological Society. During his 32 years in office, the number of Fellows doubled and the annual figures for attendance of Zoo visitors increased from 700,000 to 2 million.

Three years earlier there had been a discovery of immense zoological interest. During its first 75 years the Zoo had exhibited many animals previously unseen, and by the end of the century all the large land animals of the world had been discovered – or so it was thought. The world was soon to be astonished by the description at one of the Zoological Society's Scientific Meetings of a hitherto unknown animal the size of a horse.

Sir Harry Johnston was an explorer of Central Africa and a keen naturalist and Fellow of the Society who had heard rumours of a 'donkey' which was known to, and being caught by, pygmies in the depths of the Ituri forest of the Congo. Horses are animals of the plains, and none was known from any rainforest so, intrigued, he travelled to the area and spoke to the natives, who told him of a rare animal they called the 'O'api', which was like a dark-coloured horse with stripes on its legs and rear. Two Europeans he met confirmed the existence of the animal, which they had never seen alive but whose meat they had eaten. They did not think it was a horse, however, as it had more than one toe on each foot. Horses, of course, have only one 'toe' (hoof), but are descended from prehistoric three-toed horses, and Johnston thought the animal for which he was searching could be a survivor of those prehistoric animals, so when his native guides showed him the tracks of an animal with two toes, he did not believe they were the footprints of the animal he was seeking, but of a forest antelope similar to the bongo.

A few days later he saw two strips of hide in a native village and was told they belonged to the O'api; because of the stripes on the skins he thought the animal to be a new species of zebra. At this point in time he had to return to Uganda, but was promised a complete skin and skull by the two Europeans when these could be obtained. In due course he received a skin and not one but two skulls, and from these he saw to his surprise that the feet had two toes each. This fact, together with a study of the skulls, showed that the animal appeared to be related, of all animals, to the giraffe!

Johnston took careful measurements and then made a watercolour painting of two specimens – paintings which are so accurate they could not be bettered from living animals today – and sent these to Professor Ray Lankester, calling the animal 'Helladotherium', the name given to an extinct member of the giraffe family. Lankester at first denounced the painting as fraudulent and a joke in bad taste, but changed his mind when the skin and skulls arrived. At a Scientific Meeting of the Society in 1901, which was more crowded than for many a month and was attended by Sir Harry Johnston himself, Lankester demonstrated that the animal was a survivor of a once-flourishing race of giraffe-like animals. He called it the 'Okapi', a slight corruption of its original native name.

This painting by Sir Harry Johnston was made from a study of an okapi skin before any living animals had been seen by him! It is a perfect representation (© *ZSL*)

The Latin name given to the animal was *Okapia johnstoni*, after its discoverer, and for his contribution to zoology Sir Harry was presented with the Society's Gold Medal – only the second time it had ever been awarded.

The okapi is a shy animal that inhabits dense tropical rainforest. In such surroundings a long neck and long legs would be a serious encumbrance, so the okapi has a much shorter neck while retaining a giraffe's short horns and long tongue with which to strip leaves from branches. Its dark coloration is also more suited to dark forests, while its stripes help break up its outline and camouflage it – and also, it has been said, help its young to follow it in the gloom. The few okapis captured and sent to European zoos in the years that followed died relatively quickly, but one given to London Zoo in 1937 lived there for thirteen years. A ban on exporting the animals was introduced by Belgium, who controlled that area of the Congo, and few exceptions were allowed. However, by the 1960s the few in zoos were breeding, and a joint breeding programme was established between Marwell, Bristol and London Zoos.

This, then, was the animal first discovered at the beginning of the twentieth century. It was a time when the Zoo (like the rest of Europe) was to face the problems of two major wars within the next forty years, but, between them, was to experience greater popularity than ever before. The introduction

After seventy-five years in central London these were the first offices in the Zoo and included the Society's library and Meeting Room. The latter was later replaced by a new building to leave more space for the ever-growing number of books in the library (© Crown Copyright. NMR)

of London's first motor bus in 1906 heralded an era of cheap public travel within the metropolis, and this in turn was to lead in 1910 to the first office, library and Meeting Room of the Society to be built within the Zoo grounds, it now being considered safe for the Fellows to venture to the Gardens after dark. This was the first building in the Zoo to use electricity. (Another fifty years on and the space in this building had also become too small, so new Meeting Rooms were built in 1965, enabling the still-growing library to expand its area.) So crowded had the building in Hanover Square become that, fifteen years earlier, Sclater had had the temerity to propose to the Royal Academy that they take over an empty site in the Haymarket (now occupied by Her Majesty's Theatre) and release Burlington House for the use of the Zoological Society and other scientific bodies.

The London Underground railway was gradually extending, and a station close to the Zoo had been proposed, but unfortunately the idea was vetoed by King Edward VII, who could not tolerate the idea of a railway station in a Royal Park. This was a great pity, as many visitors have since walked a mile from Regent's Park station in the mistaken assumption that this is the nearest station to the Zoo. (Camden Town and Chalk Farm are in fact the nearest stations.)

About this time the Zoo received the first proboscis monkey to come to Europe, adding to a collection of monkeys of which they were proud. However, when the Shah of Persia visited the Zoo soon afterwards, he said that while monkeys were 'amusing animals', they were not worth keeping, and he strongly recommended to the Superintendent that they 'be abolished'. He also said that hippopotami, being of no real economic value, 'ought to be shot and exterminated'. He was eager to buy the large snakes (and had to be tactfully, but firmly told they were not for sale) and wanted to know whether the giraffes were good to eat! Had Frank Buckland still been alive he could perhaps have told him.

The Zoo's sealions had for many years had a rather miserable pool, little more than a basin in the ground with a wooden shelter at one side, but in 1905 a large pool was constructed with a grass surround and a large, over-hanging artificial rock from which the animals could dive, below which were their night quarters. Behind the rock a new aviary was built, which from the 1930s included herons in its collection. Forty years later their presence encouraged wild herons to settle in Regent's Park itself, where they now regularly nest. Often some could be seen perched on top of the aviary, hoping to snatch uneaten fish thrown to the sealions, giving visitors the impression they had escaped from the aviary.

The Zoo first tried the innovation of keeping penguins and sealions together in the new enclosure, and all went well for a while. One feeding time, however, the largest sealion and a small penguin went for the same fish, grabbing opposite ends, and the sealion swallowed not only the fish, but also the penguin! This seemed to give him a taste for penguin, and the birds had to be hurriedly moved to other quarters.

A concrete column was later built on the summit of the sealion's rock, with an opening near the top. Visitors could insert sixpence into a box on the enclosure railings and, after a certain amount of whirring, pieces of whiting were flung out of the column towards the centre of the pool. In this way visitors had the pleasure of personally feeding the sealions while at the same time contributing to their upkeep. Of course, not all the sealions' food was provided in this way, which was just as well because, when they heard the whirring sound, the sealions would swim to the centre of their pool in readiness, and the large male would be the lucky recipient more often than not, so the food given by the keepers each day ensured fair shares for all. The automatic dispenser has itself now long been dispensed with, and in 1997, after over 90 years as the sealion pond, the pool was linked to a nearby enclosure and used for the rare pygmy hippos.

Constructed in 1901 for sealions, feeding time at this pool was one of the 'don't miss' events of the day; it is now occupied by pygmy hippos. In later years wild herons could often be seen standing on top of the aviary at the far end, hoping to snatch fish from the sealions (© *Crown Copyright. NMR*)

While the fish dispenser was a novel idea, and was followed by a similar machine which dispensed grain to the mountain goats, being able to feed the animals had been a great attraction ever since the Zoo first opened, and the sale of 'monkey nuts' in packets can still be remembered by some. The Zoo made quite a profit by selling such animal food, having first started with buns which were left over from the previous day's sale in the tea pavilion.

Unfortunately, staff began by merely labelling them as 'stale buns', which one of the comic papers of the day misinterpreted, in the words of the 'Revd Stiggins':

> Honesty, my son, is ever the best policy. Refreshment caterers at other places of amusement will sell you stale buns, but do they tell you thereof? Not much! Here these worthy people tell you their buns *are* stale. Great will be their reward.

The early years of the new century saw the arrival of many zoos, from Scotland to Hagenbeck's panoramic zoo in Hamburg. Others opening in Europe included those at Rome, Genoa and Zurich, as well as several more in Germany, while new zoos also started as far away as China, Japan, New Zealand and the USA. The zoo habit was catching on fast, and zoos drew on the long and hard-earned experience of London Zoo, but one way in which few other zoos copied London was in layout. In the relatively small area it occupied, London Zoo had grown piecemeal, adding what was necessary wherever possible; so, for instance, while giraffes and hippos shared the same house, the Small Cats' House was at some distance from that for the larger cats, the Lion House. Most new zoos were designed more reasonably, often by grouping the animals by geographical distribution or by relationship (classification). But there was one curious exception.

The first Insect House in the world had opened at London Zoo in 1881 (called the Insectorium), but in 1912 Sir James Caird donated money for a new Insect House – which was built and used as such for 85 years. This house was built near the new offices, and was again a 'first' in that visitors walked in a darkened corridor, viewing well-lit tanks – a principle later copied in the new Aquarium, the Reptile House and, years later, carried to extremes in the Moonlight World for nocturnal animals. This method of lighting became known as the Aquarium principle. Adjoining the Insect House a new house for small mammals was built, but, because of space restrictions and a steep slope to the kangaroos' enclosure, the new house was added at an angle, making the combined building 'L'-shaped. Chalmers Mitchell tells of an amusing result:

> The buildings were much admired by the authorities of another well-known zoological Institution, who sent their architect to base plans for one of their houses on ours. Like the famous Indian tailor who made a new pair of breeches with a patch on the seat, following an old pair which he had been given as a model, the architect designed, and the Institute constructed, its new house on our 'L'-shaped plan.

Flattery indeed!

Keeping unusual pets had become a craze, and at about this time Fulham Public Library in London attempted to display an ants' nest. The Zoo followed suit, and soon a London department store started selling concrete 'nests' with earth and a supply of ants! But the 'ants' nest in your home' craze quickly ended, as did the nest in Fulham Library. (To this day many foolish people try to keep undomesticated animals, such as snakes and tropical spiders, as pets, without having any idea what they need in order to be kept alive.) The Zoo, however, retained a nest of wood ants in the Insect House from the time it was built and, more recently, achieved the almost impossible task of keeping a nest of the fascinating, tropical leaf-cutter ants, also experimenting with a visitor-operated video camera to see them in close-up.

Collections of animals continued to arrive at London Zoo. The Prince of Wales visited South Africa and was presented with many animals which he in turn presented to what was recognized in all but name as the *national* zoo, where they arrived in 1911. The Prince had, five years earlier, been offered a collection of animals from Nepal, and had offered them to the Zoo, according to the Minutes of a Council meeting, '... on condition he shall not be called upon to pay the cost of bringing the collection to England'. This cost was personally borne by the Duke of Bedford, who was the Society's President at that time.

The Prince's father, King Edward VII, when he himself had been Prince of Wales, had also brought back to London a very large collection of animals, after a four months' tour of India in 1875. That collection arrived in May the next year and included two elephants, which it was decided should not accompany the other animals on a train from Portsmouth Dock to London, partly

1902. By the end of the century the North Gardens contained the world's first Insect House (43) as well as houses for small cats, anteaters and sloths (45–47). In the Main Gardens the Bear Pit (15) was still in use but better cages had been built beside it – the hyænas' and bears' dens – and further development included the Reptile House (33) built with money from the sale of Jumbo. A new Ape House had also been built (from which Jacob escaped!) (© ZSL)

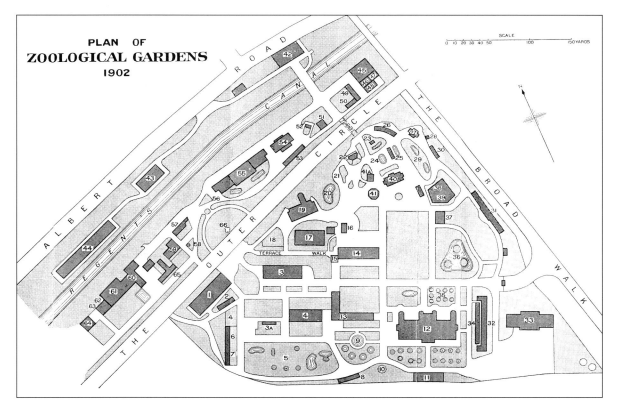

because a keeper had been crushed to death by an elephant in a railway truck only a few years earlier and partly because one of the two elephants had already damaged a rail truck while travelling to the coast in India. For these reasons it was decided to *walk* the two elephants to the Zoo. While, as mentioned elsewhere, it was common practice to walk elephants from London docks to the Zoo, such a long journey as that from Portsmouth had not previously been attempted. They set off accompanied by their two mahouts, a keeper from the Zoo, and a Royal Marine (the reason for whose presence is not known), and the journey appears to have been largely uneventful except for a claim by the *Illustrated London News* that at one point the elephants were 'challenged to a race by a dog-cart, and won'. The journey was completed in two days, the party staying overnight in Godalming at what is now the King's Arms.

The new century was to see many changes in the Zoo. Cars would change people's travel habits and affect attendances; new building techniques, pressures to retain old buildings no longer suited to animal husbandry, and enclosures without bars would all influence development of the Zoo; and two wars were to affect the Zoo directly for the first time. Above all, from being a place where animals were kept for observation, London Zoo (and the Zoological Society) grew to be among the pioneers in developing the principles of animal conservation, by breeding animals verging on extinction, reintroducing animals to the wild when conditions became favourable, and helping animals to survive in their natural habitats.

The work of the Zoo was to spread far beyond the confines of its little area in Regent's Park.

9 War – and After

During the First World War the Zoo, as with the country generally, had to 'tighten its belt' and also deal with a somewhat reduced number of visitors. The Society allowed members of the armed forces to have free admission to the Zoo, and there was a reduction in the numbers of animals – not, as in the next war, to remove those which could be dangerous if they escaped, but to keep fewer of the large herbivores in order to help conserve the nation's supply of fodder. However, several members of staff were within call to deal with any emergency, and metal shutters were fitted every night to the glass fronts of the venomous snakes' tanks in what is now the Bird House.

The Secretary was appointed to the Intelligence Division of the armed forces, and in this position was able also to deal with those (luckily few) bureaucrats who were trying to create difficulties for the Zoo. In his own words:

> I used to send civilians who were making difficulties for us at the Gardens, to the War Office, in which, having been kept waiting for a sufficient time in a corridor under the cold eye of a sergeant, they became more accommodating.

One of the earliest effects of the war was the loss, albeit temporarily, of the Zoo's sealions, which were commandeered from London and other zoos to be trained to detect submarines. The animals were trained at swimming baths in London to swim underwater and to ignore fishes that had also been released, wearing leather muzzles to help them do so. They were then taught to come to the surface and bark when a buzzer sounded, and, finally, when the best had been selected, they were taken to Lake Bala in Wales, where a steam yacht had been fitted out for them and their controllers. To avoid losing sight of them altogether, a red float was tethered from their hips. At last they were taken to the North Sea and the English Channel on active service. In the meantime, however, the hydrophone had been perfected, and the sealions were not, in the end, required after all. They were returned to the zoos concerned, where they resumed their entertainment of the general public.

Various practical displays were set up in the Zoo to alert people, and particularly troops, to the dangers of unhygienic conditions. A great Rat Exhibition was held, demonstrating their dangers and how to take precautions against them at home and in the trenches; the Curator of Insects, Professor Lefroy, arranged a special exhibition on the health dangers of flies and the best means of controlling them, while lectures were given to medical and sanitary authorities, both military and civilian. Chickens and ducks were reared, and the eggs sold to hospitals; in addition, over two hundred pigs were reared and sold, as were tomatoes, which were grown in the Zoo's greenhouses and flower-beds. An innovation brought about by the war was a permanent First Aid post, which was retained after the war. Nowadays it is difficult to think how a place like the Zoo could have existed without such a safety facility, particularly as animal feeding was allowed and members of the public therefore had much closer access to potential injury than they now have.

In 1917, a Miss Elinor Cheeseman, one of Professor Lefroy's pupils, had the distinction of being the first woman to be employed by the Society. We are now well familiar with women holding senior posts in the Society (as, for example, the Head of Public Relations, Head of Education, or Senior Librarian), as well as many keepers, but Miss Cheeseman was the first, being made Assistant Curator of Insects, under Prof. Lefroy, and later, when he resigned, appointed Curator. Prof. Lefroy died a few years later as a result of experiments he carried out with disease-carrying mosquitoes. Miss Cheeseman later became a writer and traveller in search of insects, travelling only with native guides into Mongolia and Papua New Guinea – no mean achievement in the 1920s.

Few new animals arrived at the Zoo during the war, but one which did was a bear deposited by a Canadian regiment on its way to the trenches in France. The tame black bear was the regimental mascot and, as they were based at Winnipeg, had been named Winnie. Bears are normally untrustworthy, despite their cuddly appearance; their faces are expressionless, their ears, unlike those of a dog, move little and they have no tails, so consequently they give no indication of their moods. Add to this their great strength and long claws, and you can see why they are respected by their keepers, who never enter their enclosures before a colleague has counter-checked the security of the doors retaining the bears.

Winnie was a one-in-a-million exception, however, and proved to be just as cuddly as she looked. She loved nothing better than to be handled, and would even allow her greatest luxury, a tin of mixed golden syrup and condensed milk, to be taken from her by a child. She was the darling of every visitor, and so tame that many children were allowed to touch her. She lived in the Zoo for a number of years, until she died of old age, and during her time there an

Winnie, the most gentle and loveable of bears, with Christopher Milne (© *ZSL*)

author brought his son to the Zoo and the little boy fell in love with her. The boy's name was Christopher Robin Milne, and when they got home his father changed the name of the bear he was writing about from Pooh to Winnie-the-Pooh, after Winnie at London Zoo.

Of the 150 staff employed in the grounds of the Zoo, 54 were mobilized for service in the armed forces or for work in munitions factories and, of the former, twelve died in active service. A War Memorial was designed and erected near the Main Gate – it was a hexagonal column on a plinth, carrying a bronze tablet inscribed with their names. After the Second World War further names were added, and the Memorial was moved to a lawn near Three Island Pond.

The number of animals in the Zoo had nearly halved by the end of the war, from 3,973 to 2,100. Almost the first animals to arrive after the war were about 200 rhesus monkeys, the only survivors from 1,000 such monkeys purchased by the Government in order to experiment upon them with poison gas. These survivors enjoyed a much better time in the Zoo, being given the freedom of a large aviary on the canal bank, from which the parrots had been removed. One of the first organizations to help the Zoo to re-establish itself was the New York Zoological Society with, first, a gift of sealions, and then a large collection of other mammals and birds.

The War Memorial was the first structure to be built after the war, and during the next year, 1920, the West Tunnel was built – nearly 100 years after the East Tunnel, which was smaller and had created problems with elephants at riding time, not the least of which had been Jumbo's panic run. Because the animals could not easily walk through the tunnel with the howdahs on their backs, these had to be hoisted on pulleys up a big oak tree near the riding area and then be lowered on to their backs, being removed again when the elephants were about to walk back to their house. The new tunnel overcame this problem, and the howdahs could be kept in the Elephant House and be strapped into place before the elephants left.

The same year saw the completion of the Mappin Terraces, about which more is written in the next chapter. Mr John Newton Mappin, in making his bequest in 1913, had asked that the proposed café at the base of the Terraces be left 'until the best possible provision has been made for the animals'. Work had begun on this last part of the Terraces shortly before the outbreak of war, and had been held up until now. It is an impressive, single-storey building in Italian Renaissance style with pairs of Tuscan columns and tall windows between, through which there is a panoramic view of the animals.

It was in 1923 that work started on one of the biggest building projects ever undertaken by the Zoo, a new Aquarium. Nowadays it has become the fashion for aquaria to be built with huge tanks of mixed fishes, often with walk-through tunnels, but seventy-five years ago the idea was, as with other kinds of animals, to have separate species in separate spaces; consequently, the new Aquarium consisted of a series of glass-fronted tanks. At the time of its opening it was the largest aquarium in the world, and it is still one of the largest in Europe. It has three halls for freshwater, sea-water and tropical fish, extending a total of 150 metres and containing over 100 tanks. The Mappin Terraces had been designed with the idea of later incorporating an aquarium, and this

The 'mountains' of the Mappin Terraces were constructed around huge wooden beams. On the floor of this one is the header tank containing water for the Aquarium below (© *Crown Copyright. NMR*)

is where it was built, below the four high rocks of the Terraces built nine years earlier. The water is contained in reservoir tanks under the floor where visitors walk, from where it is pumped up to smaller holding tanks in the 'mountains' above and, from there, is fed by gravity through the fish-tanks before being filtered and returned to the reservoirs. These hold 60,000 gallons of fresh water and 120,000 gallons of sea water, the latter being topped up by pumping replacement sea water each year, originally from barges carrying

This diagrammatic picture used to hang in the entrance to the Aquarium. It shows the water tanks underground and in the Terraces above (© *Crown Copyright. NMR*)

water from the Bay of Biscay, but nowadays from road tankers bringing water from the North Sea.

Full use was made of the idea first developed in the Insect House of lighting the exhibits while visitors walked in virtual darkness. For many years an extra charge was made for those visitors wishing to enter the Aquarium, as with the Children's Zoo, but since the 1970s there has been no additional charge to enter any building in the Zoo. More recently, some of the smaller tanks have been combined to make long tanks for the more colourful tropical

fishes and for the inhabitants of coral reefs. In the darkness of the Aquarium, labelling the tank contents could have been a problem, but an attempt was made to overcome this by angling the labels below so that light from the tank illuminated the label. This was not completely successful, but seventy years later modern technology provided a solution with the use of fibre optic lights.

Outside, in the rest of the Zoo, labelling each cage or enclosure had been a problem as the weather had a habit of reducing the clarity of the wording to invisibility, but a Mr Swan found the answer by providing the information on glazed tiles.

The Society's new offices were warmed by a central coke boiler, and it was in the boiler-room, below the offices, that Swan prepared his label tiles, colouring and glazing them, and then firing them in a small kiln beside the boiler. They were highly successful – and were also such minor works of art that some unscrupulous visitors made off with them, making it necessary for the tiles to be very securely wired to the cage fronts.

L.G. Mainland, who was employed by a newspaper, had been among the

The 'Aquarium Principle' of lighting, first used in the Insect House, is clearly seen here inside the Aquarium. This is part of one of the three aquarium halls (© *Crown Copyright. NMR*)

first to publicize the building of the new Aquarium, announcing that the Zoo's old 'fish house' would be closed and its inmates would be looking for new homes. Hundreds of readers then contacted the Zoo, offering a home for some of the fishes, and temporary staff had to be employed to return the many cheques and stamps that the readers had enclosed to cover delivery!

Shortly afterwards, Mainland started broadcasting on the BBC's *Children's Hour*, recounting news of what was happening at the Zoo and thereby becoming the first man to bring a zoo into the radio era. In those first days of broadcasting, the BBC was experimenting with outside broadcasts, and Mainland took part in 'live' transmissions from the Zoo. Nowadays we are familiar with shoulder-carried or hand-held cameras broadcasting coloured pictures from around the world, but in the mid-1920s the transmission of sound radio required a covered, hand-pushed cart with three masts. The masts had wires between them, some being radio aerials and others just to keep the masts upright. Officially called a 'wireless pram' (despite all the wires), it weighed about three-quarters of a tonne, required a number of men to push it around the Zoo from one broadcasting point to another, and was much too unwieldy to be taken into an animal house, having to stay outside while Mainland did his broadcast from inside with a microphone on the end of a *very* long cable.

Joan Procter, the Curator of Reptiles, who had drawn up the original plans for the new Reptile House, had designed the rockwork in the Aquarium tanks and then she designed two large rockeries destined to be Monkey Hill. When in use, this was to prove a great attraction, with a large colony of sacred, or hamadryas, baboons occupying it, to the immense pleasure of visitors. Monkeys are invariably amusing, particularly active ones, and the baboons were no exception, chasing each other around and darting for the food thrown to them by visitors, while the mothers carried their youngsters about or watched them play. Alas, this was an attraction that could not last, as the Zoo would learn from its experience. Monkeys fight, particularly the males, and with such a large potential harem the males' fights were serious and resulted in some bad wounds. Even the removal of all the females did not entirely resolve the problem so, after only a few years, Monkey Hill was then used for goats during the next war, and then rhesus monkeys for three years, after which time it was closed down.

Those post-war years saw a tremendous amount of building work, and the same year that Monkey Hill opened, work started on a new Monkey House. This was another building which today would no longer be considered adequate, consisting, as had the Lion House when it was built forty years before, of a series of cages (about fifteen down each side of the house), and housing some forty different species of monkey and ape. But, at the time, it was again a step forward in keeping animals in a healthy state and, to a large extent, was a success, as the inmates were healthier than they had been in their previous house.

There had been a two-year trial of a full-sized model of three sections of the proposed house, and this was the first animal house in the Zoo to use electricity; this was used to light quartz incandescent lights above the cages to give artificial sunlight when the weather outside did not encourage the animals to venture out. The monkeys had complete freedom of access to their outside cages, having swing flaps through which to pass whenever they wished – another innovation – while the floors outside as well as in had pipes below, through which steam could be used to heat them. The trial was a complete success, and the full-sized house was therefore built, opening in 1927. A little later, large panes of glass were fitted inside the house, between the visitors and the apes, as experience over the years showed that these animals were particularly prone to human illnesses such as colds and even tuberculosis.

Before the new Monkey House was opened, the Zoo started one of the most popular entertainments in its history – the Chimpanzees' Tea-Party. Three or four young chimps would be taken to one of the lawns, where they would sit on chairs around a table and have tea, drinking fruit juice (poured out by a keeper from a teapot) and eating fruit from a plate. There was, of course, much stealing of bananas from a neighbour's plate, climbing on to the

Monkey Hill, home to a colony of hamadryas baboons, provided much amusement for visitors but had to be closed after too many injuries were caused by fights (© ZSL)

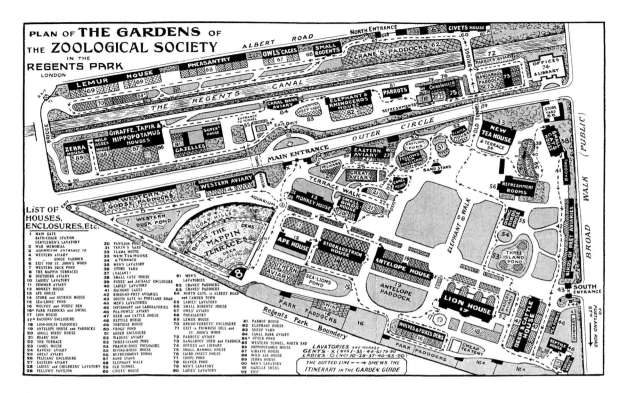

PLAN OF **THE GARDENS** OF THE **ZOOLOGICAL SOCIETY** IN THE **REGENTS PARK** LONDON

1923. The Mappin Terraces (8) were built just before the First World War on additional land given from Regent's Park 'provided the animals are visible from the park' and therefore they face the park; the Aquarium had just been added beneath the Terraces. A great wave of building was about to start – the relatively new Ape House (13) was to be replaced by a new Reptile House and the old one (48) was to become the Bird House replacing No. 20 which would become the Tortoise House, while the Western Duck Pond (7) was the site where the new Monkey Hill was to be built. The Refreshment Rooms (56) would house even noisier inmates – parrots

table, drinking from the teapot, and such general misbehaviour, which was greeted by roars of laughter from the watching crowd, particularly from children, who enjoyed seeing the 'admonitions' by the keepers lead to no better behaviour.

To create this amusing show, the keepers had themselves eaten round a table with young chimpanzees. The chimps would first copy them and then, once they had learned the procedure, tire of behaving well. As a chimp grew older, it could no longer be allowed outside near the public and would have to be replaced. Because at that time no chimps were born in zoos, new chimps were needed from the wild. Thirty years later, when chimps were being kept in natural family groups and it was proving difficult to introduce an 'outsider', the problems of available enclosures, as well as by then the unethical capture of wild-born chimpanzees, led to the cessation of the tea-parties. In addition, the Society now considered it quite inappropriate to display chimpanzees in such an unnatural way. However, it would be many years before visitors ceased to ask at what time the chimps' tea-party was due to take place, so very popular had the display been.

The year 1926 also saw the arrival of a 'white' elephant, on loan from Burma. White elephants are albinos, having pink skin and blue eyes, and with their few hairs white. In Burma they were held to be sacred, so the arrival of one at the Zoo was a rarity. About this time Sayaid Ali came to the Zoo. He was an elephant keeper and trainer, and was introduced specifically to train Indiarani, an elephant that had become somewhat untrustworthy. Elephants in a zoo must be obedient in order that action can be taken when necessary, for example to examine their feet for cuts which may cause them pain, or to ensure they come in out of the cold before a winter's night – after all, you can hardly *push* an elephant when you want it to go indoors! Sayaid Ali was a highly skilled mahout and a big, friendly man, and he quickly became popular. He enjoyed drinking lemonade, and trained Indiarani to pick up a glass of it and hand it to him without spilling a drop. After this, Indiarani became known as the 'Cheerio' elephant!

After its period at the Zoo, the white elephant went to the USA for a short display, and among the accompanying keepers was a young Burmese handler by the name of San Dwe. The elephant returned to London Zoo on its way back to Burma, and San Dwe asked to join the Zoo staff and stay on in London. He, also, became very popular, sharing Sayaid Ali's room above the Elephant House and becoming known to the other staff as 'Sandy Wee'! But, to everyone's astonishment, some time later San Dwe murdered the older man; the reason was never discovered and the incident remains unique in the history of London Zoo. At about the same time, the white elephant died in Burma. It was rumoured that there was a connection with the murder – a highly fanciful supposition.

Then came the centenary of London Zoo, and with it celebrations. The creation of Whipsnade Zoo was to be the greatest and best celebration of the Society's first one hundred years, but in London a banquet was held for about two hundred guests connected with the Zoo or with zoology (which, it will be recalled, was the province of amateurs alone when the Zoological Society was started). Now zoology was a thriving science with which many professional scientists had been, and were increasingly, associated. When the Society had been formed, the theory of evolution had not yet been propounded, but now there were branches of zoology undreamed of a hundred years before – heredity, genetics, ecology, behavioural science, and so on – while animal conservation, originally unnecessary and unheard of, had now commenced and, after a further fifty years, would start changing the face of London Zoo and other zoos around the world.

10 The New Zoo

Wibba was the little-known ruler of the ancient Saxon Kingdom of Mercia, yet his hunting ground, or 'sneade', is now known to millions of people around the world. For the name of 'Wibba's sneade' became distorted over the centuries and, whereas it was still an unknown village in 1930, a year later there was no one in England who had not heard of Whipsnade.

The story of Whipsnade Zoo really starts in 1903 at the Annual General Meeting of the Zoological Society which, as already explained, did not turn out to be as straightforward as had been expected. At that AGM the Fellows voted for a new Secretary to the Society, as this position had become vacant. As Chief Executive, the Secretary's position was highly responsible, having not only overall control of activities within London Zoo, but also, for an enthusiastic holder of the office, responsibility for the formulation of policies which, if he gained the Council's support, he could then implement to the benefit (or otherwise) of the Zoo's future. The election of a Secretary was therefore a major matter, and on this occasion the person elected to the position was Dr Peter Chalmers Mitchell.

This was to be a milestone in the annals of the Society, for Chalmers Mitchell proved to be far-sighted and enthusiastic. His term of office lasted 32 years, until 1935, and at the time of his retirement *The Times* said that he had transformed the Zoo 'into a place of really enthralling experience'.

He was an advocate of 'fresh air' for animals, and earlier had been very impressed by Carl Hagenbeck's Tierpark at Hamburg. Hagenbeck was an animal dealer who had so many animals in his possession at any one time that he decided to make them accessible to the public. He built his zoo in the country at Stellingen, a suburb of Hamburg, and incorporated his ideas of an open-air zoo by building, in addition to some more normal animal houses, four 'panoramas' where animals from one area could be seen out of doors in apparently close proximity.

His African panorama, for example, had a small lake and grassy area for birds such as flamingos, behind which, at a higher level, was an enclosure for zebras and antelopes; behind that, and again higher, was an arc of rocks retaining lions. The front of each enclosure was separated from the visitors' sunken pathway by

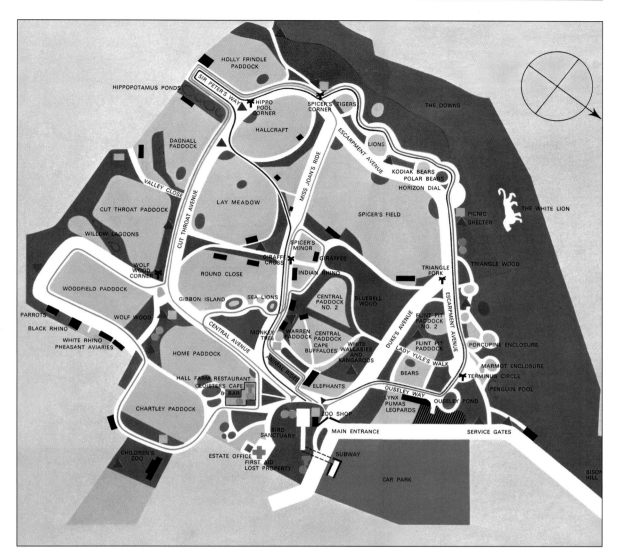

HOLLY FRINDLE PADDOCK
HIPPOPOTAMUS PONDS
SIR PETER'S WAY
HIPPO POOL CORNER
SPICER'S TIGERS CORNER
THE DOWNS
HALLCRAFT
DAGNALL PADDOCK
ESCARPMENT AVENUE
LIONS
VALLEY CLOSE
MISS JOAN'S RIDE
KODIAK BEARS
POLAR BEARS
HORIZON DIAL
LAY MEADOW
CUT THROAT PADDOCK
CUT THROAT AVENUE
SPICER'S FIELD
THE WHITE LION
WILLOW LAGOONS
SPICER'S MINOR
PICNIC SHELTER
WOLF WOOD CORNER
GIRAFFE CROSS
GIRAFFES
TRIANGLE WOOD
ROUND CLOSE
INDIAN RHINO
TRIANGLE FORK
WOODFIELD PADDOCK
GIBBON ISLAND
SEA LIONS
CENTRAL PADDOCK NO. 2
BLUEBELL WOOD
PARROTS
WOLF WOOD
CENTRAL AVENUE
MONKEY TREE
WARREN PADDOCK
CENTRAL PADDOCK
DUKE'S AVENUE
FLINT PIT PADDOCK NO. 2
ESCARPMENT AVENUE
PORCUPINE ENCLOSURE
BLACK RHINO
WHITE RHINO
PHEASANT AVIARIES
CAPE BUFFALOES
WHITE WALLABIES AND KANGAROOS
FLINT PIT PADDOCK
MARMOT ENCLOSURE
HOME PADDOCK
BEARS
LADY YULE'S WALK
TERMINUS CIRCLE
HALL FARM RESTAURANT
CLOISTERS CAFE & BAR
ANIMAL RIDES
ELEPHANTS
OUSELEY WAY
PENGUIN POOL
CHARTLEY PADDOCK
LYNX PUMAS LEOPARDS
OUSELEY POND
ZOO SHOP
BIRD SANCTUARY
MAIN ENTRANCE
SERVICE GATES
CHILDREN'S ZOO
ESTATE OFFICE
FIRST AID
LOST PROPERTY
SUBWAY
CAR PARK
BISON HILL

a ditch, not bars, so that from the bottom of the panorama, one could see only a vista of various animals and birds without any apparent barrier between them.

Chalmers Mitchell set about making a similar panorama within the relatively limited area of London Zoo, incorporating part of the additional four acres of land that had been granted by the Crown authorities soon after he took office. This additional land was a strip down the west side of the Zoo, given on condition that the animals would be visible from the park outside the Zoo! Hence the new panorama was designed to face the park. Mitchell persuaded John Newton Mappin (of Mappin & Webb, the silversmiths and jewellers) to make a generous financial gift to the Society with which a series

1970. Whipsnade Park Zoo after 40 years of development. The original farm is now unrecognizable but many enclosures follow the shapes of the earlier fields and thickets have been cleared from the woods (© ZSL)

of terraces could be built incorporating open-air enclosures for the bears, which had been restricted to a row of cages and only one jointly used outdoor enclosure ever since the demolition of the original bear pit.

The new series of terraces had at its lowest level a pool for penguins, then paddocks behind (originally intended for deer, but occupied by such animals as bighorn sheep and musk ox), above which were six enclosures for bears with a moat in front instead of bars. Above these again rose four rocky crags for mountain goats and sheep, such as ibex and Barbary sheep. The Mappin Terraces were completed in 1914 (except for the café at the lowest point), and by the end of the century was still one of the main landmarks of the Zoo, although by then it was called Bear Mountain. Not only did the terraces provide good (and larger) enclosures for the animals concerned, but also they made far greater use of the restricted land available as they were designed so that, as has been seen, an aquarium could be incorporated at ground level below the rock peaks.

But from his earliest days as Secretary, Chalmers Mitchell must have been thinking about the limitations of space in a city zoo which, even after inclusion of the additional land, was only 36 acres in size. In 1909, in an article on 'The future of the Zoological Society', he wrote: 'Regent's Park, on clay soil, in the smoky atmosphere of a great city, can never be an ideal place for animals ...', and went on to discount the suggestions of moving it to another area of London. He then wrote:

> But there is an alternative that the Society no doubt will bear in mind. There is still cheap and good land to be obtained within twenty or thirty miles of London. The Society ought to acquire several hundred acres of such land and gradually develop it, not as a zoological exhibition, but as a farm for growing suitable food and a breeding and recuperating ground for animals.

The first of these suggested uses was unlikely to be advantageous as so much specialist food was required for the Zoo animals (fruit, insects, rats and mice), and little but hay and vegetables could be specially grown. The third suggested use – that of a place for recuperation – was in fact tried in the earliest days of Whipsnade, some animals being sent for a 'summer holiday', but the trauma to the animals of their transportation counteracted any good that a few weeks in the country had done. The animals had hardly got used to their different surroundings before being moved back again, so this practice was quickly dropped. However, excellent conditions for breeding many species of animals could be provided, and this was demonstrated very successfully, as will be seen.

It took Mitchell 15 years of pushing his ideas for developing an area in the country before he achieved success. First, the extra four acres of land granted by the Crown had to be developed and the Mappin Terraces built; then came the 1914 – 1918 war, followed by a period of refurbishment at the Zoo. Once this was completed the Aquarium was constructed, and a new Reptile House built. But finally, with good financial reserves accumulating, in 1926 the Council agreed to celebrate the Society's centenary by buying some land, and in December of that year, after inspecting a number of sites, they negotiated the purchase for £13,480 of Hall Farm at Whipsnade with its 600 acres – over 15 times the size of London Zoo and much larger than the whole of Regent's Park.

So, 100 years after the start of London Zoo, Whipsnade Zoo Park was born – a completely different sort of zoo and, like its forerunner, again the very first of its kind in the world.

The land lay along the top and down one side of Dunstable Downs in Bedfordshire. It was bordered on two sides by roads, and included one field on the other side of one of these roads, which was to be developed as a car park. The farm was not in very good condition, and much work was necessary on the farmhouse itself to turn it into offices and an attractive restaurant. The land consisted of heavy clay containing many flints, and below was chalk; a great deal of effort had to be made to create roads and footpaths, to quarry chalk, build shelters, clear undergrowth from the woods, and so on. It was the time of the 1930s Depression in the country and unemployment was high, so the Ministry of Labour arranged for 150 unemployed men from areas particularly badly affected to work at Whipsnade, changing over the men every two months and paying a proportion of the costs.

Gradually the new Zoo took shape. Fields, the largest of which was the same size as the whole of London Zoo, were bordered with wire mesh to become animal enclosures; chalk was excavated to form large dells for the big cats, surrounded by bars curving inwards at the top; pools were made in some fields, and dirt tracks were surfaced to create nearly four miles of roadway and footpaths. Shelters were built in the new enclosures to give protection to the animals in the worst weather (it can be very bleak and cold on top of the Downs in winter), and a few animal houses were built for the more delicate animals, such as giraffes, although only one of these, the Elephant House, was constructed to enable visitors to go inside.

The famous 'White Lion' was carved out of the chalk slope on the side of the Downs, and this is visible for many miles, as anyone who travels to Liverpool or Manchester from London can see from the train. A high, metal-barred fence was erected all around the six-mile perimeter of the Zoo. This had an overhang turned inwards to ensure that should any fierce animal escape, it would still remain within the confines of the Zoo; however, within a short time it became apparent that, while no dangerous animal escaped *from* the Zoo, so many native animals, particularly foxes, got *into* the Zoo that the overhang had to be reversed to protect the birds which were breeding in the Zoo, and this has been the position to the present day.

The jammed country roads on the day Whipsnade opened its gates in 1931 meant that many travellers never got there that day! (© ZSL)

As the grounds became ready, stocking with animals took place. Some animals came from London Zoo, but as the conditions at Whipsnade were so different, they were quite unsuitable for most of the numerous smaller animals kept in London which, if introduced to Whipsnade, would neither have been seen nor survived a winter in the open countryside. One exception was the prairie marmot, or prairie dog, from North America, a rodent looking rather like a cheeky guinea pig. This animal lives on the open prairies where it burrows, coming out to feed and forever sitting up to watch alertly for predators. A group of them were put in a dell dug out of the side of the chalk Downs, with a huge grassy mound in the centre in which to burrow their tunnels. The colony thrived, and eventually one of their tunnels took them under the surrounding concrete wall and on to the Downland; today they can be seen busily scampering around the hillside near visitors having a picnic in the Zoo, enjoying complete freedom.

Other zoos provided animals, and some were obtained from the wild, so that herds of mixed stock could be established of antelopes, bison, deer, camels and many other species, thus avoiding inbreeding from only one pair of related animals. Those that came from the wild were ones that had never, or hardly ever, been bred in the more usual kind of zoo, the idea being to try to establish breeding herds – at the start more, it must be said, because of the difficulties of regularly trying to obtain wild replacements than with any real idea of conservation, now the objective of all good zoos.

And how successful Whipsnade has been in the breeding of wild animals! Within its first 50 years it imported 357 animals, and during those same 50 years it bred the quite astonishing total of 18,561 animals! Many of these were sent to other zoos throughout the world to help establish other captive breeding groups, in the hope of saving species from total extinction and possibly to reintroduce a species to its country of origin when conditions for it became more favourable.

After five years, at last the new Zoo was ready to receive visitors, and it opened its gates for the first time on 23 May 1931 – and what a day that was.

Whipsnade had received much publicity in the newspapers as it developed, and members of the public were keen to see with their own eyes the only 'open' zoo in the world, where animals roamed relatively freely instead of being caged or in small enclosures. It was Whit Sunday, and the weather was warm and sunny, and, as a consequence, within hours a huge traffic jam had formed. The narrow country roads leading to Whipsnade became so clogged with cars and coaches (or charabancs, as they were then called) that, of the thousands of people trying to make their way to the Zoo, many never got there at all.

The next morning the papers were full of photographs, not only of the Zoo, but also of the miles of traffic jams; but, far from being discouraged, people seemed more determined than ever to pay a visit. Buses plied between Dunstable and the Zoo, and London Transport soon started a new 'Green Line' service to Whipsnade from Baker Street, within a mile of London Zoo.

The basic layout of Whipsnade Wild Animal Park (as it was later renamed) has changed little since those first days, when the admission price was one shilling (5p) and half-price for children. The animals occupying them may have changed, but the enclosures still carried the names of Hall Farm's origi-

Brown bears were amongst the first occupants of Whipsnade and this is one of the four which still live and breed in this enclosure (*Colin Whyman*)

nal fields – Holly Frindle Paddock (originally a fringe of hollies), Cut Throat Paddock (probably a corruption of 'cut through it paddock' – a short cut for the farm hands!) and Home Paddock, beside the old farmhouse which now contains the Discovery Centre containing reptiles and fishes. New names have been added as well: Wallaby Wood, Tiger Falls and Bison Hill.

A sad story lies behind one name. Joan Procter, London Zoo's Curator of Reptiles in the 1920s, was a brilliant zoologist and had designed and supervised not only the new Reptile House, but also Monkey Hill, and she had also designed many of the tanks in the Aquarium. In the Reptile House she devised cages of all sizes, from little cages for chameleons and other small lizards, to ones five metres long and as high as the roof for pythons. Some large areas had only a barrier in front for such reptiles as crocodiles and Komodo dragons. The doors to the poisonous snakes were placed high up the rear wall, accessed from a galleyway in the central keepers' area, providing safety for the keepers at feeding times, and incubation rooms were planned for the first floor. It was an innovative house and, although it had faults by modern standards, was very cleverly designed, and when it opened in 1927 it was far more suitable than any house used previously. Joan Procter had a brilliant future ahead of her.

Following a severe illness she recuperated near Whipsnade and, for a period, rode a pony every morning from Hall Farm House to the edge of the Downs; but, sadly, she died in 1931 at the early age of 34. A bust of her can be seen in the entrance to the Reptile House in London Zoo, and at Whipsnade the track which she used with her pony was named 'Miss Joan's Ride' in her memory.

Other people's names have been recorded in the roads and paths within Whipsnade Zoo. One such was Lady Yule, who donated money for the construction of the Brown Bear's Pit – not a pit like the original one at London, but a large area of grassland filled with bushes and trees; she also presented her pet bear, Teddy, as its first inhabitant, and the path along the front of the enclosure was named 'Lady Yule's Walk' after her.

Teddy arrived in 1929, and the following year an old female brown bear named Mary was transferred from London as company for him. The change to the country surroundings of Whipsnade rejuvenated Mary, who astonished everyone by producing cubs in 1931, the year the Zoo opened, and continuing to have cubs almost every year for over twenty years!

11 The Zoo Park

It would be wrong not to tell the stories of three different species of animal which have all benefited from Whipsnade in one way or another, so before we return to the main story of London Zoo, here are those stories – of Père David's deer, the cheetah and the African white rhinoceros.

Running alongside Whipsnade Wood is Duke's Avenue, named after the 11th Duke of Bedford, President of the Society, who presented many animals to the new Zoo from his herds at Woburn. One of the most interesting of these was Père David's deer, which demonstrates one of the success stories of animal conservation. Père David was a French missionary in Peking (now Beijing) who was most interested in natural history; it was he who had discovered the Giant panda, and in 1865 he also learned of the existence of the deer that now bears his name. These deer were kept inside the huge Imperial Hunting Park, which was surrounded by a high wall; no visitors were allowed inside, and although the deer had probably existed there for hundreds of years, they had become extinct in their natural home, the marshlands of eastern China, possibly a thousand years before.

Père David climbed the high wall and saw a large herd of the deer a long way off. Even at that distance he recognized them as differing from any known deer, and he tried hard to obtain the skin of one through official channels, but without success. In a letter to the Paris Museum of Natural History, he wrote:

> Luckily I know some Tartar soldiers who are going to do guard duty in this park and I am sure, by means of a bribe, that I shall get hold of a few skins which I shall hasten to send you. The Chinese give this animal the name SSEUPOU-SIANG, which means the four odd features, because they consider that this deer takes after the stag by its antlers, the cow by its hooves, the camel by its neck and the donkey by its tail.

Eventually the skin and bones of one male and one female were passed to him over the wall and these, once back in Europe, gave confirmation of the unique character of this deer. Unlike most other deer, which have a pair of small hooves on each foot, Père David's deer has two large hooves which spread apart, originally evolved to help the animal in its swampy surroundings; they spread so much that they click together as they are lifted when the deer walks. The only other deer with similar hooves is the reindeer, whose feet have similarly evolved to stop them sinking in snow. The tail of Père David's deer is longer than that of any other deer (which usually have very short tails indeed) and ends, also unlike other deer, in a long clump of hair like the tail of a zebra. In addition, the antlers differ from all deer except the reindeer. In a typical deer, each antler grows high and branched (the beam) and has a forward-facing spike low down (the brow tine); in Père David's deer, the brow tine also develops into a large, branched antler almost duplicating the beam behind it.

These three features together make Père David's deer unique in the deer family and therefore of great interest zoologically.

The British Envoy in Peking and the French Chargé d'Affaires made many strenuous efforts to be given permission to obtain some live deer, and over the following three years were given several deer, which were sent to various

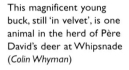

This magnificent young buck, still 'in velvet', is one animal in the herd of Père David's deer at Whipsnade (*Colin Whyman*)

European zoos. After 1870 no more could be obtained, but luckily a few of the ones in Europe bred, so they were still in existence there when disaster struck in China in 1894.

That year saw floods in China which were so serious that they breached the walls of the Imperial Hunting Park. Some of the Père David's deer were drowned, and those that got out of the Park were killed and eaten by starving Chinese peasants. A few survived within the Park, but the Boxer Rising happened six years later and those few left alive of the Park herds were slaughtered by the troops, making Père David's deer extinct in China.

The Duke of Bedford, a keen naturalist with herds of various kinds at Woburn, persuaded all the zoos with specimens to let him have their deer, and he formed a herd of 18 at Woburn Park – the only Père David's deer remaining in the world. This small herd grew to several hundred in 40 years, when the Duke's son (then himself the Duke of Bedford and President of the Zoological Society) discussed with the Society's Council the possibility of creating a second herd at Whipsnade.

There were many difficulties initially, not least being the problem of capturing such large animals, which were roaming relatively freely, without injuring

Muntjac deer are one of the seven species of mammals and birds having complete freedom within Whipsnade Wild Animal Park (*Colin Whyman*)

them – the days of tranquillizer darts were still in the future – so it was agreed that two newly born calves would be hand-reared at Whipsnade. This was successfully done in 1944, and further calves were hand-reared the next year, forming a herd which produced its own first calf in 1947 and has continued to grow ever since. By 1983, 40 years on, the Whipsnade herd numbered about 70 deer, including 20 births in that year alone. During those 40 years, many had been sent to other zoos and a number of other herds were established throughout the world.

So, Père David's deer has been rescued from extinction and is now thriving. In 1956, two pairs were sent back to the marshlands of China – the first in their country of origin for over half a century, and the first in their natural habitat for many hundreds of years.

Ever since the opening of Whipsnade, many animals have been given complete freedom. We have already mentioned the prairie marmots, and the wallabies are well known to visitors, roaming at will on the grassy slopes of the Downs and through the woods – between 300 and 400 wallabies are present at any one time. Jungle fowl, the ancestors of the common chicken, are also given their freedom, as are peafowls, of which over a hundred are at liberty, and in the springtime many peacocks can be seen displaying to the hens in Bluebell Wood while wallabies hop over the carpet of flowers.

In the early days macaws, the largest and most colourful of parrots, were also allowed their freedom. They used to fly down to Whipsnade Village, but so many complaints were received of dirty laundry, because the macaws removed the clothes pegs from washing-lines, that their freedom was ended. Another parrot allowed to fly freely was the Quaker parakeet. These are the only parrots to build nests, as opposed to using holes in trees, and, being highly communal birds, they build a communal nest of twigs in the branches of a tree. They add twigs to it each year, each pair of birds having their own hole in it, until the nest can grow to the size of a garden shed. Unfortunately, the colony died out during the war of 1939 – 45, and has never been replaced.

Cranes used also to fly at will in the Zoo, but they seemed to have difficulty finding their way back if they left the Zoo, and also seemed unaware of the dangers of landing in the enclosures of bears or lions! For this reason, such valuable and increasingly rare birds now have their wings clipped, but cranes do not normally fly unless food becomes scarce, a predator appears, or they are a species which migrates, so being earthbound is no hardship to them.

There are usually about ten different species of deer at Whipsnade, ranging from the axis deer of India to reindeer. Two of the smallest kinds (none taller than two feet in height) have the freedom of the Zoo grounds, and a visitor will often see one or another in the woods or hedgerows; they are the muntjac and the Chinese water deer. The latter are found on the banks of the Yangtze Kiang river and grow no antlers, not even the single two-pronged antlers of the muntjac, but instead have a pair of short tusks which are quite obvious, if you can get near enough.

About a year after Whipsnade first opened its gates to the public, a tragedy occurred. Stanley Stenson, aged 26, was employed as a driver in the catering department, and he tended to boast to visitors about how friendly he was with the lions, of which four adult males occupied the one enclosure. One day a visitor called his bluff and, throwing his bowler hat into the enclosure, bet Stanley £500 he would not get it. Lions are lazy by nature, even in the wild, being active only when hunting, and resting or sleeping for some 18 hours out of every 24; so Stanley saw only four peaceful lions dozing, and he climbed over the high-level barrier and under the overhanging hooks at the top of the bars; then he climbed down, walked across the enclosure, retrieved the hat and walked back. He was still some steps away from the bars when a lion suddenly charged and grabbed his leg, tripping him. It is believed Stanley died from hitting his head on the concrete area, which was probably a blessing in disguise as it was some time before the keepers could drive off the lions.

These four male lions look very calm, and so thought someone who climbed over the bars to retrieve his hat. He did not climb out again! (© ZSL)

One of the great success stories of any zoo must be Whipsnade's remarkable achievements with cheetahs. Sadly, these lovely animals, which used to exist throughout the grasslands of Africa, the Middle East and India, are now to be found in relatively few areas. The fastest moving of all land mammals (reaching speeds of 70 miles an hour for short bursts), unlike all other cats their claws cannot be retracted, but are permanently extended in order to give a firmer grip on the ground when they run, like the spikes on an athlete's shoes. In addition to diminishing in numbers in the wild, zoos had found them impossible to breed in captivity until recent years at Whipsnade.

Several factors are believed to have contributed to the cheetah's previous non-breeding in zoos, but subsequent successful breeding at Whipsnade. The stimulus in the wild for a cheetah may be the ability to see long distances, over vast open spaces, something which is impossible to achieve in the confines of a town zoo; they must not be able to see or hear other big cats (lions and leopards being the cheetah's greatest enemies because they kill any cubs they find). It has also been found that separating male and female cheetahs for a period invariably results in matings after they have been reintroduced. Whatever the reason – space, seclusion or separation – Juanita, a cheetah presented to

This large enclosure for penguins at Whipsnade, with its two pools, contrasts with the pool designed by Lubetkin at London Zoo (*Colin Whyman*)

Whipsnade in 1966 by a retired Naval Commander, bore three cubs the following year – the first time any had been born in England. She reared them herself and this was only the second known time a captive cheetah had done so anywhere in the world. She gave birth to three more cubs the next year, and by 1971 Whipsnade was sending cheetahs to other zoos for potential breeding. In 1972 one of the cubs born to Juanita four years earlier had a cub herself; this was yet again a record, as it was the first time in the world that a cheetah cub had been born to a captive-born parent.

Year after year the cheetah breeding record went from strength to strength until the deaths in 1981 of three of the most prolific breeding females. For the next two years the number of births declined, but in 1983 five litters were born to four young females, three of whom had not previously borne cubs. By 1984, a hundred cheetahs had been born at Whipsnade within 17 years, and the breeding record had passed through three generations, since when the record has continued almost uninterrupted!

Whipsnade Wild Animal Park is now nearly 70 years old, and during those years it has gained a well-earned reputation for its breeding successes with many species of animal. While London Zoo has itself had successes with

Rockhopper penguins are some of the occupants of the Whipsnade Pools (*Colin Whyman*)

endangered animals, Whipsnade has been able to concentrate on animals better suited to the different circumstances of a zoo park. Obviously, animals that in nature live in large groups are more likely to breed under conditions more closely resembling those in which they normally live than in a town zoo where only two or three specimens can be kept; antelopes, gazelles, deer, cattle and horses usually live in herds, so a group of ten or more is more likely to reproduce. Whipsnade's breeding record for only one year (1998) included live births amongst the following animals:

Among the deer: 8 Axis deer, 8 Barasinga, 8 Sitatunga, 12 Père David's deer (still going strong) and 3 Greater Kudu,
And among others: 10 Yak, 8 Scimitar-horned Oryx and 3 Bactrian camels.

Many, also, were the hatchings of birds that live in flocks, such as penguins, scarlet ibis and flamingos.

White rhinos tend to live together in groups, unlike black rhinos which are far from sociable, but until a few years ago they had never bred in zoos. At Whipsnade, however, where a group of these animals is kept in one large enclosure, nearly every year sees at least one birth. All varieties of rhinoceros are endangered, but in 1983 each of the three kinds then kept at Whipsnade was accompanied by its young – the white, the black and the great one-horned – another 'first' for any zoo.

The white rhinoceros is the larger of the two African rhinos, and an old animal can have a horn two metres long. For years these animals have been killed for their horns, which in the Far East are ground up for use in traditional medicine and in some Arab countries are carved to make dagger handles. Both kinds of rhino have been killed so ruthlessly that these days few rhinos live to sufficient an age to grow these very long horns; as an illustration, by 1970 there were believed to be no more than 65,000 black rhinos left in the whole of Africa – this may seem a lot, but it is only equivalent to the human population of one town – but so dreadfully did their slaughter continue that by 1993 there were thought to be fewer than 2,500 still alive. While the black rhino browses on leaves, having a pointed upper lip to strip the leaves off bushes in the scrubland, the white rhino is a grazer and therefore inhabits the open plains and has a pair of wide, flat lips for cropping grass. The Boers of South Africa called it the 'wijd' rhino, meaning 'wide', because of its wide mouth, and this name was mistranslated into English as 'white'; the other rhino was therefore named 'black' – although both these animals are in fact grey!

The story of Whipsnade's herd of white rhinos is quite unique. By the middle of the twentieth century, the white rhino had been hunted almost to extinction and the Natal Parks Board in South Africa made a determined effort to preserve the animals left alive in their own country. As a result, while the animal had all but disappeared from most areas of the continent, by careful management and strict protection Natal succeeded over a few years in establishing them securely in South Africa. However, they realized that, even with the best will in the world, disasters such as famine, flood or disease could decimate their carefully preserved animals, so in 1968 they began a survey to find a suitable place elsewhere in the world to establish an independent group of white rhinos in order that the species could survive any such disaster in Africa (as, indeed, occurred 15 years later, when the plains were parched by a three-year drought which killed countless thousands of grazing animals).

Of all the places they visited during their world survey, they thought that Whipsnade would provide the most likely chance of establishing a herd of these animals securely, and the Zoological Society of London and the Natal Parks Board began planning the details of how such a massive operation could best be carried out – a white rhinoceros can weigh up to three tonnes and it was proposed to capture 20 animals from the Umfolozi area, accustom them to humans and then transport them more than 8,000 miles to England! The details of the months of work, with their attendant problems and hardships, were filmed in Africa and shown on BBC television in a programme entitled *It's a long way from Umfolozi*.

The operation's successful conclusion was reported as follows in the Zoological Society's Report for 1970:

> The arrival in August of the White Rhinoceros in a balanced group of all ages, from fully adult to newly-weaned young, was clearly the event of the year. Joined by the pair of White Rhino which were already resident, the group of 22 animals has from the start shown a docility which is in complete contrast to the picture of power and aggression which their size and shape suggest as they lumber around their 30 acre paddock. After some six weeks in crates – from the time of their capture in the Umfolozi Game Reserve, through a long Atlantic sea journey, made even longer by a dock strike in Britain – the animals thundered out into the Whipsnade dusk as naturally and easily as if suddenly disturbed by a tourist car on an African plain.

Because of the size of the rhinos' enclosure, a light-railway line was laid to take visitors through the middle and was named the Umfolozi Railway.

But transporting the herd was only the first step towards conservation – breeding had to occur if the herd was to become really established. The first baby was born in 1971, but to a female who had been pregnant already before leaving Africa the previous year; it was only the second white rhino ever to be

The first white rhinos ever seen in the UK arrived at London Zoo in 1955 and fifteen years later a herd of twenty arrived at Whipsnade from Natal. Here, three of that herd remain unconcerned as the Umfolozi Railway slowly makes its way past (© ZSL)

born outside Africa (the first having also been conceived before leaving Africa). The following year there were no births, and disappointment must have grown, but in 1973 two males were born, creating history in the animal world and justifying all the time, effort and cost which had gone into the creation of the Whipsnade herd.

The next year, six young were born, of which three unfortunately died at, or soon after, birth; but in the nine years that followed only two died out of 18 that were born, and after 13 years there had been 27 births, showing that the only herd outside Africa was solidly established. The herd's population was maintained at between 15 and 20 animals to ensure sufficient territory was available to them, surplus rhinos being sent to other zoos to try to establish breeding groups elsewhere. After 20 years their numbers have now been reduced to between eight and ten, as a larger herd is no longer required since births are being recorded in several other locations.

The story of London Zoo would be incomplete without mention of Whipsnade Zoo, which grew out of the knowledge gained, and the shortcomings experienced, by London. Before we return to the main story, let us see how Whipsnade has also learned by experience and grown from being merely a great idea to a Zoo Park which stands head and shoulders above most. So, briefly, what else happened at Whipsnade by the end of the century?

Amur, or Siberian, tigers breed well in this wood at Whipsnade (*Colin Whyman*)

They had learned that an Elephant House should not divide a group of these animals every night – and neither being designed by Berthold Lubetkin (of London's Penguin Pool fame), nor later becoming a 'Listed' building, made the house any more suitable for elephants. So a large, 5-acre enclosure, the largest in Europe for elephants, is now devoted to the 'herd' of six Asiatic elephants, and the new Elephant House has been adapted to hold a young male from Cincinnati Zoo, which it is hoped will soon result in young born to the females. In the meantime, their previous enclosure has been landscaped to provide a large area for lemurs, and was dedicated to the memory of one of the best-known animal conservationists, Gerald Durrell, who started his working life as a keeper at Whipsnade Zoo.

Tigers have also benefited from a better enclosure, Tiger Falls with its trees and water being altogether more suitable than either the relatively small enclosure on the edge of the Downs, or the rocky Tiger Dell.

The gibbons have been removed from their island where, however natural the island's appearance, the animals could not swing through the two trees (or 'brachiate', as their swinging is called); they have been replaced by a colony of squirrel monkeys, who are much more at home there.

The chimpanzees have had a much larger enclosure added to the outside of their house; this is surrounded by an electrified wire, and the adult male was the first to experience its effect – it was comical to see him warning all the other members of his group that they must not go near! And some marmosets, the smallest of the monkey family, have now joined the ranks of 'free' animals in a wood, returning to their shelter every night to be fed and for safety.

Many Indian deer and antelopes, as well as camels and yaks, inhabit a huge drive-through area which has a man-made hill with a picnic area for visitors on top where they can watch the animals and eat at the same time, and this has caused the Ordnance Survey maps to become out of date as the hill is now higher than the point marked on maps as being the highest on Dunstable Downs!

Many other, smaller changes have been made over the years, including the change of name to Whipsnade Wild Animal Park. It is a zoo of open spaces, a Zoo Park ideal for breeding groups of camels, wild horses, zebras and bison, but inhabited not only by foreign animals, but also by many British animals: British birds are nesting in the wood sanctuary, a breeding colony of the rare barberry carpet moth is being cultivated, and pairs of the increasingly rare (and now misnamed!) common dormouse are now breeding within the Zoo Park. Indeed, part of the Park has been nominated a Government SSSI – a Site of Special Scientific Interest.

It is a zoo that started with the aim of supporting London Zoo, but had for many years to be subsidized by London Zoo; a zoo that over 70 years has developed into a zoo in its own right, complementary to London and standing on its own feet – a never-ending experiment in animal conservation, and a model on which newer zoo parks throughout the world have since been based.

12 The End of an Era

While the development of Whipsnade was in full swing, London Zoo was experiencing its worst time since the war. The Depression of the early 1930s had helped Whipsnade by creating many unemployed people who could work there at relatively small cost to the Zoological Society, but at the same time it reduced the number of visitors to London Zoo by nearly 200,000 in one year. The pay of a keeper was three shillings (15p) a day, which was good compared with many other wages of the time.

Nevertheless, funds were adequate to allow many building works to progress, including the conversion of the old Tortoise House into a house for humming-birds. These tiny birds, which could make their nest in a teaspoon and lay eggs the size of peas, were a great attraction. Having been first displayed in stuffed and mounted form in the house specially built for Gould's collection nearly a hundred years earlier, they had since been seen only sporadically in the Zoo. Their new house enabled them to be free-flying amongst the visitors and the tropical plants (in which it was hoped they would nest, and from which were hung the little feeding-bottles where they sipped while on the wing). But humming-birds are strongly territorial, and the males, though small, show no cowardice. It gradually became apparent that the house was only big enough for one or two pairs, so other small tropical birds were also introduced. Forty years later the Zoo authorities admitted defeat and decided that the death rate was unjustifiable so, after a period with only a single pair of humming-birds, the house was eventually closed and later pulled down.

The Zoo had a large number of cats; it not only had the now 50-year-old Lion House, with some twenty-five occupants, but also a Small Cats' House, containing a number of species of wild cat as well as related animals such as civets and genets. Cat distemper was surprisingly common in the land at the time, so to deal with the occasional outbreaks among the Zoo's own cats, big and small, a special isolation ward was built.

Money was also found to build a house for two young gorillas that had arrived, named Mok and Moina. This house was the first to be designed by a young Russian emigré, Berthold Lubetkin, who later designed the Penguin Pool, as well as the Elephant House at Whipsnade and another Elephant House which never got built in London, together with other buildings commissioned by the Society.

The new Gorilla House was a departure from the 'natural' principles of design for animal enclosures which were becoming established, such as the Mappin Terraces, and was the first of Lubetkin's very modern, functional buildings. His firm of architects, Tecton, was introduced to the Society by Solly Zuckerman, who had recently joined the Zoo as a research student. Chalmers Mitchell wanted a building for the gorillas which had convertible open caging, so that in summer the two apes could have the benefit of fresh air, and in winter the interior of the building could be increased in size when the animals were not allowed out. This complex brief was interpreted by Lubetkin in a novel way: he planned a circular building with one half being an outside cage, but the other half having a double outer wall, one part of which could be rolled round to enclose the outer half in winter. All sorts of complications had to be overcome, including pivoting the rolling wall around a central steel column and installing a high-level steel track with rollers from which the wall was suspended, high-level windows, and special heating and ventilation systems to keep the apes

Lubetkin's unique design for the Round House, built for gorillas, enabled a revolving side to be rolled round to enclose the outside semi-circle and double the usable indoor area in winter (© *Crown Copyright. NMR*)

The strange aye-aye from Madagascar, one of the many occupants of the Round House that resided in it from time to time. Note its thin third finger. (© ZSL)

healthy. The inside cage was so designed that the gorillas found it more comfortable to be near the front, giving visitors a better view of them.

Mok and Moina, a big draw for visitors for several years, have now long departed this world, and the house built for them has since housed a young chimpanzee called Dick, who stayed there during the Second World War, and later a variety of animals including orang-utans, koalas, binturongs, sand cats and even, for a short period, an elephant. At the time of writing it houses a pair of those remarkable animals from Madagascar, aye-ayes.

Sir Peter Chalmers Mitchell, who had done such great work for the Society during his 30-year term as Secretary, retired from office in 1935 and was succeeded by the biologist Dr Julian Huxley, who a few years later became well-known to millions when he joined the broadcasting panel of radio's *The Brains Trust*. His grandfather, Thomas Henry Huxley, had himself been a biologist, and a great supporter of Darwin and his theory of evolution; indeed, so great a supporter was he that he was called 'Darwin's Bulldog' and, at one meeting of the British Association for the Advancement of Science in 1860, when the bishop of Oxford asked whether the apes were on his grandmother's or grandfather's line, Huxley retorted that he would rather have an ape as an ancestor than a wealthy bishop who prostituted his gifts.

Julian was a more mild-mannered man, who popularized biology by writing about it in a clear and understandable way. He co-operated with H. G. Wells and his son Dr G. P. Wells (another biologist) in compiling a massive volume entitled *The Science of Life*, in which complex subjects such as evolution and heredity were clearly explained, comparing 'Mr Everyman' with 'Mr Everymouse' (with charming illustrations contributed by L. R. Brightwell). Before Julian Huxley became Secretary he had worked alongside Chalmers Mitchell the previous summer and had then spent time visiting various zoos in Europe, Canada and the USA. He spoke enthusiastically of his ambitions, of plans to modernize the Zoo and of his dislike of bars on cages.

He began planning for greater scientific research in the Zoo by encouraging the study of animal behaviour, but at the same time worked towards educating the public about animals by writing slim, popular books which used animals as examples – *The Stream of Life, At the Zoo*, etc. The glazed labels produced so laboriously by Swan a few years earlier showed only the animal's popular name, its Latin name and its country of origin; Huxley gradually introduced other labels, giving more information about the animals.

He also wished to encourage artists, and proposed a Studio of Animal Art. This was approved and was another of the buildings designed by Lubetkin. Finally opened in 1937, the studio had received financial support from two County Councils and advice from the Royal College of Art and from the sculptor John Skeaping. At first it appeared to be very successful, being attended by about a hundred art students each week, but within a few months various difficulties became apparent, from lighting problems to high running costs and little revenue coming in from private students. There were also difficulties with the animals, many of which resented being prised from their normal territories and would not settle down long enough in their relatively short time in the Studio – not to mention the time and trouble necessary on the part of the keepers to catch and box them and then repeat the process later in the day when the animals were to be returned. Such dealings with the animals were not without danger, either, especially when handling some of the stronger 'artist's models'. The Studio fell into disuse after only two years and was pulled down in 1962.

During his first year in office, Huxley prepared plans for what was to lead to one of the most popular of all Zoo innovations and prove to be his most lasting project, now copied in many zoos around the world – a Children's Zoo. In August of that year, 1935, he arranged for a small, experimental Pets' Corner to be opened on the Fellows' Lawn, where tame animals would be taken by their keepers: there were lion cubs, a chimpanzee, ponies, a small python, a baby yak and a giant tortoise which gave rides on its back. The entrance fee was one shilling, and this entitled each child to be photographed with an animal of their choice.

Pets' Corner was an immediate success – except with the Fellows, who strongly objected to such use of their sacrosanct lawn! They aired their views at one of the monthly General Meetings of the Society, where Huxley defended his action by saying 'While the Society relied on income from the public, the public should be given what pleased and amused them', a principle which, with limitations, should always be remembered.

Council welcomed the success of Pets' Corner and approved it for a second year, but met the Fellows' objections by insisting that it be on a different site. There was still criticism from some of the Fellows, so a special committee was set up to report back to Council and this recommended that it not be opened for a third year. Council accepted this report, but obviously had reservations because it *did* approve a revised scheme – for a Children's Zoo as an educational exhibit with a separate charge for photos, though Huxley was instructed that no apes were to be used. This Children's Zoo, the first in the world, was opened by Edward and Robert Kennedy, two of the sons of the American Ambassador; and they both became US Senators, and Robert, like his brother President John Kennedy, was eventually assassinated.

Huxley was brimful of ideas and their initiation, but had little interest in their implementation or their day-to-day management. He negotiated with Odhams Press for the production of a monthly magazine to be available through newsagents and to be called *Zoo Magazine*, the Zoological Society receiving a guaranteed minimum sum each year in advance and payment of 20% of any net profits – a 'can't lose' arrangement for the Society. There was a six-year contract and the first issue, in April 1936, had a circulation of 100,000 copies. It did much to popularize animals and London Zoo, with many features on both topics; there was, of course, much to write about the Zoo as new animals were arriving every month. *Zoo Magazine* was published monthly until June 1941, when wartime paper shortages caused it to be incorporated in another Odhams magazine and it never survived.

In 1935 a Zoo birth was to capture the public's imagination thanks to the popular press. One of the chimpanzees, Booboo, gave birth to the first baby chimp ever to be born in London Zoo. Chimps are now kept in large family groups as they do in their natural state, and few are the years when at least one is not born to such a group; however, in earlier years they were kept in pairs, as were most zoo animals, and as such were not in a 'natural' arrangement conducive to breeding, so the Zoo authorities were delighted at this first chimpanzee birth. To ensure the survival of the baby, an obstetric surgeon from St Thomas's Hospital was present at the birth and visited the chimps several times afterwards to keep an eye on their progress. As happens all too often when an ape gives birth to her first offspring, Booboo did not at first know what to do with her baby and there was a danger that she would neglect it, but she soon got the hang of things and proved to be a model mother. That year saw the celebration of the silver jubilee of the reign of King George V, and consequently the new baby was named Jubilee. People thronged to the

Zoo to see her, and gifts poured in of baby clothes and even a christening mug! Hardly a day passed without a photograph or at least a paragraph in the newspapers, and the press cameras were still clicking when Jubilee was one year old and was given a birthday cake at a full press reception!

Many other London Zoo chimpanzees had become well-known to the public of their day, but none were known to so many people, or were regarded with the same degree of affection, as the mother and daughter, Booboo and Jubilee.

The period 1935 – 6 gave rise to concern regarding the finances of the Society (neither for the first time, nor the last). Despite an easing of the economic Depression of the previous years, and the fact that visitors to London Zoo had reached nearly two million in number and at Whipsnade nearly half a million, expenditure had exceeded income at both zoos. Economies were called for, and projects such as the Children's Zoo were required to be postponed or cancelled. Huxley resisted many of the economies and wanted instead to abolish the two posts of Curator of Reptiles and Curator of Insects, both to be absorbed by the Director of the Aquarium, E. G. Boulenger (another name familiar to readers of popular books on animals and the Zoo). In this decision, Huxley incurred the disagreement of staff, and a written plea from all the keepers with more than ten years' service asked for Leonard Bushby to be retained as Curator of Insects, while Professor McBride, a Council member, protested regarding the other post.

Other members of Council, however, were on this occasion supportive of Huxley, but at the Annual General Meeting in April 1937 there were serious protests from Fellows and a resolution from two, who were also on the staff of the Natural History Museum, 'instructing Council to reconsider'. This took the members of Council aback and the scheme was revised, with the result that Bushby retained his position. Huxley was not pleased! Neither was he pleased at the rejection of his plan to build a cinema to show natural history films. In this case the Society's Treasurer said: 'Let us devote our time and energies to the display of our menagerie … so that we can say that we have the best-run and most complete exhibit in the world', which they undoubtedly did have. However, a film unit was allowed, which in two years made six films for schools and twelve for commercial showing, as well as much footage of scientific interest.

Huxley was growing increasingly irritated with the complaints and grumbles of the Fellows, whom he regarded as interfering with his business. It should be remembered that the Fellows had always been (and still are) the owners of the Society, and therefore of the Zoo, and it was they who elected the Council to whom the Secretary reported, but Huxley was not only inclined to disregard *their* views, but also he was becoming increasingly intolerant of Council itself.

In 1936, the Duke of Bedford retired as President after 37 years in office. He was a remarkable man and a keen conservationist; he had his own deer park at Woburn where Père David's deer had been saved from extinction and

August Bank Holiday in the 1930s, and crowds swarmed to the Zoo. Here they are near the entrance to the Lion House (© ZSL)

which had played a large part in also saving the European bison, and he held Whipsnade dear to his heart. He was by now 78 years old, and in view of his great achievements and his long period in office he was presented with the Society's Gold Medal by King Edward VIII; and the medal is still, at the time of writing, on display at Woburn Abbey. He was also made an Extraordinary Member of Council, an Honorary Vice-President, and a permanent member of the Whipsnade Committee.

Huxley, however, had only formal relations with the Duke, found him diffi-cult, and did not like his grand, Victorian manner. Indeed, Huxley's relations were not good with Council members generally, and in the autobiography he wrote later he showed a certain contempt for many of them, describing the Duke as 'aged and eccentric', Lord Onslow as 'pompous but kindly in a rather patron-izing way', H.G. Morris as 'with a typical Civil Service outlook', and Professor McBride as 'my scientific enemy, because I had publicly attacked his belief in the inheritance of acquired characteristics'. Collectively he described them as 'alto-gether a curious assemblage … a tight group in love with their authority, self-perpetuating and autocratic'. Small wonder that there were disagreements!

For their part, Council disagreed with him over his role, saying that he should act as a Club Secretary and be ready to see Fellows at any time, but Huxley could not appreciate that the Fellows, because they owned the Society, were therefore, through Council, his employers; instead he found himself increasingly irritated by them, and impatient with their complaints. Council was also becoming very concerned at the amount of time Huxley was spending outside the Society writing, broadcasting and lecturing; he was a member of other important committees, was Scientific Correspondent for *The Times*, and wrote articles for the press on many subjects.

To be fair, he suggested that his salary of £1,200 a year as Secretary be reduced by half, and he continued to publicize the two Zoos in a number of ways. He produced a 'booklet' of six small cardboard gramophone records, at a price which children could afford, called 'Zoo Voices', which contained many animal sounds recorded at London and Whipsnade, each introduced by Huxley, finishing with his own pet grey parrot, which had its home in the kitchen and could talk and count, 'though not always correctly', as Huxley said. He also contributed to what was described as 'the first sound book', *Animal Language*, written by him with animal photographs by Ylla and two discs recorded at London and Whipsnade by Ludwig Koch.

Eventually Council laid down the rule that 'no outside work may be undertaken by this officer which would in any way interfere with the proper discharge of his duties'. Huxley agreed to the ruling – and ignored it. The rift continued to grow.

Visitors to the Zoo were, of course, quite unaware of these conflicts. They came to see what was universally acknowledged to be the finest collection of living animals in the world, and to this collection was added an animal that drew in the public even more than had Booboo and Jubilee, and whose name became as great a household word as had Jumbo's eighty years before – Ming.

Found only in the Szechwan province of Western China, where it is estimated that fewer than a thousand such animals remain, the Giant panda was unknown to the Western world until London Zoo had already been in existence for forty years. This animal was at first called the 'Particoloured Bear'. The study of their skeletons years later caused scientists to regard it, though bear-like, as in fact more closely related to the little Red panda of the Himalayas, whose name comes from its Nepalese name *Niyalya-Ponga*, meaning 'bamboo-eater'. The Giant panda also eats mostly bamboo shoots, for which its digestive system is actually poorly constructed to cope, and this shows the animal's origin as being partly a meat-eater – it still enjoys meat when it can find it, but being a slow, ponderous mover, the Giant panda rarely has the chance unless it comes across an already dead animal. To this day there remain doubts as to the Giant panda's correct place in animal classification, and current thinking has now come full circle, again considering it to be a closer relative of bears!

The very first live Giant panda to leave China was a baby kept by an American, Mrs Ruth Harkness, who had been living in that country. She later took the panda home with her to the USA in 1936. Two years later, London Zoo purchased three without realizing how difficult these animals are to keep – as so often before, the Zoo was first in the field and had to build up its knowledge from personal experience. Tang and Sung were males, who both died, but the third was a female, Ming. Such a cuddly looking animal had not been seen before, and crowds flocked to the Zoo to see her. It was due to Ming that panda toys became all the rage for many years, at one time almost ousting teddy bears from the height of popularity. Ming was succeeded by Lien Ho, but he never captured the public imagination during his four years at the Zoo and it was to be nearly twenty years before they had another popular Giant panda, Chi-Chi. Her story will come later.

During the 1930s, Solly Zuckerman, the young university graduate who had introduced Huxley to Berthold Lubetkin, was working in the Zoo as the Anatomical Research Fellow of the Society in three small rooms above the Bird House. In 1932 he published a book that is still considered to be a major contribution to our knowledge of primates, *The Social life of Monkeys and Apes*. Forty years later he was to become Secretary of the Society himself, and later still its President.

The most famous of all the buildings designed by Lubetkin at London Zoo must be his 1934 Penguin Pool. One of the earliest examples of 'modernist' architecture, it demonstrated the potential of reinforced concrete, particularly with its two curved ramps, which are completely unsupported. Now one of the Zoo's listed buildings, it cannot be altered, even by the addition of netting overhead to stop seagulls stealing the penguins' food or by provision of a handrail for children's safety!

A new Elephant House, also designed by Lubetkin, was proposed in 1935. It was to be built on the site still occupied by the 1869 house, in the Middle Gardens where Jumbo had resided, but many were the problems to be encountered. It was two years after the building had been proposed before the foundation stone was laid. The Maharaja of Bhavnagar promised £5,000 towards the cost of the building, and another £5,000 if it was named The Edward VIII Coronation Elephant House; Council had no problem with this – until Edward abdicated before his coronation! Luckily, King George VI officially approved the name, so the money was assured. However, before building work could commence there were further hold-ups: changes in detail, increasing costs requiring economies of plan, delays in receiving local authority building approval – all played a part, and so it was another 18 months after the foundation stone had been laid before the old house was pulled down and work could start on the new one. It was now April 1939, and in September the war started. Work on the house stopped again when only the foundations had been laid. Plans for a new Rodent & Anteater House nearby also came to a halt, and neither building ever saw the light of day.

The Penguin Pool. One of Lubetkin's designs in London Zoo, this famous enclosure (now a listed building) is made of reinforced concrete – even the unsupported, curved ramps, which are as strong today as when built in 1934 (*Roger Tomlinson*)

Another Huxley project that came to grief was his proposal to erect a statue at Whipsnade: *Humanity*, by Eric Gill. The statue was owned by another sculptor, Eric Pinnington, who no longer had room for it and was prepared to offer it to the Zoological Society for £100. Both Huxley and Pinnington thought the statue would be an asset to Whipsnade, and Huxley wrote to a number of people for grants, raising £70 towards the £100 needed. But only then did Huxley report to the Whipsnade Committee, who were very doubtful about the project and referred the matter to Council. The President objected strongly to a nude female figure being exhibited by the Society, and he was supported by Chalmers Mitchell, who had been co-opted to the Whipsnade Committee and had become one of Huxley's strongest antagonists.

Council vetoed the project, deciding that statues 'unconnected with zoology' were unacceptable, and Huxley was once again warned against taking action on Council's behalf before referring the matter to it. The statue was eventually bought by the Tate Gallery.

The public continued to visit the Zoo in numbers which totalled well over a million visitors a year until the outbreak of war. But with the war came a downturn in the affairs of the Zoo, and it took many years for a full recovery.

13 Wartime Again

There can be no doubt that the Second World War had a very serious effect on the future of London Zoo, even after its finances had again been put in order. It had for many years maintained an excellent record for animal births, and in 1938 births included seven lions, five tigers, two leopards and a lynx, a record which is enviable even by today's standards. By the end of that year the Zoo had bred 149 mammals, 73 birds and 11 reptiles, and the number of animals in the collection totalled 3,624, excluding all the fishes and invertebrates. Over 1,800,000 visitors came – fewer than the previous year, largely because of the 'disturbed international situation in September' as the annual report said, but the Zoo was still enjoying its heyday.

But on 3 September of the following year, war was declared and the Government of the day instructed that all places where crowds were likely to congregate must close, and this, of course, included the Zoo.

It was the first time in its history that London Zoo had closed other than on Christmas Day each year. The animals never seem to like the Zoo being closed, missing the public who play such a large part in their lives, and this is particularly the case with the primates, so when day followed day and the public was not present, the effect on the animals became noticeable. However, help was close at hand in the shape of some soldiers billeted in an empty house on the edge of Regent's Park, and the War Office kindly arranged for them to visit the Zoo each day until they should be required for active service. The soldiers no doubt enjoyed themselves – after all, it was better than being given 'fatigues' to occupy their time – and the animals certainly welcomed their presence.

After ten days the order was relaxed, and the Zoo again opened its gates, but everyone was conscious of the possibility of invasion, and by the end of that month attendances had dropped to 11 per cent of the attendances for September of the previous year. Gradually figures improved; the total number of visitors for the year was 1,707,443 – the thirteenth best year ever, partly due to the popularity of Ming – and, despite having to survive largely on their reserve funds for the last four months, the Zoo's financial surplus at the end of the year was almost £60,000, their largest bar only one exception. The decision was therefore taken to try to stay open throughout the war.

Contingency plans had been drawn up for some time in anticipation of the outbreak of war. Wire netting had been stored at Whipsnade to be able to create enclosures there for some of the animals from London, although there were, of course, many animals for which Whipsnade was quite unsuitable; the many small mammals could not be housed there, there was no adequate provision for reptiles or fishes, and any animals requiring heated houses could not be accommodated. There was also a shortage of space for animals such as big cats, for which wire netting was hopelessly inadequate, but the elephants and rhinos had already been transferred there while their new house was being built, and it was decided that London Zoo's two Giant pandas would be moved to Whipsnade, but that one or both would return to London for the summer. With the cancellation of non-essential bus services, such as that from London to Whipsnade Zoo, and the introduction of petrol rationing, Whipsnade received virtually no visitors when the war started; indeed, visitor numbers continued to be low

throughout the war, so it was decided initially to close Whipsnade because of its catering losses and free staff for agricultural work. However, it remained closed for only three months, reopening in February 1940.

When the war started, all poisonous snakes and invertebrates at London Zoo were killed because of the danger from escapes following possible damage

Lien Ho was a gentle Giant panda who, during the war, was allowed on to one of the public lawns. Bamboo shoots were supplied for her from Cornwall. Her keepers had tried to tempt her with alternative leaves but she always refused them. She did, however, eat some vegetables and, occasionally, a little meat (*J. Barrington-Johnson*)

to their houses, and the Aquarium was closed because of the danger from broken glass. Food was an obvious problem, as even *people* had their food rationed, so large parts of Whipsnade not open to the public were ploughed up in order to grow crops suitable for herbivorous animals such as zebras and antelopes resident at both Zoos.

The library was also a big worry. It was the largest collection of its kind in the world and contained many valuable manuscripts, original drawings and paintings, and rare editions, but the Duke of Bedford offered to store them at Woburn for the duration of the war. Building of the new Elephant House was cancelled, and it was to be another 25 years before London Zoo again had such a house.

Fellows of the Society rallied round at this time. Some suggested that they 'adopt' their favourite animals, and by the end of the first year 180 had been adopted. This was the beginning of what has since become a standard adoption scheme at the Zoo, and it has been copied by others throughout the world – another 'first' for London Zoo. There were restrictions on what could be photographed by the public in wartime, although it was still possible to obtain a limited number of films for cameras when available, so a photographic competition was held at the Zoo (where there were no photography restrictions, of course) in conjunction with *Amateur Photographer* magazine, and this helped to increase attendances. A 'War Utility' exhibition was arranged, for the public to see how to keep animals for food production – poultry, goats, rabbits, pigs, carrier-pigeons(!) and bees – and one of the trees which can be seen to this day on the Fellows' Lawn, the 'Snowy mespilus', was purchased with the proceeds from the sale of pullet eggs during the war. This tree is a native of the eastern USA and produces delicate white flowers in April/May before its leaves are fully open and, later, maroon-purple fruits resembling small rosehips.

Other changes which occurred in the few months of that first year of war included allowing members of the armed forces to come into the Zoo at half-price and free on Sundays (which had for many years been Fellows' Day), while their accompanying families could enter at half-price any day. Julian Huxley suggested that senior staff be put on half-pay and that the posts of Assistant Curators be suspended; Council agreed, although full pay was brought back a year later and the post of Curator of Insects was reinstated at the same time, when the Insect House was reopened after having been shut when the poisonous invertebrates were killed. Seth-Smith, the Curator of Mammals and 'Zoo Man' on BBC *Children's Hour*, and F. Martin Duncan, librarian for 20 years, retired early, while E.G. Boulenger went to work in the War Office.

Also working for the Government shortly afterwards was the scientist who had started his career at the Zoo as a graduate in 1928, Professor Solly

Zuckerman; during the war he was chosen by Winston Churchill to be Scientific Adviser to the Cabinet Office.

Despite all the problems that occurred in 1939, London Zoo had an income of £113,600 and expenditure of £90,000 – a surplus of £23,600; Whipsnade had a surplus of £2,300, so the year ended reasonably satisfactorily for the Society. But this was, of course, only the beginning of a very difficult period, and the following year saw attendances drop to little more than one-third, creating a financial loss of £19,000; there was, however, still a cash reserve of £34,300, but this would disappear altogether within two years at the present rate. The situation was grave.

A sad loss in 1940 was the death of the Duke of Bedford, who had done so much for the Society. He had been a Fellow for seventy years, since 1870, a member of Council since 1896, and President for 37 years from 1899 to 1936. He had made many gifts of animals to the two collections, including European bison, Siberian tigers and Mongolian wild horses, as well as trees and plants for Whipsnade. In addition he had paid for the transportation to London of two large collections of animals presented to the Prince of Wales by the Government of Nepal in 1906 and 1911 (which, as with all royal gifts of animals, were deposited at London Zoo, regarded as the national zoo), and

The European bison, or wisent, stands taller than the American bison and was one of the occupants of the deer and cattle sheds. The Second World War drastically reduced their numbers in Europe but the animal has been saved by captive breeding groups like this one at Whipsnade (*Colin Whyman*)

had been one of two guarantors of the cost of building the Aquarium under the Mappin Terraces in 1922.

By August it was decided to open London Zoo to the general public on Sunday afternoons (mornings were still reserved for Fellows and members of the armed forces), and in that month Sunday takings amounted to one-fifth of the month's total income. But the war was beginning to affect the two zoos more directly. In the last three months of the year, large-scale air raids began; there were nine air raids in which bombs were dropped in Zoo grounds, six occasions at London Zoo and three at Whipsnade, involving a total of five high-explosive bombs, over 70 firebombs and two oil-bombs. Considerable damage resulted, and one giraffe 'died of a dilated heart due to over-exertion caused by fright'. Some antelopes had also died of fright, and a few birds escaped and were lost, but the only buildings destroyed or badly damaged were the Rodent House and the Zebra and Wild Horse House, though four others, the Camel House, Ravens' Aviary, Aquarium and Monkey Hill, suffered some damage such as broken glass, but were all quickly repaired.

Huxley became personally involved the night the Zebra House was bombed and a zebra stallion set off along the Outer Circle road. He helped shepherd the animal back and into the stores yard before it reached Camden Town, and later wrote in his autobiography that 'Every time the AA guns went off he backed violently. I was frankly alarmed that he would kick me in the stomach.' When, the next day, he told the zebra keeper about the incident, 'he looked at me rather pityingly. "Cor, bless you, sir, you needn't have been frightened, 'e's a biter, not a kicker"!'

The Zoo had again to be closed, for ten days at the end of September, because of unexploded bombs in or near it, and at about the same time an Emergency Fund was started for contributions from Fellows 'for any emergency purposes either during or immediately after the war'. Whipsnade, being in the country, did not suffer to the same extent, although it did not escape bomb-free; it had far fewer buildings than London, and none of them was damaged, but Council notes record that 'some of the bomb-craters will be lined to serve as dew-ponds, thus saving the Society the cost of excavation'.

The next year, 1941, saw only 513,000 visitors, the lowest number since 1864. Still the bombs fell, with 130 incendiaries, but although they caused some damage, there were no animal losses. The Aquarium Overseer had been able to keep a large number of tropical and other fishes in improvised tanks in the Tortoise House, and one side of the now nearly empty Reptile House was adapted for them. Other tanks in that house were modified for rodents (whose house had been destroyed the previous year) and for aardvarks.

Julian Huxley went to the USA to lecture, taking three months' unpaid leave to do so, and the next year he resigned as Secretary and from Council. Perhaps Council was relieved after all the controversies during Huxley's term of office, but it must be said that he had initiated many things which were beneficial to the Zoo during his seven years. From then on the post of Secretary has been an unpaid, honorary one.

Because of paper restrictions, the Annual Report was very brief in 1942, and after the Annual General Meeting a Liaison Committee was set up to receive suggestions and criticisms on policy from Fellows, but no constructive suggestions were put forward. The year 1943 saw the suspension of Scientific Meetings, but joint meetings were held with the Linnaean Society instead. The Freshwater Hall of the Aquarium was reopened, with an admission charge of sixpence, and the number of Zoo visitors increased for the second year running, reaching well over one million, partly because people wanted a change from their normally drab wartime existence; however, things were about to take a downward turn once more when the following year brought the advent of the Flying Bombs.

During the summer and autumn of 1944, one of these bombs fell inside the Zoo and a further eighteen close by. The one falling within the Zoo exploded early in the morning on the south bank of the canal, seriously damaging the Owl's Aviary and the Pheasantry on the opposite side of the canal; records show it was considered that both of these, as well as the Hippo House, would have to be rebuilt. All external windows in the Zoo were broken, and this included the glass roof which covered the whole Monkey House, the floor of which was littered with broken glass in both the public area and inside the many cages – and yet not one monkey had been cut! The glass roofs of the Reptile House and other buildings were also broken, and a peacock was seen strutting along the roof of his house.

The effect of the Flying Bombs on visitor attendances was disastrous; between June and October of 1944, the start of the Flying Bomb period, there were only 266,658 visitors, and fewer than 750,000 came in the whole year. The admission price had to be increased (but still with half-prices on Mondays and for the Forces), while, to make matters worse, Ming the Giant panda, who was the biggest draw in the Zoo, died.

At long last, however, after six years, the war in Europe came to an end in June 1945, and the public flocked back to the Zoo – over 2,200,000 visitors came that year. It was decided to reinstate the Fellows' privilege of exclusivity on Sundays, but for the mornings only, as it had been shown that the Zoo's finances gained considerably from Sunday admission of the public. It was not many years before the Fellows again lost their right to have the Zoo reserved for them, for even part of a day, but this time it was permanent.

Only a few weeks after the war ended, someone rushed into the Zoo's offices to say that an elderly gentleman had been knocked down by a taxi outside the building. Staff were horrified to find that the victim was Sir Peter Chalmers Mitchell and that he had been killed in the accident. He died on the very day

SIR PETER CHALMERS MITCHELL
C·B·E·F·R·S·
SECRETARY
ZOOLOGICAL SOCIETY OF LONDON
1903-1935
THROUGH WHOSE VISION AND BY WHOSE
WORK WHIPSNADE BECAME A ZOOLOGICAL PARK

Mitchell Monument. Sir Peter Chalmers Mitchell worked wonders for ZSL. Whipsnade Zoo was his great inspiration and this monument to him can be seen on a lawn near the entrance to Whipsnade (*Colin Whyman*)

that was the seventeenth anniversary of the granting of Royal Assent for the development of his personal dream, Whipsnade Zoo. He was cremated, a relatively rare occurrence in those days, and he had arranged for his ashes to be buried within Whipsnade Zoo, beneath a monument of four rough stone pillars surmounted by cross-pillars. This 'Little Stonehenge', as it came to be known, was placed on his instructions at the spot where he had started his tour of Hall Farm with Council members in 1926. Sadly, at the time of writing, this spot is inaccessible for visitors, being on the edge of the Asian drive-through area and some way from its entrance, but recognition has been given to the achievements of Chalmers Mitchell in the form of a pillar erected to his memory, near the entrance to Whipsnade Zoo.

With the ending of the war, life at London Zoo slowly returned to normal. Animals began to arrive again – monkeys (four of which were new to the collection), bush-babies (two new), a sub-species of serval that had just been discovered, as well as caracal lynx, genets, antelopes and squirrels. A quarterly magazine was started, *Zoo Life*, devoted mainly to illustrated accounts of animals to be seen at London or Whipsnade. But the financial difficulties were not easily to be overcome. The Planning and Priorities Committee estimated that the cost of building repairs and reconditioning essential services such as roads and paths, water pipes, drains and fencing, would total £400,000 for London Zoo alone, and the Post-War Development Fund stood at only £177,221. The long, uphill struggle was beginning.

14 The Post-War Years

The year after the war ended, 1946, saw a phenomenal increase in the number of visitors to London Zoo. After all the cares of wartime, and with few alternative forms of 'outing' available (particularly ones not involving much travel, petrol still being rationed), people flocked to the Zoo as never before – a total of over 2¾ million visitors. This was the highest number in the Zoo's history, exceeding by half a million the previous highest number in 1928.

The number of animals also increased, by 1,100; the Society had organized five collecting expeditions, and many other animals were presented by people. But while income rose, expenditure rose even more, and at the end of the year the surplus was only £15,753 – less than half that of the previous year. Despite good attendances for several years thereafter (peaking at over 3 million visitors in 1950), this was to be the sad story for many years as maintenance and repairs were so great a liability following the war.

At the beginning of the war the Zoological Society had started a remarkable publication with the off-putting name of *Nomenclator Zoologicus*. Published in four volumes, this was no less than the names of all animals discovered since the days when Linnaeus first started the logical classification of animals, and covered the years from 1758 to 1935. The first supplement was to be published in 1949, covering the years 1936 to 1945, and the intention was to issue further supplements each year or so, updating the volumes with the growing number of animals discovered in the intervening years. Those first four volumes were financed privately by Dr Sheffield Neave (the Society's Secretary) and Mr R.W. Lloyd. This new publication filled a gap long-felt by scientists the world over, and by 1946 the income from world sales showed a surplus of £1,200, which was presented to the Society, together with a stock of about 1,000 copies of each volume, to form a fund to finance future supplements.

The year 1946 also saw the death of E.G. Boulenger, who was by then the Curator of Reptiles, and his place was taken by Jack Lester, the man who was to be the unwitting cause of introducing to television audiences a man who became the best-known presenter of animal programmes – David Attenborough. The central block of enclosures in the Reptile House houses the dangerous reptiles, such as the large constricting snakes and venomous snakes, and was so designed that any escaped animals would remain separate from the public area; a concrete staircase within this central block leads to the upper floor where breeding tanks are located, and Jack Lester's office was also on that floor. One day, while working in his office, Jack heard a commotion downstairs and then a keeper shouting for help. He opened his office door to see a python coming up the stairs towards him with two keepers holding on to its tail; Jack ran to help and told me later that it had taken the three of them the best part of half an hour to manhandle the snake back into its enclosure.

The wedding of Princess Elizabeth was in 1947, and as a wedding present from the Society she was offered Life Fellowship. As Queen she later became Patron of the Society, and also twice presented them with new Royal Charters over the following fifty years.

At the same time, the Zoo's financial position was becoming ever more serious and, in the words of the Secretary, gave rise to 'considerable anxiety'. This was to be a recurrent theme over the next 45 years and I do not intend to refer to it continually, but this fact should be kept in mind since it was to create a slow build-up to the financial climax which resulted in the decision to close the Zoo in 1992.

As we saw, David Seth-Smith, the BBC 'Zoo Man', had been the first Zoo employee to become clearly connected in the public's mind with London Zoo, and he was followed by Julian Huxley. Now the next personality appeared, George Cansdale.

Cansdale had for some years been employed by the Gold Coast Forestry Department, and he was a Corresponding Member of the Society (that is, a Fellow who, because of distance, was unable to attend meetings of the Society or visit the Zoos, but was nevertheless a supporter). He had given many collected animals to the Zoo; in 1946 alone he had presented them with 148 reptiles and birds. The following year he was appointed Assistant Superintendent of the Zoo, and he took up his duties in 1948. He was to become the Zoo's first television personality. He used to talk on television about one or other of the Zoo animals and then produce it and handle it in front of the cameras. In those days all programmes were transmitted 'live', and a big fascination for the viewers was in waiting to see whether the animal would relieve itself over George or whether it would first bite him! On one memorable occasion a squirrel he was displaying escaped and for several weeks kept making unscheduled appearances in various other BBC productions!

With much backlog maintenance work necessary and a number of animal houses due for updating or replacement (the Zoo still had no Elephant House since the one pulled down before the war), it was decided to draw up plans for a complete revision of the Main Gardens. Stengelhofen, the Society's architect, drew up a draft plan for a 'two-tier' zoo with an upper walkway providing access to the upper storeys of two-storey animal houses as well as cover for visitors at ground level. The idea behind this innovative plan was effectively to double the number of inside cages without requiring any extension of the Zoo into Regent's Park. This was continuing the previous, pre-war Zoo principle of housing as many different species of animal as possible, but this idea was going out of favour with some of the Fellows, who were rethinking the justification for zoos, and the proposed plans did not materialize.

The idea of conserving animals that were becoming threatened with extinction was replacing the prevalent public view of animals as only being on earth for the use or entertainment of mankind, or for his hunting pleasure. It needs to be remembered that the Zoological Society and London Zoo were first formed with the express intention of studying animals; this they had now been doing for a century and a quarter, during which time a vast amount of information had been discovered about the living world – not least that evolution was an ongoing process which had led to many extinctions by a natural process of adaptation to changing conditions. But now it was being realized that man had been *causing* unnatural changes and the extinction of species *without* the evolution of better-suited replacements and, furthermore, that man's unnatural impact on wildlife had increased during the last hundred years and was still accelerating. Zoos were beginning to be regarded not so much as a display of as many species as possible, but as a possible refuge for rarer animals.

Over 60 years earlier, the idea of conservation had begun and the Zoological Society had been recognizing the work of early conservationists. As early as 1890, Council awarded its Silver Medal to representatives of two families for their work on the Scottish islands of Uist and Foula in protecting the great skua, commenting in the Annual Report:

Council have been influenced by the consideration that extermination of various species of animals, which has been going on with increasing rapidity in so many parts of the world, will in a few years form a serious detriment to the progress of zoological science. The total extinction with which several forms of animal life are inevitably threatened in several of the British Colonies will ever be deeply regretted by future investigators, and steps taken for their protection should accordingly be worthy of reward.

Again, in 1893, the minutes of a Council meeting record:

That the Council of this Society have learnt with great satisfaction the steps that were proposed to be taken by the Earl of Onslow, when Governor of New Zealand, and by the Houses of General Assembly, for the preservation of the native birds of New Zealand, by reserving certain small islands for the purpose, and by affording the birds special protection on these islands.

That Council venture to suggest that, beside the native birds to be protected in these areas, shelter should also be afforded to the remarkable ... Tuatara Lizard, which is at present restricted to some small islands on the north coast.

That copies of these resolutions be communicated to the Earl of Onslow, and to His Excellency, The Earl of Glasgow, the present Governor of New Zealand.

These were the early signs of the Society's involvement in conservation work, which was to be the most important of its functions one hundred years later.

Julian Huxley is largely remembered as a well-known radio broadcaster, but after the war he gave a series of three television lectures on animal patterns and shapes. The young producer of Sir Julian's three programmes was David Attenborough, later also to be knighted, and he arranged for the lectures to be illustrated with animals from London Zoo; in doing so he first met the Zoo's Curator of Reptiles, Jack Lester. Jack was not a professional zoologist, although he had a deep interest in animals; before joining the Zoo staff he had been in the overseas branch of a bank and had for some time worked in Sierra Leone in West Africa, where he had collected reptiles and become extremely knowledgeable about these animals in particular.

Shortly after the Huxley lectures, David approached Jack and discussed with him his ideas for an animal collecting expedition to be mounted and to be filmed for television. In his book, *The Zoo Quest Expeditions*, David described himself as being at the time 'a twenty-six-year-old novice television producer with two years' broadcasting experience and an unused zoology degree, anxious to make animal programmes'. His idea was to direct film sequences of Jack searching for an animal and capturing it, followed by studio handling by Jack of the same animal; in this way the animal-handling sessions which had proved so popular with viewers would be linked with film of the animal's native habitat.

Jack was equally enthusiastic about the idea, but the two of them then had the job of persuading first the Zoological Society that they would benefit from mounting a collecting expedition, and then the BBC that such a series of programmes would be of public appeal. Both parties readily agreed, and because of Jack's knowledge of Sierra Leone and its animals, that was the country chosen.

Thus were the *Zoo Quest* series of programmes born, and in each series some seven or eight programmes were devoted to the animals of a particular part of the world – after Sierra Leone came Guyana, Indonesia and Paraguay. The first *Zoo Quest* took place in 1954 and involved ten weeks of field work;

as well as the films for the BBC, a large collection of animals was brought to the Zoo, including many snakes and birds, bush-babies and mongooses. The first programme was transmitted in December with Jack handling the animals as planned, but the next day he went into hospital and for the following programme David stepped out from behind the cameras and took his place – as he was obliged to do for the remainder of the series.

The next year saw another expedition for the second of the *Zoo Quest* series, and Jack accompanied David although he was far from well. On his return, Jack Lester was presented with the Zoological Society's Silver Medal 'for outstanding services in leading expeditions to collect animals' between 1948 and 1955, the second *Zoo Quest* expedition; but Jack Lester never fully recovered from his illness, and died in August 1956. However, he had been the unwitting cause of presenting to the nation's view the most popular of all animal programme presenters, David Attenborough, whose years of television work in educating the public about animals were recognized by the Zoological Society at the end of the century when they made him an Honorary Fellow.

A few years earlier had occurred the story of Cholmondley (pronounced Chumley), a chimpanzee. Keeping family groups of chimps in zoos enables them to breed – which is essential if they are to be saved for the future. Before the war, however, this was not recognized, and in zoos they were kept in pairs, while young chimpanzees were occasionally even kept as pets. In Cholmondley's case, he had been kept by a lady in a London flat and had been brought up as a member of the family, wearing clothes, eating at the table and generally behaving as a human being, and he undoubtedly regarded himself as such – after all, he had never even seen another chimpanzee, and had only humans for company.

As happens with chimpanzees, particularly males, on reaching maturity he became unpredictable and strong-willed, and, being such a strong animal, he had to be regarded as potentially dangerous; so in 1948 he was given to the Zoo. Unwilling to mix with any of his own kind, Cholmondley was lonely. He had to be kept caged, his clothes were taken from him and he was certainly not allowed to smoke cigarettes any more, but he loved human company and was well liked both by staff and regular visitors to the Zoo. On one occasion, while temporarily in the Zoo hospital, he managed to escape: he got out of the Zoo, walked across the corner of Regent's Park, and hailed a bus in Albany Street. Having got on the bus, he sat down next to a lady and put his arm round her shoulders. He then – probably because the lady was having hysterics – bit her!

He was a lonely, misplaced animal who considered himself to be human and, I believe, never got over the indignity of having his clothes removed. Sadly, he survived in the Zoo for only three years.

Later, a bird which became well-known was made popular by accident. In February 1965, a golden eagle escaped from the Birds of Prey aviary and flew into the park. For nearly two weeks it remained free, becoming ever hungrier,

Goldie, the golden eagle known to everyone in the UK after his escape (© ZSL)

and the public became more enthusiastic about it as time went on. When the media learned about it, the eagle became front-page news; birds being so numerous in the Zoo, usually few are named, and this one was no exception, so when asked for its name by the media, a rather harassed Zoo official hurriedly dreamed up the name of 'Goldie'. The name stuck, and during the following days Goldie captured the public imagination to such an extent that the Zoo received over a thousand letters about him, as well as telephone calls, telegrams and presents including meat. It is said that the BBC included news of Goldie in 65 radio bulletins, and he was seen on over one hundred television broadcasts, while people flocked to the Zoo to give advice on his recapture.

A little food was supplied in the hope that he would stay near the Zoo, and this appeared to work, but not too much was given in order that he would be easier to capture. But eventually his hunger led Goldie to attack a small dog, whose irate owner rushed at him, swinging her handbag, and it became obvious that drastic steps would have to be taken. Luckily, only a day later he was recaptured and returned to his aviary, where he received a good meal and lived healthily for years – with his hurriedly acquired name prominently displayed.

Pipaluk with his mother – the second polar bear cub to be born in the Zoo (© ZSL)

The new magazine, *Zoo Life*, which had been launched when the war ended, never gained the popularity of its pre-war equivalent, *Zoo Magazine*. Sales were never high, and it was discontinued after 11 years, in 1957. But one of the Zoo's periodically popular animals made an appearance in 1950 – Brumas, the first polar bear cub born in the UK. Named after two bear keepers, Bruce and Sam, when Brumas made an appearance after many weeks in the inner den with its mother, the public flocked to see it. Baby animals always have great appeal, and in the year Brumas was born, 3 million visitors flocked to the Zoo. Shortly afterwards, the Zoo's second polar bear cub was born, Pipaluk, but not being the first-born, Pipaluk never commanded the same interest as Brumas.

In 1953, the post of Superintendent of London Zoo was abolished; George Cansdale was the last person to hold the position. It had been in existence for 125 years, and for nearly one third of that time had been occupied by Abraham Bartlett.

Three years later, in 1956, keeper training was formalized, with the aim of obtaining a Diploma in Animal Husbandry. The Ashover Zoological Gardens, owned by Mr Clinton Keeling, had pioneered education in British zoos (indeed that was Mr Keeling's prime objective), but the training in London Zoo and Whipsnade was the first time keepers had been trained towards a specific degree instead of having informal training by other keepers and 'learning on the job'. It was a new beginning and would lead, in 1969, to a two-part course lasting two years, organized in conjunction with Paddington Technical College. For many years now the Zoo Animal Management course has been run by the National Extension College and leads to a City & Guilds Certificate of Animal Management. This qualification has become standard for all British zoos and for overseas keepers trained at London Zoo; it can only be taken by those currently employed in a keeping capacity and still involves 'learning on the job' in addition to completing written assignments. Every new keeper is required to take this course, and anyone failing the examinations is unable to call himself or herself 'Keeper'.

During the late 1950s a young Zoo chimpanzee named Congo became very familiar to thousands of children, many of whom had never been to London Zoo, when he appeared regularly on television with Dr Desmond Morris, who, in 1956, had been appointed by Granada Television to the newly created post of Head of the Television and Film Unit at London Zoo. This unit was set up in association with London Zoo, and was resident in the Zoo, where it created many programmes for television. Its popularity during its first year was exemplified when a children's competition attracted some 65,000 entries. Congo was a regular 'star', endearing himself to children by his demonstrations of intelligence and affection. He also spent some time creating paintings – although these were less intelligible than those of a 3-year-old human child. However, over a period of two years Congo completed 384 abstract paintings and drawings, some of them admired by foreign artists as renowned as the American William Copley and Picasso, both of whom wished to own specimens of Congo's paintings. But when Congo became too adult to continue his freedom, he would not, in common with Cholmondley, integrate with other chimpanzees. Desmond Morris, as Curator of Mammals, determined to try to avoid the future 'humanization' of animals.

It was only a few years later that the popular Chimpanzees' Tea-Party was

Chi-Chi, the Giant panda who was too friendly with people (© ZSL)

ended. This had been an innovation of the 1930s and was restarted after the war, but, with animal welfare becoming of ever greater importance, the Society decided that however popular with the public, the Tea-Party had to come to an end. Shortly afterwards, the old Monkey House was replaced by the Sobell Pavilions, where chimps were kept as a family group (which had at least one baby almost every year). These Pavilions covered the area previously occupied by the Monkey House, the Tortoise House, the pelican enclosure and an aviary, and consisted of only thirteen enclosures instead of the previous house's numerous cages, giving the occupants very much more space. Despite their friendly appearance, chimpanzees in a family group are effectively 'wild' animals. This was amply demonstrated years later when, ignoring the warning notices, a mother lifted her child over the safety barrier 'to get a better look'; the child put her hand through the bars and had much of it bitten off by Johnny, the leading male.

Then came Chi-Chi, the Giant panda, who arrived by a quirk of fate, but became as famous as had Ming twenty years before. An Austrian animal collector, Heini Demmer, had been commissioned by an American zoo to negotiate with China an exchange of animals from East Africa for a Giant panda. He took a large collection of animals to Peking Zoo, where three pandas were exhibited, and after lengthy discussions an exchange was arranged. Of the pandas offered to him, he chose Chi-Chi, the youngest and the only female, who had been captured nearly a year earlier by a Chinese collecting team and had since been looked after by a Chinese girl who had lived with her day and night, resulting in Chi-Chi being extremely friendly towards humans.

However, by the time Herr Demmer left with Chi-Chi, the United States had broken off relations with China and had imposed an embargo on the importation of all Chinese goods – and pandas were classed as 'goods'! Left with a very valuable animal on his hands, Herr Demmer took her on a tour of European zoos, ending at London Zoo four months after first obtaining her. During their three-week visit, London Zoo negotiated Chi-Chi's purchase for about £10,000, with the assistance of Granada Television. America's loss was London's gain, and Chi-Chi lived in the Zoo for 14 years, during which time the Society estimated that she had been visited by some 25 million people.

No Giant panda had then been born outside China and because they were so rare the Zoological Society was anxious to encourage captive breeding. Moscow Zoo had a male Giant panda, An-An, and the two zoos agreed that Chi-Chi be flown to Moscow in March with London Zoo's Senior Veterinary Officer and a Head Keeper, but, to everyone's horror, when the two animals were introduced to each other they fought and had to be separated. In the wild, pandas are solitary animals. They live entirely separate lives until a female comes into breeding condition, when a male will follow her scent trail (perhaps for several days) until he catches up with her; they mate over the next day or two and then go their separate ways again. Should two pandas meet at any other time, they are likely to fight, and this is what had happened in Moscow, but until 1966 little was known about their lifestyle or breeding habits.

It was decided to leave Chi-Chi in Moscow until the autumn, her next anticipated period of sexual activity, and then to try putting the animals together again very carefully after a period in adjoining cages when they could become familiar with each other. She came into breeding condition in October, and this time Dr Desmond Morris, who was by then London Zoo's Curator of Mammals and was known well by Chi-Chi, flew to Moscow to be present – for Chi-Chi was a very valuable animal of a rare species, and Desmond was ultimately responsible for her. This time there was no fighting when the two pandas were introduced, but although An-An showed great interest in her, Chi-Chi refused all his advances. Whenever Desmond Morris appeared, however, Chi-Chi would make sexual advances to him, presenting him with her rear! It was another case of an animal having become too 'humanized', and after another week it was decided to abandon the attempt to mate the two pandas and Chi-Chi returned to London.

15 Of Apes and Men

Apes have been firm favourites among London Zoo visitors from the time they were first seen in the Zoo in 1835. The first ape was Tommy, a chimpanzee, who came by stagecoach from Bristol, where the keeper sent to collect him had difficulty booking a seat for him! He survived for only six months. A later arrival, Sally, lived in the Zoo for eight years. Arriving in 1883, she was quickly recognized as having not only a sense of fun, but also intelligence. She was credited with being able to count to ten, although her keeper claimed she could count to twenty when alone with him. The *Daily News*, when writing her obituary, said she would count out the number of straws asked for, putting each one in her mouth, and then hand the correct number to the person asking for them. She apparently also knew left from right. Bartlett was convinced that a number of differences between Sally and other chimpanzees '… cannot fail to distinguish this animal from the (common) chimpanzee'; it seems likely that Sally was in fact a specimen of what was later described as a pigmy chimpanzee and is now recognized as the fifth ape, the bonobo.

Possibly because they are quieter, less energetic apes than chimpanzees, orang-utans have never enchanted the public in the same way. In fact they can be every bit as amusing, in a rather ponderous way, and, while very strong, they are not inclined to the violence of adult chimpanzees. Orangutans are found in only two places in the world, the islands of Borneo and Sumatra, having become extinct on the mainland. They lead solitary lives, only joining up for mating, and the mothers usually have a baby up to the age of three with them, as well as a slightly older youngster also in tow who learns from the mother what foods are to be found where. They clamber about in trees very slowly, using their strong arms and rarely coming to the ground; when they do touch the ground, they walk on the outside edges of their feet, which are shaped like hands with an opposable big toe for grasping tree branches securely.

If you visited London Zoo in the 1980s, you would have seen Suka, the orang-utan. She was one of the prospering collection of these apes which had for some years been breeding very successfully. Because they are solitary animals they need to be kept segregated, and this means that several separate enclosures have to be reserved for them. Not many zoos can spare the space and facilities necessary, so breeding orangs in captivity is a relative rarity, despite the increasing need for this as their rainforest homes are disappearing. But London Zoo had some twelve orangs eventually, including two breeding males – in itself an achievement, for if the males can see each other only one is likely to develop into a fully mature adult. Their breeding record started in 1961, and over the following 22 years exactly the same number of young orangs was born (22), as well as several births to females sent from other zoos to be mated with London Zoo's males.

Suka was by then a grandmother, but was still having babies – one every four years or so is normal for orang-utans. She was a gentle and affectionate animal, and Esther Rantzen, the television personality, went into the enclosure with her as part of the film she was making for the BBC (*A Day at the Zoo*), a thing which could not be allowed with a chimpanzee of a similar age. Suka was also intelligent, as are most orangs, and she learned while young that when the Zoo vet came to see her, he gave her a sweet to occupy her while she was being examined. She learned to walk around her enclosure while holding a hand over her ear so that the vet would come to see what was wrong and give her a sweet in the process. Despite a number of examinations, he never found anything the matter with her ear and so her attempts to fool him wore off, but even when getting rather old she would often walk holding her ear – more in hope than expectation. Orangs seem to be mechanically minded, and Suka, when she was quite young, succeeded in completely dismantling her climbing frame and hiding the fixing nuts from her keeper!

Another example of the mechanical ability of orangs occurred in 1903, when Jacob made his name by escaping from the old Ape House, located where the Reptile House is currently situated. His keeper had carelessly dropped his bunch of keys beside the orang's cage when leaving, and Jacob had reached it and must have tried each key in turn until he found the right one to fit the lock of his cage, despite not being able to see the keyhole, which faced away from him. Having opened the door, he climbed on top of the cage and broke a skylight by throwing a flowerpot through it; once on the roof he climbed into an adjacent tree, where he built a large nest of branches and twigs, just as his wild cousins do. There he slept until he was discovered by keepers the next morning, when he was easily persuaded to return to his cage for breakfast.

A larger-than-life bronze statue by William Timym can be seen near the restaurant and canteen; this is in memory of another ape who became well-known – Guy the gorilla. It is amusing to read the first mention of Guy in the Annual Report for 1947, as it gives no hint of the popularity to come in later years:

Special mention must be made of the young male gorilla acquired in November in exchange from Paris Zoo, so that the higher apes are once more fully represented in the Society's collection.

At that time the Annual Report, issued to all Fellows of the Society, was still written in a rather dry, formal manner. The above entry was the last sentence under the heading 'Collection', which covered little more than half a page and was the only reference to living animals in the first eleven pages of the Report, which by then had already covered 22 other subjects, including scientific publications, the library, catering facilities and an obituary!

The 'young male gorilla' was 18 months old when he arrived, clutching a hot-water bottle. Like the baby hippo, Guy Fawkes, born 75 years earlier, the date of Guy's arrival, 5 November, determined his name. He was to live 31 years in the Zoo, unlike its first gorilla, Mumbo, whose diet in 1887, in addition to fruit, included sausages, beer and cheese sandwiches. Not surprisingly,

One of the Zoo's all time favourites was Guy, the gorilla. After his death this larger-than-life statue of him was presented to the Zoo by its sculptor, William Timym (*Colin Whyman*)

he sadly died within a few months. Nevertheless, it was food which indirectly caused the death of Guy also, because at that time feeding animals in the Zoo was still allowed, and the sweets given to him when he was young had made his teeth bad. It was because he needed treatment to these that he was taken into the Zoo hospital, and he died of heart failure while under the anaesthetic. At the time he died, in 1978, Guy had an armspan of six feet and weighed 32 stones (twice the reasonable weight for a large man!). Unlike the brief entry in the Annual Report when he arrived, the 1978 Report said:

> For many years he was the best known and most popular animal in the Zoo – both nationally and internationally. Many thousands of photographs as well as films, portraits, and sculptures portrayed his physical magnificence.
>
> He never sired any young and it was found at post-mortem that he was infertile.

A later male, acquired while adult from Chessington Zoo, was Kumba. Gorillas do not normally look directly at each other and one day, when a number of schoolboys were laughing and pointing at him, Kumba appears to have become impatient and charged, thumping the glass dividing him from the public. Even though this barrier was of 5-ply laminated glass, it cracked from top to bottom and, needless to say, the boys fled, not waiting to see that the window did not shatter!

Christmas lectures were given each year during the Christmas holidays for the children of Fellows and their friends, and in 1959 the Zoo started what would prove to be the highly popular XYZ Club – Exceptional Young Zoologists' Club – which was open to all children between the ages of 11 and 18, not just those whose parents were Fellows. The XYZ Club continued for many years and enabled children to see 'behind the scenes' and have their own special events, learning about animals in an enjoyable way and encouraging their interest in animals. This was the first step in this direction, which by the 1990s was being continued by the junior section of Lifewatch, the Animal Adoption scheme, the 'Art Cart' run by Zoo Volunteers (where children of all ages are encouraged to sketch animals in the Zoo, being given the necessary paper and pencils or crayons, and having their picture exhibited for the rest of the day), and eventually the official Children's Committee, which consisted of children and regularly met to discuss and advise on future Zoo plans from children's points of view.

The Coronation of Queen Elizabeth II was in 1953, and the year was marked at the Zoo in a number of ways. Many of the houses in the Gardens were given a new coat of paint; the flower-beds (always a feature) were extra colourful and contained, in addition to flowering plants, over 30,000 bulbs; gaily striped awnings and umbrellas gave the restaurants and outdoor cafés a continental appearance, and flagpoles placed down either side of the main walk and at the entrance to the Zoo flew flags of British Commonwealth countries. A number of the animal cages received new labels lettered in gold and bearing a crown to indicate a Coronation collection of animals; these had some connection with the Commonwealth or were donated by someone from a Commonwealth country, such as a Barbary ape from the Governor of Gibraltar, and a Malayan tigress presented by a platoon of Gurkhas. There was a special falconry display on a lawn, a small herb garden was formed of the type popular during the reign of Elizabeth I, and the Zoo was floodlit on Wednesdays and Thursdays throughout the summer, remaining open until 11 p.m. with an orchestra playing.

A special gift from Australia to commemorate the Coronation, and the visit of the Queen to Australia, was made jointly by four zoos: Sydney, Melbourne, Adelaide and Perth. This gift consisted of a collection of Australian animals and was assembled at Taronga Park Zoo, Sydney, and generously shipped at the expense of the President of Taronga Park Zoological Trust, Sir Edward Hallstrom, who was also a Corresponding Member of the Zoological Society of London. The collection arrived at London Zoo in 1954 and was accommodated in specially erected enclosures in what was normally the outdoor enclosure for the blackbuck herd. It included 40 mammals, 146 birds and 10 reptiles, including a number of cockatoos, emus, black swans, kangaroos, dingoes, wombats, Tasmanian devils and an echidna.

It was in the same year as these animals arrived that a new use was made of the West Tunnel in the Zoo. A team of students from the Royal Academy of Arts school made copies of the famous prehistoric cave paintings at Lascaux and Altamira, and reproduced these, life-size, on the tunnel walls. They showed the animals with which prehistoric man was familiar in Europe, and among many others can be distinguished wild horses, European bison, and the giant cattle, aurochs.

Also that year another of the benefits enjoyed by Fellows was withdrawn: this time the issuing of free tickets annually for Fellows' friends. This was done as an alternative to increasing their annual subscription, and was decided after a referendum was held. But when, two years later, the decision was made to open the Zoo to the public on Sunday mornings, so that no longer was any time to be set aside for its exclusive use by Fellows, the bubble burst. As we know, for some time after the Zoo first started only Fellows were admitted, after which members of the general public were grudgingly admitted at first on Mondays only. In view of this growing source of revenue, members of the public were later admitted every day except Sunday, and after the war it was agreed that the public would be admitted on Sunday afternoons. But there were growing objections in the newspapers that this national exhibition was closed to the public for part of one of the only two days of the week when most people were able to go there. (It is ironic that it was regarded as a 'national' exhibition when, to this day, the nation makes no contribution to its successful running!)

From having covered all the costs of starting and running the Zoo all those years before, Fellows' contributions were now only a relatively small proportion of the total revenue, and when even Members of Parliament began questioning the right of a body which stood on public land to withhold admission, Council bowed to public pressure and in 1957, despite strong opposition from the Fellows, opened the Zoo on Sunday mornings also, although the admission fee was 5 shillings in the morning compared to three shillings in the afternoon. The Fellows were incensed, and wrote letters of complaint to the newspapers, and an Ordinary General Meeting held in January 1958 was almost reduced to chaos for a time.

The problem was again one of finances. The Society had, in 1930, received a large bequest, and at that time had decided to test whether it was regarded as a charity in the eyes of the law; if it was not then the gift would become void. The decision went in favour of the Society and, also, as a charity the Society (and therefore the Zoo) was from then on exempt from paying taxes (although the later tax of VAT was excluded for a time). As a charity, however, the byelaws laid down that 'no dividend, gift, division or bonus shall be paid or made ... to ... any of its Fellows'. In addition, whereas in its early years the whole Zoo income came from the Fellows, three years after the Zoo was opened to the public for part of each week (in 1847) the Fellows' proportion of the annual income was now only 40%; a hundred years later the proportion was down to 6%, while public admissions and other charges, such as entrance to the Children's Zoo and the Aquarium, accounted for 80% (the balance being derived from refreshments, sales from the Gift Shop, scientific publications etc.). It was apparent that no longer could the Zoo be considered the sole preserve of Fellows at any time.

Furthermore, in order to avoid what Council described as a disastrous rise in the burden of the Society's rates, it wished to register as a Scientific Society under an Act of 1843 in order to qualify for exemption from rates (and as the Zoo is split down the middle between two different local councils, it paid two lots of rates, as well as the rates for Whipsnade). In order to ensure that the Society qualified to register as a Scientific Society, a new class of Fellow was created, that of 'Scientific Fellow' for professional zoologists, at half the proposed higher annual subscription required of 'Ordinary Fellows', as the original Fellows were to be known henceforth. (Subscriptions were raised from the £3 a year set in 1832 to £4 for Scientific Fellows and £8 for Ordinary Fellows.) Because of the difference in subscriptions another category was also created, 'Associates', with fewer privileges than Fellows, though this category of member was to vanish forty years later when the whole basis of Fellowship was again reviewed. In the words of the Annual Report for 1957:

> The stage had been reached in the history of the Society in which the Fellowship was threatening to be a financial impediment to the discharge of the purpose of the Royal Charter, and was therefore threatening the very existence of the Society itself.

From then on Council would consist of an equal number of Scientific Fellows and Ordinary Fellows, thus overcoming the (largely imaginary) objections of many Fellows that the majority of Council consisted of professional scientists.

One final, but very important, addition that occurred during the year of 1957 was the introduction of an education scheme for schoolchildren in the Zoo. This covered lecture-demonstrations, and was launched with a grant from the Nuffield Foundation.

The first, experimental, term of January to March 1958 was anticipated to be attended by at least 10,000 schoolchildren, and led to the creation of a permanent Education Department, based at first in the (by then empty) Small Cats' House. Later developments led to the teaching of children of all ages, a similar department being created at Whipsnade, courses for adults, in-house training of junior keepers, and, in 1981, the introduction of a Zoo Volunteer scheme. This scheme started as the training of volunteers to be Teaching Auxiliaries, who took primary school pupils on one of several tours of selected animals and told them a little about them, but by the following year they became called Zoo Volunteers.

Numbers grew to about 150 volunteers, and they were at the Zoo either for one day each week or one day each fortnight if they were members of the weekend teams. Within a few years they were staffing the Zoo's Information Kiosk, taking various 'handling trolleys' around the Gardens (which enabled the public to handle animal skins and bones, as well as see items confiscated by HM Customs), staffing a Brass Rubbing Centre and badge-making facility, as well as giving talks to the public outside the animal enclosures (the talk outside the pythons' cage at feeding time was always well attended!). They were helped with these, and many other, aspects by running their own Steering Group from 1986 to 1992, which set up the system of Daily Team Leaders and also Liaison Volunteers, who maintained contact with a particular animal house in order to keep all the other Volunteers up-to-date with news of the animals.

16 Buildings Galore

Few people have had such a profound influence on the Society as Professor Sir Solly Zuckerman. Starting as a research graduate in London Zoo in the 1930s, and later selected by Winston Churchill to be Scientific Adviser to his War Cabinet during the Second World War, in 1955 Zuckerman was asked to become Secretary of the Zoological Society. He remained Secretary for 21 years, then becoming President when Prince Philip retired after 16 years in that office. Prof. Zuckerman retired in 1983, having devoted a total of 28 years in those two offices to the welfare of the Society – and what changes were seen during that time!

His period of office was one which saw a fall in the number of visitors to the Zoo from over 2 million in 1955 to a little over 1¼ million by 1983, despite the attractions of the many new houses that were opened during that time. The Society experienced a very difficult time financially during the years Solly (as he was popularly referred to) was in office, but this would undoubtedly have been much worse but for his influence in obtaining financial support from a number of people. His contacts and his enthusiasm were of great benefit to the Zoo, and it is as a tribute to him that this chapter is devoted to the buildings erected during his term of office.

In 1956 a new animal hospital was built which was at the time considered to be the finest in Europe and was at the forefront of such buildings for many years after. Among the animals in the Zoo there were inevitably many illnesses and accidents, just as there are with people in any town. The difference here is that each animal has its own requirements: stomach ailments, for example, are very different between tigers, antelopes, hornbills and cobras, and so are the animals' treatments and handling needs. A wide knowledge had been acquired by the Zoo over 150 years, from Bartlett's rough but efficient lancing of Jumbo's cheeks, through the handling of a sick python by eight men in the 1920s, to anaesthetics appropriate to each kind of animal, the use of darts, and, later, the introduction of 'crush bars' to restrain big cats, which avoided having to remove the animals from their enclosures for a simple treatment such as applying disinfectant to a cut. If an animal needed to be inspected or given simple treatment it could be retained in the 'crush-cage', which was slowly narrowed until the animal was restrained sufficiently; this saved the more traumatic experience of the animal having to be sedated by a dart or needing to be removed altogether and transported to the animal hospital for a relatively minor matter.

In the new hospital, with its operating theatre and recovery rooms, animals were treated more successfully than ever before, and in the following years many animals from other collections, and even from the public, were treated by the Zoo's veterinary surgeons and nurses, although only animals referred to the Zoo by vets were accepted in order to ensure time was spent only on animals requiring specialist care that was not otherwise available.

In 1961 grants were received from the Nuffield Foundation and the Wellcome Trust towards two animal research centres, which nearly twenty years later were to be combined with the Veterinary Departments at London and Whipsnade to form the Institute of Zoology. There, some forty scientists were to be employed at any one time, carrying out more research into animal welfare than was carried out in all the zoos of the United States put together.

Next were built the Cotton Terraces for hoofed animals – antelopes, zebras, camels, tapirs, bison – again made possible by the generosity of a benefactor, this time Mr Jack Cotton. These Terraces embodied the original Giraffe House built 130 years earlier by Decimus Burton, whose building was by now the oldest in the Zoo still housing the kind of animal for which it was designed, and in which giraffes were still being born almost every year. The inside was modernized with tiles, but externally it was unchanged. One feature of the old house which disappeared during the modernization was a supporting pillar beside the public barrier which had carried a large dent and a notice saying this was caused by the horn of a giraffe that had aimed a blow at its keeper. (The incident was not typical of these animals, which are normally very docile and gentle, although easily frightened.) Keeper Robinson was employed by the Zoo for 43 years, much of that time spent working with giraffes, of which he became Head Keeper. He loved his charges and, when he retired in 1971, requested that when he died his ashes be scattered in the giraffe paddock. He died in 1979 and his wishes were met, so he is still with his beloved giraffes.

The Cotton Terraces were the last of the houses designed for a relatively large number of species, going against the trend of those later years when houses were erected for a small number of animals, giving them a large amount of space. Consequently, it was only a few years later that the lower parts of the Terraces, devoted to antelopes and deer, were closed to the public and several inside cages combined for a few animals who spent their days in very large outdoor paddocks. Shortly after that change, the two buildings erected either side of the Giraffe House, for camels and other large hoofed animals, were also closed to the public and again used for relatively few animals, their outdoor paddocks being combined into larger ones.

By the 1960s the Zoo had not had an Elephant House for twenty-five years, although one African and one Asiatic elephant had been in a small enclosure which had a peculiar 'sunshade' on a post, presumably to give the animals some protection from the sun and rain. At one stage an elephant had been kept temporarily in a stall beneath the Mappin Terraces with no outdoor enclosure at all, while another time the Round House built in the 1930s for Mok and Moina was pressed into service for two more elephants. In 1965, however, this state of affairs was corrected by a new house designed for these animals and for rhinoceroses by Sir Hugh Casson, who had, in 1956, been commissioned to prepare a site plan for the whole Zoo.

His building is not to everybody's aesthetic tastes, with its textured concrete walls, but it was as impressive as its occupants, and these walls were certainly safe from damage by them.

At the end of the century the elephants had been moved to Whipsnade and the building was considered unsuitable for rhinos, but it is an imposing memory of the days when these giants were in occupation. Its style has been described as 'Zoomorphic New Brutalism'! It has been said that, from the outside, the building represents a group of elephants round a waterhole with their trunks raised. In fact, the 'trunks' are all vents and lantern towers directing daylight into the animal areas inside the building, and members of the public walk in a darker central area (almost an extension of the 'aquarium effect' described earlier), creating, in its turn, an impression of standing in a jungle watching animals in sunlit glades. The Casson Pavilion contained two enclosures for each kind of animal, as well as a sick bay on each side of the building, keepers' quarters, a large storage area below, and an enclosure with a pool which, by the time the young elephants received for the house had grown up, was no longer large enough for them and so housed instead pygmy hippos in the winter when a new, large pool was constructed outside for the elephants.

Two sad incidents occurred in this house, the first leading to a permanent change in the Zoo. An African elephant was leaning over the outside dry-moat, with its trunk extended to take a bun being offered to it, when it toppled into the moat. Unfortunately it landed on its back – a most unnatural position for an elephant and one which quickly ruptured some of the animal's internal organs before a hoist could be erected to lift it out. The animal died, and the Zoo authorities decided that this incident was the final justification for feeding of all animals by the public to be forbidden. This had always been a popular pastime, but the death of this elephant, followed by the death of Guy the gorilla, confirmed that it was not in the interests of the animals to let it continue. Afterwards, the health of animals such as monkeys, elephants and bears improved once they were no longer being filled with bulk food such as buns, leaving more space in their stomachs for natural and healthier food. The elephants no longer tried to reach over the dry-moat, which was then used by a group of agoutis, a rodent from South America, who quickly settled into their new home below such monsters!

Another elephant was to die a few years later. Named Pole-Pole (pronounced to rhyme with 'slowly, slowly' – which was what the name meant), she had been used, when a youngster, to make a film in Africa called *An Elephant Called Slowly*. After the film was complete, the animal could not just be released back into the wild, but it had not received the appropriate, steady training to suit it for a zoo either, a necessity for any elephant which has to be handled, particularly African elephants. It is essential that an elephant obeys its keepers if it is to be allowed outside into the zoo for walks and at such times as it is necessary to inspect its feet, which are always subject to cuts, and to trim its toenails regularly. In the case of Pole-Pole, who had received no such training, London Zoo was hesitant to take responsibility for the animal, but as she could not just be set free again, the only alternative to placing her in a zoo would have been to put her to sleep, so the elephant did come to London, to share the outside enclosure with the Asiatic elephants, in the hope that she would learn from them because of the herding instinct.

She did not. In fact she became rather aggressive towards them and had to be separated, and this meant she could not be allowed outside as there was only one large enclosure for elephants. It was later decided to transfer Pole-Pole to Whipsnade, where the elephants were older, to see whether she would then become more tractable, but she refused to enter the travelling crate put at the enclosure entrance. It was left in place for a few days so that she could become used to it, but, unfortunately, one day when she moved towards the crate she tripped, lying in an awkward position where a crane could not be positioned closely enough, and she died. Stopping the feeding of elephants by the public, the later installation of electrically operated doors, and the enlargement of the elephants' outside enclosure, all contributed to the avoidance of such accidents, but the later move of the elephants to Whipsnade was a permanent solution.

In a lighter vein, during the months Pole-Pole was inside the house, I used to give talks on elephants to the public from in front of her enclosure, standing at the bottom of the steps from the public area with my back to the elephant so that the public could see her while I was speaking. One day Pole-Pole must have been annoyed with me for facing away from her, so she picked up a large clump of hay with her trunk and threw it over me, much to the amusement of the visitors. The next time, she threw something much more objectionable, but luckily it missed me, the droppings hitting the side wall and spattering over the nearest visitors – who were not so amused as the other observers! (Somewhat similar incidents used to occur when I talked to a tour group outside the chimpanzees' enclosure, when the senior female, Koko, would take offence at my not talking to her, even though I was facing her while speaking, and would launch herself at the bars from a height and spit at us all. Towards me alone she was very friendly, and would come to the windows inside the house to crouch closely and study my face, but I always had to be careful if we were not alone together!)

The year before the new Elephant House was built saw the opening of the new giant aviary designed by Lord Snowdon and named after him, the result of another benefaction by the generous Jack Cotton. It is a remarkable construction, standing as it does on only two points, one at each end. From each of these points rises a pair of supports which splay outwards as they rise, and from each support hangs what I can only describe as an aluminium skeletal pyramid, the whole held together under tension by steel cables and covered in wire mesh. The design of the structure is often not noticed by visitors to the Zoo, but a moment spent studying it is rewarding, particularly from the other side of the canal. (Other designs in the Zoo are also frequently overlooked by visitors but are worth more than a glance, for example Burton's entrance to the East Tunnel, or the building at the base of the Mappin Terraces, or – perhaps most ignored of all – the reptile sculptures by George Alexander on the architrave around the entrance to the Reptile House.)

The Snowdon Aviary was built on the steeply sloping canal bank, and advantage was taken of this to provide different habitats for different species of birds – a rock face for pigeons, a pool for seagulls, flat areas for pheasants, and trees for such birds as ibis. The aviary appears to be floating in the air, particularly seen from the inside, where visitors may enter and walk across a cantilever bridge over a small waterfall, from where they can look down on to the trees growing in the lower area (these trees have become quite large after 30 years), all providing good nesting and roosting facilities. The wire mesh created a problem because it had to be large enough to allow snow to fall through as otherwise the weight of snow could cause the structure to collapse, but consequently, while retaining the aviary's large occupants, the mesh is not small enough to exclude sparrows and starlings from entry, many of which seem now to live permanently inside, enjoying free food!

When it first opened, the Snowdon Aviary contained 150 birds from Africa and India, while some thirty years later it is intriguing to note that in addition to such birds as the sacred ibis, the aviary also contained a pair of bataleur eagles, and they all lived together in complete harmony. The eagles could be seen from the bridge by looking down into the trees – they never seemed to take advantage of the huge space above them to spread their wings in flight.

No sooner had these last two structures been erected than work began on a new house for small mammals. In recent years, these animals had led a very mobile existence, being put wherever space could be found for them. A Small Mammal House had been built as a wing of the Insect House, but it had never provided enough space or sufficient cages. There had also been a house for small cats, although this had contained, in addition to civets and genets, which could be regarded as close relatives of cats, such animals as monkeys, kinkajous and binturongs, the latter two being mammals with prehensile tails. During the war, many small mammals had also been moved to what had been the Giant Tortoise House, with squirrels occupying cages not much bigger than budgerigar cages. Obviously this had to be changed as soon as possible, but there was added pressure because a further area was needed to replace the Monkey House, and this would require a great deal more space, including that taken up by the Giant Tortoise House.

So, with considerable financial help from Sir Charles Clore, the Clore Pavilion for Small Mammals was built. And small mammals had never had it so good! The new building contained some 250 animals (more than in some zoos' entire collection) in 110 'cages' and three enclosures. The building is irregular in shape and has a large number of glass-fronted cages, with the glass sloping to avoid light reflection; in addition there are a variety of shapes and sizes to meet varied requirements, clever skylight arrangements to leave the pedestrian areas shaded, and a number of different furnishings of the cages, from sand and rocks to tree-top canopies. From the time it was occupied, breeding successes abounded, some being by animals that had never previously bred in captivity in this, or any other, country.

Below the main building was the Moonlight World, which contained nocturnal animals that had rarely been seen (as they were asleep when visitors came into the Zoo). Now, however, after a trial of several years in a small building in the Children's Zoo, where two aardvarks and some other animals had been kept, the Moonlight World brought to life many wonderful animals during the daytime – nocturnal squirrels, fennec foxes from the desert, the egg-laying echidna of Australia, douroucoulis (the only nocturnal monkey), bats, and even, for a few years, the timid kiwi from New Zealand. All these animals were induced to be active during daytime by the simple expedient of turning all the cage lights on overnight, so the animals would think it was daytime and promptly go to sleep. When the Zoo opened its gates in the morning the animals' lights were dimmed and they woke up, only sufficient light being present to simulate moonlight, while visitors walked in virtual darkness to enable their eyes to become adjusted to the dim light in the enclosures.

Upstairs, many other animals could be seen such as porcupines, mongooses, bush-babies, sloths, marmosets and an animal unknown until relatively recently, the naked mole rat. This hairless and blind animal lives its entire life below ground in the African grasslands, where it uses its large front teeth for digging and is the mammalian equivalent of the ant, having only one breeding 'queen' for the entire colony! For a time, even vampire bats were to be seen, but in 1972, after eight years, the last one died, and, their quarters no

The Regent's Canal passes through the centre of the Zoo and here it passes the huge Snowdon Aviary, the whole structure of which rests on two points, one at each end of the aviary (*Colin Whyman*)

longer complying with the requirements of rabies quarantine, none have since been seen in this country.

All the building work over the past few years had changed the appearance of the Zoo for the better and improved the conditions for the animals, but little of the work would have been possible without the financial help of benefactors. Visitors to London Zoo may wonder at some of the names given to particular houses or areas, but these are in recognition of the help given by

For many years since its conversion from a Reptile House, one side of the Bird House included many small cages – no bigger than budgerigar cages. This poor state of affairs was corrected by constructing several large, glass-fronted cages where the birds could fly and nest (© ZSL)

their benefactors and donors. Donations had always been welcomed, but during this particular period they enabled the Zoo to update itself as would otherwise have been impossible. The Annual Report for 1969 states:

> With the completion of well over half of the development plan adopted in 1958, three-quarters of the mammals in the collection have now been rehoused in eight new major pavilions and houses, together with their surrounding paddocks, terraces and new public walks. The Snowdon Aviary provides excellent new quarters for many of the birds in the Collection, as well as a fascinating display in an area which, for many years, had been a steeply sloping, overgrown bank, totally inaccessible to the public … During 1969 a further step forward became possible when Mr Michael Sobell promised … to meet the cost of a new Primate House.

The Sobell Pavilions for Apes and Monkeys were yet another innovative structure. They had five separate buildings, having a total of thirteen outside enclosures, each of which contained a natural group of the animals concerned, with each group having access to an inside 'room' ('cage' does not seem applicable) with a window of laminated glass through which visitors could see and photograph them. At first sight the outside enclosures seem to be very artificial, containing much in the way of overhead metal bars, but this was a deliberate attempt to provide an overhead climbing substitute for a natural tree canopy that, in such a relatively restricted space, would be quickly destroyed by its users. The tubular metal was used by the apes and monkeys for walking, swinging and clambering in a way that had not previously been possible for them, and the gibbons could 'brachiate' (in other words, swing along underneath the bars) just as they do in their natural forests.

These new Pavilions covered an area previously occupied by the Monkey House built some forty years earlier, which was itself a great advance in keeping healthy monkeys. But that earlier house had contained over forty cages instead of the thirteen new enclosures, while occupying only half the area now allowed, as the new Pavilions also took over the ground previously occupied by the Giant Tortoise/Small Mammal House, a large aviary, the pelicans' enclosure and the very old Bear Dens. They also swallowed up one of the original parts of the Zoo – the Fellows' Terrace, where, 150 years earlier, Fellows' wives would walk up and down with parasols and talk, back in the days when 'The OK thing to do on a Sunday afternoon is walking in the Zoo', as the old song said.

The Sobell Pavilions were completed in 1972, and their opening saw the end of the demonstrations of chimpanzee intelligence which had been given in the Children's Zoo for some years and which, like the Chimpanzees' Tea-Party, would conflict with the principle of leaving a family group of these apes undisturbed. Two rather elderly chimps had been together in the old Monkey House for a number of years: Dick and Abena. Sadly, Dick, then over thirty years old, did not take to the change of accommodation and died shortly after, but Abena was successfully introduced to the new group at the estimated age of 27 years. She had given birth to a baby nineteen years earlier, and amazed everyone by having another baby two years after her move.

The last of the big new building plans was the construction of the New Lion Terraces in 1975. This was again an innovation replacing an old house – the Lion House built a hundred years before. That house had gained a surprisingly good breeding record, but had long outgrown its justification as a place to keep animals, despite providing one of the most popular displays in the Zoo – feeding time for the big cats. Of those who saw it, who can ever forget the rumble of the heavy trolley arriving, and the snarls and roars of the animals as the keeper poked a joint of meat under the bars for each one? But 'the old order changeth', and, just as for the primates, a greatly enlarged area was taken over and a 'natural' habitat provided for the cats, with only seven enclosures instead of some fifteen cages, and also spread over the space previously occupied by the Deer and Cattle Sheds, and an aviary (though a new, smaller aviary for wading birds was incorporated into the area). The Deer and Cattle Sheds had been occupied by such animals as bison, buffalo, camels and reindeer, which were now housed in the new Cotton Terraces, so this area was available for redevelopment.

One new refinement in the new house was the introduction of 'crush bars' between which the cats had to pass when entering or leaving their inside quarters, enabling inspection of them or the treatment of minor ailments to be carried out easily.

Unlike their domestic relatives, many big cats enjoy swimming, as well as being expert climbers, so their enclosures were all contained and roofed with wire mesh except for that of the lions. Lions hate water, and a pool in front of their enclosure (with a high wall between it and the public) was all that was considered necessary to retain them safely. Some years later, in 1990, it was decided not to keep African lions any longer because they were so numerous and bred too readily in captivity, making the youngsters hard to place. Instead the Zoo was to keep Asiatic lions, of which there were only 300 left alive in the small Gir forest of India. Originally they were common throughout much of Asia and the Middle East, but they had been hunted to the point of extinction, so it was considered appropriate to keep them in London Zoo, which was developing primarily as a conservation centre.

Two pairs of Asiatic lions were received from an Indian zoo, and after their six months' quarantine one pair was transferred to one of the other enclosures until they were ready to go to another zoo, while the other pair was allowed out into the large lion enclosure. The lioness thought the duckweed that covered the surface of the pool was grass, and sprang into the middle of it! Startled, she swam to the outer wall at the visitors' side of the pool and started trying to climb out of the water up the ivy-covered wall. Luckily the keepers were alert, having only just released her, and while one keeper kept her away from the wall with a pole, the other hurriedly cut away the hanging ivy. The lioness never made that mistake again, but the ivy was from then on kept short – just in case! Her mate, the male, had lost part of one ear, which had been bitten off when he was a cub, so with only 'alf an ear he was named 'Arfur'.

Prince Philip became President of the Zoological Society in 1961, and he arranged for one of the Council meetings to be held in Buckingham Palace, the only time this has happened. Fifteen years later, Prince Philip was still President, and Queen Elizabeth had been the Patron for 24 years when the Society celebrated its 150th anniversary in 1976. What better way to highlight the celebrations than to invite them both to open the New Lion Terraces, and this was done on 3 June. Their arrival was greeted by a fanfare played by trumpeters of the Royal Military School of Music and composed for the occasion by Sir William Walton. Guests included Ambassadors, Government ministers and representatives of many bodies, including other zoos, and among the guests was Sir Charles Clore who had not only covered the cost of erecting the Clore Pavilion for Small Mammals, but also had generously

As the big cats enter their house at night they have to pass through crush bars. When it is necessary for a vet to examine them, the bars hold them still – much better than sedating them and moving them to the Zoo hospital (© ZSL)

contributed to the cost of the New Lion Terraces. Other celebratory events that year included the holding of a symposium entitled 'The Zoological Society of London 1826 – 1976 and beyond', a Children's Day at London Zoo for over five thousand underprivileged children, and an exhibition of Zoo photographs dating from 1911 to 1930 in the Casson Pavilion. Many books about London Zoo were published that year, and a film was produced by David Attenborough, *The Zoo: A Portrait of an Institution.*

A rather less happy occurrence that year was a drought, when London had an almost unbroken period of hot, dry weather from May to August, during which rain fell on only twelve days, mostly at the beginning and end of that period. This was the second dry summer in succession and, apart from a ban on the use of hoses, which caused problems to flowerbeds as well as to the newly installed trees and shrubs in the New Lion Terraces, the drought was probably the major cause of piping becoming cracked by ground movement, which affected heating and water supply systems and, in one case, a gas main, although corrosion to the pipes must also have been a contributing factor.

Arfur died in 1995 while still young, but he had already fathered cubs. He had appeared in the newspapers when he attacked a man who had climbed over the high wire-mesh fencing at the side of the enclosure. The man said he only wanted to stroke the lions as they were his friends, and he took them two frozen turkeys! Although mauled, the man recovered after a stay in hospital. At the Zoo an overhang was put on top of the wire mesh, projecting outwards to avoid a repetition of such an incident, but eighteen months later a second man did a similar thing, carrying a Bible and claiming this would protect him. But he was no Daniel and this time the two cubs joined in the attack. One newspaper described how 'Arfur shook his victim like a rag doll'. The man was rescued by keepers firing blank shots to frighten the lions into running inside their night quarters, and he was then flown to hospital by air ambulance. Having been bitten on the neck and legs, amazingly he also survived. The Zoo tries to ensure that the public is safe from escaping animals, but after this second 'invasion' of the lions' domain, they gave up trying to keep the public safe from themselves!

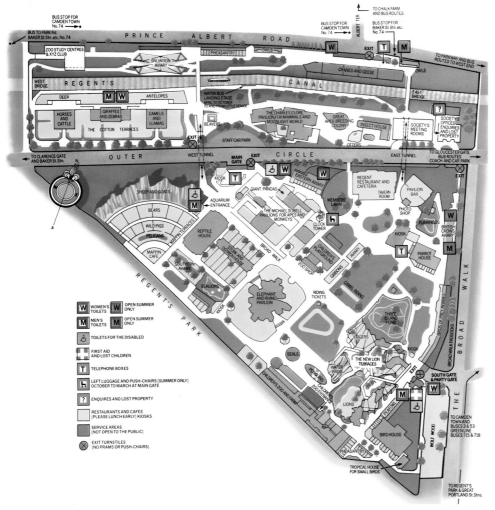

1985. By now the Giraffe House area had been modified to become the Cotton Terraces for hoofed animals and many new structures had appeared: In the North Gardens the Snowdon Aviary, in the middle Gardens the Clore Pavilion, including the Moonlight World, and in the Main Gardens the Elephant and Rhino Pavilion and the New Lion Terraces. Fifteen years later the Insect House would be demolished and the Web of Life exhibition would appear in the new Millennium Building near the Bird House (© ZSL)

17 Conservation and Consultation

The Zoological Society, anxious to improve the way animals were kept in zoos throughout the country, some of which did not have the Society's own high ideals, had taken part in advising on the formation of the Federation of Zoos in 1965, and this in turn led to the Government-sponsored Zoo Licensing Act in 1981. Inspectors visit all zoos and have the power to refuse to reissue a licence if conditions for the animals are not satisfactory and are not quickly corrected. This is, of course, in addition to the other Government and Local Government controls such as Health and Safety.

Other organizations were also trying to conserve animals; some, such as the Fauna and Flora Preservation Society, in their early days had the help of the Zoological Society, whose address and meeting rooms they used. One conservation organization, started in 1961, was the World Wildlife Fund (WWF), later to change its name to the Worldwide Fund for Nature, and as President of the Zoological Society, Prince Philip accepted the position of President of Trustees of the British National Appeal which was set up. In addition, Jack Cotton, who had already helped London Zoo so much with money for the Cotton Terraces and Snowdon Aviary, now gave £10,000 to the new Fund through the Zoological Society. More and more people were becoming conscious of the need to protect wildlife as never before, and zoos were becoming co-operative in trying to rescue species facing extinction.

One now historic example was the attempt to save the Arabian oryx. This small antelope was perfectly adapted to its life in desert areas. Standing at only half the height of a man, it had two long horns which, when seen from the side, appeared to be one, and this is believed to have given rise to the mythical animal, the unicorn (demonstrating for how long a time the oryx had been known to man). But by 1963 the Arabian oryx had been hunted almost to extinction. The Fauna and Flora Preservation Society had sent an expedition to Aden where they captured two males and one female oryx, and another female was presented by Kuwait. These animals, together with the only specimen in London Zoo (another female) and two from other zoos, were all sent to Phoenix Zoo in Arizona, where conditions resembled the animals' home territory. In all, seven oryx arrived there to form the tiny nucleus of the World Herd, while in the wild the animal had become extinct. 'Caroline', London Zoo's oryx, gave birth the next year and that started what was to be a resounding success in building up the herd.

Some years later, when the herd had grown considerably in number, animals were passed to several other zoos to establish the species elsewhere, but London was unable to receive any as it was unlawful to import hoofed animals from America. The Zoo therefore had to wait a little longer, until, in 1983, two oryx which had been born to the animals sent to East Berlin Zoo were sent to London to become the nucleus of another herd. Two years later a calf was born in London, the first ever in Britain. The World Herd now numbered over 250 animals in 20 different institutions. In 1986 the female in London Zoo died after giving birth to a second male calf, but another male and three females, born in Zurich and Hanover Zoos, arrived to swell the group.

Due to the co-operation of zoos around the world, this pretty antelope had been saved from extinction, and, after guarantees had been received that hunting would be forbidden and that special areas were to be treated as reserves, with help from London Zoo a number of oryx were returned to the Middle East. After a period in captivity there, when the animals were able to learn how to survive in the heat and without drinking water (oryx gain what moisture they need from the foliage they eat and from the morning dew), they were released back into their original homelands and have since thrived. Having become extinct in the wild in 1972, but now once again thriving in their original homeland, the Arabian oryx is an example of the need for captive breeding programmes for survival, and illustrates what is being achieved by the co-operative action of zoos.

Another example was in 1985, when a near relative, the scimitar-horned oryx, was reintroduced to Tunisia where it had died out early in the twentieth century. It had probably become extinct throughout its Sahara range, as none had been seen for several years. A herd, started by Marwell Zoo in 1970 and jointly owned by Marwell and the Zoological Society of London, now numbered 72 and was dispersed through four zoos including Whipsnade. Ten of these animals were sent to Tunisia after it set up a reserve where the oryx were to be protected from hunting and from where goats and camels would be excluded, enabling vegetation to grow. Another 15-year zoo programme to save an animal from extinction had met with success! Incidentally, at Whipsnade their successful breeding of cheetahs led that year (1985) to the birth of their hundredth cub. There had been 30 litters of cubs over three generations, starting with two arrivals in 1967.

The very next year, the Congo peafowl at London Zoo started breeding. This rare bird had only been known since 1936, when two mounted specimens in the Congo Museum in Belgium were recognized by J.P. Chapin as having been wrongly identified as blue peafowl. Peafowl are all native to Asia except this one, but Chapin realized the Congo peafowl was a sub-species new to science for which he had been searching for 23 years on the evidence of only one feather! It was not known how many there were in the Congo, but the fact that they had remained undiscovered for so long indicated that there may not be many surviving there, so successful captive breeding was to be encouraged. By 1985 there were still only some 60 birds in captivity, and London Zoo's were the only ones in Britain, having arrived in 1984 and the next year laid four eggs. These were removed to encourage the pair to lay a second clutch; three of the eggs hatched, and the chicks were hand-reared. Ten years later, London Zoo had its first chick from a captive-bred mother.

In 1971, decimal currency was introduced to the UK and the locks on all the ladies' toilets in the Zoo had to be changed in order to accept the new money! It was another eleven years before charges were finally dropped for toilets, as well as for both the Children's Zoo and the Aquarium after it became apparent that the cost of manning the entrances used up most of the proceeds. Nowadays everywhere in the Zoo is free once the visitor has entered.

One February afternoon in 1971 there was an animal escape. Though relatively rare, it is not unknown for one or other animal to escape; cranes have occasionally flown out of their enclosure when their flight feathers have been allowed to grow too long before being clipped, or a flamingo has managed to reach the public path from Three Island Pond. A bateleur eagle escaped from the brand new African Aviary within a week of this aviary being opened because it was able to squeeze through the 'piano wires' that roofed it; this bird was quickly recaptured. But this February afternoon the escape was of a potentially dangerous animal – a wolf, which had managed to get into the area between its enclosure and the public barrier. The 'escape drill', which was regularly practised (but happily not often needed), was put into operation and, despite only half the staff being on duty as it was a Sunday, the wolf was recaptured within half an hour without anyone, or it, being injured.

While animals occasionally escaped, people sometimes broke in. Most years saw attempts to steal birds' eggs and in 1971, according to the Annual Report:

> The annual scourge of egg-stealing by vandals or misguided collectors was rather worse than usual … the eggs of Cattle egret, Sacred Ibis, Gallinule, Barnacle Geese and even penguins were stolen.

The following year was even more terrible, with the theft of eggs from sarus cranes, penguins again, and white storks being considered 'especially frustrating'. The Annual Report went on:

Sadism could have been the only reason why five birds in the Snowdon Aviary were killed on a dark and wet January afternoon.

In 1974, London Zoo was to see not only the deaths of a snowy owl and two eagle owls and the loss of their eggs, but also money stolen from a security van by four armed men. A few years later, an aracari (a small toucan) was stolen from the Bird House, but such was the publicity given to this incident on television that a lady was able to recognize the bird when she saw it for sale in west London's Shepherd's Bush Market. She bought it and presented it back to the Zoo as a gift. This story illustrates the two contrasting faces of the public! Cameras linked to monitor screens in a central Security Room have since greatly improved security in the Zoo and helped to avoid such occurrences.

Two Giant pandas from China arrived in 1974, presented to Mr Edward Heath as a gift 'to the British people from the peoples of the Chinese Republic', and, in return, London Zoo gave Peking Zoo a pair of young white rhinoceroses, both of which had been born in Britain. The pandas were carried by British Airways, who arranged for one of their aircraft on the regular freight flight to Hong Kong to fly on to Peking and back. In order to avoid the animals flying in the heat of the day, the return flight to London was altered to pass across India and the Persian Gulf by night. The pandas' names were Chia-Chia and Ching-Ching, and both were about two years old. It would be four years before they reached maturity, but, sadly, although they were in the Zoo for ten years, they never produced any offspring; this was thought to be because Ching-Ching had an intestinal complaint from her early days, from which she eventually died. Neither was Chia-Chia's visit to Washington successful in 1981. He was sent to the National Zoo there in the hope that he would mate with their female, but when they were introduced to each other, they fought and had to be separated in case the female was seriously injured, so Chia-Chia came back home in disgrace! However, he did unknowingly father a baby in Madrid Zoo, where their female was artificially inseminated, a scientific development by the Zoological Society which avoids the stress caused to large animals when transporting them around the world.

Chia-Chia, however, was transferred to Chapultepec Zoo, Mexico City, in 1988, after the death of Ching-Ching, as it was recognized by the Society that, however much of a 'crowd puller' a panda might be, it would be wrong to deny the potential to breed with such a rare animal. This transfer was yet another example of co-operation between zoos helping to protect endangered animals. Mexico had a breeding pair of Giant pandas that had two daughters, so London Zoo made Chia-Chia available to them. But although it was successful with breeding pandas, the Mexican zoo was not rich and had insufficient space or resources to house another panda, so Chia-Chia was sent first to Cincinnati Zoo for three months. They donated all the extra revenue earned from him to Mexico, where better panda facilities were able to be built. At least one cub was the result of this co-operation, so London Zoo's loss of its greatest visitor attraction at the time turned out to be a gain to the world's conservation of these endearing animals.

Considering how 3 million people had flocked to the Zoo to see Brumas, the polar bear cub, in 1950, imagine what the attendance might have been 25 years later if a baby panda had been born!

There were several interesting occurrences in 1980. The Zoo's Education Department had its one millionth pupil, and Sir David Attenborough presented him with a copy of his book *Life on Earth*. Elm trees in the Zoo were becoming infected with Dutch elm disease, as was happening throughout the rest of the country, and were having to be cut down, but in 1980 an addition to the trees in the Zoo was a Turkey Oak, given by the Duke of Wellington, who was a member of Council. This tree had been grown from an acorn of the tree that had been planted years ago over the grave of 'Copenhagen', the charger ridden by the first Duke of Wellington at the Battle of Waterloo.

'Cocky', a sulphur-crested cockatoo, had been in the Zoo longer than any other bird and was thought to be at least 56 years old – he was presented with a medal and certificate by the Burlington Arcade Association in London for 'so ably entertaining visitors for over 50 years'. The following year, the family who had originally donated Cocky to the Zoo advised them that he had been with them from the beginning of the century and was therefore at least 80 years old! Another event was the hatching of a snowy owl whose father was Eros, a male owl presented to the Zoo 30 years earlier. Eros must by then have been well over 30 years old as he was already fully grown when in 1950 he had landed, exhausted, on a ship in the North Sea. This chick was his 39th offspring to have been hatched in the Zoo, but he went on to father a total of 57 chicks by the time he died in September 1993.

Pelicans had been kept for many years in St James's Park in the centre of London, but in 1981 two of the birds began disgracing themselves by catching and eating live birds! The authorities were made aware of this by members of the public, who complained in no uncertain terms, so they asked the Zoo to take the two pelicans, and, as the birds would not have the opportunity to practise their delinquent behaviour in the Zoo, they were accepted and caused no further trouble.

A few years later, another bird in a public area gave cause for official concern: Hector, one of the ravens at the Tower of London. There is a belief traditionally held that should the ravens forsake the Tower, it will fall to a foreign power. Hector had been resident at the Tower for a number of years. He had been reared in a flat in south London where he had learned to say such endearing things as 'Give us it 'ere then', in a deep voice with a 'sarf-London' accent, but his chatter eventually proved too much for the neighbours and his owner gave him to the Tower, where for twenty years he behaved himself – more or less. Once he pecked the surface off a guardsman's boots, and on another occasion he tore the windscreen wipers off a Bentley, but the last straw came when he attacked an American lady from Little Rock. Whether it was her blue-rinsed hair or whether he just could not stand people who said 'Have a nice day' we shall never know, but he zoomed down on her and knocked her flowered hat from her head, tearing it to pieces with his beak and (so it has been said) laughing as he did so! Hector was therefore dispatched to the Zoo, where for many years he would say his name to the regular visitors whom he got to know: 'Hect*aw*'. But he never gave up his ways, and his keeper said he was the only bird it was too dangerous to go into the cage with.

The first of four orphan elephants arrived in 1982. Dilberta was a baby Asian elephant from Sri Lanka who had been found abandoned, wandering in the forest, two years earlier. She was taken to Colombo Zoo, and presented to Prince Philip during his visit to Sri Lanka. From there she was flown to London by British Airways, whose Junior Jet Club adopted and named her. She was trained using Sri Lankan words of command so that she would not obey, or be confused by, members of the public shouting commands in English, and the same was done with the other young elephants who arrived in the following years.

The orang-utan collection was thriving, and 1982 was memorable in being the twenty-first birthday of Bulu, the first orang to be born and reared in Britain. His birthday coincided with the birth of his grandson, who was the first orang to be born in Britain to two captive-born orang-utans, his mother being Suka, who was mentioned in an earlier chapter.

All Fools' Day, 1 April, has long been a reason for hoax telephone calls to the Zoo from people persuaded by their friends or working colleagues to ask after Mr L.E. Phant, Mr P. Cock, Mr C. Lion or any other of a number of Zoo inhabitants, but in 1984 the Zoo got its own back with the help of a popular BBC television programme, *That's Life*. Esther Rantzen, the programme's presenter, who had done much to publicize the Zoo with her BBC film *A Day at the Zoo*, arranged with London Zoo for a BBC crew to film a new arrival, the label outside its enclosure reading:

LIRPA-LOOF

Eccevita mimicus

Eastern Himalayas

and beside it a map of Asia showing a large red patch as the animal's habitat, north of Bangladesh.

The Lirpa-Loof was hailed (tongue-in-cheek) by David Bellamy, the botanist well-known to television viewers, as a great acquisition, and the watching crowd laughed as the shaggy animal ambled towards the front of the enclosure and then stood on its hind legs and waved to the crowd. The children clapped, and, to everyone's astonishment, the animal applauded as well; after all, its Latin name was *mimicus*! The television crew filmed its every move – and also filmed the watching audience's reactions to the animal copying everything they did. The film was shown on *That's Life* and over the next week the Zoo answered 1,000 telephone calls, the BBC received hundreds of letters, and even the Natural History Museum had 500 enquiries. On *That's Life* the following week, Esther Rantzen, George Callard (the animal's keeper) and even the Lirpa-Loof itself, sang a song including the words 'if you were fooled, we apologize'. For the original programme had been transmitted on 1 April – and 'Lirpa-Loof' spelled backwards did, after all, read 'April Fool'!

A postscript to that story is that up to five years later, visitors (who had obviously not seen the second BBC programme) were still asking at the Information Kiosk where the Lirpa-Loof was – one of them being a Chinese visitor who could speak very little English!

When we think of animals verging on extinction, our thoughts invariably turn to tigers, rhinos and other mammals. But these large animals are not alone in becoming rare, and 98% of all the known animals in the world are invertebrates (animals without a backbone); indeed, insects alone outnumber all the vertebrates – mammals, birds, reptiles, amphibians and fishes. The Insect House in the Zoo, built 60 years earlier, was renamed the Invertebrate House because it contained not only ants, cockroaches, crickets and other insects, but also many kinds of spider, millipedes, land crabs etc., and even, at times, such animals as the upside-down jellyfish. The keeping staff were at least as enthusiastic about their animals as other keepers around the Zoo, and a good illustration of this is the leech.

Leeches are blood-suckers, and will live on nothing else. Medicinal leeches were on show in the House, and so many had been taken from the wild in the earlier days of medicine (for 'bloodletting') that they had become scarce. Later destruction of their natural habitat had made them very rare – so rare that they had been entered into the 'Red Data Book' of endangered species. So, in the words of their Acting Head Keeper at the time, Paul Pearce-Kelly:

> It was with unbounded joy that we noticed baby leeches swimming in our leech display. This is as far as we know the first breeding of medicinal leeches in any zoo. This success could be due to their diet of ultra high-quality fresh blood. How do I know this? Easy – it's mine!'

Such dedication! (A few years later, Paul Pearce-Kelly had become the Curator of Invertebrates – and the leeches had been persuaded to drink from a saucer, but the blood they drank was still provided by their keepers.)

The dedication of keepers in this section is perhaps illustrated most clearly by the story of the partula snail. This little snail with a pretty shell is found only on the Pacific island of Moorea, and the island is divided by mountain ranges into a series of valleys, each valley containing a different sub-species of partula snail, each with different shell markings. No other snails were to be found on the island, and man had lived there for hundreds of years with no significant effect on the snail population. However, in the 1960s, man introduced the giant African snail as potential food, but specimens escaped and before long they became a major agricultural pest, eating the crops and becoming so numerous that on one occasion two wheelbarrow loads of snails were removed from the walls of just one house. In 1978, in an effort to eradicate them, the authorities introduced euglandina, a carnivorous snail from Florida, but as with so many man-made animal introductions, the plan went sadly awry. Euglandina did not relish the tough hide of the giant snail but thought the little defenceless partula particularly tasty, and in next to no time all the sub-species of partula were on the verge of extinction.

Three professors from Nottingham, Virginia and Perth Universities were studying the partula snail and decided that the only way the animal could be saved was by captive breeding. Since 1986, London Zoo has co-ordinated the breeding of 12,000 of these little snails, of 33 sub-species, in 17 institutions. Later, after a trial release in the Palm House in Kew Gardens, the staff of the Invertebrate House took some back to Moorea and set up the world's smallest conservation area – only metres across, with protection to stop euglandina intruding. This first attempt was unsuccessful, but a later attempt had more luck and small colonies are now surviving in the protected areas.

In 1988 the same staff went on another rescue mission, this time to St Helena in the Atlantic Ocean, to try to save the giant earwig. After an exhaustive search, they could find none and reluctantly decided that they must have been too late and the animal, over three inches long, was already extinct. Another animal becoming increasingly rare is the Mexican red-kneed bird-eating spider, so many having been caught for the pet trade that it is very scarce in its natural home. Here again the keepers have managed to rear the young bred in the Zoo, and it is difficult to appreciate the problems involved in keeping 100 little carnivores in separate glass jars, each of which must be opened once a week to feed the youngsters! Even some of Britain's own invertebrates are becoming endangered, and the Invertebrate House has had successes in saving from extinction the British field cricket and the wartbiter cricket, so named because in the Middle Ages it was thought to heal warts by biting them; both species of cricket have now been reintroduced to protected areas on the South Downs and are doing well. Little animals as well as large ones are the concern of London Zoo!

The Invertebrate House had yet another function in addition to exhibiting animals and trying to breed the endangered ones – it provided food for those animals around the Zoo that were insectivores, including a number of birds and reptiles as well as marmosets and mongooses. In 1980 it was recorded that about 7,000 locusts were supplied *each week*, as well as fruit flies and blow-fly larvae. Figures for the quantities of other foods needed are breathtaking. By 1988, the 2,900 animals in the Zoo, of over 800 species, needed 12,500 eggs and 10,000 pints of milk each year, as well as 100 tonnes of hay and clover, 35 tonnes of carrots, 31 tonnes of potatoes, 10 tonnes of greens and nearly four tonnes of tomatoes. Fruit requirements included 23 tonnes of bananas and 11 tonnes of oranges, while the carnivores needed 40 tonnes of meat and over 20 tonnes of fish. Some food bill!

Every day a van delivers the food in bulk to each House, as well as the animals' additional vitamin and mineral supplements, and the keepers then make up each animal's requirements. Extras are also needed; the elephants and giraffes enjoy branches of evergreen oak, donated by several people from their estates, and when Giant pandas were in the Zoo they needed regular supplies of their main food, bamboo shoots, which were cut on an estate in Sussex and sent by train weekly to the Zoo. Several years earlier, supplies of bamboo were cut by the Polkerris boy scouts for Chi-Chi. Birds with pink feathers, such as flamingos and scarlet ibis, can be kept healthy on quite ordinary foods, but lose their pink colour unless they are fed on carotenoids which are present in their natural shrimp food. When koalas were kept in the Zoo, they required a variety of eucalyptus shoots, some of which were sent from Cornwall while others were flown in from San Diego Zoo in California, from where the animals had come, and the kiwis in the Moonlight World ate about 400lb. of earthworms a year each. The organization needed for the food aspect alone of the Zoo is mind-boggling.

Unusual animals were still arriving. In 1964, for the first time, the Zoo received two giant pangolins, a kind of anteater covered in scaly plates like a reptile and able to curl up in a ball like a hedgehog, and the next year, when the Secretary, Solly Zuckerman, visited Taronga Park Zoo in Sydney with Earl Mountbatten, he was presented with a collection of 23 birds of paradise. In 1983 a group of young paddlefish arrived from Alabama, and, though they were at that time only five inches long, they were capable of growing up to five feet in length; these remarkable fish were again being exhibited for the first time, and they swam around their aquarium tank with their mouths wide open, swallowing the water fleas placed in their water – these did not have so far to come as had the fish, being collected from the moat surrounding the Giraffe House. A number of animals, particularly reptiles, were given to the Zoo each year by the Customs authorities, having been illegally imported, but two Chinese mitten crabs that came had been found wandering in a London suburb, and no one knew how they had arrived.

Consultation and co-operation between zoos was increasing, and in 1960 the Zoological Society had started a publication intended to be referred to by zoos around the world, who would also make contributions to it in the form of articles about new houses and methods of keeping animals, breeding successes, etc.; this publication was the *International Zoo Yearbook*, and its appendices included lists of rare animals in captivity, and details of zoos and their speciality collections. It went from strength to strength and is recognized throughout the zoo world as an indispensable work.

By the 1970s the Society was being consulted by zoos and city authorities around the world more frequently, and in 1976 alone London Zoo's architect helped design a national zoo in Khartoum, while Tripoli, in Libya, was given advice for a new zoo there also. So many bodies abroad were consulting the Society that eventually a separate Division was formed for that express purpose and to assist with conservation projects around the world. The Division's successful expertise is well illustrated by the year 1984, when new zoos were planned in Sharjah and Bahrain and the Doha Zoological Gardens were opened in Qatar with 800 animals supplied from London, Whipsnade and Marwell, nine members of the Society's staff being engaged in the contract. The Field Conservation & Consultancy Division, as it was later to be named, was the personal achievement of David Jones, who had for some years been the Senior Veterinary Surgeon in the Zoo and was then made Director of London Zoo, eventually becoming the first Director General of the Zoological Society. He developed many contacts around the world who asked for advice and help from London Zoo, and, when he left some years later to become Director of North Carolina Zoo in the USA, it was thanks to his able young deputy, Alexandra Dixon, that the work he had started was continued. So ably did she follow in his footsteps that she was quickly confirmed as Director of the Division, which continued to flourish greatly as time went on.

Over the same period covered by this chapter, not all was good news. Dutch elm disease had already destroyed a number of trees in the Zoo, and the winters of 1971 and 1972 saw difficulties caused by strikes by workers in the electricity industry, with Zoo staff facing many problems trying to maintain warmth and lights for the animals' welfare. Another problem was repairing the mesh of the Snowdon Aviary; it was impossible to reach all of it from scaffolding, and for some weeks a crane had to be employed from which was suspended a cradle. A very expensive business! Wire was also behind the escape of some squirrel monkeys. Someone opened a small, wire door used to scatter food for them, and six monkeys escaped, climbed to the top of a very large tree nearby, and went to sleep in a crow's nest. Keepers eventually coaxed them down with their favourite titbit, mealworms, but not before one of the monkeys had fallen out of the tree and was killed. The little door was wired shut to stop any other member of the public doing the same thing again.

Wartbiter crickets. These were so named because it was thought their bite cured a wart! Both they and field crickets have become rare but are being bred in the Web of Life Centre for release in protected areas (*Terry Dennett/ZSL* (above left) and *Rod Williams* (above right))

Whipsnade, too, had not been without its problems, and it had to be closed from November 1967 until the spring of 1968 in order to avoid the accidental introduction of foot-and-mouth disease which was prevalent in large parts of the country at that time. A happier note at Whipsnade was when, to celebrate its fiftieth anniversary in 1981, the admission price on Saturday 23 May was reduced to one shilling (5p) – the same rate as on the day it opened.

On the night of 16 October 1987 came the great storm known to all who experienced it as 'the hurricane'. Trees in London Zoo suffered severely, and damage was widespread, so much so that, for the first time since the war, the Zoo was closed the following day in order that cleaning-up could be done. A total of 45 trees were either blown over or were so seriously damaged and insecure that they had to be felled, and about 250 others required attention, such as the lopping of branches left dangling. Two notable losses were a black walnut tree on Three Island Pond and the Tree of Heaven which was home to the pair of Red pandas, who had a shelter built around its trunk. Luckily, the male Red panda was in the Zoo hospital at the time and the female had been removed the day before in anticipation of the tree suffering in the forecast high wind, although no one had expected the wind to be quite as strong as it in fact became. The canvas cover over the arena where 'Meet the Animals' was held was also badly damaged, and had to be replaced, a new one having to be made in Germany.

The next year saw the birth of another animal destined to be a Zoo personality – 'Rosie'. Rosie was born underweight and her mother, a black rhinoceros who had successfully reared calves previously, rejected her, so an attempt had to be made to hand-rear Rosie. Rhinos' milk is very different from cows' milk and, of course, is not readily available at supermarkets, so her keepers managed to 'milk' the mother, send the sample to the Society's Institute of Zoology for analysis, and then make up a special milk for Rosie. She thrived on this milk, and quickly became popular with visitors, who watched her running around one of the lawns with her keepers each day. Rosie grew up to be a healthy adult who, it was hoped, would herself raise calves in due course.

But the most serious news at London Zoo concerned its increasing financial problems, and, while I have avoided continual references to this, no book on the Zoo, or indeed the Zoological Society, would be complete without information on the state of affairs which almost resulted in bankruptcy.

Field crickets being released on the South Downs after being bred in the Zoo. Hundreds have now been released and have become re-established on protected parts of the South Downs (*Dave Clark*)

18 Black Clouds

LONDON ZOO WILL CLOSE

Such were the headlines that hit the newspapers one summer's day in 1991 and caused a stir not only in England, but also in zoological circles throughout the world.

Many factors had led to this state of affairs, starting as far back as the last war, when so much maintenance work had been left undone for several years, increased by damage caused by the many bombs which fell in and near the Zoo. Some of this work was rendered unnecessary by the building of new Houses, but while during later years there were generous donations towards new buildings, these gifts rarely covered *all* the costs or the charges for any modifications later found to be necessary, nor did they cover the subsequent maintenance of these buildings, for example when expensive repairs were necessary to the wire mesh of the Snowdon Aviary in 1980.

Further major drains on the income of London Zoo were the subsidies made to other parts of the Society. Whipsnade had regularly to be subsidized, as did the Institute of Zoology, and the Zoological Society itself could not operate on its income from Fellows alone, even though all its publications (the *Journal of Zoology*, the *International Zoo Yearbook*, the *Zoological Record* and *Nomenclator Zoologicus*) largely recovered their costs; but the library did not, and much work on preserving the valuable older books was becoming necessary. A small but growing source of income was generated by the advisory and consultancy services given, although here again they were far from breaking even. In 1980 alone these services covered many matters (not all being a source of income, by any means) ranging from advising on the design and stocking of a national zoo in Kuwait, another in Libya and a third in Syria, as well as advice to Newham Council in London on a proposed City Farm, to giving lectures on behalf of the World Health Organization in China, Hong Kong, Nairobi, Peru and the USA, training university staff from Thailand and Kenya, veterinary consultancy services both abroad and in the UK, and advice to children seeking help regarding their pets!

In 1980 it became apparent that London Zoo, and indeed the Society itself, was in a period of serious financial difficulty. Professor Lord Zuckerman, then President, wrote in the Annual Report to Fellows:

The situation is now much more serious because our present revenue is not sufficient to cover even our basic running costs ... It no longer seems possible that the Society can continue to be solely responsible for the running of a major national institute without help from the central or local government.

Such further large-scale economies as we can introduce in addition to those we have already made could only be at the expense of the care of the animals and of the services we provide for the public. We are, in effect, up against a brick wall.

Unlike most other major zoos and, indeed, all other national zoos we are not in receipt of any annual subvention from central or local government. More than half the running costs of the Paris Zoos are borne by the French Ministry ... the Washington Zoo is a Federal institution and the New York Zoo is maintained by the City and also receives capital support from the Federal Government of the USA ... Berlin, Rotterdam, Amsterdam, and many others are all heavily supported by public funds. The Moscow Zoo is a government institution.

But the London Zoo, still the pre-eminent institution of its kind in the world, has been maintained and built up as a charitable venture for all the years of its existence.

The President's remarks led to the appointment of a Commercial Manager and the setting up of a Committee of Members of the Society, who made a number of proposals during the following years and took an active interest in setting up several exhibitions and other events. Within two years the committee had raised £50,000, of which £10,000 was used for the functions they organized and the balance donated to the Society. But in view of the fact that no other national zoo in the world had to manage without government help, and of the unlikelihood of the Society continuing to function successfully without such help, negotiations to this end were put in hand and led to a statement in Parliament by the Minister involved that a study of the Society's finances would be made and financed jointly by the Government and the Society, and that limited financial help would in the meantime be given.

But the financial position continued to worsen. It is not intended to detail all the growing problems the Zoo experienced during the years following 1980; suffice it to say that the limited financial help given by the Government over those years was not intended to *clear* the bank debt, but only to help avoid future losses of income – and in this it was unsuccessful. In his last Annual Report as President, in 1983, Lord Zuckerman made the following rather bitter comments:

> The Society itself has had to raise the money for animal houses and garden amenities. In the past thirty years it has all but rebuilt the 36 acres it occupies in Regent's Park … Over the years the Society has set standards of animal care for all other national and all major civic zoos but, unlike them – as Council has never ceased to point out – it does not receive regular and assured financial support from governmental sources. It is a curious British anomaly that the public can visit the Natural History Museum to study dead animals free of charge, but has to pay to look at the living animal in our national zoo. Today the Society does not have the money to carry out even all the essential maintenance work needed, let alone provide new buildings.

It is sad that Solly's last year, after he had been so long in office, should have led to such a comment because he must personally be credited with having obtained so many millions of pounds in the way of financial support both from

Molybdenum wires have replaced wire mesh in the African Aviary, making photographing the birds much easier. The wires are held under tension
(*Colin Whyman*)

private individuals and from large foundations such as the Nuffield, Ford and Wolfson Foundations and the Wellcome Trust. As early as 1970 were his efforts recognized, when the Society granted him its Gold Medal after his first 15 years as Secretary, and at that time Prince Philip, who was then President, said:

> During his tenure of office Lord Zuckerman has breathed new life into the Society. It is through his enthusiasm and planning and his positive genius for extracting money in large quantities that we have been able to achieve so much rebuilding in the Gardens … He has had not only the vision of what should be done, but the determination to see it through despite the many, many difficulties which have been faced during the last years.

However, Lord Zuckerman's continuous pressure on the Government for funding led to help for a limited period. In July 1984, in answer to a question in the House of Commons, the Secretary of State for the Environment gave the following information:

> The Zoological Society of London has recently informed me that they do not believe it to be a realistic proposition that the Society could return

Occupants of the African Aviary include a pair of ground hornbills; the aviary wires can be only faintly seen (*J. Barrington-Johnson*)

to financial self-sufficiency by 31 March 1986 as had been envisaged …
They have therefore sought an assurance of Government support on a
longer term basis … The Government agree that there is a need for both
short and long-term support.

Unfortunately, the 'long-term' support never materialized, except in the form
of help from the Higher Education Funding Council for England, which paid an
annual Grant to the Institute of Zoology, amounting to over £1 million a year,
which at least removed one financial liability from London Zoo. In 1988, when
temporary financial help from the Government was coming to an end, the
Secretary of State stipulated that London and Whipsnade Zoos be run by Andy
Grant, an American who had, a few years earlier, been employed as deputy
director at San Diego Zoo, California, and prior to coming to the Society had
been responsible for putting Leeds Castle, Kent, back on its feet. Grant had set
up his own company, from which he was seconded to be Managing Director of
the new company, Zoo Operations Ltd, and he appointed several members of
his previous team as a management team of directors in the new company.

The Secretary of State, on receiving agreement to these innovative changes
from the Society and from the Clerk to the Privy Council (as amendments
would be necessary to the Charter), offered a once-for-all capital grant of £10
million to end the Government's involvement, as well as a new 60-year lease
for the Regent's Park land, and confirmed that a further ten acres of land
granted many years earlier would still be made available when required. It was
ironic that not only was the Society not to receive any more Government
money, but also the additional 10 acres never materialized and the new lease
was not ready to be signed eleven years later.

The new company, Zoo Operations Ltd, quickly prepared a report on how
it proposed to act to set London Zoo firmly back on solid ground. By no
means all of the Government's £10 million was available; part of it was to
cover the shortfall in income, and only the balance could be used towards any
capital project. The plans produced by Andy Grant and his team were
complex, and even at that stage there were some people who were doubtful
whether those plans could be brought to fruition without a very large amount
of additional funding. The plans included the whole of the Stork and Ostrich
House and its enclosures being absorbed into the Sobell Pavilions to create a
huge exhibit for gorillas; the Mappin Terraces, which had been closed for four
years, to be transformed to provide waterfalls, woodlands, bamboo thickets
etc. for Giant pandas and a number of other animals, the re-landscaped area
being called 'The Szechuan Experience', and the aquarium below being modified to include floor-to-ceiling tanks and huge display tanks for coral reef life
and sharks in an open ocean setting. The disused Parrot House would be
transformed into 'The World of Invertebrates' and would, outside, have a

tropical rainforest built on one side and a British country garden on the other.

The first area to receive attention was the walking area around a great oak tree, surrounded by the restaurant, the gift shop and the old Parrot House. This was to become Fountain Court, a large patio area round a fountain with seats and fast-food outlets; it was intended later to move the Zoo entrance here. The area was developed, and a pool with fountains installed, with financial help from the Barclay brothers, but the Zoo entrance was never moved. The model elephant placed in the centre of the pool and later moved to the Elephant & Rhino Pavilion was donated by Liberty, the Regent Street department store.

Not one of the other projects was to materialize.

A few years before, a membership scheme called Friends of the Zoos had started, and by 1989 there were some 7,000 Friends. These were now split into two groups, one being attached to London Zoo, and the other to Whipsnade. Friends had free admission to the Zoo of their choice, and theirs was a cheaper form of membership than being a Fellow or an Associate Member, but carried few other benefits. The London Zoo Friends became known as Lifewatch members – a term which was in time to be developed by the Society as a whole. The Lifewatch symbol consisted of the same four animals which had for 160 years been represented in the Society's coat of arms, but here they were running, swimming, or flying, instead of their formal presentation in the arms – a lion, a zebra, an osprey and a salmon. (It is intriguing to note the complete coincidence that these animals share the initials of the Society – Zebra, Salmon, Osprey, Lion: Zoological Society of London!)

There was another way in which the new team was unsuccessful: it failed to gain the support of local inhabitants for its plans. It proposed to develop six of the further ten acres of Regent's Park which the Government had confirmed would be made available, but did not discuss their proposals before publication with those people living nearby, who strongly objected to the take-over of the 'walking areas for their dogs' (even though they would still have 360 acres left for this purpose). Even more opposed were they to plans for a night-time show of illuminated model animals which it was being proposed should float down the canal, and on this point they were supported by many of the Fellows, who rejected this 'Disney' approach.

The Society's loss that year (1989) rose even higher, to over £2 million, despite the new management and Government help. Nevertheless, attempts were still being made to introduce new or improved facilities. A new incubation unit for birds had been started the previous year with money mainly donated by Fellows, although this was never to become the large bird-breeding area originally envisaged, covering a large part of the north canal bank. A major grant from the Clore Foundation enabled the Clore Pavilion to be extensively renovated, and construction work started on creating a modernized Eastern Aviary. This was to open the following year with four large outside enclosures instead

Above the 'Animals in Action' displays demonstrate the natural behaviour of animals, such as the silent flight of a barn owl low over the heads of the audience (*Mike McQueen*) or *right* a kookaburra 'killing' a rubber snake without being bitten, by holding it behind the head while banging it to insensibility (*Roger Tomlinson*)

of the previous eight, and with wire mesh replaced by 'piano wires' of stainless molybdenum developed for North Sea oil rigs, allowing much freer photography. The wires along the top were held under 40 tonnes of tension to keep them taut, but as they did not succeed in retaining a bateleur eagle (which was quickly recaptured) they were then reinforced with wire cross-struts. A total of 15 miles of 1mm wire, seven times stronger than steel, was used in the aviary which, first built in 1864, was renamed the African Aviary.

So far as animals were concerned, for the first time in many years two female koalas were on display, lent by San Diego Zoo. Fresh shoots of eucalyptus trees were flown each week from San Diego, while shoots grown in Cornwall were also given to the animals until San Diego Zoo was satisfied they would thrive on these. A small Australian marsupial, Leadbeater's possum, thought for many years to have become extinct, had been rediscovered a few years earlier, and London Zoo had been given a pair by Australia. Their breeding success in London had been so great that several were now being supplied to other zoos to continue the work of conserving this still very endangered animal. Two pairs of a highly endangered bird, Rodrigues fody, were lent by Jersey Zoo, which had been breeding them, in an attempt to establish a second breeding group as only 200 birds had survived in Mauritius, the only place in the world where they exist in the wild. So, despite the troubles, the invaluable work of London Zoo continued.

An even greater conservation project was started the following year – elephant tracking by satellite. This involved fitting a radio collar to one of the leading animals of a herd of African elephants and tracking the herd's movements to find its main routes, particularly where these clashed with human populations. The signals were picked up by satellite and transmitted to Toulouse, in France, from where they were sent by landline to the Institute of Zoology. A model demonstrating the route was erected in the Elephant House, where talks were given daily by Zoo Volunteers, illustrated by a short film projected on to a large screen.

This project was opened by the Queen, who also met Berthold Lubetkin by the Penguin Pool he had designed sixty years earlier. The Queen then presented prizes to the winners of a Schools' Art Competition organized by the Zoo. Prince Philip, in the meantime, had been touring the Animal Hospital and the Institute of Zoology where he was told of the conservation projects being carried out, some of them in conjunction with the WWF of which he was President, before meeting the Queen again to enjoy tea with a number of Zoo benefactors and others.

Highly popular 'Animals in Action' shows developed from the 'Meet the

Animals' events we have already read about. These displayed animals behaving as they do in the wild – Quaker parakeets building their communal nest, an owl hunting by sound, a kookaburra killing a (rubber!) snake. Lemurs, coatis, macaws, burrowing owls, even brown rats, all helped to educate children (and adults) about the wonders of the animal world, without resorting to circus tricks. Shortly afterwards, other displays of birds were given on a nearby lawn, involving hawks, serimas and even emu chicks displaying natural actions. These displays proved as popular with visitors as had the Chimpanzees' Tea-Party sixty years before. An added bonus was the ability to use the hawks to frighten away pigeons waiting to descend on food scattered for the occupants of Bear Mountain, as the Mappin Terraces were renamed.

But money troubles continued, and it was decided to ask McKinsey & Company, Inc. to undertake a study of the Society to review their activities; McKinsey agreed, and provided their entire services free of charge. Their subsequent report recommended that a core group be set up to prepare plans to secure the future, giving priority to avoiding bankruptcy, and that to overcome a picture of confused purpose in the minds of the public, the Society adopt an unambiguous mission. The Mission Statement subsequently prepared was:

> To promote the worldwide conservation of animal species and their habitats by stimulating public awareness and concern through the presentation of living collections, by relevant research and by direct action in the field.

This Mission Statement was later expanded to show more clearly the total work of the Society.

The ruling Council in 1991 included ten professors, two lords, and three knights (of whom one was a County Court Judge), in addition to a Member of Parliament, the Leader of Westminster Council, the Director of Edinburgh Zoo and a banker – a knowledgeable group of people, with much acumen between them; but it was not to save the Zoo from near-bankruptcy. At its meeting at Whipsnade on 9 July 1991, Council learned that at the present rate of loss the Society would be bankrupt within fourteen months, and the decision was taken to 'reluctantly close Regent's Park Zoo to the public in September 1992'. This was the wording in a letter sent to all Fellows, which went on: 'This decision could be reversed if adequate private sector funding becomes available …' All the steps taken in recent years had proved ineffective. Lord Peyton felt unable as Treasurer to remain associated with Council policy, and resigned along with four other Council members.

Even though the Society was a charity, it had to act in much the same way as a business company, and therefore could not continue trading for many more weeks without becoming illegal, as it would then have been incurring debts knowing they could not be repaid. Not only that, but also it would by then be unable either to cover the costs of transporting the animals to alternative homes or to pay redundancy money to the staff, many of whom were loyal employees of many years' standing.

It was with heavy hearts that the decision had been taken, on the advice of the Society's auditors and solicitors, to close London Zoo, concentrating resources on Whipsnade where there was much more space for development, fewer costs, lower charges from builders, and, above all, land that belonged to the *Society*, not a Government department, and which contained (at that time) no listed buildings.

19 To the 21st Century

The following fourteen months were the most disturbing time in the Society's history. The Fellows were understandably horrified at the prospect of London Zoo's closure, and during those months five meetings were called. Fellows, staff and many other people gathered together to start a 'Save Our Zoo' campaign.

In February 1992, the President, Prof. Mitchison, resigned because he had been appointed to a position in Berlin and could no longer attend Council meetings. He was succeeded by the recently retired Field Marshal Sir John Chapple, and it was he who then had to lead the Society through the troubled days ahead. Steps were already being taken to try to put the financial affairs in order. London Zoo had twice as many animals as the next biggest UK zoo, and their numbers were reduced by sending some to other collections, thereby lowering the feeding costs and also the number of staff required to look after them, although even after this reduction London Zoo still had far more animals than any other zoo in the country. Many of the animals that left were sadly missed by their keepers, and one young elephant who went to Chester Zoo caused his keeper to shed some tears – captured on film.

The film was being made by Molly Dineen, who had created a name for herself with two half-hour films she had made for BBC television. She had wanted to make another half-hour film, about the relationship between animals and their keepers, and, having persuaded the BBC to back the film, had approached the Zoological Society, who gave her complete freedom to film. She not only did all the filming herself, but also interviewed in an unobtrusive way, and her only help was her sound recordist, who also held her clapper-board! Shortly after she started, the furore over closure began and she switched the theme of her film. Molly filmed in places to which even the Fellows, let alone the media, were not normally given access, such as meetings of the ruling Council, as well as a meeting called by the Fellows. The end result was a wonderful record of the human side of the troubles, extending over four one-hour programmes on BBC television, entitled *The Ark*.

A group of six Fellows had formed a Reform Group the previous summer,

The author talking with Molly Dineen, who made a film of the troubles of London Zoo in 1991/2, shown as four one-hour BBC television programmes under the title *The Ark* (*J. Barrington-Johnson*)

which proposed that the Zoo dispose of its 'common' animals and build up a collection of only endangered animals, but many Fellows, while sympathetic to the principles of keeping endangered animals, disagreed with such an extreme policy of keeping *only* such animals, and Sir David Attenborough was quoted as saying, 'Who can imagine London Zoo without giraffes?' The Reform Group blamed senior staff and members of the Council for the present state of affairs. Sir Barry Cross was Secretary of the Society at that time and he said:

> The Zoo has been insolvent for at least 20 years. Recently we have looked at at least a dozen plans, involving reductions in costs, staff, or species. None has so far produced a viable option that would keep us open for more than another six to 18 months.

There followed many months of uncertainty. Council, in coming to its decision, had realized that the plans could be reversed if a viable option emerged within a short time, and had immediately embarked on the tough, cost-cutting exercise which resulted in making some staff redundant, arranging for some animals to be transferred to other collections, and achieving a balanced budget. But while in January 1992 the President expressed a hope that closure could be averted, in June the Council confirmed its decision of 12 months earlier that the Zoo had to close.

And then the storm broke!

The daily newspapers were full of the story. 'End of the Zoo', said the *Evening Standard*, 'Gates will shut in September after 166 years'. 'A corner of London will die', claimed another. 'Zoo's "bright future" ends Sept. 30', wrote *The Daily Telegraph*, while *The Times*'s headline read 'Raffles' Ark falls victim to law of the theme park jungle'.

It is strange to relate that it was the announcement of the intended closure of London Zoo which eventually helped to save it. It seemed as though the public realized for the first time what a public asset London Zoo was and how it would be missed. Not only that, support came from around the world in the form of letters from other zoo authorities writing to say, in effect, 'What on earth does your government think it is doing not to support London, one of the greatest zoos in the world? Everyone realizes that no national zoo can survive these days on gate money alone, and London, of all zoos, is an inspiration to all others.'

An immediate response to the announcement of closure was a gift of £1 million from the Emir of Kuwait, 'from the children of Kuwait to the children of London', as a 'thank you' for the help that country received from Britain during the Gulf War.

The 1992 Annual Report of the Society stated:

Council debated … and concluded that … it did place moral pressure on the Society to look further at survival options for the Zoo. Accordingly, Professor Peter Jewell … kindly agreed to chair a working party to evaluate in all some eight proposals which had been received. The Chair was later assumed by Mr Barrington-Johnson. The Committee's recommendation … was accepted by Council 15 October 1992.

Later, the Society awarded the Emir its rarely issued Gold Medal in recognition of the invaluable help he had given in the Zoo's hour of need.

Further splendid gifts followed, one being from Dr Swraj Paul (later Lord Paul), whose young daughter, Ambika, had died of leukaemia, but during her life had loved to come to the Children's Zoo. He promised £1 million for a new Children's Zoo, which would not only be a much larger and better one, creating a great attraction, but also would avoid the repairs which had become necessary to the old one. After its completion, an attractive fountain, showing a young girl feeding the birds, was placed nearby in memory of Lord Paul's daughter.

An unusual gift was promised by David Blackburn. He told the President that, provided he could be kept informed of the financial position of the Zoo and make his views known, he was prepared to subsidize the Zoo by up to £250,000 every three months for the next two years! The money was intended to help cover any shortfall which was incurred through no fault of the Zoo, for example exceptionally bad weather. Because of his generous offer, which gave some stability to the Zoo's finances for the following two years and, with the other gifts, enabled longer-term plans to be made, David Blackburn was honoured by being made Stamford Raffles Patron of London Zoo.

So great was the public's concern, that people came to the Zoo in increasing numbers, attendances rising by 50%. They not only attended the Zoo in greater numbers, but also sent cheques from £10 to £100. Many children must also have emptied their money-boxes to help, because donations as small as a ten-pence coin stuck to a card were arriving with every post. A total of £440,000 was received from the public, and this money was later used to build a large aviary for macaws, with special nesting facilities inside the attached building where the relative quiet would be conducive to breeding.

As Sir John Chapple, the President, said, the generosity of so many people created a breathing space in which to try to set matters straight, and so it came about that eventually Sir John was able to make a welcome announcement:

> My message today is that London Zoo will remain open and, although we have a number of things to resolve, we can now look forward confidently to a bright future.

London Zoo had achieved this without financial help from the Government or the Town and City Councils of London, unlike all other national zoos in the world, and without employing any 'outsiders' such as they had been forced to employ in earlier years in order to receive Government help. The Society had reduced its running costs by £1.7 million a year, mainly by reducing the Society's staff of 400 to 310, 52 losses of which had been at London Zoo itself, and by reducing the number of animals by some 15%.

One animal loss was unforeseen. A pair of hyacinth macaws, Gus and Betsie, had been in the Zoo for several years and now, for the first time, were nesting. Hyacinth macaws are the largest of all macaws and one of the rarest, so the fact that this pair had at last laid two eggs was welcome news, but one night their enclosure was broken into and both the birds as well as their eggs were stolen. Their rarity made them valuable (probably in the region of £7,000 to £10,000 each), but also very difficult to dispose of, as the thieves no doubt discovered for themselves, because a few days later the birds were discovered on a rubbish dump. The female was dead and the male was in a sorry condition, but he made a complete recovery back at the Zoo. However, after several years already spent forming a pair-bond it looked likely that, with a new female, it could again be years before nesting was to be seen with this particular bird. Eleven years later the new Macaws' Aviary contained four pairs of these rare birds.

While there had been many cuts in staffing, at the same time Council decided to make a new appointment of a Director General of the Society, partly to take some of the weight of responsibility from the shoulders of the Secretary (an unpaid post since the departure of Sir Julian Huxley, and therefore filled on a part-time basis), and partly to pull together the different Divisions of the Society. These were London Zoo, Whipsnade Wild Animal Park, the Institute of Zoology, the Field Conservation & Consultancy Division, and, of course, the learned Society itself. The Society had grown tremendously since those early days some 166 years before, when it had consisted only of London Zoo, the Society and, for a few years, a museum.

Ever since the creation of Whipsnade, the different and increasingly numerous divisions had tended to 'do their own thing' – even though they were all reliant to some extent on the income of London Zoo. Now, a Director General could link together the various departments and ensure that all were not only reliant on each other, but also that each should become self-funding (except for capital projects for which some central funds could be made available). These dual objectives were not easily achieved, as they tended to conflict with each other; as examples, the veterinary facilities were part of the Institute of Zoology, but were relied on by the two animal collections, and the Field Conservation Division, when later trying to protect sea-horses, needed help from the Aquarium to breed them in captivity.

The many details of that difficult period, which lasted for many years towards the end of the twentieth century, have been much abbreviated, but let us now return to matters more directly concerned with the story of London Zoo and its animals.

Throughout the Zoo's history there had been animals escaping – in more recent years, luckily non-dangerous animals only – and this happened several times with the pelicans when they were housed on Three Island Pond.

On a number of occasions, members of the public had reported that two or three pelicans were wandering about on the nearby lawn, and the birds had to be herded back. As a result, they were returned to the pool they had been kept in earlier, which was surrounded by a wire barrier instead of only a stream-filled ditch one foot deep, leaving Three Island Pond to the flamingos and ducks. Eventually, a low barrier, sufficient to keep the pelicans in, was erected round Three Island Pond and the birds were returned there. But one morning the reverse thing happened: their keeper was, as usual, counting the 15 pelicans but kept arriving at a total of 16 birds. Overnight a stranger had joined the Zoo's own birds! This new pelican stayed for two weeks, enjoying the free food, and then flew off again; where he came from and where he went remain a mystery.

With the approach of the new millennium several applications were made to the National Lottery funds for funding to help develop London and Whipsnade. One such application, for example, was for money to modify several areas in order to make them more accessible for wheelchairs, but the

National Lottery Charities Board did not make funds available, even for an invalid ramp for the newly reopened Mappin Terraces, renamed Bear Mountain, so the money therefore had to be provided by the Society. The Zoological Society also applied for funding towards a proposed National Aquarium at Docklands in London, which was not granted; the Docklands Commission and the local Council were both in favour, and although only half of the necessary £100 million would have been necessary from the National Lottery, promises for much of the remaining 50% had been obtained. This would have been not only the largest aquarium in the UK (indeed, one of the largest in the world) but also the first aquarium in which animals that died would not be replaced from the wild but instead by animals bred within the aquarium or in London Zoo. The application was eventually turned down after the expenditure of much money on plans and supporting statistics which had been required, but ten years later, in the new century, plans for a world-class aquarium in Docklands were to become reinstated.

Another application was made, for funding towards a new Millennium Building within London Zoo, and in this case the money was granted because it was for an educational project – although there was a delay of a year or so while the new lease for London Zoo was granted by the Ministry, as money could not

Millennium Building. Caught in the light of sunset, the strange but conservational Millennium Building is now home to 'BUGS' (Biodiversity Underpinning Global Survival), the renamed Web of Life exhibition
(*Colin Whyman*)

be made available to an organization which might not be there if no lease was provided! But construction of the new building commenced, and it was completed by the time the lease was eventually signed on behalf of the Government, some four years after the previous lease had expired! In the meantime the Society had to make money available to cover almost the whole of the £4.4 million needed, instead of only their half, but they were helped considerably by the builders, who granted them a four-year loan of £1 million free of interest.

The Millennium Building was to house a living exhibition named 'The Web of Life', to demonstrate the extraordinary range of animal life (or biodiversity) and its reliance on every aspect of its surroundings. The exhibition pressed home the necessity for conservation of living things, and illustrated how the Zoological Society was helping around the world. It was another innovative move for London Zoo because, instead of building an animal exhibit and then adding interpretations in graphics, the story of animal diversity in various locations, such as tree canopies, seas etc., was illustrated almost entirely by *living* animals. There are 65 live animal exhibits, and the opportunity was taken of using mainly invertebrates, since these account for 98% of all animal life. It had long been a desire to replace the old Insect House (recently renamed, more correctly, the Invertebrate House) and the use of invertebrates in The Web of Life enables visitors to see the invertebrate conservation work of the Zoo.

The building was itself conservation-conscious in that it was highly efficient in the way of heating and air conditioning, the air being heated almost entirely by the body-heat of visitors and partly also by sunlight through its huge plate-glass walls. If the temperature rose too much, blinds automatically covered the windows, while heat exchangers below ground retained summer warmth for use in winter. While the air was recirculated, stale air was extracted, but before ejection was used to warm the fresh air entering the building, and a constant temperature was also maintained by having boreholes below ground and tall ventilation 'chimneys' overhead (a system perfected many millions of years ago by termites in their mounds). In these ways, the use of fossil fuels and production of pollutants were minimized – a truly environmentally friendly building.

Invertebrates on display included the very successful nest of leaf-cutter ants, which had been in the Invertebrate House, but was now shown to much more eye-catching effect by the use of ropes between nest and food supply, along which the ants clambered in the public domain; there were also Upside-down jellyfish and robber crabs, while other animals included fishes, golden lion tamarins, flightless rheas, and giant anteaters from the Pampas of South America. Conservation work undertaken by the Zoological Society as a whole was emphasized, and it was possible to see 'behind the scenes' through windows to the breeding of endangered invertebrates. The whole exhibition was mounted within a framework of partitions which could be moved or replaced, giving great flexibility for any subsequent variation to, or complete change of, the exhibition within.

The Web of Life was the Zoological Society's largest conservation education project, and a new venture in zoo exhibition design. It was opened in 1999 by the Society's Patron, Queen Elizabeth.

During the last decade of the century, which had started with such bad news, the Zoo had still been a world leader. It had mounted an exhibition of extinct animals – dinosaurs, mammoths, sabre-toothed cats – interspersed with the living animals around the Zoo. It had introduced 'behavioural enrichment' to keep animals alert and active, for example honey-filled holes in a tree trunk which the bears had first to unplug, nuts and small fruits in a tube which the chimpanzees had to poke out with sticks, and maggots dropping occasionally from the roof of the mongoose enclosure. Behavioural enrichment is now a standard consideration of ordinary animal husbandry within London Zoo and many other zoos around the world.

The Zoo had extended the idea of mixed species in an enclosure: cranes with the pygmy hippos, now occupying a greatly enlarged area including the old sealion pond, gazelles and even little meerkats in the giraffe enclosure, and ducks, langur monkeys, gibbons and muntjacs with the sloth bears, which together occupied the whole of the panoramic Bear Mountain except for the mountain peaks themselves (although the muntjacs had later to be removed after one was killed by an overprotective mother bear!). By 2004, in the Middle Gardens a 'Happy Families' area had been built for enclosures of families of otters, meerkats and marmosets, and the canal bank wood had been turned into a country walkway for encouraging British wildlife – birds to nest, hedgehogs to roam, caterpillars to feed on such as nettles, and bats to roost – while in the Main Gardens a (new) house was (being) built to be occupied by Komodo Dragons, who would be part of zoos' worldwide conservation breeding of these reptiles. The male was the first to arrive, followed some months later by a female who tried to climb the artificial cliff temporarily separating her from the male, but fell, and died, setting the breeding programme back until the cliff is modified and a second female can be obtained. The penguins had been removed from their Lubetkin pool, which had never been suitable for these birds to breed (almost all hatchlings having had to be hand reared), and there were plans to reduce even further the number of enclosures in the Sobell Pavilion for primates in order to give a much greater area for breeding Lowland gorillas. Breeding successes in the Zoo abounded and 2003 saw many births, including okapis, Malayan tapirs, bearded pigs and two species of anteaters – the giant anteater and the tamandua – as well as many bird hatchings – including toucans.

So London Zoo was again leading the world.

At the same time its offspring, Whipsnade Wild Animal Park as it is now named, was busily making improvements, including the provision of a new

An area near the Sobell Pavilion for small mammals is devoted to 'families'. The family of meerkats keeps at least one lookout on duty on the false termite rock for the many enemies they suspect will attack them, even in the Zoo!
(*Colin Whyman*)

enclosure for its elephants (the largest in the UK), where in 2004 Whipsnade's first elephant calf was born; she stood 1 metre tall and weighed 149 kg – over 23 stone! Other improvements included the expansion of the area for hippos and pygmy hippos and yet another large area devoted to lemurs, while a band of marmosets was given freedom to roam throughout one of the woods where visitors walked. Yet another area was provided for the young Asiatic one-

horned rhinos which had arrived to join the Park's older pair (given by Nepal as thanks for the Society's work in that country), the chimpanzees were enjoying a much enlarged island enclosure where they may be joined by the chimps from London Zoo to form a larger group of these apes, the penguins' enclosure had been doubled in size, with two large pools, and plans were being drawn up for a large lion enclosure with hidden barriers between them and the antelopes – a more life-like view of Africa. And in 2002 the herd of White rhinos which had arrived at Whipsnade from Natal 30 years earlier produced their forty-ninth and fiftieth calves.

With the turn of the decade it finally appeared that the long lasting financial troubles were at last conquered, as each year a relatively small but steady surplus was being made to be put towards funding the ongoing capital investments necessary in both zoos. Also, in 2003 a welcome addition to the funds was made. In Chapter 15 reference was made to London Zoo being a charity run by unpaid trustees and therefore exempt from taxes, but for a number of years VAT had been charged on admission fees. Towards the end of the last century the EU made the decision that charitable zoos should not pay VAT but

Renamed Bear Mountain, the Mappin Terraces are now home to a pair of sloth bears, a colony of langur monkeys and a pair of gibbons (to be seen at the top of a post) who call loudly morning and evening (*Colin Whyman*)

for several years HM Customs & Excise did not recognize this ruling in the UK and appealed, first to the High Court and then to the European Court of Justice, both of which ruled in favour of the ZSL (which fought the test cases on behalf of, and in co-operation with, other charitable zoos in the UK). From then, early in 2003, London Zoo no longer paid VAT on admissions, but it was the end of the year before HM Customs & Excise agreed the refund of VAT paid since the legislation should have been implemented.

So it was that in 2003 not only did the Society make a surplus of over a million pounds but a refund was also received from the government of £9.5 million paid since the correct legislation should have been implemented, putting the two Zoos on an even firmer financial footing for the future.

The Zoological Society, started by a man of vision assisted by gifted amateur zoologists, which had grown and, after 120 years, introduced the professional membership of Scientific Fellows, was demonstrating how it was now well and truly back on its feet and well placed to continue providing advice and support to the zoological world, and to the concerns of animal conservation in particular, into the new century as it had done throughout the previous two. Within two years of the start of the new millennium, the Zoological Society, now known as ZSL, was working on, or assisting with, conservation and research projects in 40 countries around the world. It had also signed an agreement with the other great Zoological Society, which owned the Bronx Zoo in New York and is now known as the Wildlife Conservation Society; this agreement was to enable both Societies to better carry out worldwide conservation by helping each other and providing knowledge, experience and facilities not necessarily available to one or the other separately.

The Zoological Society of London, the oldest Zoological Society in the world, was continuing to live fully up to the Latin words on its coat of arms – *Curae genus omne animantium*, which can be loosely translated as 'Every living thing is our concern'.

And along with the Society went London Zoo, saved for the next century and determined to continue setting ever better standards for zoos around the world as it entered the new millennium.

Appendix A

The Zoological Society of London Council Members

1826

Sir Stamford Raffles (President)
Earl of Darnley
Earl of Egremont
Earl of Malmsebury
Viscount Gage
Bishop of Carlisle
Lord Stanley
Sir Humphry Davy
Sir Everard Home
E. Barnard, Esq
H.T. Colebrook, Esq
Davies Gilbert, Esq
Rev Dr. Goodenough
Thos. Hosefield, Esq, MD
Rev. W. Kirby
T.A. Knight, Esq
T.A. Knight Jun., Esq
W. Sharp MacLeay, Esq
J. Sabine, Esq
N.A. Vigors, Esq
Chas. Baring Wall, Esq

December 1999

Sir Martin Holdgate (President)
Harry Wilkinson (Treasurer)
Prof. R. McNeill Alexander (Secretary)
Sheila Anderson
John Barrington-Johnson
Dr. Brian Bertram
Jonathan Boyce
Roger Ewbank
Dr. Tony Fincham
Prof. Mike Hassell
Martin Jiggens
Dr. Nancy Lane
Ken Livingstone, MP
Dr. Sophie McCormick
Martin Rowson
Ken Sims
Ted Smith
Peter Stevens
Jane Thornback
Prof. Roger Wheater
Robert Wingate
Prof. Paul Racey (co-opted)
Prof. Jeremy Rayner (co-opted)
Neville Reyner (co-opted)

Appendix B

The Zoological Society of London Honorary Fellows

1999

HRH The Prince Philip, Duke of Edinburgh
HM The Emperor Akihito of Japan
Prof. Jean Anthony, Museum National d'Histoire
    Naturelle, Paris
Sir David Attenborough
Prof. Jean Dorst, Museum National d'Histoire
    Naturelle, Paris
Prof. Ernst Mayr, Harvard University, Massachusetts,
    USA
Prof. Dr Milton Thaigo de Mello, Universidad de
    Brasilia, Brazil
The Hon. Miriam Rothschild
Prof. Knut Schmidt-Nielsen, Duke University, North
    Carolina, USA
Prof. Edward O. Wilson, Harvard University,
    Massachusetts, USA
Prof. John Maynard Smith, University of Sussex

Appendix C

Listed Buildings in London Zoo – 1999
Casson Bridge
Clock Tower
East Tunnel
Elephant & Rhino Pavilion (now Casson Pavilion)
Giraffe House
Mappin Terraces (now Bear Mountain), including the
    Aquarium, Goat Hills and Mappin Café
North Gate Kiosk
Penguin Pool
Primrose Hill Footbridge
Raven's Cage
Round House (Gorilla House)
Snowdon Aviary
'K3' Telephone Box

Index

Page numbers in italic refer to illustrations

British Watercolours
from the
Oppé Collection

*with a selection of drawings
and oil sketches*

Anne Lyles and Robin Hamlyn

with contributions by
Peter Bower, Tabitha Barber
and Diane Perkins

Tate Gallery Publishing

front cover:
*A Bridge on the River Ticino, near Polleggio c.*1770
(no.46, detail)

back cover:
The collector's mark used by Paul Oppé

Measurements
Height is given before width, centimetres before
inches

Abbreviations
PRO Public Record Office, London
repr. reproduced
DNB Dictionary of National Biography

Published by order of the Trustees 1997
to accompany the exhibition at the Tate Gallery
10 September – 30 November 1997
and touring from September 1998 – June 1999
to the Royal Albert Memorial Museum and Art
Gallery, Exeter; The Fitzwilliam Museum,
Cambridge; The Whitworth Art Gallery,
Manchester; and the National Museum and
Gallery of Wales, Cardiff

Published by Tate Gallery Publishing Ltd
Tate Gallery, London SW1P 4RG

1 85437 240 8

A catalogue record for this book is available from
the British Library

Designed by James Shurmer

Colour photography by Tate Gallery
Photographic Department

Printed and bound in Great Britain by
Balding + Mansell, Norwich

Contents

Foreword

In 1996 the Tate Gallery acquired the Oppé collection of British drawings and watercolours. Formed by A.P. Oppé between 1904 and his death in 1957, this collection had long been one of the most important and wide-ranging of its kind. It was also one of the most famous left in private hands. Paul Oppé was a discerning scholar who used his collecting as the basis for much distinguished research into British art at a time when there were relatively few students of the subject. He had always been a very generous lender to exhibitions in Britain and abroad so many of the works in his collection were well known. So when at the end of 1994 the Oppé family first approached the Tate with a view to selling the collection to the gallery we were presented with a unique opportunity. The collection could be saved for the nation and the Tate's existing holdings of watercolours could be transformed at the very moment we were planning for the Tate Gallery of British Art. In the circumstances it was even tempting to think that there was an historic inevitability about this offer because of Oppé's own involvement with the Tate. In 1928 when the Thames flooded the Tate he was among those who helped rescue the Turner Bequest drawings. He had frequently lent to Tate exhibitions, as indeed had his son Denys after he inherited the collection.

That we were finally successful was due to the combined efforts of many people. Of these I would first single out Charlotte Oppé and her mother, Jean Oppé (who sadly died just as this book was going to press) who wished the collection to come to the Tate; and Sir Jack Baer and Lindsay Stainton of Hazlitt, Gooden and Fox who voluntarily gave an immense amount of their time to negotiating on our behalf with Sotheby's, who were acting for the Oppé family, and also to valuing the collection prior to our bid for special funding. At an early stage our efforts had the invaluable support of our colleagues in the British Museum and the Victoria and Albert Museum as well as the Fitzwilliam Museum, Cambridge. Inevitably, however, in order to acquire the collection we were heavily reliant on outside funding and we are therefore especially grateful to Lord Rothschild of the Heritage Lottery Fund and his Trustees, as well as Robert Dufton, Head of the Fund, who gave the greater part of the funds required not only for the purchase but also for conservation, cataloguing and touring costs to regional venues; Sir Nicholas Goodison and David Barrie and the committee members of the National Art Collections Fund who purchased two works from the collection for the Tate, and the Friends of the Tate Gallery who contributed towards conservation costs as have also a number of private individuals. Within the Tate I would also want to single out for mention my colleagues Robin Hamlyn and Anne Lyles in the British Collection and Richard Hamilton and Belinda Davies of the Development Office who nursed this exciting acquisition through from beginning to end.

This book celebrates both the acquisition of the Oppé Collection and also accompanies the exhibition of works from it which opens at the Tate before touring to four regional venues. The exhibition has been selected by Anne Lyles with a view to including many of the collection's acknowledged masterpieces and also to reflect the range and depth of Paul Oppé's collecting activities and his scholarship. The bias is, inevitably, towards works from the second half of the eighteenth century, reflecting the collection's greatest strength and Oppé's own particular contribution to British art history. In this sense both book and exhibition celebrate Paul Oppé's remarkable achievement.

Nicholas Serota, *Director*

Acknowledgements

Inevitably, with an exhibition embracing so many different artists, the authors have sought help and advice from a wide range of scholars, researchers, curators, conservators and dealers. They would like to single out for special thanks Lindsay Stainton of Hazlitt, Gooden and Fox who made many invaluable comments on individual drawings in the collection; Aydua Scott-Elliott whose catalogue of the collection was indispensable; Sheila O'Connell at the British Museum, especially for her help on Hogarth, Chatelain and John Inigo Richards and for allowing access to the unpublished manuscript copy of *British Drawings in the British Museum*, vol.2, by Edward Croft-Murray; Jane Munro of the Fitzilliam Museum who helped on a wide variety of queries, and to whom we are greatly indebted for reorganising the Oppé collection when it was on deposit in Cambridge; Shelley M. Bennett at the Henry Huntington Library and Art Gallery, San Marino for her valuable advice on Stothard; Camilla Baskcomb for her skilled conservation work on the one hundred works in this selection, her extraordinary patience and remarkable good humour; and to Charlotte Oppé in particular for all her support and enthusiasm, as well as for generously allowing access to the family papers.

We should also like to thank the following people who have helped in various ways: Maureen Athill, Roseline Bacou, Emma Chambers, Karen Dalton, Stephen Deuchar, Judy Egerton, Veronica Evans, Ian Fleming-Williams, David Fraser, Susan Hamlyn, Brian A. Harrison, Colin Harrison, Ralph Hyde, Susan Lambert, Michael Liversidge, Briony Llewellyn, Christopher Newall, Patrick Noon, Charles Nugent, Felicity Owen, Roger Quarm, Terry Radley, Jeremy Rex-Parkes, Barbara Ross, Emma Savino, Emma Scrase, David Scrase, Kim Sloan, John Sunderland, John Tavener, Martha Tedeschi, Tony Tibbles, Jane Wallis, David Wardlaw, Henry Wemyss, Janet Whittaker, Timothy Wilcox and Andrew Wyld.

Within the Tate Gallery, we are grateful to the following: Rob Airey, Ann Chumbley, David Clarke, Sarah Derry, Elizabeth Einberg, Jim France, David Fraser Jenkins, Tim Holton, Matthew Imms, Shulla Jacques, Carolyn Kerr, Susan Lawrie, Heather Norville-Day, Leslie Parris, Graham Peters, Sue Smith, Rod Tidman, Piers Townshend, Ian Warrell and Andrew Wilton.

In Pursuit of the Abstract and the Practical

A.P. Oppé and the Collecting of British Watercolours and Drawings in the Early 1900s

Robin Hamlyn

It was probably sometime during the 1930s or 1940s that a curator in the museum world thought of the following limerick:

> An eager collector from Smyrna
> Once thought he'd discovered a Turner
> But he showed it to Oppé
> Who pronounced it a copy
> Palpably the work of a learner[1]

To be commemorated in a limerick, and moreover one which has survived to be passed down over half a century or more, is a rare distinction. It is also a vivid reminder of just how influential a collector, scholar and connoisseur its subject, Paul Oppé, was – not specifically as a collector of Turners but as a collector of British drawings and water-colours as well as old master drawings. But in its own informal way this limerick brings home to us what should also not be forgotten – what Sir Kenneth Clark described as 'the humour, humanity and generous width of sympathy which were the complement to [Oppe's] rigorous intellect'.[2]

Paul Oppé's collection of British works was started, tentatively, in 1900 and by the time of his death in 1957 it amounted to more than three thousand items. When he began collecting, the English school of watercolourists, for long regarded by the British as their greatest and most original contribution to European art, was only just beginning to receive the sort of attention which now constitutes the essence of art-historical studies: an appreciation of the aesthetic qualities in a work of art combined with the construction of accurate biographies and chronologies out of dated and undated works in order to establish both an individual's stylistic development and his or her contribution to a school or movement. From very early on Oppé's contribution to the creation of this modern discipline, certainly as far as British art was concerned, was substantial; it was also, perhaps not least to himself, unexpected because he arrived at it after much soul-searching and via his study of ancient Greek art. A good idea of the impressive range and nature of Paul Oppé's taste and scholarship can be found among the selection of works in this book. However, what first shapes a collector, then forms his taste and finally what drives the formation of the collection itself are always fascinating matters and the purpose of this essay is to throw some light on the background to Oppé's collecting.

Paul Oppé was born in London in 1878, the son of Siegmund Armin Oppé who was in business in Lyons silk and feathers, and Pauline, the daughter of D.J. Jaffé, a Belfast merchant and warehouseman in linen. Paul was the third son and the fifth of eight children. In 1886, when Paul was eight years old, Siegmund died suddenly at the family home in Denmark Hill, the result of overwork in consolidating his business interests. To begin with Paul was educated by a Miss Steffans at a local school. The family moved to Frith Hill, Godalming, in 1889 and Paul went on to gain a junior scholarship to nearby Charterhouse in 1891. However, at just this time he began to show signs of a 'digestive weakness' which was to trouble him for the rest of his life and, unable to sit for a senior scholarship in 1893, he left Charterhouse after only a short period. One way of coping with this physical problem was, apparently, taking long walks outdoors every day and many short ones when he was indoors. In time this regime was to become an important way of fixing on purposes and stimulating thought.[3]

With a complete change recommmended Paul, then barely fifteen, was taken by his mother, along with an elder sister and twin brothers, on a voyage to New Zealand. Paul arrived back in England in 1895, a few months after his mother and siblings, bringing with him 'cases of curios', many of which he had collected in Japan. He studied a few terms at the University of St Andrews, a period which produced his short, prize-winning, published work on Greek drama, *The New Comedy*, and in 1897 became an Exhibitioner at New College, Oxford. He graduated with a double first in *Literae Humaniores* in 1901, was a short period at the University of Berlin and then spent, as a result of a shipwreck while on a cruise, four months in Greece attached to the British School at Athens. In the autumn of 1902 Oppé returned to St Andrews where he remained in the Classics department until 1904 when he took up, though only for a term, a lectureship in Greek History at the University of Edinburgh. Under Baldwin Brown, Professor of Fine Art at Edinburgh, Oppé's interest in European art grew, though typically for the time, it was in the direction of the Italian Renaissance rather than British art. Brown was to recommend Oppé as the author of a monograph on Raphael which eventually appeared in 1909.

In 1905 (though, as the account below shows, it was by no means a smooth or obvious progression), Oppé entered the Board of Education in London and, the Victoria and Albert Museum being then that department's responsibility, he was both an advisor (1906–7) and then Deputy Director (1910–13) in that institution. Apart from these secondments and a period during the war when he was in the Ministry of Munitions, he remained in the Board of Education until his retirement, after eight years as Principal Assistant Secretary, in 1938.

During the whole of this period Oppé was collecting and writing about British and European drawings and he continued after he had retired. His salary as a civil servant (and even his office hours) allowed him to take full advantage of the flourishing London market at a time when real treasures could be bought cheaply. By the time of his death in March 1957 Oppé had written some thirty articles and books on art, each of which made an original contribution to art history.[4]

If, in the 'cases of curios' which A.P. Oppé brought back to the family in Godalming in 1895 we can spot the first evidence of the impulse to collect, then it is in buying his first British watercolour while he was up at Oxford in 1900 that we can divine the specific direction in which his collecting was eventually to take him, and even the method which guided it. His first purchase is a slight work by an unidentified artist (fig.2) though Oppé nonetheless carefully annotated the back of it with the date and place of purchase and details of how much it cost.[5]

However, it is the notes Oppé made in Greece when he was studying Greek antiquities and thinking about his research into the history of the Oracles – his 'First Greek Notebook', covering the period 21 May to 11 July 1902 – which first tell us about the nature of the mind and eye which were at work a few years later when he started seriously collecting British drawings and watercolours. In the first entry, which

described the eruption of a volcano which had occurred a few days earlier on Martinique, Oppé suddenly saw that historical events become real through being illuminated by the events of the present day and mans' place in them. This, he writes, is 'the only way we can get to learn the past'. The point is telling because, as the first entry in his notebook, it becomes his reason for starting it. By looking at the possibilities offered by historical enquiry beyond the amassing of dry facts, Oppé saw that generalisations about the past could be revised through taking account of the part played by the individual. His description of an event which reshaped the landscape also anticipated Oppé's later preoccupation with representations of landscape in drawings and watercolours. Having discovered a basic methodology, Oppé was later to take it to its logical conclusion in his chosen field of art history, by garnering and studying the evidence – the works themselves – in order to rediscover the lost history of British watercolour art. So in the notebook entry of 21 May 1902 he writes of the violent volcanic eruption as an event which 'lets us know what happened at Pompeii. Not a sudden catastrophe overwhelming the pleasure and business in a second. Rather the picture is that of men anxiously watching; of eager argument; of scornful bravado expressing itself in vulgar pleasure seeking; and of brave if stupid negligence. But in this case there was more excuse: Vesuvius burns always. None the less the picture is much more terrible if one imagines that it was the expected, the expected for wh[ich] one is unprepared, that happened'. The watching, the argument, the bravado, even the negligence, become a way of measuring the significance of a historical event; by marshalling the evidence of these and other actions it is possible to interpret history.

This same notebook also reveals Oppé's love of and eye for colour and its suggestiveness: on the prow of the boat which took him to the island of Crete were 'two men in their dark blue and red and a girl with reddish yellow hair, red collar and cuffs and green dress. Against the sea – bright-dark, or dark-light in the sun – effect purely Titianesque. But it sparkled and was brighter than any great painted colour' (p.2). In another possible allusion to Titian (his *Bacchus and Ariadne* in the National Gallery comes to mind), 'There isn't much doubt what the blue of the sea suggests. It is the pink of flesh' (p.9).

The second British picture Oppé acquired, after a gap of some four years, was a watercolour by one of the great acknowledged masters of the British school, John Sell Cotman, and we know from Oppé's diary of 1904 that the year itself and this one purchase in particular marked a turning point in his life, when his mood changes from melancholy to happiness and when nagging uncertainties about his future begin to be resolved in a moment of quiet, but passionate, exultation.

Even without the evidence of the diary, an article 'The Chasm at Delphi' in the November 1904 issue of the *Journal of Hellenic Studies*, his second and last published contribution to classical scholarship, can now be seen as the proper coda to his first career, because he had exhausted this particular vein of research. In this article 'the poverty of the evidence' sustaining traditional accounts of how the Oracle in the temple at Delphi worked was criticised and existing literary, architectural and topographical evidence subjected to rigorous re-examination in pursuit of what might actually have happened. It was exactly the discipline which he later brought to bear on his collecting.[6] The portrait of the scholar-collector in the making that is captured in Oppé's own record of 1904 interestingly shows a man who is both an innovator and of his time.

On March 1904 Oppé was in Edinburgh at the Royal Scottish Academy viewing the James McNeill Whistler retrospective exhibition, firstly for an hour with Baldwin Brown, and then alone for a further hour, taking notes on the pictures: 'I must make myself do so whenever I see pictures', he urges in his diary. A week later he was in London, visiting the exhibition of the International Society of Sculptors, Painters and Gravers at the New Gallery where, among works displayed (with 'deplorable lack of taste' according to the *Studio* critic), he would have seen Barbizon landscapes, drawings

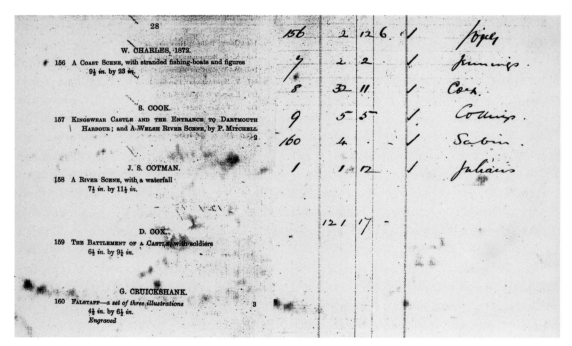

fig.3 Excerpt from the clerk's copy of *Catalogue of . . . Ancient and Modern Pictures and Watercolour Drawings*, Christie, Manson & Woods 16 and 18 April 1904 (second day) showing lot 158, J.S. Cotman, now titled *Llangollen*, bought by Cox for A.P. Oppé *Courtesy Christie's*

by Whistler and Rodin's sculpture *The Thinker*.[7] After lunch there was a 'loaf about [the] Tate Gallery'. Oppé was struck by the 'new experience' of 'London in idleness', for it was 'pleasant & may be useful' and a sharp contrast to what he described on 9 April as 'the barrenness & stolidity' of St Andrews.

The question that pre-occupied him was 'What could I do? Scholar, I hate reading. Fiction. I don't judge character. Politics, no chance & I hate dirt. Business ... or the law ... perhaps' (29 March). His gallery-going at first offered him very little in the way of answers to this question, though one is very conscious of the fact that such an activity was possibly 'useful' to him during this vacation trip. The practice of art, once an ambition, was still at this time an option for Oppé.[8] He even seemed to see London through the eyes of Whistler and Monet: 'I only care in London for the river in the fog' (29 March). The landscape paintings of Le Sidaner at the Goupil Gallery had 'some pleasant moments & some bad colour' (30 March). In the National Portrait Gallery 'the portraits are all bad' with, as an afterthought, G.F. Watts's 'symbolical characters ... beastly' (2 April). On 9 April he went to the exhibition of the Royal Watercolour Society with his mother but was 'not much interested' (9 April). Later the same day he travelled down to Haslemere in Surrey to stay with a friend, the artist Thomas Cooper Gotch. He was selling very few works and it appears that Gotch's situation[9] initally added to Oppé's sense of self-doubt and then partly helped to clarify his thoughts. At the beginning of his brief stay he asks in his diary 'Do I know what I want?' and replies 'Certainly not'. After a conversation with Gotch on 11 April he wrote, succinctly, 'the miseries of a painter's life', and he can identify what needs to be avoided – of one day reaching a point, arrived at by the depressed Gotch, of no return. He travelled back to London on 12 April, dropping in at the Law Courts to watch a case. A career at the bar was, then, still a possibility but art still tugged at him.

On 13 April 1904 his diary notes 'walk to Christies where fell in love with a blue Cotman & a "Turner"'. It was a typical watercolour sale of the time with some ninety framed and unframed eighteenth- and nineteenth-century English works – mostly of rather middling quality – on the walls and in portfolios. The work by John Sell Cotman that had caught Oppé's eye was lot 158 in the following Monday's sale (fig.3). The economy of Cotman's style would have immediately appealed to Oppé the classicist, just as its sombreness would have matched his mood (fig.4). Over lunch at the Savile Club, still churning his future over in his mind, Oppé told Baldwin Brown that he was 'very full of the art criticism idea & very keen on pictures'. Brown was encouraging and the following day, with his spirits lifted, Oppé went to Christie's again, noting that he was 'as keen as ever' on the John Sell Cotman. His own view that his lectureship at St Andrews would lead nowhere was now reinforced by friends, and he was more-or-less finally dissuaded by them from studying for the bar. With his own perception of himself as one torn between the 'abstract & practical' confirmed by another friend (16 April), this London trip was about to end with the matter of his future still unresolved: 'perhaps all my restlessness & energy will be devoted to the oracles'.[10] But Oppé's visit to Christie's the previous day had in fact set in train a thrill of possession that would not be denied: '"My" Cotman shines'. And so Oppé, instead of returning to Scotland on that Sunday, stayed on until the Monday. He wrote afterwards, 'made my way circuitously to Christies via [the] Savile [club] … & via Bank etc. Christies again admired, asked for an expert who priced [the Cotman] at 12 gns. I said 40 & he seemed surprised. Then loafed about … & I talked & chaffed [to another Oxford man] as finally the Cotman appeared & Cox bought it against Agnew 25 [gns] & Permain 30 [guineas].[11] I wasn't a bit excited because I knew I shd get it. I meant to.' He walked home 'very cheery' and shortly afterwards the picture was delivered, 'finer than ever'. He paid 'on the nail with no regrets & admired'. 'One thing', he noted, 'rejoiced me' and that was the 'very fine' frame on the work which was for him 'proof that the late owner held it a jewel'. On his train journey back to St Andrews almost immediately afterwards, still full of doubts about a future there, he asked, 'Why did I buy the picture for more than I should?' and answered '(i) I admired (ii) I wished to back my choice (iii) my excited state made me commit an action & something of strength'.

When Oppé returned to London at the beginning of July he once again went to Christie's where he thought about bidding for a fine watercolour by David Cox, though because he 'was thinking of it as an investment' he decided against it (2 July). On the 28 July, however, he visited the British Museum Print Room where, to use his own word, he 'BMused' on his April acquisition, looking at a book of Cotman's drawings as well as the works by him on display: 'I don't yet follow his chronology but I see he was far more versatile & more cultivated than any other of his school', he concluded, adding 'my painting is perhaps faded but it is most beautiful'. Afterwards, Oppé walked back home to Chelsea across one of the parks and in the same diary entry he shows his awareness, just as he had in Greece and was to again in the future (see no.17, for example), of that enduring link between art and nature, past and present, which guided him towards the certain truths to be found in English landscape drawings: 'admired Cotman's eye and hand & the trees in the park'.

Oppé was, of course, from the very beginning a private collector. But if the Cotman purchase was guided chiefly by instinct his collecting thereafter could not take place in a vacuum. For what this Cotman purchase had brought about was his first visit to the Department of Prints and Drawings at the British Museum where, as we can understand from his comments, he could see the artist in context and reach conclusions about his status.[12] It is therefore interesting to consider the state of scholarship and public awareness of British drawings and watercolours at about this time. One of the most striking features is how the early scholars in the field, such as Paul Oppé, effectively created a new discipline out of well-established tradition of connoisseurship.

The South Kensington Museum, now known as the Victoria and Albert Museum, housed the national collection of watercolours. This had been established in 1857 'with the intention of forming an historical series of paintings in water-colours, and was the first attempt to bring together and exhibit to the public the works of those native artists who were the founders of a school peculiarly English in its aims and characters'.[13] By the 1890s the watercolours were housed in three galleries 'grouped together under the names of the painters as far as possible in strict historical sequence', beginning with the early painters of topographical views such as Paul Sandby and ending with examples of exhibition pieces by members of the Old Watercolour Society, with the collection being steadily added to by purchases and donations.[14] But for A.J. Finberg, in about 1904, this display was 'little short of chaotic; the drawings are crowded together upon the walls without reference to historical or aesthetic considerations'; nor, he pointed out, was there even a catalogue available. Finberg voiced these complaints in the Preface to his pocket-sized history of 1905, *The English Watercolour Painters*, the stimulus for which was a combination of this state of affairs, his recent explorations among the mass of unexhibited Turner Bequest material in the National Gallery and his conviction that a popular guide to the English watercolours at South Kensington and the British Museum in particular was needed.

The contents of the Print Room at the British Museum, first established in 1808,[15] were, inevitably, the focus of research, although it was not until 1888 that the Department of Prints and Drawings actually had space in the museum to put on exhibitions.[16] The collection was formed out of gifts, bequests and purchases with the aim of making it 'as complete for the purposes of historical study as means and opportunities allowed'. Specimens 'by every hand of note in the British School' were added 'so that no name mentioned in the annals of our native art, or at any rate as few as possible, may remain unillustrated'.[17] The catalogue of all these works was in manuscript with no distinction between the watercolour artists and those who were engravers and draughtsmen. The watercolours themselves were stored in solander boxes on shelves, which was convenient enoughfor the purposes of study though, as Gilbert Redgrave pointed out, 'they cannot be seen by the public so readily as they would be if framed and arranged on the walls of a picture gallery'.[18] However, the Prints and Drawings Gallery did display in wall and desk cases a representative selection of drawings and sketches from the collection, changed every two or three years, including, in 1891, a group of works by British masters including Flaxman, Stothard, Rowlandson, Constable and De Wint, and then in 1904 a significant group of Cotmans, a sign of Oppé's particular interest coinciding with a wider trend.[19]

In an age of specialist art-historians it may strike some people as surprising that at this time the scholars who pioneered the analytical study of works of art which is taken for granted today were, like Paul Oppé, grounded in quite different disciplines, and sometimes even torn between several professions. Laurence Binyon (1869–1943), who was supervising the Print Room at the British Museum that 28 July when Oppé made his first visit, had as a boy shown an equal interest in poetry and painting. He arrived in the Department of Prints and Drawings in 1895 via the University of Oxford – where he had won the Newdigate prize for a poem in English and gained a first class degree in classical mods – and the Museum's Department of Printed Books.[20] If Binyon's name is not remembered by other than a few specialists in English or Oriental art (his other specialism), one single piece of his writing is known throughout the land and has assured him immortality; it has nothing to do with watercolours even though it is to do with a kind of decided nationalism which could be associated with an interest in English art – it is that patriotic poem *For the Fallen* which was first published in the *Times* in September 1914 and part of which is still read every Armistice Day.[21] Much earlier, in 1898, he had published the first of four volumes (the last appeared in 1907) which catalogued the British Drawings in the British Museum, the research for which coincided with that for two separate monographs on Crome and Cotman, published in 1895 and 1897. At least one review of this first volume (artists A–E), describing Binyon's entries as 'bald and dry', incidentally highlighted the nature of the work – the immense amount of matter-of-fact documentation – that was necessary before scholars and collectors could make a fair assessment of any one artist's achievement, let alone the achievement of the British school as a whole. The same reviewer was also impatient about some of Binyon's slips – such as the spelling of Van Dyke's name as 'Vandyke' – and questioned the statement that Alexander Cozens was the son of Peter the Great (an issue taken further by Oppé in 1919; see no.15). This demand for accuracy down to the last detail was a sign of things to come.

A particularly striking feature of this revival of interest in the early 1900s in what had always been hailed as a specifically English contribution to art, and most specifically, landscape art, is the way in which it apparently coincided with a growth of interest in exploring, retrieving and defining other areas of 'Englishness' through its past. Such revivals never start suddenly nor, when they happen, is it easy to pin the label of patriotism to them. If one is looking for an important early sign of renewed interest in the history of English watercolours then J.L. Roget's *History of the Old Watercolour Society* of 1891 must be singled out. But if one is looking for the first 'official' signpost pointing in the same direction then the most obvious is the opening of the National Gallery of British Art (that is, the Tate Gallery) in Queen Victoria's diamond jubilee year of 1897. However, when it came to showing watercolours, the Tate was sadly deficient: only a few were shown in an upstairs gallery,[22] though by 1907 some more had gravitated down to the corridors by the main galleries.[23] While the Tate did not quite live up to its name as the National Gallery of British Art in this respect, the British Museum, with its displays complemented by Binyon's work, effectively carried the flag. If we are thinking of broader notions of searching for a British (though actually English) identity at this time, and moreover one concerned with the very landscape the watercolourists had depicted, then there is another 'monument' which was very consciously an idea conceived as a celebration of the Jubilee. This was the record of the history and antiquities of every county, the *Victoria History of the Counties of England*, the first volume of which appeared in 1900.[24]

But the death of Queen Victoria at the beginning of a new year and only just over one year into the new century, in January 1901, created a very real sense that a new era had indeed begun. John Galsworthy, in the second volume of his 'Forsyte Saga', *In Chancery*, published in 1920, catches something of just how this mood must have settled on the country at the time of Victoria's funeral when he has Soames, witnessing the procession, musing 'There it was – the bier of the Queen, coffin of the Age slow passing!' A brusquer commentary, also written with hindsight but nonetheless reflecting his desire at the time for a new beginning, coupled with his feeling that the 1890s had already been 'fixed on the dawn of a new era', comes from the art critic Frank Rutter who recalled the place of honour given to Victoria's portrait at the 1901 Royal Academy exhibition, adding that 'it is annoying to think how clearly I remember it, though it was and is of no particular significance.'[25]

Thereafter, it is possible to discern a pattern of explorations of the nation's heritage into which a newly awakened interest in the history of British art seems to fit quite naturally. Attributable as these explorations are to the efforts of a few individuals, such a pattern cannot be detached entirely from some sort of sense that a new reign, that of King Edward VII, required a re-confirmation of what 'Britishness' – which effectively meant 'Englishness' – meant. Perhaps in the case of the fine arts these explorations were partly attributable to a rejection of what was happening in contemporary art – specifically, of course, the French Impressionism that was on view, to a generally hostile reaction, at the Grafton Galleries in London in the Spring of 1905; possibly they can be interpreted as a search for reassurance that the native school was still capable of great things at a time when its official leader, the Royal Academy, was held in low esteem. Oppé's own response to this, in 1902, is pertinent, for when he visited the Academy exhibition he came away feeling that 'the strange thing is the absence of direction in modern English art. Mostly portraits, either Sargent and imitators, or wild and uninteresting naturalism falsified. Little or no landscape – what there was except for small pictures – bad. Subjects varied. You would say there was no demand for pictures and no desire for any kind of thing'.[26]

One of these explorations which comes unexpectedly to mind is the similarity between the new interest in historic British art in these first years of this century and the more-or-less simultaneous revival of interest in English folk-song. Although the individualism of the watercolour artist is akin not to folk-music rooted in rural traditions but, rather, to composed 'art-music', the comparison is not altogether unapt, since, from 1916, if not earlier, Oppé was a friend of Cecil Sharp (1859–1924), the pioneer in this field who, inspired by hearing a folk song in Somerset in September 1903, went on to collect many others 'to be preserved for the benefit of future generations'.[27] The composer Ralph Vaughan Williams defined a folk song as 'an individual flowering on a common stem',[28] a phrase which dovetails neatly with how British watercolours were, and still are, viewed in the context of European art. Sharp's travelling up and down the land in search of words and music was an adventure which finds a curious parallel in what A.J. Finberg was doing on paper from April 1905 onwards when he was attempting to catalogue the drawings and sketchbooks in the Turner Bequest in the National Gallery. In order to reconstruct one of Turner's English trips he brought together the lists of places he visited and 'then drew up a sketch map of the tour', and with this as a clue 'was able to draw together' those works made during the tour which were scattered randomly in the Bequest.[29] Finberg's account of map-making across known but largely uncharted home terrain might perhaps stand as a metaphor for the way in which he and Paul Oppé, among a few others, searched for and finally rediscovered a source of British genius which needed to be identified. Oppé himself was a founder member of the Walpole Society for Promoting the Study and Appreciation of British Art which was established in April 1911. The Walpole Society recognised that 'British Art, as a whole, does not occupy the place it deserves in general estimation, either here or abroad'. Its unashamed ambition was to make its annual volumes of published research into 'our National Art' a 'worthy monument to the artistic genius of our country'.[30] In this the process to which Paul Oppé had contributed so much over relatively few years finally bore fruit and, it might be argued, with his collection now finding a home in the Tate Gallery, his ambition has been achieved.

1 Communicated by David Fraser Jenkins of the Tate Gallery who heard it from Rollo Charles (1916–77) of the National Museum of Wales, Cardiff (1946–77), who may have heard it from Sir Karl Parker (1895–1992) of the Ashmolean Museum, Oxford (1945–62) or Edward Croft-Murray (1907–1980) of the British Museum Department of Prints and Drawings (1933–72).

2 Sir Kenneth Clark in the Foreword to the catalogue *Exhibition of Works from the Paul Oppé Collection*, Royal Academy of Arts, 1958, p.v.

3 The composer Benjamin Britten (1913–1972) described similarly productive walks 'thinking walks', an expression which sums up their purpose for Oppé extremely well (Humphrey Carpenter, *Benjamin Britten. A Biography*, 1992, pp.58, 200). The obituary for Oppé in *The Times* (1 April 1957, p.14c) referred to his 'occasional capriciousness, which his friends were inclined to attribute to uncertain health'.

4 These biographical details are taken from James Byam Shaw, 'Paul Oppé 1878–1957', *Proceedings of the British Academy*, vol.64, pp.459–65, and notes made by Oppé's brother E.F. Oppé in 1958 and his daughter Armide, kindly made available by the Oppé family, along with details from A.P. Oppé's diaries and journals which are quoted below. A list of Oppé's principal publications is given on p.vi of the 1958 exhibition of works from his collection (see note 2 above).

5 'St Clements May 22nd 1900 6d'.

6 A.P. Oppé, 'The Chasm at Delphi', *Journal of Hellenic Studies*, vol.24, part 2, 1904, pp.214–40.

7 Reviewed in the *Studio*, vol.31, no.131, Feb. 1904, pp.59–68.

8 In a note prefixed to an early diary of about 1900 Oppé wrote of himself, 'Had he could, he would have been a painter, finding certainty & rest in the things of sense'. There are also some miscellaneous notes on Titian, an artist whom Oppé occasionally mentions in his Greek Journal. This early interest in old masters manifested in his collection of old master drawings and in books on Raphael (1909) and Botticelli (1911).

9 Gotch (1854–1931) at the beginning of his career lived in Newlyn and was a painter of *plein-air* landscapes. From the 1890s onwards his subject matter was more decorative and allegorical. At an unknown date in 1904 Oppé bought two watercolours from him.

10 Diary entry for 17 April 1904. The mention of 'the oracles' probably refers to the article that was published in November 1904; see note 6 above.

11 Agnew and Permain were both firms of picture dealers. Cox, probably a dealer, was bidding for Oppé at this sale.

12 Oppé's visit is recorded in the *Visitors Book Print Room*, vol.17, 25 June 1905–30 Dec. 1905. Lawrence Binyon is noted in this book as being on duty in the Print Room on 28 July.

13 Samuel Redgrave, *A Descriptive Catalogue of the Historical Collection of Water-Colour Paintings in the South Kensington Museum*, 1877, p.1.

14 Gilbert Redgrave, *A History of Watercolour Painting in England*, 1892, p.244.

15 Antony Griffiths and Reginald Williams, *The Department of Prints and Drawings in the British Museum: User's Guide*, 1987, p.1.

16 Op.cit., p.16.

17 Sidney Colvin quoted in Gilbert Redgrave, op.cit., p.245.

18 Gilbert Redgrave, op.cit., pp.245–6.

19 Antony Griffiths and Reginald Williams, op.cit., p.16; Gilbert Redgrave, op. cit., p.246.

20 *Dictionary of National Biography* 1941–1950, pp.79–81.

21 The first line of the fourth stanza, 'They shall not grow old, as we that are left grow old', also appears on many war graves.

22 Edward T. Cook, *A Popular Handbook to the Tate Gallery 'National Gallery of British Art'*, 1898, p.9.

23 *Descriptive and Historical Catalogue of the Pictures and Sculptures in the National Gallery, British Art*, 1907, p.5.

24 R.B. Pugh (ed.), *The Victoria History of the Counties of England. General Introduction*, 1970, p.1.

25 Frank Rutter, *Art in My Time*, 1933, pp.39 and 74.

26 Oppé's 'Second Greek Notebook', p.[16]. This notebook covers the period 12 June 1902 until his return to England, via Marseille and Paris, on 22 or 23 July 1902.

27 A.H. Fox-Strangways with Maud Karpeles, *Cecil Sharp*, 1933, pp.48–9.

28 Ralph Vaughan Williams, *National Music*, 1934, p.60.

29 A.J. Finberg, *A Complete Inventory of the Drawings of the Turner Bequest …*, 2 vols, 1909, vol.1, pp.xiii–xiv.

30 Preface to *Walpole Society, First Annual Volume*, 1911, pp.v–vi. The Walpole Society still publishes its annual volumes of research.

The Transformation of the British Landscape Watercolour *c.*1750–1805

Anne Lyles

'Better adapted to the amusement of ladies than the pursuit of an artist.' The painter Joseph Wright of Derby's dismissive remark about the role and function of watercolour is a reflection of the entrenched prejudice against the medium which persisted for most of the eighteenth century.[1] In expressing an opinion such as this as late as 1795, however, Wright was apparently out of touch – or, perhaps, swimming against the tide of historical circumstances. For towards the end of the century various factors, such as the establishment of public exhibition bodies and the rise of artists' colourmen, had helped to make watercolour a more independent and respectable art form. At the hands of a number of highly talented practitioners, such as J.R. Cozens (nos.59–61), watercolour was now being transformed into a much more expressive and painterly medium. By 1802, indeed, such was the passion for watercolour among the artist friends of the collector and connoisseur Sir George Beaumont that the latter could declare that 'all the rising and promising young men give themselves up to it'.[2]

When Wright stigmatised watercolour, declaring it more suited to the female dilettante than the serious artist, he was no doubt meaning to imply that, compared with oil painting – the context, indeed, in which his comment was originally made – watercolour was not especially arduous and was therefore an ideal leisure activity for the fairer sex. One could rephrase his remark to say that he thought watercolour 'better adapted' to the amateur than the professional. Though generally preferring to make landscape drawings in monochrome washes (no.29), Wright did in fact occasionally practise watercolour himself.[3] However, he appears never really to have got to grips with the medium, writing at one stage to a friend that 'I dare say when the application of [watercolours] are understood, it is pleasant work'.[4] Pleasant, perhaps, but as Wright here implies, perhaps after all not so easy to master as meets the eye.

Whilst the oil painter works with opaque colours, and generally proceeds from dark tones to lighter ones, with ample opportunities to make revisions, the watercolour painter uses transparent colours and can only work from light tones to dark. Not only does this mean that, in pure watercolour at least, there are no opportunities for making corrections, but since the lights are created by leaving the white of the paper blank, the process requires a great deal of anticipation and forethought. The luminosity of pure watercolour derives from the fact that the transparent colours never quite hide the white surface of the paper. It is also dependent on the paper's granulous surface, whose hollows and projections reflect different amounts of light.

The application of transparent layers required practice. As the eighteenth-century topographical draughtsman Edward Dayes pointed out, the artist first had to 'to choose ... the most transparent colours'.[5] But he also had to learn how to anticipate colour values in advance, making allowance for the loss of tone when the water (used to dilute and spread the colour) had evaporated.[6] Oil painters who never took up watercolour tended to underestimate the skill it required. 'Sir Joshua Reynolds, from observing the clearness in transparent drawings', wrote Dayes, 'thought it impossible to foul or muddle them; but his mistake arose from his never having practised in that way'.[7]

Watercolour had first been used in Britain in the middle ages to illustrate manuscripts, and by the sixteenth and early seventeenth centuries it was also adopted for painting portrait miniatures (or 'limning' as it was then known). In both these cases the medium was employed in rather dense and concentrated form. It was only from the middle of the seventeenth century that watercolour was first taken up by artists – and used in more transparent form – to colour landscape, which at this date almost invariably meant works of topography.

The technique of the 'stained' or 'tinted' drawing, as it became known, was first introduced into England in the seventeenth century by the Bohemian artist Wenceslaus Hollar, and was widely used by artists for topographical views throughout the eighteenth century – by Chatelain, for example, and by Grimm, Marlow and Pars amongst others (nos.11, 27, 38, 46–8). The topographer's brief was to describe with clarity and accuracy the features of a particular place, city or town. He would pay careful attention in the first instance to detailed underdrawing in pencil, which he would then usually reinforce afterwards in pen. In most cases, he would then add grey or brown washes with the brush to indicate light and shade (usually in dilute indian ink); and then over this 'dead coloring',[8] as it was called by Edward Dayes, the draughtsman would finally superimpose delicate layers of restrained watercolour washes. The classic topographical view was presented in clear, crisp daylight, 'unobstructed by clouds or shadows' which might detract from the presentation of accurate information.[9] The emphasis was on detail, precision and control, not freedom of artistic expression.

Though widely practised by oil painters as well as watercolour draughtsmen at this date, topography was perceived as one of the lowliest of subjects in which an artist could specialise. As late as 1801, lecturing in his capacity as Professor of Painting to students at the Royal Academy Schools, J.H. Fuseli famously dismissed it as 'that kind of landscape which is entirely occupied with the tame delineation of a given spot'.[10] Instead of such 'map-work', as he labelled it, Fuseli recommended to them the ideal landscapes of the old masters, of Nicholas Poussin, Gaspard Dughet and Claude Lorrain, for example, or those of Britain's own painter of classical landscapes, Richard Wilson (no.13). And, indeed, throughout the eighteenth century many artists preferred to specialise in this more 'serious' and elevated branch of landscape painting.

However, if the practice of topography offered no promise of artistic respectability, it did at least provide some guarantee of a regular income, as a large proportion of topographical drawings in this period were made with the specific purpose of being reproduced as engravings for sale, either as singly issued prints (no.11), as illustrations in antiquarian books (no.27) or, as was the case for so many of the prints produced after J.M.W. Turner's watercolours, sold by subscription in instalments (no.78). Indeed, in the early days, topographical draughtsmen were almost entirely dependent for their living on commissions received from print publishers, or else on their abilities as teachers – J.B.C. Chatelain (no.11) being an example of a mid-eighteenth-century draughtsman who relied on both activities. It was not until the advent of public exhibition bodies in the 1760s, such as the Society of Artists, the Free Society and especially the Royal Academy, that topographical draughtsmen had an opportunity to sell their work to the sort of wealthy and cultured patron hitherto only accessible to the oil painter.[11] Paul Sandby (no.25) was a founder member of the Royal Academy and a regular exhibitor there, thus greatly helping to elevate the status of watercolour as a medium.

Given that so many topographical drawings were destined to be translated into monochrome engravings, one might well ask why colour was added to them in the first place. The two preliminary drawings for engravings by Barlow and Hayman of animal and figure subjects (nos.2 and 10), for example, are executed in pencil and monochrome washes alone. This was a question which concerned the naturalist Gilbert White who commissioned illustrations from S.H. Grimm (see no.27) for his celebrated publication, *The Natural History of Selbourne* (1789). When White was allowed to watch Grimm gradually working up some of his watercolour 'scapes' using the method of the tinted drawing, he concluded that 'they looked so lovely in their indian-ink shading that it was with difficulty the artist could prevail on me to permit him to tinge them; as I feared the colours might puzzle the engravers; but he assured me to the contrary'.[12] Even if, by implication, the engravers were well capable of translating colours into their tonal equivalents, the fact remains that they did not actually need the colours at all.

It would seem that the most likely explanation for the draughtsman's use of colour in topographical drawings such as these is that it reinforced the notion that they were views of real places. In theories about art, colour had often been associated with verisimilitude and lifelike imitation. In particular, there had been a long-running debate, originating in Italy in the sixteenth century, about the relative merits of drawing and design (*disegno*) on the one hand, and colour (*colore*) on the other. According to this debate, *disegno* was associated with invention, with the concept or idea originating in the artist's mind, whereas *colore* was equated with nature and the real world, its diversity, variety and above all its particularity. The former tended to be seen as as an intellectual and rational activity, and was associated in particular with Florentine practice, the latter as a manual and practical one, and equated above all with Venetian painting.[13]

Sir Joshua Reynolds's *Discourses* on art, delivered at the Royal Academy between 1769 and 1790, were to a great extent dependent on concepts such as these, and can only have served to underline them for an eighteenth-century audience. His own guiding principle was that artists should strive to rise above the 'particular' in nature, with all its blemishes and defects, and attempt to achieve instead a 'general' representation of the natural world through a process of idealisation. And he tended to prefer what he saw as the intellectual approach of the Florentines (and their Bolognese successors) over what he perceived to be the inferior, more 'ornamental' style of painting practised by the Venetians.[14] In this theoretical context it would not have been unreasonable for the landscape draughtsman to assume that colour was a local matter, to be used for describing particular objects, and that monochrome by contrast was the appropriate vehicle for imaginary and more 'elevated' landscapes. Indeed, in one of the *Discourses*, Reynolds actually recommended reducing colours to 'little more than chiaro scuro' the better to achieve 'grandeur of effect' in painting (see no. 83).

Most of J.B.C. Chatelain's drawings, for example, are invented landscapes executed in pen-and-ink and monochrome washes or black chalks, often featuring rock formations apparently composed from lumps of coal.[15] Gainsborough is said to have admired Chatelain's drawings, and his own late pastorals in black chalks were often similarly composed from ingredients assembled in the studio (see no.23).[16] However, Chatelain chose to add colour to his *View of the Wrekin Hill in Shropshire* (no.11), a topographical drawing made with a view to publication as an engraving.

Much of the imagery of Gainsborough's late drawings – and for that matter, of Chatelain's invented landscapes too – provides interesting parallels with the theoretical writings of the Picturesque movement.[17] The Revd William Gilpin, one of the movement's chief proponents, famously defined the 'Picturesque' as 'that particular quality which makes objects chiefly pleasing in painting', and to achieve this pleasing effect, he instructed artists to work 'from the general face of the country' rather than from 'any one particular scene'.[18] His own landscape drawings concocted according to this maxim as well as his other Picturesque principles are, like Gainsborough's, almost invariably executed in monochrome media (usually grey washes). William Marlow was acquainted with Gilpin and there are examples of grey wash capriccio landscapes by him in the Oppé collection, one of which could almost pass as Gilpin's own; they stand in distinct contrast to Marlow's better-known topographical watercolours (no.38).[19]

In an early sketchbook used in Rome in 1746, Alexander Cozens made reference on one page to 'collouring from life' and on another to 'Water Collors 30 in all in bottles' which were available to him for sketching – and indeed a number of drawings made by him in Italy that year are landscapes painted in watercolours with indian ink and pen or pencil (see no.15).[20] On his return to England, however, he worked almost exclusively in monochrome washes. This can in no way have been connected with the poorer range of colours available in England. As early as 1674, W. Gore's *Art of Limning*, as well as mentioning three kinds of black and six kinds of white, had listed thirty-one colours from which 'all other colours necessary and useful … may be composed'.[21] Rather, Cozens chose to work in monochrome washes because his interests turned increasingly towards teaching and the theory of landscape, and he was beginning to evolve his famous idea for composing imaginary landscapes using ink blots (nos.18–20).[22]

The use of monochrome in Alexander Cozens's work was probably also connected with his concern to represent nature purely through mass and tone rather than outline. For in his *New Method of Assisting the Invention in Drawing Original Compositions of Landscape* (1786), he defended his famous 'blot' technique on the grounds that it enabled the invention of 'accidental forms without lines', explaining that 'in nature forms are not distinguished by lines, but by shade and colour'.[23] Paul Oppé argued that actual colour is suggested in Cozens's monochrome blot drawings both through association and through the impact of contrasting tonal values, even providing 'a greater range' than colour itself.[24]

Cozens's emphasis on tone and mass in drawing was taken up by the Oxford drawing master John Baptist Malchair, who would have been familiar with his ideas through those pupils – George Beaumont for example – who had come to him straight from Cozens's tuition at Eton.[25] Indeed Malchair directly echoes Cozens in his own unpublished treatise, *Observations of Landscape Drawing … Intended for the Use of Beginners* (1791) when he writes that 'natural objects have strictly speaking no outline'.[26] Malchair recommended that outlines should be made to 'disappear … when the discriminating powers of Shade and complexion take place', and his own work (no.24) and that of his pupils such as W.H. Barnard and William Crotch (nos.72 and 76) usually reflects this advice, as well as generally being executed in monochrome media, and despite the fact that they were drawing real landscapes more often than imaginary ones.

The topographer Edward Dayes, by contrast, went out of his way to refute Cozens's statement that 'shade and colour' were pre-eminent in the natural world, asserting by contrast his belief in 'a perfect contour in Nature', and those who thought otherwise he dismissed as 'ignorant people (who cannot draw)'.[27] Of course Dayes had reason to feel defensive. The 'tinted drawing', of which he was himself an exemplary practitioner, was heavily dependent – in the detailed underdrawing – on the use of outlines for representing form. The picturesque theoriser William Gilpin associated outline with the technical aspect of drawing.[28] And indeed it has recently been convincingly argued that the prominent pen-and-ink outlines in Francis Towne's topographical watercolours were added by him deliberately to reinforce the fact that these were the very sketches he had made 'on the spot', as he so often inscribed them, and then coloured up afterwards.[29]

If in the middle part of the eighteenth century, then, there was something of a gulf between the ideal, imaginary landscape on the one hand and the real and more literal topographical 'view' on the other, there were nevertheless a number of artists who, like Chatelain, practised both. The influential oil painter George Lambert, for example, one of the 'founding fathers' of the British landscape school, painted two very distinct types – classical landscapes in imitation of Poussin and Gaspard (fig.5) and views of actual places, be these ruined abbeys and castles or country house estates. In later life the water-colourist Paul Sandby (no.25) was to add generalised classical landscapes to his repertoire of topographical drawings and many of these, no doubt destined for exhibition at the Royal Academy, were painted in the denser medium of gouache (also known as body-colour) – that is, watercolour mixed with an opaque white pigment. Gouache was seen

fig.5
George Lambert,
Classical Landscape
1745, oil on canvas
Tate Gallery

fig.6
William Taverner,
Richmond Reach
?*c.*1750–65, watercolour
on paper
Oppé Collection,
Tate Gallery

as a more 'classical' technique than watercolour and thus (like monochrome) more suited to ideal landscape.[30] Works executed in gouache were often framed like oils for exhibition, whereas 'tinted drawings' were usually mounted on a second sheet of paper and given a simple washline border (like those which Pars supplied for his patron, Lord Palmerston, nos.46–8) and then stored away in portfolios.[31]

Those artists who worked in Lambert's circle, such as Jonathan Skelton (who may have been his pupil) and the fascinating amateur, William Taverner, tended to pursue a similar distinction between imaginary and real landscape. Nevertheless their drawings sometimes show a blurring of the boundaries between the two and are usually executed in watercolours. For example, Taverner's naturalistic watercolour sketch *From Camberwell* (no.8) stands at the opposite pole from his ideal, Italianate compositions (no.7), some of which were in fact executed in gouache. It also heralds a more direct way of looking at the world and a more spontaneous and atmospheric use of the watercolour medium. However, in his large panorama of *Richmond Reach* in the Oppé collection (fig.6), the naturalistic and the ideal are held in a sort of tension.

The way in which artists struggled to resolve the apparently competing demands of the real and the ideal at this date is especially well illustrated in the work of Jonathan Skelton. The inscription on the back of his watercolour of *Greenwich Park* (no.33) clearly states that 'The Parts of this Drawing are in Greenwich Park' – that is originally observed and sketched by him there – but then 'Grouped together at Fancy'. Skelton lived in Rome from the end of 1757 until his death in 1759, and his correspondence written at that time to his patron (see no.32) reveals him searching out examples of paintings by Gaspard or Claude to copy,[32] but also sketching in oils and watercolours directly from nature. English Grand Tourists who were shown examples of his work in Rome differed in their opinions as to which of the two – art or nature – they most closely resembled: 'Mr Light ... said that ... I was something in Claudes Manner. Mr. Stephens ... something in Mr. Lamberts Manner' but 'Lord Brudenell ... could not tell what Master I immitated, He thought my Manner very like Natures Manner'.[33]

For the generation of watercolourists following in Skelton's footsteps to Italy in the 1770s and 1780s – Thomas Jones, for example, and his sketching companions Towne, Pars and 'Warwick' Smith – it was similarly 'Natures Manner' that was to prove the dominant influence. Like Richard Wilson and Skelton before them, these landscape artists came above all to visit those sites in the Roman Campagna celebrated for their classical associations or represented in the paintings of Claude, Poussin and Gaspard.[34] Jones was a pupil of Richard Wilson, whose own canvases and drawings (no.13) had done so much to endorse the image of the area as 'classic ground'[35] – and indeed he felt his experience of these sites the more enriching for his prior familiarisation with them through his master's work (see no.44). Jones no doubt also spoke for the rest of his generation when he wrote of the inspiring qualities of the Italian terrain itself: 'this Country ... seems formed in a peculiar manner by Nature for the Study of the Landscape-Painter'.[36] The sheer beauty of the Italian countryside provoked in these artists an intensity of response which encouraged a more vigorous and experimental approach in their drawing. It helped liberate them from the constraints of their previous training, prompting from them new levels of technical assurance.

Jones had trained for two years with Wilson in London, learning to make drawings in his master's preferred media, that is to say 'black and White chalks on paper of a Middle Tint' – for Wilson 'did not approve of *tinted* Drawings ... which, he s'd hurt the Eye for fine Colouring' (see no.13).[37] Before his departure for Italy in 1776, Jones had already abandoned chalks for pencil and watercolour (despite Wilson's prejudice against it) as well as adopting the oil sketch (no.43). But once he arrived there, it was above all the small oil study that he was to bring to a pitch of such outstanding technical resolution (no.45 and fig.7).

Jones's sketching companions in Italy, Pars, Towne and 'Warwick' Smith, mean-while, similarly modified and refined their watercolour techniques in response to the stimulating scenery they experienced there, or saw in France or Switzerland *en route*.

fig.7
Thomas Jones,
Naples: The Capella Nuova outside the Porta de Chiaja 1782,
oil on paper
Tate Gallery

Pars, though still essentially wedded to the methods of the 'tinted drawing', brought a new vivaciousness and looseness of handling to his watercolour technique, as well as a greater atmospheric subtlety (no.46). For Francis Towne, the intensity of the Italian sunlight brought out a new vividness in his rendering of contrasts of light and shade, brilliantly captured, for example, in his *Wood near Albano* (no.34) – the latter perhaps inspired by the drawings made there a few years earlier by the portraitist, Towne's Devon acquaintance, John Downman,[38] whose Italian subjects in the Oppé collection represent almost his entire landscape *oeuvre* (see nos.54–5). But Italy, and above all the Alps, also elicited from Towne a heightening of his intuitive sense of structure and form, giving rise to some of the most austere and formally compelling works that have ever been produced in British landscape art (no.35 and fig.8).

One of the most significant factors affecting the subsequent evolution of the British landscape watercolour, however, is that most of these artists using the medium in Italy in the late 1770s and early 1780s at one stage or another – and to a greater or lesser degree – abandoned the conventional monochrome underpainting of the 'tinted drawing' in favour of pure and directly applied watercolour washes. One of the artists to do so most consistently in Italy, and who is sometimes said to have been assigned

fig.8
Francis Towne,
The Source of the Arveyron with Part of Mont Blanc 1781,
watercolour with pen and brown ink
Victoria and Albert Museum

the chief credit for the development in general,[39] was John 'Warwick' Smith. As one writer has recently emphasised, colour washes in Smith's Italian landscapes are applied directly on to the paper, and the broader effects of light and shade sub-sequently created by him with grey or brownish wash over the colour (nos.51–2).[40] By applying transparent dark colours over light ones, thus enriching and deepening tones and colours – a process known as 'glazing', and described in some detail by Edward Dayes – the watercolourists had now learned that the paper would still act as an illumi-nant.[41] Although this development had already been anticipated to some extent by Taverner and Skelton, the way was now open for watercolourists to develop it as an entire manner, especially after the beginning of the nineteenth century.[42]

It seems chiefly to have been under the influence of his fellow artists in Italy that 'Warwick' Smith had been emboldened to experiment with watercolour in this way. For on his return to England in 1781 he reverted to the more traditional method of the stained drawing.[43] The true revolutionary in the vital transition from tinted drawing to watercolour painting at this date – and conceivably the prime influence on Smith himself (see no.51) – was Alexander Cozens's son, John Robert Cozens. For despite generally adopting a restrained palette of blues, greens and greys (but see no.60), it was John Robert Cozens who was the first British watercolour painter genuinely and con-sistently to model form using colour rather than line. This enabled him to express atmosphere and spatial recession in an entirely original way (nos.60–1). The fact that in the first histories of British watercolour it was Smith rather then Cozens (or any of the other artists working in Italy at this time) who was given the credit for the invention of direct colouring was probably because Smith was the only one regularly to exhibit his drawings in London on his return.[44]

Unlike Smith's work, that of John Robert Cozens was rarely exhibited in public, being mostly commissioned by private patrons (see no.60). Nevertheless it was deeply appreciated in quarters of equal, if not greater significance. For his work was especially highly thought of by the physician and amateur artist Dr Thomas Monro who cared for Cozens in the 1790s when the latter was suffering from an incurable mental illness. About this time Monro established an informal 'academy' at his house in London, where promising young landscape artists were invited to sketch. It served as an important training ground for landscape artists at a time when the Royal Academy Schools only taught drawing from the life and from the antique. Girtin and Turner (nos.77–8), and also Cotman, Edridge and Cornelius Varley amongst others (nos.85–6, 74, 84), came here to study and copy watercolours by the topographers Edward Dayes and Thomas Hearne, for example, but especially by John Robert Cozens himself.[45]

From the 1790s until well into the following century the Continent was more or less closed to travellers owing to the French revolutionary and Napoleonic Wars. Landscape artists were now forced to rely for their subject-matter on scenery which could be found at home, and in the 1790s Girtin and Turner travelled extensively thoughout England and Wales. Their earlier watercolours tended to be dependent on the tinted drawing method used by Dayes and Hearne, but as they absorbed the more tonal and painterly approach of Cozens, they too gradually began to shed their monochrome layers of underpainting in favour of directly applied watercolour washes. Girtin's *Trees in a Park* (no.77), which combines grey washes for shading alongside areas of local colour, is something of a transitional work in this respect.

Many years before, William Taverner had discovered the suitability of watercolour for describing views of unadorned nature (no.8). Now Girtin and Turner came to realise that, given its inherent luminosity and the speed with which it could be applied, watercolour was the ideal medium for capturing transient atmospheric effects. Girtin, indeed, seems to have favoured colouring in the open air (see no.77),[46] something for which watercolour was more convenient than oil, being more portable and rather quicker to dry. In adopting this practice, he set a particularly important example for other members of the Romantic movement – Cornelius Varley and John Constable, for example – who were beginning to scrutinise nature's individual forms and changing moods more intensely than ever before.

For Varley, this might mean making a study of a tree trunk at close quarters (no. 84), for Constable an atmospheric sketch over Epsom Downs (no.81), or for Joshua Cristall a richly evocative watercolour overlooking fields at sunset (no.73). For John Sell Cotman, however, this closer scrutiny of nature resulted in a more analytical approach to his subject, and in the production of semi-abstract images whose status is rather ambiguous (no.86). Just as with Francis Towne's reductive and simplified designs (no.35), one finds oneself pausing to consider whether Cotman's watercolours made on the banks of the River Greta are in fact nature studies at all.

Around 1780, the firm of Reeves first supplied colours in small, hard, soluble cakes,[47] an invention which no doubt facilitated (if not actually encouraged) the practice of sketching in colours in the open air. Prior to this date, it had been customary for watercolour artists to prepare their own colours, grinding and washing them, and then mixing the pigments with the appropriate proportion of gum arabic. This was a laborious business, and since it required knowledge about pigments as well as skill in mixing them, it tended to be associated with the practice of the artisan (oil paints, by contrast, had been available ready-made some one hundred years before).[48] Reeves's invention was followed in the 1830s and 1840s by Winsor and Newton's marketing of moist colours for watercolour painting in metal tubes.[49] By taking over the more mundane tasks of the watercolourists' practice, the artists' colourmen helped to place them on a similiar professional footing as oil painters, since the watercolourists could then justifiably claim to be practising a 'liberal' rather than a 'mechanical' art.[50]

The problem for many of the watercolourists was that things did not seem to be changing fast enough. They were now in the vanguard of developments in landscape, and in the forefront of new responses to nature. Moreover, watercolours were among the most powerful and original works to be exhibited at the Royal Academy in the early years of the new century, such as Girtin and Turner's large-scale representations of Welsh, Yorkshire or Swiss scenery – and these were often the more expressive and monumental for being executed in sombre tones recommended by theorists of the 'Sublime'.[51] However, though watercolours had been admitted for exhibition on the Academy's walls since its earliest days, at the turn of the century they still tended to be relegated to subsidiary rooms, and to be ill hung or poorly lit. Above all, it was clear that watercolour could only suffer when compared (as it inevitably was) with the more forceful medium of oil.

In 1804, therefore, a group of sixteen artists, including Cornelius Varley (no.84), and his elder brother John, came together to found a separate society exclusively devoted to practitioners in watercolour. By the time the Society of Painters in Watercolour (as it was called) held its first exhibition in London's Lower Brook Street the following year, others – such as Barret, Cristall and Havell (nos.71, 73 and 87) – had joined them. They were mostly landscape artists and some of them had got to know each other, and developed their ideas and aspirations about landscape, at meetings of the Sketching Society only a year or two before (see no.83). However, the latter's leading spirit, Girtin, had died in 1802. Nor was the Society of Painters in Watercolour able to recruit Turner since, as a Royal Academician, he was not eligible for membership. Then in 1806, John Sell Cotman, one of the most promising new talents of his generation, was mysteriously 'blackballed' when he applied to join.[52] Seen from this perspective, it was not an entirely auspicious start. However, the Society's first exhibition was a remarkable popular success.

The foundation of the Society of Painters in Watercolour opened a completely new chapter in the story of British watercolour. At long last freed from direct competition with oil paintings, the watercolour now ironically began to rival them in density, power and strength of colour – indeed, watercolours even began to be framed like oils. In the early years, the Society's members generally restricted themselves to watercolour alone, though they would now apply it more densely so that it tended to obscure the white of the paper beneath, with the result that they then developed a new range of techniques such as sponging and scraping chiefly designed to bring back the lights (no.71). At this stage the bias of their art was still towards landscape, though their imitations and pastiches of the old masters (no.71) were supplemented from about 1820 with Picturesque views on the Continent, now that artists were again free to travel abroad.

From the 1820s, indeed, not only did their colours start to get much brighter (and during that decade some new pigments, such as emerald green, were introduced), but some watercolourists, such as W.H. Hunt and J.F. Lewis (nos.94–6), began to take up the more opaque medium of gouache. They employed gouache, either on its own or in combination with watercolour, for a now much wider range of subject-matter, embracing, for example, still-lifes and flower pieces, historical interiors and subject pictures (no.95) and even, in Lewis's case, exotic scenes from the Middle East (see no.96). To some extent these artists were tailoring their subjects to a new sort of buyer. For times and tastes were changing. As the wife of Thomas Uwins (no.88) remarked, the 'old nobility and land proprietors' were being replaced by the 'railroad speculators, iron mine men and grinders from Sheffield etc.', and the latter seemed to want something rather more decorative and undemanding than their predecessors.[53] However, W.M. Thackeray felt that the watercolourists' reliance on gouache was a reflection of their 'endeavouring to carry their art further than it will go'.[54] And indeed in 1858 the twice-serving President of the Society, J.F. Lewis, resigned, having decided to abandon his laborious gouache technique and to concentrate on the financially more rewarding sphere of oils instead.

There was, however, another factor contributing to the decline in watercolour (for a decline was how many contemporary critics saw it) – the proliferation of drawing masters and the growth in popularity of the medium amongst amateurs. These later amateur practitioners were rarely as accomplished as their eighteenth- and early nineteenth-century forebears, such as Girtin and Turner's pupil, Lady Gordon (no.75), or those who took tuition from J.B. Malchair (nos.58, 72 and 76). In 1859, the art critic John Ruskin attributed the large bulk of indifferent work at the Society's exhibition that year partly to the support of amateurs who 'concern themselves with art without being truly interested in it; and … enjoy being taught to sketch brilliantly in six lessons'.[55] Joseph Wright of Derby may have been out of touch when, in the 1790s, he dismissed watercolour as better suited to the amateur dilettante than the serious, professional artist. But he surely did not realise that, in due course, his words might come to seem prophetic.

NOTES

1 Letter to John Leigh Philips, 29 May 1795, quoted W. Bemrose, *The Life and Works of Joseph Wright ARA commonly called 'Wright of Derby'*, 1885, p.95. The full remark reads 'Paper and camel hair pencils [i.e.brushes] are better adapted to the amusement of ladies than the pursuit of an artist', and was made in the context of their mutual friend, William Moss Tate, having recently resumed oil painting after a period experimenting with watercolours. It was Tate's success with watercolours the previous March which prompted Wright's other remark about them, that once their application was understood, it was pleasant enough work (see note 4).

2 Beaumont to William Gilpin, original letter in Bodleian Library, Oxford; quoted L. Stainton, 'A survey of English Watercolour Painting from the Seventeenth Century to the Present Day' in *Watercolours from Leeds City Art Gallery*, exh.cat., 1995, p.19.

3 Examples of Wright's work in watercolour are in the Derby Museum and Art Gallery, e.g. *House Built on Top of a Wall, Cascade at Tivoli, Dovedale and View near Cromford* (repr., B. Nicolson, *Joseph Wright of Derby: Painter of Light*, 1968, 2 vols., pls.147, 251, 254 and 297).

4 Letter to John Leigh Philips, 30 March 1795, W. Bemrose, op.cit., p.95. See also note 1.

5 [Edward Dayes], *The Works of the late Edward Dayes*, 1805, p.299 (*Drawing and Coloring Landscapes*).

6 Leslie Worth in conversation with Judy Egerton; see J. Egerton, *British Watercolours*, Tate Gallery, 1986, p.6.

7 E. Dayes, op.cit., p.299 (*Drawing and Coloring Landscapes*).

8 E. Dayes, op.cit., p.301 (*Drawing and Coloring Landscapes*).

9 R. and S. Redgrave, *A Century of Painters of the English School*, vol.1, 1866, p.374.

10 J. Knowles, *The Life and Writings of Henry Fuseli*, London 1831, vol.2, p.217.

11 M. Hardie, *Water-colour Painting in Britain*, 3 vols., 1966–8; see vol.1, p.102.

12 Quoted M. Hardie, op.cit.; see vol.1, p.166.

13 For a useful summary of this debate, see C. Pace, 'Disegno e Colore' in J. Turner (ed.), *The Dictionary of Art*, vol.9, 1996, pp.6–9.

14 See M. Kitson, 'Reynolds' in D. Bindman (ed.), *The Thames and Hudson Encyclopaedia of British Art*, 1985, p. 202.

15 E. Dayes, op.cit., p.199 (*Essays on Painting*).

16 Ibid.

17 L. Stainton, op.cit., p. 15.

18 For Gilpin's definition of the 'picturesque', see *Three Essays: On Picturesque Beauty; On Picturesque Travel; and On Sketching Landscape*, 2nd ed., 1794, p.6; the other phrases come from his *Landscape Scenery* (quoted M. Hardie, op.cit., vol.1, p.77).

19 Marlow was probably introduced to William Gilpin by his brother, the painter Sawrey Gilpin, who was working in Samuel Scott's studio during Marlow's own apprenticeship to Scott. Marlow later contributed two drawings to Gilpin's manuscript *Tour of the Lakes* (see M.J.H. Liversidge, 'Six Etchings by William Marlow', *Burlington Magazine*, vol.122, 1980, p.553). The two capriccio landscapes by Marlow in the Oppé collection are the oval *Composition, Tivoli*, T09171 (which is very close to Gilpin) and *Composition: Scene on the Coast*, T09170.

20 A.P. Oppé, 'A Roman Sketchbook by Alexander Cozens', *Walpole Society*, vol.16, 1927–8, pp.88 and 90 (Cozens's pp.10 and 14). For examples of Cozens's coloured Roman drawings (in the British Museum) see K. Sloan, *Alexander and John Robert Cozens: The Poetry of Landscape*, New Haven and London, 1986, plates 19 and 20; plate 21, *A Villa*, in dry colours and bodycolours, is now in the Oppé collection, T08864.

21 M. Hardie, op.cit.; see vol.1, p.12.

22 For a discussion of the use of monochrome by eighteenth-century British draughtsmen (especially Alexander Cozens) in relation to the theory of landscape, see A. Wilton, 'The Structure of Landscape: Eighteenth-Century Theory' in *The Great Age of British Watercolours 1750–1880*, exh.cat., Royal Academy, 1993, pp.36–9.

23 The text of the *New Method* is given in full in A.P. Oppé, *Alexander & John Robert Cozens*, 1952, p.170 (Cozens's pp.8–9 of the *New Method*).

24 A.P. Oppé, op.cit., 1952, p.105.

25 A.P. Oppé, 'John Baptist Malchair of Oxford', *Burlington Magazine*, August 1943, p.194.

26 Quoted by Ian Fleming-Williams in *Constable: A Master Draughtsman*, exh.cat., Dulwich Picture Gallery, 1994, p.64.

27 Dayes, op.cit., p.282 (*Drawing and Coloring Landscapes*). There can be little doubt that Dayes is here having a dig at Cozens and the *New Method*, even though he dosen't refer to it here – or to Cozens – by name. In a biographical profile of John Robert Cozens, Dayes famously dismissed Alexander as 'Blotmaster-General to the town' (*Professional Sketches of Modern Artists*; see Dayes, op.cit., p.325). And in his *Essays on Painting*, Dayes similarly dismisses 'various schemes ... to assist the powers of imagination', such as a 'system of blotting', again without actually mentioning Cozens's name (Dayes, op. cit., pp.198–9).

28 T. Wilcox, *Francis Towne*, exh.cat., Tate Gallery, 1997, p.15.

29 Ibid.

30 A. French, *Gaspard Dughet called Gaspar Poussin 1615–75; a French Landscape Painter in Seventeenth-Century Rome and his Influence on British art*, exh.cat., Kenwood 1980 p.15. It has been argued that whilst Sandby's early work in gouache was probably

influenced by a Flemish tradition transplanted by artists such as Jan Siberechts and Peter Tillemans, his later work in gouache (often imaginary subjects) was influenced by the work of the Italian artist Marco Ricci (1676–1780), especially the latter's thirty or so gouache capriccios acquired by George III in 1764 and now in the Royal Collection (see B. Robertson, *The Art of Paul Sandby*, exh.cat., Yale Center for British Art, New Haven 1985, pp.10–11).

31 For a general discussion of this subject, see P. Mason, 'The Framing and Display of Watercolours' in *Watercolours from Leeds City Art Gallery*, exh.cat., 1995, pp.29–30.

32 He seems not to have been able to track down a suitable Gaspard or Claude to copy, so had to settle for a Vernet instead. See B. Ford (ed.), 'The Letters of Jonathan Skelton Written from Rome and Tivoli in 1758, together with Correspondence Relating to his Death', *Walpole Society*, vol.36, 1960, p.40.

33 B. Ford (ed.), op.cit., pp.54–5.

34 L. Stainton, op.cit., p.16.

35 Ibid; and see also D. Bull, *Classic Ground: British Artists and the Landscape of Italy, 1740–1830*, exh.cat., Yale Center for British Art, New Haven 1981.

36 A.P. Oppé (ed.), 'The Memoirs of Thomas Jones', *Walpole Society*, vol.32, 1951, p.66.

37 A. P. Oppé (ed.), op.cit., 1951, p.9.

38 T. Wilcox, op.cit., p.73.

39 For example, Martin Hardie wrote that 'Warwick' Smith had been given undue 'prominence ... for his alleged invention of the application of local colours without under-painting' (op.cit., vol.1, p.88). However, what the critics seem actually to have singled out in Smith's work was his so-called 'depth and richness of colour', not specifically the abandonment of monochrome underpainting; see, for example, Ackermann's *Repository of Art*, 1812 and Arnold's *Library of the Fine Arts*, 1833, both quoted by Hardie, op.cit., vol.1, p.116.

40 T. Wilcox, op.cit., p.16.

41 E. Dayes, op.cit., pp.309–10 (*Drawing and Colouring Landscapes*).

42 M. Hardie, op.cit., vol.1, p.14.

43 J. Bayard, *Works of Splendor and Imagination: the Exhibition Watercolor 1770–1870*, exh.cat., Yale Center for British Art, New Haven 1981, p.16.

44 Ibid. As Bayard points out, Pars died in Rome in 1782, and J.R. Cozens showed a drawing publicly for the last time in 1771 – although of course Beckford's collection of drawings by Cozens came up for sale at auction in 1805. Towne did not exhibit his drawings, except at his one-man show in London in 1805 which seems to have gone more or less unnoticed by artists and critics alike; and in any case, as Tim Wilcox has pointed out, it was not generally Towne's custom to use monochrome underpainting in combination with local colour, since his works tend to be painted *either* in shades of monochrome wash *or* in colour (op. cit., p.11).

It should, nevertheless, also be pointed out that the Italian subjects 'Warwick' Smith exhibited at the Society of Painters in Watercolour on his return from the Continent would almost certainly not have been the original watercolours he made in Italy, but variant versions produced – when he had already reverted to monochrome underpainting – specifically for exhibition and sale. See also note 39.

45 Monro seems temporarily to have gained possession of some of Cozens's drawings during this period, since he did not acutally own any until he acquired a number at the Beckford sale in 1805 (see note 44 and *Dr Thomas Monro (1759–1833) and the Monro Academy*, exh. leaflet, Victoria and Albert Museum, 1976).

46 One of Girtin's early biographers recorded that 'when he had made a sketch at any place, he never wished to quit until he had given it all the proper tints' (see J.L. Roget, *A History of the 'Old Watercolour Society'*, 1891, vol.1, p.95).

47 M. Hardie, op.cit., vol.1, p.18.

48 J. Thristan, 'Notes on Technique and Watercolour Painting' in *Watercolours from Leeds City Art Gallery*, exh.cat., 1995, p.40.

49 The new moist colours were listed in Winsor and Newton's catalogue in 1832, but it wasn't until about 1847 that they were put into metal tubes (M. Hardie, op.cit., vol.1, pp.20–1).

50 J. Thristan, op.cit., pp.40–1.

51 L. Stainton, op.cit., p.20; Edmund Burke recommended 'sad and fuscous colours, as black, or brown, or deep purple, and the like' in *A Philosophical Enquiry into the Origin of our Ideas of the Sublime and Beautiful* (1757), see section no.XVI.

52 According to the wife of Cotman's patron, Francis Cholmeley of Brandsby Hall in Yorkshire (see 'Introduction: Cotman's Life and Work' in M. Rajnai (ed.), *John Sell Cotman 1782–1842*, exh.cat., Victoria and Albert Museum, Arts Council, 1982, p.13).

53 S. Uwins, *A Memoir of Thomas Uwins R.A.*, 1858, vol.1, p.125; quoted and discussed by L. Stainton, op.cit., p.22.

54 W.M. Thackeray in G. Ray (ed.), *Contributions to the Morning Chronicle*, Urbana 1955, pp.135–7; quoted J. Bayard, op.cit., p.23.

55 E. Cook and A. Wedderburn (eds.), *The Works of John Ruskin*, vol.14, 1903–12, p.246; quoted J. Munro, *British Landscape Watercolours 1750–1850*, Fitzwilliam Museum 1994, p.15.

'Displaying the Colours to Advantage'
The Papers Used in the Oppé Collection

Peter Bower

Most artists have left no record of their thoughts about the papers on which they worked. But the evidence exists in the sheets themselves. Close examination of the individual papers in this catalogue can tell us much about the source of the sheet and the use for which it had originally been designed. Much of the work in this book was executed away from home, either travelling in Britain or on the Continent. The identity of the maker or mill that produced a particular paper widens our understanding of an individual artist's working practice. Some artists preferred to take papers that they knew and understood away with them on their travels. Others seem to have relied on finding papers along the way and some artists, of whom Turner is perhaps the best example, commonly took paper with them, both as loose sheets and as sketchbooks, as well as regularly buying various quantities of paper at the different places he visited.

Most of the works in this catalogue have been executed on papers that were not designed either for drawing or watercolour.[1] For most of the period there were no purpose-made drawing or watercolour papers. Artists worked on those papers that suited them, choosing from the great variety of papers made by the small mills that supplied the artists' colourmen and stationers. 'Drawing' papers, which included papers for watercolour as well as those for pencil, chalk and ink, were quite simply those papers

fig.9 Detail from a trade card from Dorothy Mercier, Printseller and Stationer of Windmill Street, London, *c.*1761. Besides advertising 'Frames and Prints in the Neatest and Genteelest of Taste' she sold 'Finest Writing Papers ... plain in all sizes' as well as 'English Dutch and French Drawing Papers'
Private Collection

on which artists found they could work, regardless of the use for which paper mills had made them.

Over the course of the eighteenth century, with more mills starting up, more stationers and colourmen in business and an increasingly discerning and sophisticated paper-buying public, a much greater variety of sizes, weights, textures and qualities of paper were becoming available (see fig.9).[2] Paper was usually described by its function: it was simply a 'Writing', 'Printing' or 'Wrapping'. It was either 'Thick' or 'Thin', 'Large' or 'Small', sometimes 'Stout', sometimes 'Coarse'. Quality might be described as 'Superfine', 'Fine', or 'Retree' (that is, substandard but useable sheets). There were various tones of white and cream, depending on the cleanliness or otherwise of the rags used to make the paper. Coloured papers were either brown, blue or drab, including a small range of browns, buffs, greys, blue-greys and olive-green papers, the colour again coming mostly from the raw materials.

The makers and countries of origin for many of the papers in this exhibition can be identified from the watermarks found, showing the international nature of the paper industry even in this period. Perhaps half the paper in this exhibition is of continental rather than English manufacture, some bought abroad but much obtained in England. The English paper industry was still in its infancy in the early eighteenth century and imported very large amounts of white papers from Holland, France and Italy, with Dutch writing papers generally proving more popular with artists both for working on and for use as mounts.

Dutch writing paper can be seen in the work of artists as varied as John Downman,[3] Wright of Derby, William Pars and John 'Warwick' Smith, using papers from Jan van der Ley (nos.29 and 55), Dirk and Cornelis Blauw (no.46) and Jan Honig (no.52). The great French maker Jean Villedary is well represented with works by Skelton (no.33) and Pars (no.48). Other French sheets were used by Oliver (no.1) and Downman (no.54). As one might expect, with so many works having Italian subjects, a lot of the paper found in this collection is Italian, bought by the artists on their travels. The identified makers are Bracciano, used by Thomas Jones (no.44), Braccini, used by Flaxman (no.63) and Guiseppe Miliani, used by Lord Leighton (no.100). One particularly fine Italian watermark, found in James Barry's work (no.40), has not yet been identified with any particular maker (see fig.10). Despite the healthy state of the Italian paper industry during the eighteenth century, considerable amounts of French, English and Dutch paper was exported to Italy during the eighteenth century and such papers were easily available at artists' colourmen and stationers in Rome, Florence, Venice, Naples, and other cities. Many of the Dutch makers, in particular, had well deserved reputations for quality. The papers were strong and white, they looked good and more importantly they worked well: artists could rely on them.

Throughout the eighteenth century a complex web of technical, cultural and economic influences operated on papermakers, paper merchants, artists' colourmen, and artists themselves, leading to the evolution of many new types of papers designed and made for very specific puposes, including those made specifically for watercolour.[4] Examples of these include papers by Edmeads and Pine in a work by Turner (no.78), two different papers from Thomas Creswick used by Joseph Farrington (no.50) and Henry Edridge (no.74) and a blue watercolour paper used by Clarkson Stanfield (no.92). The introduction of these new papers coupled with changing sensibilities and aspirations in the artists themselves had a dramatic effect on the working practices of individual artists and their expression of their vision.

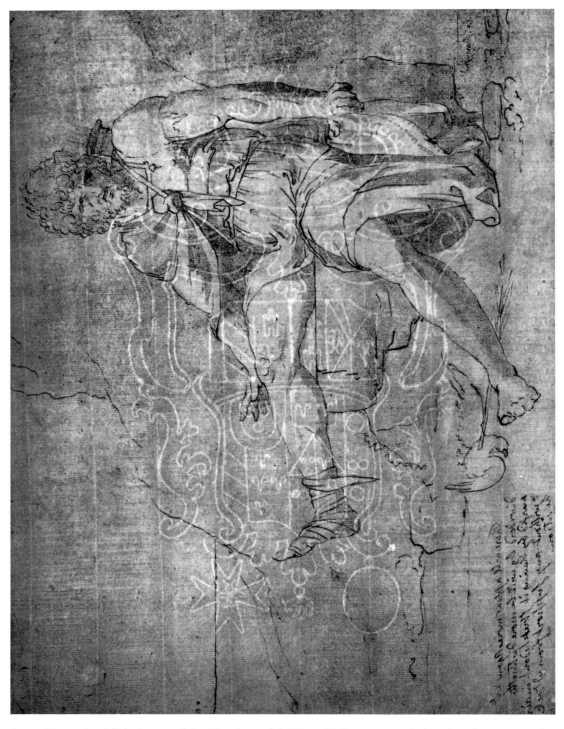

fig.10 Transmitted light image of the Kingdom of the Two Sicilies watermark found in the paper used by James Barry for *Philoctetes* (no. 40) which also clearly shows the horizontal laid lines and vertical chain lines left by the wires making up the surface of the mould upon which the sheet of paper was made
Private Collection

Any work of art on paper is an intimate object, meant to be seen close to. The interplay of the surface with the marks made on it is an integral, often crucial part of the visual effect of the work, though the importance attached to this depends, to some extent, on the concerns and intentions of the individual artist. Subtle qualities of texture, tone and the three dimensional nature of any mark made on the surface are often ignored when examining a picture, though, in a purely physical sense, they are the work. Watercolour, in particular, depends for its success on a deep and vivid understanding of the nature of particular surfaces and the ways that those surfaces can be worked. The ability of an individual paper to satisfy the demands the artist makes on it depends quite simply on how it was made. The colourmen knew this and sought out those writing and wrapping papers that would suit their customers.

English drawing and watercolour before 1800 was generally based on the use of the better types of white or off-white laid writing papers which had the necessary surface strengths and light-reflecting capabilites. Besides the best known English makers like James Whatman, used by several artists in this catalogue for drawings or backings (e.g. nos.3, 12, 21, 25, 28, 35 and 53), and the Portals, used for example, by Thomas Girtin (no.77), many of the smaller English mills particularly from Kent and Hampshire are well represented: Francis Towne uses Clement Taylor (no.37), Fuseli uses Charles Wilmott (no.42), Paul Sandby uses Robert Williams (no.25)[5] and John Constable uses William Allee (no.79), John Gater (no.81) and Pine and Thomas (no.82).[6] The colourmen also stocked the stronger grades of buff, blue and grey wrapping papers for those wishing to work on coloured grounds. Examples of these can be seen in the work of Thomas Jones (no.43), George Garrard (no.70), John Sell Cotman (nos.85–6)[7] and William Havell (no.87). For those preferring a much smoother surface various glazed boards were also available (see George Barrett, no.71).

Artists have always chosen a paper to suit their particular needs. If they could not find what they wanted then they simply altered the sheet. Several examples of such prepared grounds can be found in this catalogue in the work of Isaac Oliver (no.1), Richard Wilson (no.13), Thomas Gainsborough (no.23) and George Richmond (no.97). The work of Alexander Cozens shows the great variety of papers available to the artist. Every sheet of his in this catalogue is different, from tracing paper (no.17) to fine writing paper (no.15), and the preparations he has given to them vary from oils (no.20) to washes (no.18). It was possible to buy already toned and coloured grounds, such as Bistre papers, from the colourmen but the highly individual nature of many prepared grounds suggests that most artists chose to prepare the sheets themselves. It was just this kind of individual usage that gradually filtered back to the papermakers, via the colourmen and merchants, and led to many changes in papermaking practice, such as the design of specific surfaces and coloured papers for artists.

The early years of the eighteenth century saw the advent of a 'new technology' throughout western European papermaking. Developments in the preparation and pulping of rags, a completely new form of 'wove' papermould made with woven wire cloth rather than the traditional laid cover that made its first appearance in the 1750s, and improvements to presses and drying lofts all contributed greatly to making a much wider range of papers. In particular, the growing use by mills of the Hollander beater (see fig.11), designed to produce more pulp and at a faster rate than the old stamping engines, soon showed that it had other advantages. Papermakers soon learnt that they could control the beating of individual batches of rags in ways not possible using earlier methods. This allowed the papermaker to develop the potential of a

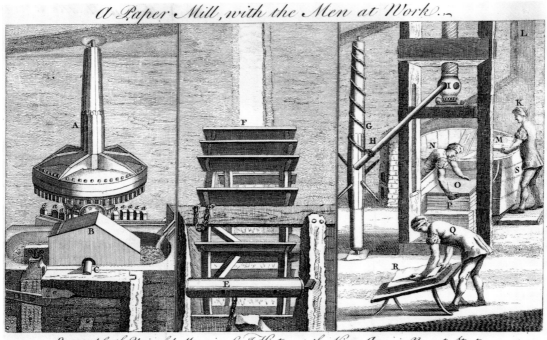

fig.11 Illustration of papermaking from *The Universal Magazine* showing the waterwheel in the centre, the Hollander beater pulping rags on the left and a typical crew making paper by hand on the right. The vatman (K) is forming the sheets, The coucher (N) is transferring the newly formed wet sheets onto the felts (P) and the layer (Q) is seperating out the newly pressed sheets, prior to hanging them up to dry *Tate Gallery*

particular rag fibre, or combinations of fibres, in highly specific ways to give the finished sheets distinct characteristics suitable for very specific tasks. The development of new types of presses, primarily to speed up production and to give greater surface strength for writing papers (which had had to change with the introduction of the steel nib in the 1780s) also benefited artists working in watercolour because the greater pressure and compaction of the surface of the sheet allowed an artist to work the colour more vigorously. Many of these changes were profound but 'invisible', only becoming apparent when the sheet was actually being worked on. Some artists such as Turner,[8] Girtin and Cotman show a deep understanding of the possibilities of these new surfaces.

Cost may well have played a significant part in the choice of many of the papers. Much of the paper seen in this exhibition is not of the finest quality, despite the often illustrious names seen in the watermarks. Quality control varied greatly from mill to mill and even within a particular mill. Makers generally packed their paper with quires of slightly substandard sheets of the same paper at the top and bottom of the ream to protect the bulk of the paper. The stationers and colourmen would seperate these sheets out and sell them at half price. But despite their imperfections, close examination shows that they were generally sound, particularly as regards the sizing of the sheet, a crucial consideration when working in watercolour. What deficiencies they had in papermaking terms were obviously never serious enough to inhibit the artist from working on them.

An artist's choice of paper was probably governed by a mixture of availability – particularly for those artists travelling on the Continent or to out-of-the-way places – and the particularities of his working methods. Some artists preferred hard-sized smoother papers, others slightly coarser and softer-surfaced sheets. The media being used and the speed and pressure of the artist's hand all contribute to the success or otherwise of a particular sheet for a particular artist.

The wonderful variety of tones and surfaces in the range of nominally white papers in this catalogue was the result of the small-scale and local nature of papermaking by hand throughout the period covered by this exhibition. Most mills were small, often only operating one, or possibly two, vats and producing perhaps between five hundred and one thousand sheets a day, depending on the size and weight of sheet. Local and regional variations in papermaking practice, particularly regarding the collection, washing and preparation of the rags, as well as differences in the cleanliness and quality of the river or spring water used by the mill, made an extraordinary range of subtly different papers available.

The journey, in terms of both papermaking and artistic practice, from the earliest sheet in this catalogue used by Isaac Oliver (no.1) to Lord Leighton's purpose-made coloured drawing paper (no.100) is a long road. One can imagine the pleasure many of these artists must have felt, particularly when travelling abroad, when they stopped at a colourman's or stationer's shop and paused awhile to buy some papers, finding a new paper they had never seen before, judging the strength and texture, the tone and weight and size of the sheet, perhaps taking the paper to the doorway to better judge the colour and surface in a stronger light. How many times, back home in England, may some of them have wished they had bought some more of a particular paper in Rome, or Venice or Naples?

NOTES

1 Further information on all the individual papers used in this catalogue is available in Bower, Peter, *Report on the Papers Found in One Hundred Works From the Oppé Collection*, unpublished report for the Tate Gallery 1997.

2 See Krill, John, *English Artists' Paper*, 1987, for an excellent introduction to the marketing of English artists papers.

3 Downman's paper usage is documented in Bower, Peter, 'The Papers used by John Downman', *The Quarterly* (The Journal of the British Association of Paper Historians), no.20, Oct. 1996, pp.7–15.

4 For further information on this development see Bower, Peter, 'The Evolution and Development of Drawing Papers and the effect of this development on Watercolour Artists, 1750–1850', *The Oxford Papers* (Studies in British Paper History vol.1), 1996, pp.61–74.

5 Paul Sandby's paper usage is well documented in Donnithorne, Alan, 'Media, Paper, Watermarks and Mounts' in Jane Roberts, *Views of Windsor: Watercolours by Thomas and Paul Sandby*, 1997, pp.138–43.

6 Other papers by other makers used by Constable are listed in Bower, Peter, 'The Evolution and Development of Drawing Papers and the Effect of this Development on Watercolour Artists, 1750–1850', *The Oxford Papers* (Studies in British Paper History vol.1), 1996, p.73.

7 Ibid. pp.73–4.

8 For Turner's paper usage in the first half of his working life see Bower, Peter, *Turner's Papers: A Study of the Manufacture, Selection and Use of his Drawing Papers 1787–1820*, Tate Gallery 1990.

ISAAC OLIVER
c.1560/5–1617

1 Charity c.1596–1617

Pen and ink, ink wash and gouache on laid paper
11.4 × 8 (4½ × 3⅛)
Inscribed bottom right 'Is: Ollivier'
T10165

Isaac Oliver is best known as a portrait miniaturist, but he was also a draughtsman of some significance in the history of British drawing. Together with the architect Inigo Jones (1573–1652), Oliver's near contemporary, he was the first artist working in England to produce a body of drawings which in their subject-matter and technique demonstrate a wide knowledge of Continental art. His subject drawings and sketches owe a great debt to the work of the French School of Fontainebleau, as well as to Netherlandish and Italian art, the influences of which he absorbed through travel abroad (he visited Venice in 1596) and through the study of prints and engravings. Oliver was also very conscious of his Continental origins. The son of a French Huguenot goldsmith, who by 1568 had fled to London with his family, he was very much part of the exiled Huguenot community there, with its extensive European contacts. Although he became a naturalised Englishman in 1606, he nevertheless made a point of signing his work 'Ollivier' instead of the anglicised Oliver.

This drawing of Charity is one of thirteen which are signed by him. That he regarded his drawings as significant enough to sign is important, as at this time in England the idea that drawings, opposed to paintings, could be works of art in their own right was only just beginning to be formed. An increasing taste for collecting drawings appears to have been particularly apparent at the culturally sophisticated courts of Henry, Prince of Wales, and his mother, Queen Anne of Denmark, who in 1605 appointed Oliver her court limner (miniature painter). Oliver's elaborate *Nymphs and Satyrs* (Royal Collection) was possibly owned by her, along with other drawings on a similar theme (Roberts 1986, p.97); and *Moses Striking the Rock*, Oliver's other highly finished drawing in the Royal Collection, was possibly also inherited by Charles I from her collection (MacGregor 1989, p.118). Oliver certainly attached much importance to his subject drawings: in his will he bequeathed to his son Peter 'all my drawings allready finished and unfinished and lymning pictures, be they historyes, storyes, or any thing of lymning whatsoever on my own hande worke as yet unfinished' (Stainton and White 1987, p.48).

It is not known if this particular drawing was executed simply for pleasure or as a commission. As is the case with the majority of Oliver's subject drawings, it is not related to any of his known large subject miniatures, although the pose of Charity is very similar to that of the Madonna in his *Madonna and Child in Glory* (Beaverbrook Art Gallery, Fredericton, New Brunswick). The date of the drawing is difficult to determine, as Oliver made borrowings from such a wide variety of sources and styles. The initial inspiration appears to have been an engraving by the sixteenth-century School of Fontainebleau artist and printmaker Jean Mignon, after a painting of the same subject by Andrea del Sarto (1487–1530), then in the collection of François 1er (Finsten 1981, vol.2, p.214, no.180). However, as far as is known, Oliver never copied directly, preferring to amalgamate influences from several sources in one drawing, thereby creating a work of art original to him – in this he was in tune with art theorists, who emphasised the superiority of invention over imitation (Stainton and White 1987, p.17). The strong hatched lines for shading possibly reflect Oliver's study of prints, a practice advocated by Henry Peacham, who, like Oliver, had some connection with the court of Henry, Prince of Wales, in the enlarged 1612 edition of his *Graphice or the Most Auncient and Excellent Art of Drawing and Limning*.

TB

38

FRANCIS BARLOW
?1626–1704

2 Turkeys

Pencil, pen and black ink with grey washes on laid paper 13.9 × 20.1 (5⅛ × 7½)
T08091

According to the engraver and art-world commentator George Vertue, Barlow was initially apprenticed to the portrait painter William Sheppard (*fl.* 1641–after 1660), but soon left his master, finding that 'his fancy did not lye that way, his Genius leading him wholly to drawing Fowl, Fish and Beasts …'. By 1656 he had enough of an established name in that genre for the diarist John Evelyn to describe him as 'the famous Paynter of fowle, Beastes & Birds'. Barlow's main reputation, however, was as a draughtsman and an etcher, rather than a painter. Vertue considered his 'Draught' far more convincing than his 'Colouring and Pencilling', and it is chiefly for his drawings, and the etchings and engravings after them, that he is admired today. Nevertheless, Barlow has the distinction of being the first native-born artist of animal and sporting subjects, as well as being the first professional English book illustrator and etcher.

In most cases Barlow's drawings are related to printmaking, but his work in this field was not confined totally to interpretations of the natural world. The 1687 edition of his famous *Aesop's Fables* (first published in 1666) contains thirty-five additional plates illustrating the life of Aesop; and he also designed satirical prints and playing cards (see Stainton and White 1987, nos.105–8 and nos.111–15). However, drawings of birds, animals and sporting scenes were undoubtedly his speciality and form the majority of his output. His series of bird and animal prints, illustrating different species, were published in collections such as his *Diversae Avium Species* (1658) and *Multae Diversae Avium Species* (1671), with the plates etched either by himself, or more usually by other professionals in this field such as Wenceslaus Hollar (1607–1677), Jan Griffier (*c.*1645/52–1718) and Francis Place (1647–1728). These collections served as working manuals for use by other artists (Hodnett 1978, p.102), and Barlow designs certainly appear in paintings by Griffier, who obviously benefited from his role as etcher. Presumably they were produced also in the spirit of scientific enquiry which marked the age, with the intention of recording some aspect of the physical world. Barlow's drawings, such as the one shown here, are accurate depictions of birds and animals in their natural habitats, sketched mainly from life, although he also reused some of his designs, incorporating them in later drawings or paintings. For instance, the turkey shown here on the fence is almost identical to the one which occurs in plate 11 of an incomplete but very early series, possibly datable before 1654, collected together with other proofs in *Multae et Diversae Avium Species Multifariis Formis & Pernaturalebus Figuris per Franciscum Barlovium …* (British Museum), reissued, with additions, in the 1671 edition mentioned above (Hodnett 1978, p.102). Two of the original drawings for this series (*Woodcocks* and *Partridges*), as well as several etchings, are in the Oppé collection.

Most of Barlow's drawings have rather deliberate and heavy outlining which is an indication that he intended them for reproduction, the hard lines being an aide in the process of transferring the image to a copper plate. This drawing was certainly engraved (an engraving of it from Bowles and Sayers's *Various Birds and Beasts Drawn from the Life by Francis Barlow* is also in the Oppé collection), and the blackened reverse with faintly discernible outlining with a sharp instrument is evidence of it. Bowles and Sayers's book was published between 1754 and 1769, the engravings taken from Barlow plates acquired from the collection of Francis Place. It was Place's practice to retain Barlow's drawings once having made plates from them, and his collection was eventually inherited by Patrick Allan-Fraser, from whose sale in 1931 this drawing originates (Tyler 1971, pp.76–7, 85). Other Barlow drawings of birds in the Oppé collection, which share the same provenance, are of the same size and are also blackened on the reverse, which indicates that they are intended as a group. So far it has not been established if the series was published in Barlow's lifetime – his series of prints exist today in confusing forms, bound in various or only partial assortments, and in his own day his volumes went through several publications, with amendments and additions, with copies or reissues appearing in the eighteenth century.

TB

SIR JAMES THORNHILL
1675/6–1734

3 A Ceiling and Wall Decoration *c.*1715–25

Pen and brown ink and brown washes over pencil on
laid paper 31.1 × 39.1 (12¼ × 15⅜)

T08143

Thornhill was the most important native-born baroque
decorative painter of the early eighteenth century, competing in a field which had been dominated previously
by foreign artists trained in the Continental tradition,
such as Antonio Verrio (?1639–1707) and Louis Laguerre
(1663–1721). From 1711 to 1727 he worked on his most
successful and imposing interior scheme, the Painted Hall
at Greenwich, which survives today as a masterpiece of
the baroque style in England. George I recognised his
achievements and status in the artistic community by
appointing him History Painter to the King in 1718,
Serjeant-Painter in 1720, and in May of the same year
knighted him.

Thornhill is at his most creative and inventive as a
draughtsman. A large number of sketches and preliminary
studies by him survive, which illustrate vividly his working procedure in the evolution of his schemes. In the first
stages of their conception Thornhill would make rapid
pen or pencil drawings, choosing and rejecting subject-
matter and compositions as he went. As the design progressed, the drawings become more detailed and finished,
and the compositions more decided, resulting finally in
an oil sketch. This highly finished design for a staircase,
painted with grand mythological scenes – the Birth of
Venus in the centre, Neptune in his chariot to the left,
and an Assembly of the Gods on the ceiling above –
although formerly catalogued simply as an unknown
wall and ceiling decoration, in fact appears to be a preliminary drawing for the oil sketch of the same subject,
minus Neptune, at the Victoria and Albert Museum.
However, even at this late stage Thornhill was changing
his mind about various elements, deciding not to ink in
the pencilled putti to the left of Neptune.

The oil sketch, along with two others thought to be
alternative designs for the same space (fig.12), have been
identified in the past with Thornhill's designs for the
staircase at Canons, Middlesex, the celebrated country
mansion of James Brydges, 1st Duke of Chandos; and a
pencil drawing depicting the same subject as fig.12, Dido
and Aeneas, is inscribed 'D.Chand. at Canons' (see Croft-

Murray 1962, p.266; Simon 1974, no.46). Begun in
1715 but pulled down within only thirty-five years, the
best architects, craftsmen and interior decorators were
employed in the design of the house. According to
records Thornhill was responsible for painting the main
staircase and the saloon, although the subject-matter is
not specified.

This association with Canons is not a certainty,
however. The dimensions of the design, particularly the
square ceiling, do not tally with the narrow, rectangular
space occupied by the staircase on floor plans of the house
(Huntington Library, California, reproduced in Dunlop,
1949, p.1952). Thornhill habitually re-employed similar
designs with minor alterations for different locations. The
same compositional format – a mythological scene framed
by double or single Corinthian or composite columns,
with coffering above – was used by him frequently, for
instance for the staircase at Hanbury Hall, Worcestershire.

T B

fig.12 Sir James
Thornhill, *Design
for Wall and
Ceiling Decoration:
Aeneas before
Dido, and the
Gods on Olympus
c.*1715–25,
oil on canvas
*The Board of
Trustees of the
Victoria and Albert
Museum*

THOMAS CARWITHAM

(*fl.*1713–1733)

4 Fantasy of Flight *c.*1713–33

Pen and brown ink and pale brown washes on laid paper
35.5 × 22.4 (14 × 8⅞); artist's mount 41.9 × 28.8 (16½ × 11⅜)
Inscribed bottom left in pen and brown ink: 'Carwitham'
T08118

Thomas Carwitham is thought to have been related to the professional engraver John Carwitham (*fl.c.*1723–1741) who worked mainly for booksellers, but who also acted independently, designing, for instance, the highly original set of plates for the 1739 publication *Various kinds of Floor Decoration* (Hammelmann 1975, p.24).

Like John, Thomas Carwitham seems to have pursued a varied career. He is known primarily for sketches illustrating scenes from classical mythology (Wark 1969, p.22; Croft-Murray 1960, p.264), mainly from Ovid's *Metamorphoses*, one of which (Victoria and Albert Museum) is signed and dated 1713. Another (Huntington Library, California, formerly in the possession of William Gilpin) has an inscription that indicates he was the pupil of the baroque decorative painter Thornhill (see no.3), and although no further documentary evidence for this has come to light so far, his style of draughtsmanship is so close to Thornhill's as to lend this theory some weight. He is not known to have executed any decorative schemes of his own, but it is possible that he was employed by others as a specialist painter of illusionistic architecture and sculpture. In 1723 he published a treatise, *The description and use of the Architectonick Sector, And also of the Architectonick Sliding Plates*, in which he is described as a history and architectural painter; and in his preface he tells us that, through his experience as an architectural draughtsman, he has for some time 'observ'd the Tediousness of Making, and the Uncertainty of Working by Scales on Paper' (Croft-Murray MS, p.2).

In appearance this sketch is more akin to a decorative design than to a religious or mythological illustration, and the tumbling figures, falling from a height, are reminiscent of depictions of the Last Judgement. However, their facial expressions lack the terror associated with the fall of the damned to Hell, and an obvious narrative element is missing from the scene as a whole. The twisted, contorted bodies and the spatial relationships between them are strangely similar to the astonishing and slightly eccentric sixteenth-century School of Fontainebleau engravings of human gymnastic pyramids, attributed to Juste de Juste, with which Carwitham might well have been familiar (Zerner 1969, p.33): it seems more likely, however, that the sketch is simply an independent artistic exercise, done as a virtuoso performance in dramatic foreshortening, and to test his skills in depicting falling human figures seen from below.

Carwitham's loose, sketchy technique and only tentative acknowledgement of the rules of human anatomy strongly resembles Thornhill's own draughtsmanship style – for example, the falling figures in his sketch *An Olympian Scene* (Victoria and Albert Museum; see Mayhew 1967, p.18, no.27). As Thornhill's pupil Carwitham would obviously have been trained in his manner and could also have attended drawing classes at the Great Queen Street Academy of which Thornhill became Governor in 1715. Unlike John Carwitham who is recorded as a member in 1713 (Bignamini 1988, p.74), it is not known if Carwitham was a subscriber to the Academy, although he was certainly interested in drawing, demonstrated by his publication of a manual, *Carwitham's Drawing-book for initiating youth …* (Croft-Murray MS, p.2). Founded in 1711, with Sir Godfrey Kneller as its first Governor, the Great Queen Street Academy concentrated mainly on the life class. In seeming sympathy with Thornhill's own approach, which was to concentrate on overall form rather than exact depiction of musculature, direct study of anatomy was not pursued (Bignamini 1988, pp.65–7). Thornhill's ability to depict the human figure was much derided by Kneller. On finding the artist Thomas Gibson (*c.*1680–1751) making sketches of a model posed in an extraordinary way, and on hearing the explanation that it was at Thornhill's request, who intended to make use of the sketches for his decorations then in progress at Greenwich Hospital, Kneller exclaimed: 'I see! I see! Mr Dornhill is a wise man. But if I was Mr Dornhill I should let Mr Gibson draw all my figures for me' (Whitley 1928, vol.1, p.13).

TB

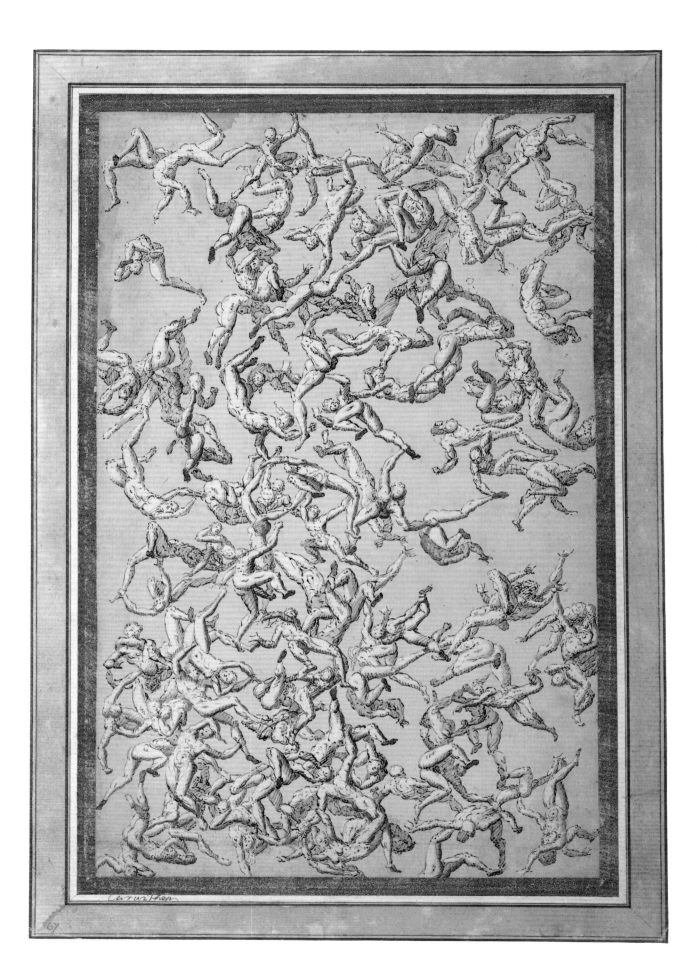

Carruthers

JOHN VANDERBANK
1694–1739

5 Equestrian Design: The Volte Renversée to the Right 1728

Pencil and grey wash on laid paper 25.7 × 17.4 (10⅛ × 6⅞)
Inscribed bottom centre in pencil: '*J Vanderbank Fecit 1728*'
T08274

Vanderbank was foremost a portraitist but he also painted history and narrative scenes, and produced drawings for engraving as book illustrations. He was the eldest son of the tapestry weaver John Vanderbank, who headed the Soho Tapestry Manufactory and held the lucrative office of chief tapestry weaver to the Crown. On his death in 1717 he left his family in comfortable circumstances, which seems to have encouraged Vanderbank into extravagances beyond his means. Vertue condemns his high living and self-indulgence 'in dressing, living keeping Horses coaches &c. town and Country ...', but admired Vanderbank's abilities as an artist. 'He might have carryd all before him', he tells us, 'but gave others room to exert. and blasted his reputation, yet still his superior merit in drawing, greatness of pencilling, spirit and composition, kept up to the last, in spite of the Blemishes of his Vanitys' (Vertue, vol.3, pp.97–8).

For extensive periods throughout his life Vanderbank was in debt, and in 1724 his financial situation was such that he was forced to leave the country for France to avoid imprisonment. His straitened circumstances compelled him, on his return, to live within the liberties of the Fleet prison, and in 1729 he suffered a spell in Marshalsea prison, again because of debt. It was during this period of intense financial insecurity that Vanderbank made this equestrian study. It relates to the 1729 publication *Twenty Five Actions of the Manage Horse*, a manual on horsemanship and dressage part-published by Joseph Sympson who also engraved the plates after Vanderbank's designs (Hammelmann 1968, pp.287–9). This particular drawing was engraved, in reverse, for plate 12: *The Volte renversée to the right, when a horse moves with his head to the centre & hind quarters without the Volte, the best lesson to make a horses shoulders pliable*. In his introduction to the work Sympson tells us that 'the better to execute his Ideas' Vanderbank 'was himself a Disciple in our Riding-Schools, and purchased a fine Horse as a Model for his Pencil'. The sketch certainly appears to have been done

from life, as do others in the same series, although the fluidity of the draughtmanship is somewhat lost in the engraving: Sympson's skill as an engraver was questioned by his contemporaries, Vertue describing him as 'from the lowest degree of that business' (Vertue, vol.3, p.20). Not all of Vanderbank's drawings of this type relate to the 1729 publication, however. *Horse and Rider* (Witt collection, 1547), for example, even depicts the same man astride the horse but is signed and dated 1730. It is possible that, as was his practice with his famous *Don Quixote* designs of which there are several series (Einberg 1987, p.76), Vanderbank was capitalising on his original success by producing further drawings for sale to clients.

Despite Vertue's colourful account of his character, Vanderbank must have approached his artistic career with a degree of seriousness. He ran a successful portrait practice which attracted royal patronage, and he took on assistants such as Arthur Pond (1701–1758) and John Robinson (c.1715–1745). As a young man in 1720 he had set up with Louis Chéron the first St Martin's Lane Academy, the successor to the Great Queen Street Academy of which he had been a member since 1711, but which had folded because of Thornhill's declining interest in it (see no.4). St Martin's Lane introduced fresh approaches to the teaching of drawing. It was the first academy to employ the female model (an innovation, according to Hogarth, purely to make the academy 'more inviting to subscribers'), and placed a firm emphasis on direct observation and anatomy (Bignamini 1988, pp.83–95). Vanderbank appears to have been dedicated to its success, paying in addition to the stipulated two guineas annual subscription an extra fifteen (Bignamini 1988, p.84). However, with his hasty flight to France in 1724 the Academy foundered – '... the treasurer [that is, Vanderbank] sinking the subscription money', writes Hogarth, 'the lamp stove etc were seized for rent and the whole affair put a stop to' (see Bignamini 1988, p.89, n.1).

TB

WILLIAM HOGARTH
1697–1764

6 George Taylor Triumphing over Death c.1750

Red and black chalk on laid paper 49.5 × 39.6 (19½ × 15½)
T08212

George Taylor, a famous eighteenth-century pugilist (boxer and prize fighter), died on 21 February 1750, and it was presumably soon after this date that Hogarth made this design for his tombstone together with its companion, *Death Giving George Taylor a Cross-Buttock* (Oppé collection T08211). Commonly known as 'Taylor the Barber', because of his other profession, he succeeded Jack Figg as Champion of England in 1734. From the early 1730s he was proprietor of the Tottenham Court Boxing Booth where great crowds gathered to see champions such as Jack Broughton fight, as well as Taylor himself who was always ready to show opponents 'the truth of a good drubbing' (Anon. 1788, p.54). Taylor also ran an academy for the science of self-defence where gentlemen were taught the arts of fencing, quarter-staffing and fisticuffs. He himself was adept in the use of the back-sword, and was particularly well known for his excellent execution of the cross-buttock fall, a move 'gained by a low hold of the waistband of the breeches with the right hand, and of the right shoulder of the left hand, by which you capsize your opponent, by throwing him head foremost over your right hip, and a part of your buttock, and is of all the falls the worst, as all the upper forms are subject to injury by it' (Anon. 1788, pp.12–13).

Both of Hogarth's designs, which when reversed join together to form the arabesque of the top of the headstone, appropriately depict the cross-buttock fall. *Death Giving George Taylor a Cross-Buttock* shows Taylor, dressed in the breeches common to pugilists and with a shaved head (although scratching, biting and kicking were not permitted during a fight, there was no rule against hair-pulling), being felled by the move that made him famous; while here, now clad in a loincloth, he is shown as the vanquisher. The mock heroism of the designs is matched by the epitaph that was intended to accompany them: 'Incorruptable and Unconquerable', the inscription reads, 'Learn | Heros of a higher Class | from his Example | to render | British Bravery | Invincible' (Oppé 1948, p.49). In fact Taylor was not invincible. Despite several attempts to defeat Broughton he failed, apparently because of his lack of 'that necessary ingredient for a boxer called

bottom' (Anon. 1788, p.72). It is not known if Hogarth's headstone was ever executed. Tradition has it that it was intended for Deptford Churchyard and Taylor was certainly from that area, having become in his retirement proprietor of the Fountain Inn there (Egan 1812; Miles 1880, vol.1, p.20). The boldness of the designs suggests that they were intended for use (unlike the initial pen and ink sketches at the Yale Center for British Art), and, indeed, a counterproof exists of *George Taylor Triumphing over Death* (Oppé collection); and both designs have been strengthened in black chalk, perhaps having been touched up after the transfer process.

Hogarth had presumably known Taylor personally. It is possible that he was a model at the second St Martin's Lane Academy, founded by Hogarth in 1735, where life drawing was a central element to the teaching despite Hogarth's personal lack of patience with it. Jack Figg is an earlier example of a pugilist who was employed as a model, certainly at the Great Queen Street Academy and possibly also at the first St Martin's Lane Academy of which Hogarth was a member (Bignamini and Postle 1991, pp.80–1). Hogarth makes reference to pugilism in several of his prints (Paulson 1970, vol.1, pp.313–14). *The March to Finchley*, for instance, depicts a contest in progress, possibly at Taylor's Tottenham Court Booth or at Broughton's nearby Amphitheatre which had opened in rivalry to Taylor's establishment; and *The Second Stage of Cruelty* makes open reference to Taylor. In the background an advertisement is pinned up for a fight between Taylor and Field at the Amphitheatre. On one level Hogarth appears to be attacking pugilism as a cruel sport – one could fight until the death – but he is also, surely, alluding to the war that was waged in the press between Taylor and Broughton in 1743. On the same day as Taylor was to take on Field at his boxing booth, Broughton advertised a series of tantalising prize fights at his new Amphitheatre. The end result was that Broughton stole Taylor's business, the boxing booth closed down, and Taylor and his men had to transfer their performances to the Amphitheatre (Anon. 1788, p.61).

TB

WILLIAM TAVERNER
1700–1772

7 Italian Composition: the Outskirts of a Town ?1750–65

Watercolour over pencil on two pieces of laid paper, joined vertically
19.5 × 46 (7⅝ × 18⅛)
T08512

Taverner holds a special place in the history of British drawing, being remembered today as 'our first regular and systematic painter of free landscape in watercolour' (Hardie 1966, vol.1, p.69). He was a lawyer by profession, inheriting his father's position as Procurator-General of the Court of Arches of Canterbury, an appeal court located in Bow Church, London to which disputed wills were sent from the Prerogative Court of Canterbury – for such matters fell within the jurisdiction of the church before the middle of the nineteenth century. Technically, then, Taverner should be considered an amateur, though he seems to have devoted most of his spare time to art. The diarist Joseph Farington recorded that Taverner 'had much quaking abt. shewing his pictures', but that this 'raised their reputation' (*Diary*, 8 February 1797, vol.3, p.765), and certainly Taverner's skills as an artist were highly regarded in his own lifetime. As early as 1733, for example, the engraver George Vertue, who kept notebooks in which he recorded extensive information about the art of his times, wrote: 'Mr. Taverner about Aeta 30 (besides his practise in the Law) has a wonderfull genius to drawing of Landskap in an excellent manner. adornd with figures in a stile above the common' (Vertue, vol.3, p.68). Vertue's estimate of Taverner's age as being about thirty in 1733 can now be revised, thanks to the recent discovery by John Tavener

that William Taverner was born and baptised at St Martin's Church, Ludgate, in London on 25 November 1700 (Tavener 1994).

The majority of Taverner's watercolours depict imaginary, ideal compositions in the manner of the great classical masters, Claude, Poussin and Gaspard Dughet (the latter was particularly fashionable with British artists in the early and middle years of the eighteenth century). This subject, for example, is an Italianate capriccio which features a classical temple in the far left-hand distance resembling that of the Temple of the Sibyl at Tivoli near Rome, although it is unusual for Taverner in not including foreground classical figures. In some of Taverner's landscapes, idealised or mythological figures are the artist's prime subject, often painted in the denser medium of bodycolour or gouache – that is watercolour mixed with lead white to make it opaque (an example in the Oppé collection, *Diana and her Nymphs*, T08520, is in watercolour and bodycolour). Indeed Taverner was one of the earliest artists in Britain to use bodycolour regularly in his work. Vertue recorded that he also painted in oil 'in a very commendable and masterly manner' (Vertue, vol.3, p.68), though only a few of his oil paintings are known today; examples are in the collections of the University of Liverpool and of the National Trust at Stourhead in Wiltshire (French 1970, p.15).

AL

WILLIAM TAVERNER
1700–1772

8 From Camberwell ? c.1750–65

Watercolour over pencil with touches of gouache on
laid paper 20 × 31.9 (7⅞ × 12½)
Inscribed on verso in pen and brown ink
'From Camberwell'
T08275

In addition to his imaginary, Italianate landscapes, Taverner painted more informal views of the English countryside. Some of these are large panoramic compositions, such as the view looking diagonally across the Thames near Richmond in the Oppé collection (T08239, fig.6). Although more naturalistic than his ideal landscapes, nevertheless many of these larger English scenes seem to retain a lingering classical sentiment. Others, however, such as this watercolour taken from Camberwell or a view by Taverner from Highgate in black and white chalks also in the Oppé collection, T08205, are much purer, direct renderings of the landscape the artist sees before him (the latter once belonged to the watercolourist Paul Sandby (no.25) who during his lifetime amassed at least twenty-five examples of Taverner's work; see Robertson 1985, p.14). A number of watercolours by Taverner of views behind Cavendish Square and in the environs of London were included in the sale of his effects in 1776 which took place four years after his death (Tavener 1994).

Indeed, Taverner's view from Camberwell has a breadth and a freedom of execution which, together with its naturalistic palette, suggests that it may well have been painted on the spot. There are few precedents in British watercolour for such expansive, unadorned transcripts of nature as these, with the exception perhaps of some of the landscape sketches produced by Dutch or Flemish artists working in England in the seventeenth and early eighteenth centuries. In particular, Peter Tillemans (1684–1734), who settled in England from 1708, painted a handful of landscape sketches which seem to anticipate those of Taverner (see Stainton and White 1987, p.244). We know from Vertue that Taverner was fully active as an artist by 1733 and it is possible that, as a young man, he was acquainted with Tillemans; certainly one writer has seen similarities in Taverner's early watercolours with Tillemans's own style of painting (Robertson 1985, p.14), and we also know that Taverner at one stage owned a battle painting by Tillemans (Tavener 1994). However, given that Taverner's work is so rarely dated and shows so little evidence of stylistic progression, it is very difficult to assess the likelihood and possible impact of artistic influences. Another possibility is that he was taught or at least greatly influenced by the landscape painter George Lambert (Einberg 1970, p.22). For Taverner would very likely have known Lambert through the theatre, his father William Taverner senior (c.1675–1731) being a playwright as well as a lawyer, whilst Lambert painted scenery for the theatre.

AL

52

SAMUEL SCOTT
c.1702–1772

9 A Lady with Hands Folded *c.1760*

Pencil and watercolour approx. 22 × 15.3 (8⅝ × 6)
on laid paper 24.4 × 15.3 (9⅝ × 6)
Inscribed in black ink on the back by Horace Walpole
'by Sam. Scott, Painter of Seapieces'

T08477

When Horace Walpole published in 1762 the first serious attempt at a survey of English art, *Anecdotes of Painting in England*, his Preface included the comment that Mr Scott was an artist 'who seems born for an age of naval glory, and is equal to it' (Walpole 1888, p.xiv). Earlier, in 1733, George Vertue had numbered Scott among 'the most elevated Men in Art' in London (Vertue, vol.3, p.61), an assessment made on the basis of a relatively small output of modest-sized oils depicting men-of-war and other craft in calm seas and a set of six pictures showing settlements belonging to the East India Company in which he painted the shipping and George Lambert (1700–1765) painted the buildings and landscape (Kingzett 1982, pp.69–72). He was so well known as a painter of seascapes and, indeed, Walpole's endorsement on the back of this sheet implies that this was really the only way his contemporaries could view him, that he was known as the 'English Van de Velde' after Willem Van de Velde the younger (1638–1707), the Dutch marine painter who worked in England from 1672 and many of whose drawings Scott later owned. However, while Scott made his reputation as a marine artist, from the early 1740s he was also sketching views of London subjects, notably views of Westminster and its new bridge. The arrival in London in 1746 of the Italian *vedutisto*, or painter of views, Canaletto, stimulated a demand for such views to which Scott responded by using these drawings as the basis for finished oils (for example *An Arch of Westminster Bridge* of *c.1750*, T01193; Einberg and Egerton 1988, no.140). Like Van de Velde and Canaletto, Scott made precise preparatory drawings for the principal architectural motifs in such works but he also made slightly freer studies, often in pen and ink and wash or watercolour, for what is called the staffage – a word used to describe the accessories or figures, which were then introduced into these scenes to bring them to life. Since Lambert has already been mentioned here as a collaborator with Scott, it is worth mentioning in this context that Lambert quite possibly adapted the figures which he put in his landscapes from drawings by William Hogarth (Einberg and Egerton 1988, p.159).

The finely dressed lady in this watercolour was introduced by Scott into the lower left foreground of three of the four versions of a large oil, *Covent Garden*, which date from *c.1760*, one of which is in the Museum of London (Kingzett 1982, pp.74–5, pl.25a), and she occurs again as a figure standing at a gate in Scott's oil painting of Broad Street, Ludlow (Kingzett, pp.68–9) which dates from after 1765. The same two pictures in addition share a horse and rider who must similarly have been based on an independent drawing. The Oppé collection also includes another watercolour study of a lady holding a basket (T08476) who also appears in the *Covent Garden* painting (Kingzett, no.D79, pp.93–4).

Samuel Scott lived in a house on the east side of Covent Garden Piazza – a house that was later inhabited by Richard Wilson (no.13) – and was as a result very much at the centre of London's burgeoning art life. Two promising young painters, Marlow (no.38) and Sawrey Gilpin (1733–1807), were his apprentices. He was a friend of Hogarth's (no.6) and in 1746 became a Governor of the Foundling Hospital. In 1755 he was on a committee, chaired by Francis Hayman (no.10), which proposed that a Royal Academy should be established. Another close friend, who lived a few doors away, was James Deacon (no.12), and they are shown together as members of a merry club, which included Horace Walpole's brother, which met at Scott's, in a tracing from a now lost painting by Marcellus Laroon (Raines 1966, pp.90, 153–4).

RH

FRANCIS HAYMAN
1708–1776

10 The Author and his Reader; A Frontispiece to *The Tatler* 1759

Pencil and grey wash on laid paper 13.5 × 9 (5¼ × 3½)
Inscribed bottom left in grey ink 'F.HAYMAN'
T08137

This drawing is one of four illustrations made by Hayman as frontispieces for a new 1759 edition (in four volumes) of *The Tatler, Or The Lucubrations of Isaac Bickerstaffe, Esq. The Tatler* was a periodical started in 1709 and edited by Richard Steele, who took on the name of Bickerstaffe, and it appeared three times a week until January 1711. Engraved by Charles Grignion (1717–1810) for volume I, this design takes its inspiration from Steele's words in the original dedication to the first volume: 'to expose the false arts of life, to pull off the disguises of cunning, vanity, and affectation, and to recommend a general simplicity in our dress, our discourse, and our behaviour', as well as those in the first issue, where he wrote that the 'end and purpose' of his paper was to instruct 'Gentlemen, for the most part … persons of strong zeal, and weak intellects' and 'worthy and well-affected members of the commonwealth' in what they should think after they have neglected 'their own affairs to look into the transactions of state'. Steele also wrote that each issue would 'have something which may be of entertainment to the Fair Sex, in honour of whom I have taken the title of this Paper' – a reference to 'tattlers', or idle talkers.

Working in the fashionable rococo style, Hayman produced nearly two hundred designs for book illustrations in the course of his career with almost half of them being engraved by Grignion (Allen 1987, pp.183–6). But he was also a leading history painter and had a flourishing portrait practice. So, in the spirit of Steele's general tone, this frontispiece gently upsets the conventions of the modern conversation piece in which Hayman himself and others customarily portrayed figures fashionably and elegantly disposed in groups – usually in handsome interiors. Hayman shows an author, his pen idle, sitting at his table, while his companion looks up from her journal: the atmosphere is one of exasperation and boredom – in marked contrast to the elegant detachment which was the currency of contemporary portraiture. The black cat, the normal symbol of the witch's familiar, can perhaps be seen as a witty allusion to Steele's references to 'false arts' and 'cunning' and maybe, even, to his female audience.

Drawings made specifically for engravings were usually executed in pen and ink and monochrome washes, as here, because engravings reproduced tone and line rather than colour. By coating the back of the drawing with graphite or something similar as this one was the design could be transferred directly onto the copper plate – hence its being printed in reverse (see fig.13) – and the indentations of Grignion's stylus where he followed Hayman's line in the course of doing this can be seen quite clearly, for example, on the author's leg.

RH

THE

TATLER;

Or, LUCUBRATIONS of

ISAAC BICKERSTAFF, Efq;

VOLUME the FIRST.

LONDON:

Printed for JACOB and RICHARD TONSON.

MDCCLIX.

fig. 13 *The Tatler* 1759, frontispiece and
title page to vol. 1
The British Library Board

JEAN BAPTISTE CLAUDE CHATELAIN
*c.*1710–*c.*1758

11 A View of the Wrekin Hill from Ercall, Shropshire *c.*1748

Watercolour over pencil with pen and black ink on laid paper
30 × 48.5 (11¾ × 19⅛)
T08125

Chatelain is chiefly remembered as one of the earliest landscape engravers in England, but he was also a talented landscape draughtsman and a drawing master of some repute. He was born either in Paris or, more likely, in London of French (Huguenot) parents. Accounts of his early life vary, one recent author claiming Chatelain was employed by the French army in Flanders in the capacity of draughtsman (Johnson 1994, p.44), another that he abandoned his career as an officer in the French army to become a draughtsman and engraver instead (Murdoch 1985, p.166). He is usually said to have died in 1771, but more up-to-date sources quote a contemporary account stating that Chatelain's demise came 'about 1758', after over-indulging in lobsters and asparagus (Alexander 1996, p.513; O'Connell 1997). He died in poverty at the White Bear in Haymarket, and was buried in the poor ground of a workhouse in central London, having converted to the Catholic faith (Murdoch 1985, p.166).

As an engraver and draughtsman Chatelain produced both imaginary and topographical landscapes – that is to say, views of actual places. The Oppé collection includes a number of his imaginary or 'fancy' landscapes, as Iolo Williams called them (1952, p.25). They are broadly classical in inspiration with, perhaps, flanking trees, a few decorative figures, a church or a castle in the middle distance silhouetted on a rocky crag with fantastic mountains beyond, and are almost invariably executed in pen and monochrome washes, or occasionally fine black chalk (Williams 1952, p.25 and pl.XXII). This view of Wrekin Hill, by contrast, is one of Chatelain's rarer and more substantial topographical drawings, and is unusual in

being coloured (another drawing by him in the Oppé collection, said to be a view of Wentworth Woodhouse in Yorkshire, T08820, is executed in grey washes). Chatelain's drawing of Wrekin Hill was engraved in 1748 with the full title *A View of the Wrekin Hill in the County of Salop taken from Birch tree Bank at Ercall 7 Miles from Y:ᵉ S:ᵈ Hill.*, though some of the image to the left was clipped in the print and the name of the engraver is not specified. Chatelain, thanks no doubt to his own experience as a printmaker (he was an especially skilled etcher), has supplied in the preliminary drawing both cloud formations and parallel ruled lines in the sky, which the engraver has followed faithfully in the print, though superimposed in parts with broken, diagonal shading.

In 1800, the German *émigré* and Oxford drawing master J.B. Malchair (no.24) told Farington that when, in the late 1750s, 'He first taught musick and drawing in London there were only 5 ore 6 drawing masters', mentioning Chatelain and Sandby (no.25) amongst them, and then adding that 'now', by contrast, 'there are hundreds' (*Diary*, 1 August, vol.4, p.1425). In his capacity as a drawing master Chatelain issued two publications, *A New Book of Landskips Pleasant & Useful for to learn to draw without a Master* (1737, published with Jean Rocque), and *Fifty Small ... Views ... Adjacent to London* (1750, etched by James Roberts I). Chatelain's reproductive engravings include a series of landscapes after paintings by Gaspard Dughet and others in British collections, issued for Arthur Pond's *Forty-Four Italian Landscapes* (1741–3) – Dughet's work being especially fashionable with British artists at this time.

AL

JAMES DEACON
*c.*1710–1750

12 Classical Landscape 1740/1743

Watercolour over pencil, varnished, on laid paper
21.9 × 23.6 (8⅝ × 9¼) on laid paper support 36 × 38.2 (14⅛ × 15)
with artist's wash-line mount

Inscribed in pencil on back of mount 'drawn by Ja⁵ Deacon
1740' and 'James Deacon fecit 1743'

T08256

Little is known about James Deacon and works by him are rare. He was the son of James Deacon, who was the Collector of the Coal Duty for the Port of London from 1716 until his death in June 1742. Just before Deacon senior died it was discovered that over many years he had defrauded the Revenue; the papers concerning this fraud, to which Deacon junior seems to have been privy, and a few notes made by the engraver-antiquarian George Vertue in his *Journal* in 1746, 1749 and 1750 are our main source of information about the artist (Vertue, vol.3, pp.132, 151, 153). In a sworn statement of April 1743, which gives us an approximate date for his birth, Deacon stated that he worked as a unpaid clerk in his father's office between about 1726 until about February 1741 (PRO Treasury Board Papers T1/312, f.15). The possibility of a charge being pressed against him led him in December 1744 to petition for it to be lifted on the grounds that 'he suffers very much by reason of [it] … and is not only deprived, by means thereof, of the good Offices of his Friends, but is reduced to great difficulties' (PRO Treasury Reference Book vol.10, T4/11, f.265). Vertue appears to have known nothing of the scandal surrounding Deacon, for when he first mentions him in 1746 he dwells chiefly on his natural genius, including his scholarship and musicianship, and singles out the 'curious Eye & … fine hand' which characterises his drawings, particularly some of his portrait heads, and he sees him as very much an amateur. J.T. Smith (Smith 1828, vol.2, p.204) notes that Deacon studied painting as an amateur under the artist Marcellus Laroon (1679–1772). In early 1746 or around March 1748 Deacon moved to the house in Covent Garden once occupied by the miniaturist

C.F. Zincke, 'expecting to thrive' in what was then the artists' quarter of London: he probably shared the house with the medallist Richard Yeo (d.1779) and he was a few doors away from Samuel Scott (no.9): Deacon's portraits of Scott and his wife are in the British Museum (repr. Kerslake 1977). It seems that on a technicality Deacon avoided prosecution but, ironically perhaps, he died on 21 May 1750 having caught gaol fever after attending a trial at the Old Bailey.

Another larger, undated classical landscape in watercolour by Deacon which belonged to the collector Charles Rogers is in the Cottonian Collection in Plymouth (Sotheby's 1979, no.61), and a small watercolour using elements found in T08256 is at the Yale Center for British Art (repr. Wilton and Lyles 1993, no.15). Both works owe a clear debt to the classical landscapes painted by Nicolas Poussin and Gaspard Dughet and very much reflect the taste of the circle of connoisseurs, among them Rogers, and artists, among them George Lambert (fig.5) and his collaborator Scott, in which Deacon probably moved. With its tight handling, its prominently placed temple and tiny figures in the middle distance dipping in the mirror-like water this work owes a greater debt to Nicolas Poussin. The second date inscribed by Deacon on this drawing may refer to the time he mounted it. Distinguished by a striking border of strips of paper painted with red lead and with the image itself varnished, it suggests that during his 'great difficulties' the artist had to find a cheap way of 'framing' his picture; small holes at each corner of the mount indicate that the picture was just pinned to a wall.

RH

RICHARD WILSON
1713–1782

13 Ariccia *c.*1754–6

Black chalk and stump on grey prepared laid paper
32.2 × 44.7 (12⅝ × 17⅝)
T08164

Born in Powys (Montgomeryshire), the son of an Anglican clergyman, Wilson spent most of his early career training to be a portrait painter. It was during his years in Italy between 1750 and 1757 that, encouraged by Francesco Zuccarelli (1702–1788) and Claude Joseph Vernet (1714–1789), he decided to concentrate exclusively on landscape. He became one of the most important landscape painters in Britain in the second half of the eighteenth century, his mature oils revealing a balance between his admiration for the works of the acclaimed masters of classical landscape – in his own words, 'Claude for air and Gaspard for composition and sentiment' – and at the same time a close attention to the actual appearances of nature.

Ariccia, situated south-east of Rome in the Alban Hills, was celebrated for its groves (thought to have been the hunting-grounds of the classical goddess Diana) and also as one of the favourite sketching sites of Gaspard Dughet; Wilson's oils of the town and its groves accordingly reveal a significant debt to that painter (Solkin 1982, p.203). However, there is no known oil painting by Wilson based on this study showing the town alone, with the Palazzo Chigi and Bernini's Church of Santa Maria dell'Assunzione. In fact most of Wilson's Italian drawings seem to have been made independently of his paintings, 'either as studies from nature, as ideas for compositions, as sketches of places visited, or as commissioned views' (Ford 1951, p.34). Some years later Wilson asked the painter Paul Sandby (no.25) to help find suitable buyers for his sketches among the latter's gentlemen pupils; however, finding a demand only for highly finished drawings, Sandby 'was induced to make the purchase himself' (Smith 1828, vol.1, p.117). This explains why Sandby's collector's mark (incorporating the initials 'PS') is found on many of Wilson's drawings, in this example in the lower left-hand corner below the mark of a later collector, A.G.B. Russell (respectively, Lugt 1921, no.2112 and Lugt 1956, no.2770a).

The majority of Wilson's drawings are executed either in chalks, pen and ink or pencil. His preferred method, first adopted in Italy from about 1753, was black and white chalks on paper of a middle tint, usually grey. He might then proceed, as in this drawing of *c.*1754–6, to soften and smudge some of the black chalk using a stump (a tightly rolled paper or leather cylinder with rounded points) to create rich areas of tone – an alternative to using a monochrome wash. This was a method Wilson was to use both for sketches and for finished drawings, such as the famous series of views of Rome and its environs made between 1754 and 1755 for the Second Earl of Dartmouth. He was later to recommend a similar method to his pupils, such as Thomas Jones (nos.43–5), so that they might be 'ground … in the Principles of Light & Shade without being dazzled and misled by the flutter of Colours' (Jones, *Memoirs*, p.9).

A L

RICHARD DALTON
1715 or 1720–1791

14 The Farnese Hercules 1742

Red chalk approx. 51.8 × 21.8 (20⅜ × 8½) on laid paper 52.9 × 36.5 (20⅞ × 14⅜)
laid down on laid paper 68 × 51.9 (26¾ × 20⅜) with artist's wash-line border
59 × 42.4 (23¼ × 16⅝)

Inscribed ΓΑΥΚΩΝ ΑΘΗΝΑΙΟΟ ΕΠΟΙΕΙ [GLYCON THE ATHENIAN MADE IT
– that is, the statue of Hercules] and 'R Dalton F- 1742' on the base of the statue
in red chalk

T08241

Dalton was apprenticed to a coach-painter in Clerkenwell and afterwards went to Rome to study drawing and painting. Among the earliest of eighteenth-century English painters to make this trip, he was there by March 1741 when he is reported by one Grand Tourist as not only 'by far the best of any of the English artists' there but also making drawings of 'some statues ... in red chalk ... for Lord Brooke' and drawings in black and white chalks on blue paper (seemingly reported by him as a technique of his own invention) of Raphael's frescos in the Loggia of Psyche and the *Triumph of Galatea* in the Villa Farnesina for the Countess of Hertford (Hertford 1805, vol.3, pp.102, 111). Like many artists in Italy he also dealt in art: in June 1743 he was in contact with Sir Horace Mann, the British envoy in Florence, about a Raphael that was for sale (Walpole 1937–83, vol.18, 1977, pp.235, 239). This is the first sign of the sort of entrepreneurship which later made him extraordinarily unpopular with his colleagues. In 1763, when Dalton, now Librarian to the Prince of Wales, returned to Italy and crossed paths with the engraver Robert Strange, Strange was moved to write to his patron that 'persecution was to haunt me even beyond the Alps, in the form of Mr. Dalton' (Dennistoun, 1855, vol.2, p.3). Dalton never lacked for good patrons, however, for in 1749 he had travelled to Greece, Turkey and Egypt with Lord Charlemont, and in 1778 George III made him the surveyor of the Royal pictures.

In all fourteen chalk drawings, all about the same size, made by Dalton from Antique sculptures are known, with thirteen of them in the Royal Collection (Oppé 1950, no.163): six, including another drawing of the Farnese Hercules, are dated 1741 and three 1742. The artist's wash-line border on this drawing suggests that it was one made for Lord Brooke. Dalton would have copied these marbles, not just because it was a commission but also for a very practical purpose: as records of great works of art they would inform his own art or any teaching he might do when he got back home. A portrait by Johann Zoffany in the Tate Gallery shows Dalton with such a drawing in his hand as he instructs his niece (Tate Gallery 1978, pp.44–5) and in 1770, just as the market for such images increased as the teaching of the recently founded Royal Academy emphasised the use of classical prototypes in pictures, John Boydell published a set of twenty prints after Dalton's drawings, including one from the Hercules (Bignamini and Postle 1991, no.23). The colossal statue of the Hercules which Dalton drew in the Farnese Palace was known throughout Europe and commented upon and copied by generations of writers and artists (Haskell and Penny 1981, pp.229–32). In Dalton's time it was not uncommon for the great and the good to be credited with classical attributes: the 1770 print of Hercules was dedicated by Dalton to Chichester Fortescue Esq. – with Hercules' legendary strength and honour linked to a surname which translates as 'strong shield'– just as he dedicated his print of Apollo, the god of medicine, to Dr Mead.

In the very act of copying, and also by drawing with red chalk, Dalton was, of course, self-consciously setting out to emulate those Renaissance draughtsmen who had used the same medium (as, indeed, they had used black and white chalk on blue paper) for the same purpose. Unlike Rubens, for example, who drew from the Farnese Hercules when he was in Italy in 1605–8 and reworked the subject for a later drawing of *Hercules Standing on Discord* (British Museum), Dalton never put his work to such a use for he never ventured into the area of history painting: in fact, Edward Edwards (1738–1806) wrote that Dalton 'as an artist never acquired any great powers' (Edwards 1808, p.182).

RH

ΓΛΥΚΩΝ
ΑΘΗΝΑΙΟΟ
ΕΠΟΙΕΙ

ALEXANDER COZENS
1717–1786

15 In the Farnese Gardens, Rome 1746

Pen and black ink and grey washes on laid paper;
image to ruled border 23.7 × 37.9 (9⅜ × 14⅞);
sheet size 24.5 × 39 (9⅝ × 15⅜)
Inscribed in pen and brown ink lower left 'Alex.ʳ Cozens.1746 Roma'

T08117

'Almost as full of Systems as the Universe' – so spoke the eccentric millionaire William Beckford of Fonthill in 1781 of his friend and artistic protégé Alexander Cozens. Today Cozens is best known for the treatises he wrote in which he attempted to categorise landscape types, the most famous of these being his last, *A New Method of Assisting the Invention in Drawing Original Compositions of Landscape* (1786), where he gave his most detailed explanation of how to compose landscapes using ink blots (see nos.18–20). Cozens was a deeply intellectual artist, and his treatises have a serious moral purpose, even if some of his contemporaries failed to grasp this, especially the topographer Edward Dayes (1763–1804) who disparagingly dubbed Cozens 'Blotmaster-General to the town'. For Cozens's systems for inventing imaginary landscape compositions were intended to produce landscapes which could evoke different types of mood and emotion in the viewer, and thus be spiritually uplifting (see under no.17). Indeed, in an era when landscape was considered one of the lowliest categories of painting (history painting being considered the most elevated), Cozens promoted the revolutionary idea that landscape was capable of effecting moral good.

Cozens was born in Russia in 1717. In the first of his articles on a British artist written in 1919 Paul Oppé confidently put paid to the long-standing rumour that Cozens was the illegitimate son of Peter the Great, surmising instead that the artist's father was Richard Cozens (from Deptford), one of the Tsar's principal shipbuilders. In his later, definitive account of the work of *Alexander and John Robert Cozens* (1952, pp.1–4) Oppé then speculated that Peter the Great may have been Alexander Cozens's godfather, something only recently confirmed (Sloan 1985, p.70). Cozens was educated in England from 1727 but appears to have returned to Russia in the early 1740s, sailing in 1746 from St Petersburg for Italy where he remained for two years. He was one of the earliest British artists to study in Rome, Richard Dalton having arrived only a few years before (see no.14).

Nearly sixty watercolours and drawings by Cozens have survived from his stay in Rome. A group of fifty-seven of them, now in the British Museum, were said to have been dropped by Cozens from his saddlebag on his way home to England through Germany, and later found and purchased by his son John Robert Cozens in Florence in 1776 (Sloan 1986, p.9). One of these is an unfinished grey wash study, *A Tomb by a Road*, on which Cozens superimposed a one-inch grid. This enabled him to transfer the design onto a second sheet, which he then worked up into this, the finished version of the composition, adding figures, clouds and careful pen-and-ink outlines to delineate form, as well as a signature and date (Sloan 1986, pp.14–15). Many years later J.R. Cozens was to make an evocative watercolour of this composition, without figures, presumably worked up from his father's unfinished wash sketch; John Robert's version is in the Fitzwilliam Museum, Cambridge (Munro 1994, p.51).

An important sketchbook also used by Alexander Cozens in Italy was published by Paul Oppé in 1928 (now Yale Center for British Art). As well as landscape and figure studies, the sketchbook contains written notes which reveal that whilst in Rome Cozens worked in the studio of the French landscape painter Claude-Joseph Vernet (1714–1789), with whom Richard Wilson was to become acquainted in the 1750s. Other notes by Cozens in the sketchbook are detailed, analytical schemes for sketching from nature, revealing a love of categorisation that would bear fruit in his later treatises on landscape.

AL

66

Alex. Cozens. 1744 Roma

ALEXANDER COZENS
1717–1786

16 Rocky Bay Scene ?c.1759–65

Oil on laid paper 16 × 18.7 (6¼ × 7⅜)
T08044

On his return from Italy (see no.15), Cozens became deeply involved in teaching drawing. From 1750 to 1754 he held the post of drawing master at Christ's Hospital, a London charity school. Then around 1763 he began teaching at Eton College near Windsor, his most famous pupil there being Sir George Beaumont (1753–1827), who later took lessons from Malchair (no.24) and subsequently became a famous connoisseur and collector. During the 1750s and 1760s Cozens began to take private pupils as well, and it seems most likely that his famous method of composing imaginary landscapes by means of ink blots evolved directly out of his teaching of amateurs. He first published the idea in 1759, in a short illustrated *Essay to Facilitate the Inventing of Landskips, Intended for Students in the Art*, though with rather rudimentary explanations (it was not until *A New Method* of 1786 that he provided a full set of instructions). Between 1760 and 1781 Cozens was also exhibiting his work, both oil paintings and monochrome drawings, at the Society of Arts, the Free Society and the Royal Academy.

Cozens would have learned how to use oils in Vernet's studio in Rome (see no.15), and in later years he is known to have shown an interest in the technical methods of oil painting. In 1768 the sporting artist Sawrey Gilpin (1733–1807) managed to obtain Cozens's 'secret' 'method of painting with tacky colours', sending a detailed description in a letter to his father that year (Sloan 1986, pp.164–5). Five years later the painter Ozias Humphry (1742–1810) wrote in his notebooks three recipes for varnishes which had been communicated to him by Cozens, as well as a light painting-oil containing finely powdered glass to secure quick drying which Cozens had probably learned in Italy (Oppé 1952, pp.82–3; all four recipes are given in Sloan 1986, p.166). Cozens seems to have been a fairly prolific painter in oils: as well as the seventeen or so examples he exhibited during his lifetime, twenty-one were included in the sale

of his effects at Christie's after his death; and ninety were included in his son's sale at Greenwoods in 1794 (Sloan 1986, p.82), the majority of these probably by Alexander since John Robert rarely painted in oil. However, only twelve examples of Alexander's work in oil are known today.

Of these twelve four are in the Oppé collection, from an album of Cozens's drawings formerly belonging to William Mackworth Praed (1756–1835), one of the artist's pupils (see under no.17). All are small coastal scenes at twilight or moonlight, and this example was regarded by Oppé as one of the most 'adventurous': 'the moon irradiates the clouds which hide it, and its light throws the more distant headlands and sea into shimmering blue, the nearer rocks and their reflections into deepest shade. With the simplest construction and the least possible detail the subtle play of light is the dominant feature' (Oppé 1952, pp.83–4). A group of five other small oils by Cozens is known which relates to an important unfinished treatise of his mid-career, *The Various Species of Landscape*, and it is possible that they were originally executed to publicise that project – in an undated letter to the Bath portrait painter William Hoare Cozens writes of his intention to paint small oils for just such a purpose (Leger 1996, pp.20–1; the letter is published in Oppé 1928, A, p.91). These four examples in the Oppé collection could similarly relate to another (earlier) treatise, or they may have been painted on commission – a different, undated letter to Hoare seems to imply that Cozens may sometimes have painted small oils for private clients (Oppé 1928, D, pp.92–3). *Rocky Bay Scene* itself is compositionally similar to a much larger and more elaborate exhibition oil by Cozens, *A Bay at Dawn*, which only recently turned up on the art market (Leger 1996, pp.16–23). His remaining two oils are views of Matlock dated 1756 (repr. Sloan 1986, p.38).

AL

ALEXANDER COZENS
1717–1786

17 The Cloud c.1770

Brown washes on laid tracing paper
23.3 × 31.3 (9⅛ × 12⅜)
T08057

Cozens was one of the earliest British artists to make the representation of skies and cloud formations a special category of study. Two important sequences of sky studies by him survive. One is an album in the Hermitage Museum in Leningrad, formerly belonging to his most celebrated pupil, William Beckford of Fonthill, containing twenty-five grey wash studies of skies in rather characterless landscapes. The second sequence comprises over twenty numbered pencil and monochrome wash drawings in the Mackworth Praed album in the Oppé collection, which illustrate Cozens's intentions for one of the categories, 'Circumstances', of a treatise he was working on in the late 1760s and early 1770s, *The Various Species of Composition of Landscape, in Nature*. This treatise was apparently never finished and was thus probably never published in full, but the evidence suggests that it was a very ambitious and complicated system indeed. Manuscript lists by students of some of Cozens's theories which relate to this project, as well as comments on it by contemporaries, indicate that the landscapes included in this system were intended to arouse specific emotions which would have a positive moral effect on those who viewed them (Sloan 1986, pp.56–61).

A list of contents survives for this treatise (repr. Sloan 1986, p.54) which shows that it was intended to consist of sixteen 'Compositions' (these were reproduced by Cozens as etchings and later copied by Constable (see no.82), fourteen 'Objects' and twenty-seven 'Circumstances'. The 'Circumstances' are especially interesting, as they correspond to the conditions which affect the atmosphere and colour or tone of a landscape – wind, fog, spring, summer, or the time of the day, for example – and thus contribute to its mood. Like the other twenty-three drawings said to be related to the 'Circumstances', *The Cloud* is also from the Mackworth Praed album – and, indeed, was originally mounted in sequence with them by the album's original compiler, Henry Stebbing (1752–1818), an enthusiastic 'disciple' of Cozens with an impressive understanding of his complex output. Although of a similar size to many of the other drawings related to the *Various Species of Landscape*, and like some of them also on varnished paper, *The Cloud* has not previously been linked with this treatise. Certainly, it is taken to a greater degree of finish than the others. However, it seems more than likely that it, too, is a composition relating to one of the 'Circumstances'; and in view of the inclusion of the sun just above the horizon to the far right, it may perhaps correspond with 'Circumstance' number 3, 'Rising-sun' or number 7, 'Setting-sun' (in fact its similarity with a recently discovered, related oil by Cozens suggests it may well represent the sunset view). Paul Oppé himself spoke especially movingly about this famous drawing, in which 'the earth is a mere stage above which the cloud makes the whole drama'; here 'Cozens allows his giant cumulus to surge up with its own force into the light from behind the dark hill, as thunderclouds rise in the height of summer ... heavy with rain but blazing with light, at once the most solid and menacing feature of the landscape and the most ephemeral. In no other drawing does Cozens reach to quite this degree of controlled but burning emotion' (1952, pp.99–100).

It has been argued that even the twenty-five sky studies in the Hermitage may have originally been produced by Cozens in connection with the *Various Species* (Sloan 1986, p.78). In the event the projected twenty-five skies were reduced to twenty and published as line-engravings in Cozens's *A New Method* of 1786, numbered 17–36 on five plates, with four to a sheet (repr. Wilton 1980, pls.20–3). In 1823 they were copied by Constable (repr. Reynolds 1984, pls.442–60). Like Cozens, Constable recognised the importance of the sky in providing the mood of a picture, famously declaring 'It will be difficult to name a class of Landscape, in which the sky is not the "*key note*", the *standard of* "*Scale*", and chief "*Organ of sentiment*"' (letter, 23 October 1821; Beckett 1968, p.77).

AL

18 A Blot: Landscape Composition *c.*1770–80

Brush and dark grey, brown and black washes with slight traces of pencil on laid paper
prepared with a yellow wash
16.2 × 20.7 (6⅜ × 8⅛)

Inscribed in pencil upper left '4', and in ink on verso 'on yᵉ other hand we ought to
have an Idea of yᵉ Whole which we want to produce | distinct from any other Whole,
but that Idea must be form'd only in yᵉ gross, without | an[y] [ex]act conception of
yᵉ Parts, or form'd so imperfectly as that nothing shall | interfere with, or hinder us
from comprehending, yᵉ Whole, & if possible that alone. | Therefore that yᵉ Pupil may
arrive at this knowledge of Parts, or more | properly speaking, be enabld to lay up a
plentifull store of ideas of yᵉ forms of | Objects which belong to Drawing, I imagine
nothing can be more conducive than a | constant use & close observation of parts of
Objects, already well represented, that | is to say yᵉ drawings of a Master, or good Prints,
but I cheifly rely upon is, their | frequency of this, & that yᵉ Method. by which it is carried
on shall be as quick | & short as possible, at yᵉ same time sufficient to make yᵉ Pupil
produce his forms | in yᵉ most perfect degree of Imitation of yᵉ Original, especially
with regard to propor:tion | nothing answers this purpose so well as Tracing which
will be explaind | '

T08114

Cozens's famous 'blot' technique was fully evolved by
the 1750s, but he did not explain it in detail until the
publication of *A New Method of Assisting the Invention
in Drawing Original Compositions of Landscape* (1786). The
idea seems originally to have been developed by him as a
teaching aid, to liberate the imagination of the student
who, he felt, spent too much time in copying the works
of others. In *A New Method* he explains that 'an artificial
blot is a production of chance, with a small degree
of design' and should be embarked on only after the
practitioners had possessed their minds 'strongly with a
subject'. He defines the 'true blot' as 'an assemblage of
dark shapes or masses made with ink upon a piece of
paper, and likewise of light ones produced by the paper
being left blank'. A blot, then, is not a drawing as
such but 'an assemblage of accidental shapes', 'forms
without lines from which ideas are presented to the mind'
and from which a drawing may be made (see no.20).
Cozens admits that the title of his treatise derives from
a passage in Leonardo da Vinci's *Treatise on Painting*
(available in an English translation of 1721), in which
the eminent Renaissance painter recommended a 'new
method of assisting the Invention ... in opening the

mind' – namely, that artists might study random stains
or marks on an old wall and thus furnish themselves with
an 'abundance of designs and subjects prefectly new'.
However, Cozens points out that his own method is an
improvement on Leonardo's, since instead of waiting for
random shapes to suggest ideas, blotting is done deliberately, the 'rude forms' which result having been made 'at
will'.

This blot is numbered '4' and broadly corresponds with
blot 5 of *A New Method*, defined as 'A narrow flat, almost
parallel and next to the eye, bounded by a narrow range
of groups of objects' – though it is not a preliminary
study, even if Cozens was constantly rearranging the
numbered sequences of his proposed treatises. The long
inscription on the reverse may be an early (abandoned)
draft for some of *A New Method's* explanatory text. Oppé
pointed out that the idea that the student might 'lay up
a plentifull store of ideas of ... forms of objects' for a
drawing (especially by tracing them) is related to the idea
in Rule IV (section 5) of *A New Method* where a pupil is
advised to make individual blots of specific objects on
separate pieces of paper and then to trace them (1952,
pp.67–8, 76 and 182).

AL

ALEXANDER COZENS
1717–1786

19 A Blot: Tigers *c.*1770–80

Brush and grey and black washes on laid paper
19.7 × 28 (7¾ × 11)
T08116

Much of the text to Cozens's *A New Method of Assisting the Invention in Drawing Original Compositions of Landscape* (1786) is devoted to expounding the idea of the 'blot' as an image of great suggestive power – by implication one as infinitely various as the cloud in the passage from Shakespeare's *Anthony and Cleopatra* (Act IV, Scene ii) which he quotes on the title-page:

> Sometime we see a Cloud that's dragonish,
> A Vapour sometime like a Bear, or Lion,
> A tower'd citadel, a pendant Rock,
> A forked Mountain, or Promontory,
> With Trees upon't, that nod unto the World
> And mock our Eyes with Air.

In theory, then, almost any subject might be suggested by a blot. In practice, however, Cozens makes it clear early on in the treatise that his brief is the 'Composing [of] landscapes by invention', and it is only landscape blots which he chooses to illustrate, along with a repertoire of skies that might be incorporated into such designs (see under no.17). Later on in the treatise, under Rule IV, section 5, he suggests that the student might make separate blots of 'single parts or objects' that might be incorporated into a landscape drawing, such as 'trees, thickets, water, rocks etc' (see also under no.18). However, judging by the blots that survive, neither he nor his pupils can often have made such specialised blots as these, least of all of animal forms – this one apparently being unique.

Oppé calls this 'the most oriental' of all Cozens's designs, and, indeed, it had a powerful impact on the Chinese author Chiang Yee when he saw the drawing in the 1930s (Oppé 1952, p.102, and Chiang Yee, *The Silent Traveller in London*, 1938, p.158). Oppé likens Cozens's procedure to that of the Chinese artist, emphasising his power of memory in retaining a subject (perhaps only casually seen for an instant), and then unconsciously moulding it into pictorial form, freed from all superfluous detail and incident. In this drawing, Oppé writes, 'Cozens omits all minor recognizable details and allows the unconscious swirl of his hand to project the mental image of the beasts with the movement and vitality of their masses' (1946, p.9). Cozens wrote in *A New Method* that 'in order to be able to make out designs from blots', 'a person must have genius', and he defined 'true genius' as the power which 'conceives strongly, invents with originality, and executes readily'. Such qualities apply wholeheartedly to this drawing, with its bold design, simplicity of form and vigorous, expressive brushwork.

As Oppé pointed out, a true blot must, strictly speaking, have no sky and be completed in brushwork in only one tone of black on white paper. This blot, however, has a layer of grey wash applied over the brushwork, whilst no.18 has both sky and additional washes. Blots were, of course, intended to be worked up by means of tracing into more elaborate and detailed drawings (see no.20). However, for quite a number of them, including nos. 18 and 19, Cozens seems to have been content just to add a sky or a wash of grey or brown, and then leave them as they stood; Oppé called these 'blot-sketches' (1952, pp.100–2).

AL

74

ALEXANDER COZENS
1717–1786

20 Mountainous Landscape with Cypresses c.1770–80

Grey and black washes on laid paper prepared with either
an oil or a mastic ground 44.8 × 57 (17⅝ × 22½)
T08240

In *A New Method for Assisting the Invention in Drawing Original Compositions of Landscape* (1786) Cozens illustrates sixteen 'blots' (engraved in aquatint, probably by himself) of various kinds of composition of landscape, as well as different sort of skies (see nos.18 and 19). These were followed by seven further plates, including two more 'blots' and five worked-up landscapes based on them (repr. Wilton 1980, pls.24–5), the latter five engraved in a mixture of aquatint and mezzotint by William Pether (1731–c.1816), the printmaker and portrait miniaturist under whom Henry Edridge (no.74) later trained. This, one of the largest and most elaborate of all Cozens's drawings, is similar to these finished landscapes illustrated in *A New Method*, and like them was probably worked up from a blot.

In Rules IV and V of *A New Method* Cozens explains how to make and then finish a sketch worked up from a blot. A sheet of tracing paper was first attached onto the selected blot, and the outlines of any figures or animals which were to be introduced were added onto the sheet in pencil. A blot survives by Alexander Cozens and by his son John Robert for a composition of *Hannibal Passing the Alps* which still has its sheet of tracing paper attached (fig.14). It shows some preliminary pencil and pen work defining a few fir trees and mountain contours, as well as being squared up for enlargement – small blots would, presumably, often have needed translating into larger drawings like *Mountainous Landscape with Cypresses*, but this is something Cozens fails to discuss in *A New Method*. The Hannibal blot is also of special interest in having been made on a sheet of wrinkled paper, for at one stage in *A New Method* Cozens recommends the option of crumpling the paper before a blot was started in order to produce a greater variety of accidental shapes; being done before any ink was applied, the crumpling of the paper did not affect the general design, as is sometimes

mistakenly thought – a misconception Oppé was at pains to correct (1952, pp.65–6).

After the pencil had been added (if at all), the sketch itself was started and was to be executed entirely with the brush in diluted drawing ink (a recipe for which Cozens gives in Rule I). Once the sketch was made, more specific details might be introduced, such as water, rocks, or trees. Cozens's own craggy peaks are reminiscent of the other-worldly rocks in the fantastic landscapes of fifteenth-century Flemish artists such as Pieter Breughel or Paul Bril (Wilton 1980, p.9), though his trees, like the cypresses here, tend to be more recognisable species, perhaps corresponding to examples published in his treatise *The Shape, Skeleton and Foliage of Thirty-two Species of Trees* (1771). The artist was then to 'adapt a sky proper to the landscape' from the selection offered in *A New Method*, and finally the rest of the composition was to be worked up to an appropriate degree of finish, paying particular attention to aerial perspective. In this example, as Oppé writes, 'Hills enclose the plain and an arm of the sea into which the river flows. Here every detail is worked out, curve balancing curve, shadow creating and contrasting with light, and the pattern receding into space with a suggestion of infinity' (1952, p.91).

Cozens's systems are often highly complex and technical, and were certainly not for the faint hearted; as Oppé says of the closing sections of *A New Method*, 'no one who reads it can ever think again of Cozens' methods as having been devised for the entertainment of fashionable idlers at Bath or elsewhere' (1952, p.69). His systems exerted an important influence on a number of contemporary and later artists, including Joseph Wright of Derby (no.29) and William Gilpin (1724–1804), but especially on Cozens's own son, John Robert Cozens (nos.59–61), as well as on John Constable (no.82).

AL

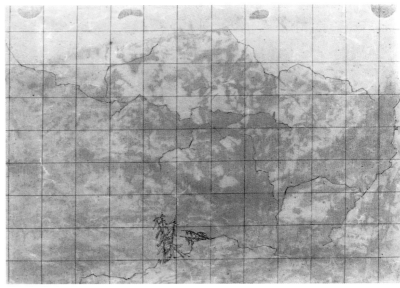

fig. 14 Alexander and John Robert Cozens, *Blot for 'Hannibal Passing the Alps'* c.1776, pencil, pen and brown ink tracing over black wash sketch
The Board of Trustees of the Victoria and Albert Museum

DOMINIC SERRES

1722–1793

21 General View of the Environs of Naples 1787

Watercolour over pencil with pen and black ink on laid paper 20.4 × 37.8 (8 × 14⅞);
artist's washline mount 26.2 × 43.5 (10¼ × 17⅛)

Inscribed lower left 'D.S.' and on verso in pen and black   ink 'General View of the Environs of Naples |
1. Elisian Fields. 2. Puzzuoli [sic]. 3. Convent of Camalduli. 4. Solfatara 5. Bay of Puzzuoli,
6. Castle St Elmo. | 7 Mount Vesuvius. 8. Posilipo. 9. Nisida. 10. Bay of Misenum. 11. Portici.
12. Ruins of Misenum. 13. Castelamare | 14. Cape Misenum, 15. Capo Minerva: 16. Mare Morto. |
D.Serres. 1787. N°. 51'

T08269

The Frenchman Dominic Serres spent the whole of his working life as an artist in England, practising almost exclusively as a marine painter. Born in Gascony in 1722, and said to have been the nephew of the archbishop of Reims, he ran away to sea to avoid a career in the Church. When master of a trading vessel to Havana he was taken prisoner by a British frigate and brought to England 'by 1758' or probably earlier (Cordingly 1974, p.83). 'Honest and inoffensive', according to one contemporary, 'though in his manners *un peu du Gascon*', Serres rose rapidly in London's artistic establishment, thanks in particular to his 'ostensibly documentary visual accounts of the sea actions of the seven years war' (Deuchar 1996, p.481). In 1768 he was one of the thirty-six founder members of the Royal Academy – the only marine painter to be so, albeit sharing minority status with two flower painters and a painter of animals (Quarm and Wilcox 1987, p.20); and in 1791 he became Marine Painter to the King.

Whilst Serres's son, John Thomas Serres (also a talented marine painter), is known to have visited Rome and Naples between 1790 and 1791, the evidence for a visit by Dominic Serres to southern Italy is purely circumstantial. In addition to this view by him of the environs of Naples, there are also watercolours of *Shipping off Sorrento* (dated 1788; Christie's 18 November 1980, lot no.18) and of *Agropoli, the Temple of Pasteum and the Bay of Salerno* (Yale Center for British Art). He also produced an oil, *Their Sicilian Majesties' return to Naples from Leghorn* (National Maritime Museum), which he specified as having painted in London in 1787 and which

he exhibited at the Royal Academy the following year. It is possible that his watercolours of views in and around Naples were executed in England as well, perhaps following a visit to Italy in 1786.

This watercolour shows the view looking towards Naples across the Bay of Pozzuoli from the west – from the basin of the 'Mare Morto' ('Dead Sea') which used to be part of the old harbour of Misenum; the drifting smoke of Mount Vesuvius can be made out on the horizon. It is a modest, gently coloured drawing which nevertheless reveals a regard for subtle atmospheric effects which Serres is said to have learned from the marine painter Charles Brooking (1723–1759). Serres has annotated the watercolour with the numbers one to sixteen, corresponding to significant landmarks in the view which are then described by him in a key on the reverse – a system he adopted, though in shorter form, for the watercolour of Agropoli as well. This provision of detailed information complete with key is commonly found on topographical prints and may indicate that Serres intended some of these watercolours to be engraved (the number '51' on the back of this drawing may indicate that it was part of a series). The combination of yellow and pink for the artist's washline mount is also used by Skelton for one of his mounts (no.32).

In later life Serres was a friend and neighbour of Paul Sandby (no.25) in Bayswater, and like Sandby formed an important collection of old master and contemporary drawings. It was inherited and then dispersed by his son J.T. Serres following the latter's marriage to the spendthrift landscape painter Olivia Wilmot.

AL

GIOVANNI BATTISTA CIPRIANI
1727–1785

22 Design for the Illumination for the King's Birthday 1771

Pen and ink and watercolour on laid paper 46 × 60.5 (18 × 23½)

Inscribed on reverse 'Illumination of the Royal Academy the first year of its
removal to Sommersethouse | on his Majestys birthnight 1771 when the mob by
throwing Squibs set fire to a part thereof | and endangered the Palace wh occasioned
the discontinuances of these elegant shows'

T08124

Cipriani was one of the earliest exponents in England of
the neo-classical style and was particularly admired in
his day for his draughtsmanship. Born and trained
in Florence, initially under the Anglo-Florentine artist
Ignazio Enrico Hugford (1703–1778), he travelled to
Rome in 1750 where he came into contact with the
architect Sir William Chambers (1726–1796) and the
sculptor Joseph Wilton (1722–1803). He was pursuaded
by them to come to England, where he arrived in 1756
and remained for the rest of his life. Throughout
his career Cipriani remained firmly associated with
Chambers, producing decorative designs for the interiors
of his neo-classical buildings, as well as for their external
ornamentation. This is certainly the case with Chambers's
Somerset House, the Strand block of which became
the new headquarters for the Royal Academy in 1780.
Cipriani was responsible for the exterior sculpture, which
was carved among others by Wilton; and he also designed
decorative panels and friezes for the interior of the
Library and for the Staircase (Croft-Murray 1970, p.189).

Cipriani was a Founder Member of the Royal
Academy of Arts which officially came into being on 10
December 1768. Membership was drawn from 'Painters,
Sculptors, or Architects, men of fair moral character, of
high reputation in their several professions'. Each year the
Academicians staged an annual exhibition and dinner and
celebrated the King's birthday by illuminating the front of
their building, after which they adjourned to dine at the
Free Masons' tavern on Great Queen Street (Hutchison
1986, p.40). This design is for the 1771 illuminations
which, according to the inscription on the reverse, were
the last of their type, the building having been set on fire
and endangered by 'the mob … throwing Squibs'.
Although the drawing is in Cipriani's hand, the creation
of the illuminations was in fact a communal effort.
Further inscriptions on the reverse make it apparent that
Sir William Chambers was responsible for the overall
conception of the design (appropriately, 'Architecture' is
represented on the left; 'Sculpture' on the right and
'Painting' in the centre, surmounted by the arms of the
Academy's patron, George III), while other Founder
Members took charge of the actual execution of individual sections of it. Charles Catton (1728–1789), George
III's coach painter, executed the royal arms; Nathaniel
Dance (nos.30–1) painted the figure of 'Sculpture';
Cipriani painted the octagonal grisaille above, as well as
the large central figure of 'Painting'; John Inigo Richards
(1731–1810) and Samuel Wale (1721–1786) painted the
decorative panels on either side; while Benjamin West
(no.26) took charge of 'Architecture'. Biagio Rebecca
(1735–1808) painted the urns and decorative swags, and
was the only non-Founder Academician involved,
although he had enrolled as a student at the Academy
Schools in 1769.

Cipriani had an abiding interest in art education.
Soon after his arrival in England he had become, jointly
with Wilton, tutor at the Duke of Richmond's Cast
Gallery in Whitehall, and had also subscribed to the
second St Martin's Lane Academy, set up by Hogarth
in 1735, out of which, arguably, the main forces for
setting up a public or Royal Academy in London grew
(Bignamini 1988, pp.95–124). He also taught at the Royal
Academy Schools. In 1775 he became 'Master of the
Living-Academy' (that is, the life class), and having had
arguments in the past with Michael Moser, the Keeper of
the Schools, concerning its organisation, it was formally
agreed that none 'shall presume to enter the Room whilst
the Visitor [Cipriani] is setting the Model' (Hutchison
1986, p.43).

During his lifetime Cipriani was widely admired for
the clarity of his drawing style, which people could
observe at the annual Academy exhibitions, and also
through the numerous engravings that his friend and
fellow Italian Francesco Bartolozzi (1725–1815) made
after his designs. After his death, Bartolozzi engraved and
published his *Rudiments of Drawing* (1786–92).

TB

THOMAS GAINSBOROUGH
1727–1788

23 Study of a Cow in a Landscape *c.*1758–9

Pencil on laid paper prepared with a yellow ground
15.3 × 18.8 (6 × 7⅜)
T08111

The Suffolk-born artist Thomas Gainsborough was one of the greatest portrait painters of his day, a significant rival to Joshua Reynolds with whom he is often compared. However, Gainsborough was also an important landscape painter – with Richard Wilson (no.13) he is considered a 'founding father' of the British landscape school – and always thought of himself as a landscapist, maintaining he only painted portraits to earn a living. Unlike Wilson, Gainsborough's landscapes are rarely inspired by classical, Italianate examples. Rather, his early Suffolk scenes combine a strong naturalistic bent with the influence of seventeenth-century Dutch masters such as Hobbema and Jacob van Ruisdael, whilst his later landscapes are pastoral idylls intended, as Constable was later to write, 'to deliver a fine sentiment'. However, like Wilson, Gainsborough was an enthusiastic and accomplished draughtsman. In fact, more drawings survive by Gainsborough than for any other landscape artist in this period.

In his early career Gainsborough's preferred drawing medium was pencil, and his favoured subject-matter plants, trees or animals, mossy banks, woodland paths and thickets. Such subjects are generally observed from a close viewpoint, and almost certainly drawn from nature – this example dating from the end of the 1750s at the close of the artist's Suffolk period, just before his departure for Bath. Drawing for Gainsborough has been described by one author as an act of love and of recreation, even a contemplative activity, rather than a means of storing up ideas and information (Hayes 1970, p.16). However,

Gainsborough did sometimes turn to these early studies for compositional ideas (they were originally made by him in sketchbooks and thus available for reference). For example, he later incorporated without alteration a very similar study of a reclining cow in the Oppé collection (T08110) into a larger more elaborate drawing, as he also did (into a different composition study) an early drawing of a sleeping sheep (Hayes 1970, p.310 and Hayes 1980, p.52). This pencil drawing has been coated by Gainsborough with a layer of fixative, which has subsequently discoloured (an effect exaggerated by the fact that he is working on a paper prepared with a yellow ground, Bower 1997, p.51). In a letter of 1773 to the painter William Hoare of Bath, Gainsborough recommended 'skim'd milk' for fixing chalk (see Hayes 1970, p.23), though whether he used the same substance for fixing pencil is not known.

Indeed, by 1770 Gainsborough had completely abandoned the use of pencil in favour of chalks, his daughter explaining that 'he cd. not with sufficient expedition make out his effects' (quoted Hayes 1970, p.22). It seems that the rapidity with which chalk could be handled was now better suited to his aims and temperament. For although Gainsborough might sometimes use chalks on coloured papers for sketching from nature, more often than not he would be using this combination of media for the picturesque landscapes he was contriving towards the end of his life in the studio from 'stones, bits of looking glass, small boughs of trees, and other suitable objects' (Edwards 1808, p.135).

AL

JOHN 'BAPTIST' MALCHAIR
1729–1812

24 Barmouth 1795

Pencil and grey washes on laid paper
31.7 × 45.1 (12½ × 17¾)
Inscribed on the verso in red chalk '52'
T08210

John 'Baptist' Malchair was one of the most influential drawing masters operating in Britain in the last two decades of the eighteenth century. Born in Cologne and by profession a musician (his instrument was the violin), he began taking pupils to supplement his income on his appointment as leader of the Oxford Music Room Orchestra in 1759. By the late 1760s he had built up a successful practice as a teacher of drawing, finding a plentiful supply of pupils amongst the undergraduates in the city. About forty of his Oxford pupils are known by name, some of whom were later to become talented amateur artists or influential patrons and collectors such as Sir George Beaumont (1753–1827) and Lord Aylesford (see no.58). Amongst his better-known later pupils are the Revd William Henry Barnard (no.72) and Oxford's precocious Professor of Music, William Crotch (no.76). The latter – 'if not a direct pupil, at least an ardent disciple'– also became a close friend, supporting Malchair in old age when forced to give up teaching on losing his sight (Williams 1952, p.91).

If Malchair's importance rests chiefly with the influence he exerted on his pupils, his own work is not without a certain understated charm and, in later life, was capable of great expressive force. Paul Oppé, whose 1943 article remains the most substantial source of information on the artist to date, defined three main categories in Malchair's output: ideal landscapes made as instruction drawings for his pupils, didactic in function and rather pedestrian in spirit; drawings made in and around Oxford, valuable for their refreshingly unconventional approach to composition as well as for their topographical content; and the late Welsh studies, especially those made, like this view of Barmouth, on the artist's final tour of the country in 1795, which reveal a new breadth and freedom of handling. (Oppé 1943, *passim*).

The change in style at the end of Malchair's life, and the fact that he was now working on a larger scale, is partly attributable to his failing eyesight but also to the dramatic impact of the Welsh scenery itself. One of the most striking drawings in the series, *Moel-y-Ffrydd* (fig.15), was described by Iolo Williams as 'a really remarkable drawing of a long, sharp saddle-back of mountain stretching and rising away from the spectator's eye' (Williams 1952, p.93). There can be little doubt that these late Welsh drawings were largely executed on the spot. Indeed, this subject is almost certainly identifiable with the drawing described by Malchair himself as 'Part of Barmouth near the harbour, here we had a great crowd of spectators ... the sea sand whirled over the houses, quite coverd our paper' (manuscript list of drawings made on the 1795 tour, collection Ian Fleming-Williams). Malchair's Welsh drawings, about seventy in total, were later owned by William Crotch and mostly numbered by him in red chalk on the back; this one is the fifty-second in the series. An interesting album containing reduced versions of thirty-nine of the Welsh subjects by Malchair himself is in the National Museum of Wales, Cardiff.

AL

fig. 15 John 'Baptist' Malchair, *Moel-y-Ffrydd* 1795,
pencil and grey wash
*Tate Gallery, presented by Ian Fleming-Williams in
1995 to celebrate the Tate Gallery Centenary 1997*

PAUL SANDBY

1730–1809

25 Rochester, Kent *c*.1785–95

Watercolour over pencil on laid paper 24.6 × 38.1 (9⅝ × 15);
artist's border 25.4 × 38.8 (10 × 15¼)

T08474

Paul Sandby is the best-known, most prolific and most versatile of a number of British watercolourists active in the second half of the eighteenth century who specialised in topography – the detailed and accurate representation of particular places or localities. He was a founder member of the Royal Academy, and one of the few artists to exhibit watercolours there in its early years. In this way he helped to raise the status of watercolour and, indeed, is often referred to as the 'founding father' of British watercolour painting, although he also worked in gouache (bodycolour) and in oils, as well as being a pioneering printmaker. His elder brother, Thomas Sandby (1723–1798), was also a founder member of the Royal Academy and its first Professor of Perspective.

The Sandby brothers were the sons of a Nottingham framework knitter, and both initially trained as military draughtsmen at the Board of Ordnance in the Tower of London. After the defeat of the Jacobite uprising in 1746, Paul was employed on the Military Survey of the Scottish Highlands, settling on his return at Windsor alongside Thomas, recently appointed Deputy Ranger of the Great Park under the Duke of Cumberland (George II's favourite son). Although Paul moved to London in 1760, he continued to visit Windsor regularly over the next decade. The watercolours he made of the Castle and Park during these years are amongst the most impressive of his entire career, with their sparkling light, crisp detail, skill in rendering different textures and inclusion of sensitively observed, well-drawn figures. The finest group are in the Royal Collection, and were catalogued by Paul Oppé in 1947 (see also Roberts 1995).

Following his appointment in 1768 as Chief Drawing Master at the Royal Military Academy in Woolwich, Sandby took lodgings at Old Charlton in Kent. In the ensuing years he was often to be found drawing in the county, at Charlton itself, at Whatman's paper mills near Maidstone and also at Canterbury and Rochester. Sandby painted several views of Rochester in the 1780s and 1790s, mostly observed from across the Medway (an example in gouache is in the Whitworth Art Gallery, Manchester), though there are other examples like this one where the city (with its prominent castle keep) is seen from a closer and more oblique angle. Like most of Sandby's later watercolours, it is freer in handling, richer in colouring (this being a sunset view), and the topographical element is less pronounced. One author even detects in these later watercolours a certain weakness in the figure drawing (Herrmann 1986, p.116), and it has to be admitted that in this composition Sandby has misjudged the relative scales of the figures to the left.

Sandby was a great experimenter with materials and techniques. He sometimes made his own pigments, once managing to create two different blacks from the burnt crust of a French loaf and from split peas parched over a fire (letter 1797; Sandby 1892, pp.110–11). His aquatint engravings of Wales (1775–7) are amongst the earliest made in Britain, and helped popularise the country at a time when it was still little visited by artists or travellers. There is a fine portrait of Sandby as a young man by Francis Cotes (1726–1770) in the Tate Gallery (N01943).

AL

86

JOHN INIGO RICHARDS
1731–1810

26 Near Charlton, Kent ?*c*.1753–65

Watercolour over pencil on laid paper
14.5 × 21.2 (5¾ × 8⅜)

Inscribed verso in pen and brown ink on attached label, probably in Richards's hand, 'Near Charlton, – Kent', and again by J.H. Anderdon 'by John Richards R.A.'

T08270

Like George Lambert (1700–1765), whose pupil he was, John Inigo Richards combined a career as both landscape and scenery painter. From 1759, like Lambert before him, Richards worked at the Covent Garden theatre, collaborating amongst others with Cipriani (no.22), and where from 1777 to 1803 he was principal painter. He was a painter chiefly of topographical landscapes, exhibiting at the Society of Artists and Free Society, and later at the Royal Academy, of which he was a founder member, in 1768. He worked quite extensively in watercolour, usually on a smallish scale as here, and in an attractive palette of greys, greens, pinks, salmon-reds, and rich, strong blues (for skies). His watercolours show a wide range of finish, sometimes being fairly elaborate with carefully applied detail, at other times more loosely painted, especially in the skies – and many show extensive and vigorous penwork. Martin Hardie felt Richards was 'ahead of his time, certainly ahead of Sandby … in diversifying the colour in his washes and in softening their edges' (1966, vol.1, p.163).

The topographical range of Richards's watercolours is quite extensive, covering locations in Kent, Surrey and the West Country and as far afield as Ireland. One of his earliest dated watercolours, a view in the British Museum of *St Regadon's Abbey, Kent* of 1753 (that is, St Radigund's Abbey), would imply that Richards was sketching in that county from the early days of his career – and this may well have been the case. However, this view by him of Charlton Wood in Kent is known in an almost identical watercolour version in the British Museum (repr. Hayes 1970, pl.272) attributed either to Lambert or to another artist working in his circle, Jonathan Skelton (nos.32–3). Richards's watercolour includes the extra detail of a figure leaning against some paling in the upper left, but

may have been copied from the version in the British Museum. Alternatively, both watercolours could have been copied after a (lost) oil of this composition by Lambert, *A view of Charlton Wood in Kent*, listed as item no.27 in the sole surviving copy of the *Catalogue of the Genuine Collection of Pictures, of … Mr. George Lambert*, 1765. The existence of these different versions highlights the difficulties which abound in correctly assessing the complex range of material in the Lambert circle. The question is also raised as to what extent Richards's watercolours in general are copied after works by others rather than being original sketches gathered on his tours around the country.

In 1788 Richards became Secretary at the Royal Academy, a post he held until his death in 1810. He is represented in a drawing by George Dance (no.41) with the Academy's printer settling the catalogue for 1795. In his capacity as Secretary Richards catalogued the Academy's collection of works of art, and in 1791 was paid twelve guineas to repair its cartoon by the celebrated Renaissance artist Leonardo da Vinci of the *Virgin and Child with Ss Anne and John the Baptist*, now in the National Gallery (Williams 1952, p.40).

This watercolour, along with nine others by Richards in the Oppé collection, came from the collection of J.H. Anderdon (1790/3–1879). They originally belonged to a set of extra-illustrated (or 'grangerised') volumes he assembled covering the annual exhibitions of the Society of Artists of Great Britain between 1760 and 1791, being disposed of by him at some stage before he presented the volumes to the British Museum in 1867. The latter still contain a further eleven watercolours by Richards, many of them annotated like this one in his hand.

AL

SAMUEL HIERONYMOUS GRIMM
1733–1794

27 Creswell Crags, Derbyshire 1785

Watercolour with pen and black ink on laid paper
25.9 × 37.2 (10¼ × 14⅝)
Inscribed centre foreground in pen and black ink
'S.H. Grimm fecit 1785'

T08113

Grimm's career, like Sandby's, is characterised chiefly by his substantial output as a topographical draughtsman, and his watercolours have a similiar precision and charm. Like Sandby, he was for many years an exhibitor at the Royal Academy (although never, like the former, an Academician). However, to a much greater extent than Sandby Grimm remained dependent for his livelihood on private patrons and the expanding market for antiquarian publications.

The son of a Swiss notary from Burgdorf, Grimm received his early training under the Bernese topographer J.L. Aberli (1723–1786) who is known for his colour prints of Swiss scenery. After a three-year sojourn in France (which included a walking tour through Normandy in 1766), in 1768 Grimm settled in England, where his working life was shaped by four antiquarians and a naturalist: Sir William Burrell, who commissioned views in Sussex; Richard Kaye, for whom Grimm made countless topographical drawings; H.P. Wyndham, whom he accompanied on a tour to Wales in 1777; Cornelius Heathcote Rodes of Barlborough Hall near Chesterfield in Derbyshire, for whom in the 1770s and 1780s he produced views of the house and surrounding countryside; and Gilbert White, for whose celebrated *Natural History of Selborne* (1789) Grimm contributed illustrations.

This watercolour features the striking ravine of limestone cliffs known as Creswell Crags which, though also painted in the 1760s by George Stubbs (1724–1806), were actually rather inaccessible to the eighteenth-century traveller (Egerton 1984, p.102). It was evidently worked up by Grimm from drawings made on one of his visits to Barlborough. In many ways it is a classic example of the 'stained' or 'tinted' drawing produced by the late eighteenth-century topographer, in which careful pencil underdrawing and layers of grey wash (to indicate light and shadow) were superimposed with 'local' colour and pen outlines to clarify form; one author draws attention to the 'neat pen-work, like minute hem-stitching' round the outlines of Grimm's trees (Williams 1952, p.46). This careful and restrained style of watercolour painting had evolved especially to suit the needs of the reproductive printmaker, and indeed this subject was engraved in 1789 for Samuel Middiman's *Select Views in Great Britain*. However, in the engraving the three endearing children on the rock in the middle distance have been replaced by two adults. Either the engraver thought the detail inappropriate, or the watercolour on which the print was based was one of Grimm's duplicate versions in which he varied the incidental figures (Clay 1941, p.41).

Grimm also produced a number of lively caricatures and satires, predominantly social subjects (Godfrey 1984, pp.60–1). Gilbert White detected Grimm's 'vein of humour' but was careful to ensure it was allowed no place in the *Natural History of Selborne*, believing 'all my plates must be serious' (Hardie 1966, vol.1, p.165).

AL

Attributed to JOSEPH WRIGHT OF DERBY
(1734–1797)

28 Study of an Unknown Man c.1751–7

Pastel and red and white chalk on prepared laid paper
45.6 × 28 (15⅜ × 10¾)
T08244

Previously thought to be a seventeenth-century portrait sketch, this drawing is now attributed to Joseph Wright of Derby (see no.29). This is on the strength of its similarity to a group of studio drawings believed to be by Wright now in Derby Museum and Art Gallery, and the fact that recent analysis of the paper has shown that it dates from the period c.1747–57, making the earlier identification impossible (Bower 1997).

The collection of Wright drawings at Derby includes studio works (some autograph, some only attributed to Wright) which cover the period from 1751, when he was a pupil in the portrait painter Thomas Hudson's studio, to 1769 by which time he had established an independent reputation (Leger 1995, pp.56–9). This drawing is extraordinarily similar, both in handling and subject-matter, to one of these drawings in particular – a portrait sketch c.1751 attributed to Wright, tentatively identified as either James, Duke of York, or Prince Rupert, and thought to be a copy of a mezzotint after a painting by Sir Peter Lely (1618–1680). Although the identity of the sitter remains conjectural and the exact source for the sketch – whether a mezzotint or an actual painting – unknown, both drawings are clearly related to each other. They depict the same sitter and follow one another in such close detail, even down to individual lines and diagonal hatchings, that it is possible that the one shown here, executed in red chalk, is in fact a version of the other, in black chalk, both done as an exercise in the use of slightly different media.

Wright studied under Hudson (1701–1779) from 1751 to 1753 and again from 1756 to 1757 (Nicolson 1968, vol.1, p.2, n.2). At this period Hudson's London studio was large and flourishing, where Wright would have obtained a solid and traditional art education. To judge from the studio drawings which date from this period this involved making red chalk studies after the Antique, detailed drapery studies, general sketches of compositions and poses, as well as drawings after old master paintings or prints such as this one (Leger 1995, p.56). Technically it is very similar to a portrait sketch he made of Hudson himself (Derby Museum and Art Gallery), but while the latter is obviously a contemporary image, the more antiquarian style adopted here (together with the sitter's Lelyesque air) serves to underline the drawing's seventeenth-century derivation.

Copying prints was a well-established teaching exercise. Although past and current London drawing academies tended to stress the life class, other academies (such as those established in Edinburgh in 1729 and 1760) placed importance on drawing after paintings, engravings and drawing manuals (Bignamini 1991, pp.8–9). According to Vertue, it was self-teaching through this method that brought Arthur Pond (1701–1758) recognition: 'by drawing and studying after painting the heads of Vandyke &c. ... and ... by Collections of drawings prints books ...', he says, Pond was now 'cryd up to be the great undertaker. of gravings paintings &c &c'. As Hudson's pupil Wright presumably would have had at his disposal for study Hudson's own large and impressive collection of paintings, drawings and prints. Hudson was one in a line of great artist-collectors such as Van Dyck, Lely and Kneller and, like theirs, his collection was as much for instruction and edification as it was for acquisition of status as a virtuoso. Sales of his collection after his death show that he possessed over eight hundred drawings and prints and over eighty paintings and pieces of sculpture, a great many of which he had bought in the 1747 sales of the collection of his former master and father-in-law, the painter Jonathan Richardson (c.1665–1745). Only a small proportion of the items can be identified today, but it is known that among them were works by Rubens and other old masters, works by his English contemporaries and near contemporaries, as well as paintings and drawings by Van Dyck and Lely (Vertue, vol.3, pp.134–5; Miles and Simon 1979). From Richardson he purchased Lely's portrait of Sir William Swan, and he also owned Lely sketches now in the British Museum (for example, *Studies of Arms and Hands* – see Stainton and White 1987, pp.126–9). Undoubtedly he would have also owned several mezzotints after Lely's portraits.

TB

JOSEPH WRIGHT OF DERBY
1734–1797

29 Inside the Arcade of the Colosseum *c.*1774–5

Brown washes over pencil with pen and brown ink
on laid paper 37.7 × 50.7 (14⅞ × 20)
Inscribed upper left in pen and brown ink '25'
T08590

Wright launched his career as a portrait painter (see under no.28), and his representations of sitters from his native Derbyshire were to remain an important source of income throughout his professional life. Today he is best known for his subjects of scientific experiment set at candlelight or lamplight, such as *A Philosopher Lecturing on the Orrery* (Derby Museum and Art Gallery) and *Experiment on a Bird in the Air Pump* (National Gallery, London); and, indeed, it was with these paintings that Wright established his London reputation in the 1760s. During a trip to France and Italy between 1773 and 1775, however, he became increasingly interested in landscape, and on his return to England landscape oils – of both Italian and British subjects – became a regular feature of his output as well.

With his pregnant wife and the two artists Richard Hurleston (d.1777) and John Downman (nos.54–6), Wright set sail for Italy in November 1773. They travelled round the coast of Spain as far as Nice on the southern French coast, disembarking there for three weeks because of bad weather (see no.54). They then continued by sea to Genoa and Leghorn (Livorno), from where they took the overland route to Rome, arriving in February 1774. Three sketchbooks by Wright are known from the trip, all apparently used in Rome; they contain studies after the Antique, figures observed on the streets, and landscape views, especially sketches of skies (Egerton 1990, pp.140–2). He also made larger, more elaborate drawings of Italian landscapes and classical ruins in monochrome media like this one, his preference for monochrome finding parallels in the work of other oil painters in this period such as Wilson and Gainsborough (nos.13, 23). However, some of these drawings may have been executed after Wright's return to England. This

subject, for example, exists in a second version (Henry Huntington Library and Art Gallery, San Marino, repr. Nicolson 1968, pl.155) which one author believes may be the original and this, the Oppé version, a later commissioned copy (Egerton 1990, p.143). However, it should be noted that the Oppé version carries one of the inscribed ink numbers found on other original sketches made by Wright on his Continental trip, such as the Nice landscape in the Oppé collection (T08253) numbered 244; and it is also executed on a Dutch paper (made by Jan van der Ley) commonly found in use in mid to late eighteenth-century Italy (Bower 1997, p.63).

The Colosseum, one of the most impressive of all the great monuments of Imperial Rome, never failed to make a striking impression on the eighteenth-century traveller. The gigantic amphitheatre was constructed between AD 72 and 80, and was used by the Romans for gladiatorial combats, games and other festivitites. Owing to its immense scale, it could be shown by artists in its entirety only if they adopted a rather distant viewpoint. Instead, some artists concentrated on the arena itself, perhaps showing – as in a watercolour by William Pars (Tate Gallery T04853) – the wooden cross and altars symbolising the stations of the cross erected after Pope Benedict XIV in 1750 declared the site sacred ground in memory of the Christians who were martyred there. However, other artists, such as Wright, 'Warwick' Smith and J.R. Cozens, chose to depict a section of the arcade from close to. Their compositions have a dramatic impact which is reminiscent of the powerful ruin etchings made by the Italian printmaker and architect G.B. Piranesi (1720–1778) and may, indeed, have been inspired by them (Hawcroft 1988, pp.41–5).

AL

SIR NATHANIEL DANCE-HOLLAND
1735–1811

30 Portrait of Hester Smith née Dance 1769

Pencil on laid paper 35.7 × 26 (14 × 10¼)
Inscribed in pencil bottom left 'Nath. Dance fecit 1769'
T08229

Nathaniel Dance, who later changed his name to Dance-Holland, was the third son of the architect George Dance senior (1695–1768) whose most famous building is the Mansion House in the City of London. Not long after Nathaniel left school in 1748 he became a pupil of Francis Hayman (no.10) and it was under his influence that his interest in painting historical subjects first developed. He travelled to Rome in 1754 and it was in a letter from there, written in 1759, that he described Hayman as 'very difficient [*sic*] in point of Colouring and Correctness of drawing, yet he certainly has Genius and a great Facility of Invention' (Goodreau 1977, no.3a): by correctly indentifying an emphasis on subject-matter over draughtsmanship and painterliness as a weakness in art Dance diagnosed what was a recurrent feature in English historical painting. He remained in Rome until about the end of 1765 and during his time there painted a pioneering work in the history of English neo-classicism, a subject from the Roman poet Livy, *The Death of Virginia*, and before he left he had received three commissions for paintings illustrating subjects from the *Aeneid*, one of which, *The Meeting of Dido and Aeneas*, is now in the Tate Gallery (T06736).

In the end, however, it was as a portraitist that Dance-Holland made his name. Inevitably, he modelled his first efforts on those of his master, Hayman. This is clear from a small double portrait of his brother, George, and their sister, Hester, as children of about 1753 (Goodreau 1977, no.1). Just as this suggests reliance on amenable sitters to help, as it were, practise in a challenging genre, so this 1769 drawing of Hester possesses similar undertones, for it is both the largest-known portrait drawing by him and dates from the same year that Dance-Holland showed portraits of King George III and his Queen, at the first exhibition of the newly founded Royal Academy.

Hester was born in 1742 and Dance shows his twenty-seven-year-old sister, who had by now been married for five years to her cousin, Captain Nathaniel Smith of the East India Company, in a relaxed pose. It is a sensitive rendering of a clearly much-loved sister. She appears, within the conventions of the age, to have acted on equal terms with her brothers, and Nathaniel left her £10,000 in his will. The book which she holds perhaps indicates something of her intellectual interests, and it is recorded that she was friendly with the poet Samuel Rogers and the eminent patron of the arts William Lock of Norbury (Stroud 1971, pp.250–1). She died in 1819.

RH

SIR NATHANIEL DANCE-HOLLAND
1735–1811

31a Four Heads ?after 1782

Pen and brown ink over pencil on laid paper
7.8 × 16.1 (3⅛ × 6⅜) (cropped corners)
T08392

31b 'And Who Are You' ?after 1782

Pen and brown ink over pencil on laid paper
12.4 × 15.9 (4⅞ × 6¼)
Inscribed in brown ink bottom left edge 'And who are you?'
T08393

In 1776 Dance exhibited at the Royal Academy for the last time as a professional artist. The picture which he showed was the *Death of Mark Anthony* (Goodreau 1977, no.38), and it must have been this work which a young Russian student, G.I. Skorodumov, had in mind in 1777 when he listed Dance among the top English artists of the time. None the less, Dance continued to paint portraits, though with his retirement to the country in 1782 he exhibited only three more times at the Academy as an 'honorary exhibitor' – an expression commonly used to describe an amateur. Although not strictly speaking an 'amateur', the principal output of his later years was very much of a type associated with amateurs – for example, Henry Bunbury (see no.53) – caricature. This was, of course, a natural extension of portraiture, and the studies of heads shown in these two brilliantly handled pen and ink sketches betray the serious portraitist's interest in physiognomy combined with an interest in the ludicrous which was not, naturally, admitted into the world of the formal portrait.

For various reasons Dance himself became the butt of a few jokes in the art world and was thus well qualified to turn the tables gently on the rest of humanity. His brother, George (no.41), described him as one who 'had very strong affections' (Farington, vol.11, p.4038) which came to the fore in his 'passionate love' for the artist Angelica Kauffman while in Italy. In a nice neo-classical gloss on modern manners the satirist and gadfly of the artists' profession Anthony Pasquin had Dance 'sighing at her feet' (Pasquin 1796, p.113) and the pair of them rambling 'to Tivoli and its classic bowers', Nathaniel pleading 'with the rapture of a Tibullus' while Angelica, 'the elegant nymph, delicately cherished his desires' (Pasquin 1796, p.42). Angelica later rebuffed Nathaniel and turned her attentions to Sir Joshua Reynolds, and Dance ridiculed them in drawing (Penny 1986, no.170). Years later Nathaniel Dance's association with a rich widow, whom he eventually married in 1783, was the subject of amused gossip. He became an MP in 1790, assumed the name Holland, after his wife's cousin, in 1800 and the same year became a baronet.

Both Nathaniel and George Dance were consummate caricaturists and their work is sometimes confused. Although Nathaniel was 'considered a singular man in His manner', his wit is preserved only in drawings such as these. By contrast, the equally observant George once caught in words the essence of his and his brother's view of other men's weaknesses. Thus, summing up John Downman's (see nos.54–6) constitutional slowness he said 'If … you were to point to a flower, & say, "There is a flower," [Downman] would lift up his eyes & after a pause say ,"Yes it is a flower"' (Farington, vol.8, pp.3029, 3133).

RH

And who are you?

JONATHAN SKELTON
*c.*1735–1759

32 A Farmstead *c.*1755

Watercolour over pencil on laid paper
14.8 × 22.2 (5⅞ × 8¾);
artist's washline border 20.5 × 28 (8⅛ × 11)
Inscribed on washline mount in pen and brown ink '73'
and 'J Skelton'
T08473

Skelton is an important figure in the emergence of a landscape watercolour tradition in Britain in the mid-eighteenth century, but like William Taverner (nos.7–8) a rather shadowy one. His surviving works all date from between 1754 and 1758, and a profile of his life and work can at present be pieced together only by examining the locations and dates on his watercolours, and by referring to the interesting group of letters he wrote in 1758 from Rome and Tivoli to William Herring of Croydon (Ford 1960). Skelton's trip to Italy was funded by William Herring, but came to an abrupt end in early 1759 when the artist died there following complications from a duodenal ulcer. Despite his premature death, Skelton is today remembered as the first British artist to have produced an impressive group of watercolours of Rome and its vicinity, anticipating by more than fifteen years the better-known Italian views of a later generation of artists which includes William Pars, John 'Warwick' Smith, Francis Towne and J.R. Cozens (Ford 1960, p.24).

Before his departure for Italy late in 1757 Skelton seems to have been a servant in the household of William Herring's cousin, Thomas Herring, the Archbishop of Canterbury (who had been painted by Hogarth in the 1740s, Tate Gallery T01971). One of Skelton's earliest drawings, *The Archbishop's Palace, Croydon* is inscribed as having been 'taken by a Footman in His Grace's family in 1754'. Furthermore, the locations depicted in many of Skelton's other watercolours correspond with the Archbishop's residences – at Lambeth in London and at Rochester on the Medway where he retained the deanery, as well as at Croydon Palace in Surrey (Stainton 1985, p.26).

A Farmstead is similar in character and size to a watercolour by Skelton of Lambeth Palace in the Victoria and Albert Museum dated 1755, and may have been painted in the same year. It shares the same rather fortuitous arrangement of features, localised colours and unpretentious charm that one author sees as characteristic of Skelton's smaller English subjects in general (Ford 1960, p.27). Like other early drawings by Skelton, *A Farmstead* also shows a close resemblance to the work of the British landscape painter George Lambert (see fig.5), especially in the treatment of foliage which in its own turn owes a debt to Gaspard Dughet (1615–1675). It is possible that Skelton was a pupil of Lambert's. He makes several references in his correspondence from Italy to a 'Mr Lambert'; and the striking combination of pink and yellow ruled borders in Skelton's washline mount round *A Farmstead* was adopted by another of Lambert's pupils, Richard de Beauvoir (*fl.* 1759–1768), for his own mounts.

AL

73

JONATHAN SKELTON
*c.*1735–1759

33 Greenwich Park, A Capriccio 1757

Watercolour over pencil on laid paper 25 × 54.1 (9⅞ × 21¼);
artist's washline border 29.3 × 58.5 (11½ × 23)
Numbered '6' lower left in pen and brown ink.
Inscribed on verso in pencil 'The Parts of this Drawing are in |
Greenwich Park But Grouped together at Fancy J: Skelton 1757'
and again in brown ink below
T08254

By 1757 Skelton's watercolours were becoming more atmospheric and more expressive, his washes were becoming looser, and he was beginning to favour a panoramic format for his English subjects like the one adopted here for *Greenwich Park*. A group of eight watercolours by him of Canterbury and its vicinity, also dated 1757 and mostly on this larger format as well, clearly reveal this tendency in Skelton's work towards a more pronounced naturalism; indeed, one of them, a view of the village at Harbledown (Yale Center for British Art), is inscribed by the artist on its old mount as having been 'drawn immediately after a heavy summer-shower'. It is clear from Skelton's letters written from Rome that he often worked out of doors in Italy using oils and water-colour, but whether he did so in England is not known. This view of Greenwich Park, however, is most unlikely to have been painted from nature, since the artist admits in an inscription that its constituent parts have been grouped together by him 'at Fancy' – and the same is likely to be true of the picture's pair in the Fitzwilliam

Museum, Cambridge (fig.16). Indeed, both Skelton's later English subjects and his Italian watercolours reveal a characteristic mid-eighteenth century tension between, on the one hand, a greater sense of naturalism and, on the other hand, the artist's evident indebtedness to the classical masters of the past, especially Gaspard Dughet.

Most of Skelton's extant drawings originated from the library at Hoveton House, Norwich, and are thought to have been collected in the later eighteenth century by one of Hoveton's owners, Thomas Blofeld (1753–1817). Numbering some eighty to ninety works, they were listed in an inventory of the library's books and drawings compiled in the late nineteenth century. The water-colours were sold in 1909, and are now widely dispersed. However, most of Skelton's known watercolours can today be identified, with varying degrees of certainty, with numbered items in the Hoveton handlist. Thus *Greenwich Park* was number 6 on the list, whilst *A Farmstead* (no.32) was probably the seventy-third (Pierce 1960, pp.13 and 20).

AL

fig. 16
Jonathan Skelton,
In Greenwich Park
1757, watercolour
with pen and
black ink
*Fitzwilliam
Museum,
Cambridge*

FRANCIS TOWNE
1739–1816

34 Wood near Albano 1781

Grey and black washes with touches of pale ochre and
brown wash with pen and black ink on laid paper
32 × 44.6 (12⅝ × 17½); artist's washline border 38.5 × 51
(15⅛ × 20⅛)

Inscribed lower right in ink 'F. Towne delt | 1781'
and on verso 'Taken in a wood near Albano | by |
Francis Towne | 1781:'

T08184

Although born and trained as an oil painter in London, in
the mid-1760s Towne decided to settle in Exeter as a
drawing master, and by the 1790s had a flourishing and
lucrative teaching practice there. In his later career he
struggled hard for professional recognition in London,
but never became an Associate of the Royal Academy,
despite making ten bids for election between 1788 and
1803. Although he probably failed adequately to court the
Academicians, Towne's prospects seem always to have
been compromised by his reputation as a provincial
drawing master (Stephens 1996, p.504). An exhibition he
held of his own work in London in 1805 appears to have
passed unnoticed by artists and critics alike (see no.37),
and for a century after his death in 1816 his watercolours
remained virtually forgotten. It was not until the 1920s
that, thanks to the writings of Paul Oppé, Towne was
'rediscovered', his austere sense of design readily appreciated by a twentieth-century audience. Today he is
regarded as one of the most original landscape watercolourists of the late eighteenth century.

The watercolours Towne made in Italy in 1780–1, and
in the Alps on his subsequent return to England, are
usually regarded as his finest; certainly these were the
years when, stimulated by the new scenery, 'his distinctive style … found its fullest expression' (Stainton 1985,
p.27). Continuing a practice he had first adopted on a
tour to Wales in 1777, Towne generally numbered his
Continental drawings in sequence (no.35, for example, is
numbered '52'), and sometimes now also inscribed them
with the time of day when made. Drawn (in pencil) on
the spot, and often so inscribed, Towne would then add
washes of monochrome or colour whilst the memory of
the scene was still fresh in his mind. He would subsequently reinforce the original pencil line in pen and ink
as if to emphasise the status of these drawings as sketches.
Signed, and then usually laid down onto his own mounts
(and then reinscribed on the reverse), the whole series of
sketches would then be retained by him to show to
patrons in the hope of receiving commissions for copies.

When painting in monochrome in Italy, Towne
tended to use brown rather then grey washes in response
to the warmth of the Mediterranean climate (Wilcox
1997, p.57). Here he has reverted to grey washes to
capture the cool and shady Alban woods, the white of the
paper brilliantly suggesting the shafts of intense sunlight
penetrating through the glades. Towne may have known
the watercolours made at Albano a few years earlier by
his Devon acquaintance and friend John Downman (see
no.55). However, he seems in any case to have had a
special fondness for woodland scenes, making other
studies in the chestnut woods at Rocca di Papa and in
Devon at Peamore Park.

AL

104

FRANCIS TOWNE
1739–1816

35 The Source of the Arveyron 1781

Watercolour with pen and brown ink and scratching out on laid paper 31 × 21.2 (12¼ × 8⅜); artist's washline border 37.1 × 27.3 (14⅝ × 10¾)

Inscribed in ink lower right 'F. Towne del^t| N$_{·}^{o}$ 52 1781', and on verso in ink 'N$_{·}^{o}$ 52 | A View of the Source of the Arviron | drawn by Francis Towne.' and, partially deleted, 'Sept ... 1781'

T08147

When Towne arrived in Italy in the autumn of 1780, a number of his artist friends were already resident there: William Pars, for example, was in Rome, funded by the Society of Dilettanti and enjoying 'a very liberal commission' to paint some views for his old patron Lord Palmerston (see nos.46–8); whilst Thomas Jones was in Naples, and the following March welcomed Towne there on a short visit when they suffered a narrow escape from the local, knife-brandishing banditti. In Rome Towne also made the acquaintance of the watercolourist John 'Warwick' Smith (nos.51–2) who became a regular sketching companion, and who accompanied him on his return journey to England across the Alps in 1781. It was on this trip that Towne produced some of the acknowledged masterpieces of his entire career. Indeed, this watercolour and its pair in the Victoria and Albert Museum (fig.8), are among the most celebrated British watercolours ever painted.

The river Arveyron is a short tributary of the river Arve and rises from the base of the Glacier des Bois in Chamonix. Thanks to the cave of ice which flowed out of it, it was one of the most famous sights in the Alps at this date (Wilcox 1997, p.101). William Pars, for example, had visited the site with Lord Palmerston on their tour of Switzerland a decade or so earlier. Towne was using a small sketchbook on this journey measuring about eight inches by six; and he drew this subject across a double spread of the book turned on its side (hence the crease across the centre), whilst the other version, numbered 53 and exactly twice as large, he tackled on two separate openings of the same book. Intent on capturing the sheer massiveness of the mountains, Towne ignores all traditional notions of perspective and recession in these drawings and essentially overlooks any foreground detail (the human figure, for example, is conspicuous by its absence). His colour, as Martin Hardie writes, has an 'enamelled clarity', and is 'imposed on nature as an arbitrary, functional part of the design' (1966, vol.1, p.122). In this, the smaller version, where two vast, almost perpendicular mountains rise from a distant valley, Towne uses simplification of form at its boldest, producing one of the most abstract of all his compositions.

Swiss subjects had already been treated by a few English artists before Towne's own visit to the Alps in 1781: William Pars had painted an important sequence of Alpine watercolours on his return from a trip to Switzerland with Lord Palmerston in 1770 (see no.47); and J.R. Cozens produced a range of atmospheric Alpine views following two Continental journeys in 1776 and 1782–3, which were to be especially influential on the young Girtin and Turner (see under no.61). However, Towne was the first to evoke the Alpine landscape's forbidding presence and to capture, in Oppé's words, 'the crushing grandeur of the mountains'.

AL

FRANCIS TOWNE
1739–1816

36 Waterfall near Ambleside 1786

Watercolour with pen and brown ink on laid paper,
37.7 × 26.5 (14¾ × 10⅜)
Inscribed verso in pencil 'Fall Rydall' and in ink 'Rose Merivale'
and, in Oppé's hand, 'one of three variants |
given to me by Miss Merivale | 13th December 1915.'
T08262

In 1786 Towne joined two Exeter friends, James White and John Merivale, on a tour of the Lake District. The area had already attracted various artists by this date, thanks in part to the publication of guidebooks by Thomas West and William Hutchinson. However, it was the appearance in 1786 of William Gilpin's influential account of his own picturesque tour of the region four years before which turned a trickle into a flood, popularising the Lake District for the amateur artist and recreational traveller in search of the 'Picturesque'. Indeed, it may well have been the publication of Gilpin's *Observations, relative chiefly to Picturesque Beauty, made in the year 1772, on several parts of England; particularly the Mountains, and Lakes of Cumberland, and Westmoreland* which provided the immediate impetus for Towne's own friends to embark on their tour that year (Wilcox 1997, p.106).

Ambleside served as a base for the party during most of their tour, and this gave Towne the opportunity of exploring the area in some depth. Panoramic views by him of Ambleside are fairly numerous (see, for example, Tate Gallery T01019). However, Towne was particularly attracted to the secluded waterfalls of Stock Gill that ran down the hillside into the town, and the three versions he made of these falls are amongst the most impressive drawings he made on the whole tour (see Wilcox 1997 nos.57–9; the two other versions are in the Ashmolean Museum, Oxford, and in a private collection). The combination of rocks and trees in a secluded corner of nature was just the sort of subject which had attracted Towne when sketching near Tivoli outside Rome, though in the Lakes he had the additional element of the waterfall to contend with. Waterfalls were stock-in-trade subject-matter for the 'Picturesque' traveller, but as Oppé points out, Towne makes almost no attempt to produce any illusion of falling water or rising spray (1920, p.121). Rather, water (corresponding to areas left blank on the paper) functions chiefly for him as a method of bringing light, variety and contrast into the pattern made by a combination of rock, foliage and tree stems. Towne's elevated and close viewpoint makes the subject both more intense and more dramatic, and the two barely discernible figures on the far left-hand rock provide a sense of scale.

White was a lawyer and uncle of Towne's most famous pupil John White Abbott (1763–1851), whilst Merivale was the father of another of Towne's students, John Herman Merivale (1779–1844). It was J.H. Merivale who, on the death of White in 1825, received Towne's entire artistic estate. Two of his granddaughters still owned the work in the early twentieth century when Paul Oppé began to take an interest in Towne, at that time an obscure and forgotten Devon artist (Wilcox 1997, p.161). Oppé has noted on the back of this drawing that it was presented to him by 'Miss [presumably Rose] Merivale'.

A L

FRANCIS TOWNE
1739–1816

37 In the Campagna, Rome, looking towards the Sabine Mountains c.1786

Watercolour over faint traces of pencil on laid paper 23.2 × 47.5 (9⅛ × 18¾)
T08266

On his return from the Continent Towne found only a few patrons willing to commission replicas of the many sketches he had made. He might occasionally receive a commission for an oil, for which he charged 25 guineas, but more often it was for a watercolour, for which he asked between eight and ten. There can be little doubt that this subject was a commissioned one, being based directly on the original coloured sketch of the same view in the British Museum. Furthermore, lacking the pen and ink outlines that are the hallmark of Towne's sketching style (no.34), this watercolour has a softer, looser handling which is characteristic of his commissioned work in general – and a reflection of his understanding that 'finished' watercolours were required to manifest the qualities of paintings rather than drawings (Wilcox 1997, p.12). Another of Towne's commissioned watercolours, *The Bay of Naples with Capri in the Distance*, dated 1786, is also in the Oppé collection (T08195).

The original sketch by Towne for this work is inscribed 'No.5 2 Miles from Rome going out at the Porta Pia from 10 o Clock till 1 o clock' and dated 26 October, 1780. It was, then, only the fifth sketch which Towne had made after his arrival in Rome that year, and perhaps partly for this reason lacks the vigour of many of the later Roman watercolours. The countryside along the old Via Nomentana to the north-east of the city was visited by a number of artists in this period keen to escape the bustle of city life, although the Roman Campagna was also remembered as a favourite sketching ground of the seventeenth-century landscape painter Claude Lorrain. As well as another sketch made in the vicinity by Towne from 'Martinelli's vineyard', there are others by Thomas Jones and John 'Warwick' Smith, the latter having lodgings here for a time, as, indeed, did John Robert Cozens (see no.51). Thanks to Towne's annotating his original watercolour sketch with the hours of the day when it was executed, it is possible from the reading of the shadows to establish that his viewpoint faces eastwards.

In 1803 Towne boasted that he had 'never in [his] life exhibited a *drawing*' (meaning a 'tinted drawing' or watercolour). However, only two years later he put on display over 190 of his original 'on the spot' sketches in a gallery in London's Lower Brook Street he hired from the artist Henry Tresham, whom he may have known in Italy (no.57). The exhibition was almost certainly prompted by his hearing of the formation of the Society of Painters in Watercolour in late 1804, and their plans for an exhibition the following year. It was, however, a critical and financial failure. Today it is still sometimes possible to establish which of his works were exhibited there; many of them, including the original sketch on which this watercolour was based, still carry the tell-tale pin-holes on their mounts where they were tacked to the gallery walls (see Wilcox 1997, p.130).

AL

WILLIAM MARLOW
1740–1813

38 Villeneuve-lès-Avignon c.1766–85

Watercolour over pencil with pen and brown ink
on laid paper 25.6 × 37.5 (10⅛ × 14¾); artist's washline
border 28.3 × 40.3 (11⅛ × 15⅞)
Inscribed lower right in pen and brown ink 'W Marlow'
T08209

In the 1750s William Marlow was apprenticed for five years to the painter of marine views and graceful London topography Samuel Scott (see no.9), and today is best known for his views of London painted very much in Scott's manner. However, the many landscapes of French and Italian subjects which Marlow made following a tour to the Continent between 1765 and 1766 – and which he exhibited in substantial numbers at the Society of Artists and the Royal Academy – contributed equally to his contemporary reputation and commercial success. Indeed, the fact that certain compositions by him are known in numerous, near-identical versions, especially views of Lyons and Villeneuve-lès-Avignon, is evidence of Marlow's popularity as a painter of 'souvenir' pictures for those who had made the grand tour (Liversidge 1980, pp.549–50).

Some travellers at this period, Downman and Wright of Derby (nos.29 and 54–5), for example, chose to make the voyage to Italy by sea, but the majority seem to have selected a route overland. One of these routes took the traveller southwards through France, via Paris and the Sâone and Rhône valleys, and this was clearly the one which Marlow himself followed, judging by the various sketches by him which have survived from his tour. An album containing some of his Italian and French sketches, now partly dismembered, is in the Oppé collection and includes a pencil study (fig.17) for this watercolour. The study is a careful topographical record of Villeneuve-lès-Avignon, seen across the river Rhône from the Île de la Barthelasse – the island situated in the middle of the Rhône which, together with the river itself, separates Villeneuve from its older, sister town of Avignon to the south-east. The watercolour, by contrast, is more elaborate and includes one of Marlow's characteristic knotty and twisted trees (very broadly indicated in the preliminary drawing), as well as figures

participating in the life of the river – the sort of differences, in short, one would expect between an original study and a finished composition.

The reverse of Marlow's preliminary drawing describes the religious foundation in the distance of this view as an Augustine convent, but in fact the artist depicts the Benedictine abbey of St André, incorporated within the fort of the same name and largely demolished during the French Revolution. Both drawing and watercolour include two of the ruined piers of the medieval bridge of St Benézét, the famous 'Pont d'Avignon' (immortalised in the song 'Sur le Pont d'Avignon') which once crossed the Île de la Barthelasse thus linking the two towns, but of which only the four eastern arches remain today. The bridge is the subject of another watercolour by Marlow in the Whitworth Art Gallery, Manchester (Nugent 1993, no.52), which is also based on a pencil drawing in the Oppé album (T09164).

From 1775 Marlow rented a property at Twickenham, moving there permanently in semi-retirement ten years later. For over thirty years he shared a house with the Curtis family and their six or seven children, some of whom Farington recorded looked 'very like Marlow' (*Diary*, 23 June 1808, vol.9, p.3302). It was presumably Marlow's financial obligations towards the Curtis family which necessitated his sometimes resuming work during this period, and in 1795 he produced a set of six etchings, *Views in Italy*, which were issued by John Curtis from Twickenham – though by this date Marlow's work (and that featuring grand tour sites in general) was no longer fashionable (Liversidge 1980, pp.549–50). In later life Marlow turned to making 'Telescopes & other Articles' (Farington, *Diary*, 10 February 1813, vol.12, p.4297), and is also said to have designed the seals for the original thirteen United States of America (Howgego 1956, p.5).

AL

fig. 17
William Marlow,
*Villeneuve c.*1765–6,
pencil and pen and
black ink
*Oppé Collection, Tate
Gallery*

JOHN HAMILTON MORTIMER
1740–1779

39 Banditti Going Out in the Morning 1773

Pen and grey and black ink over some pencil
21.3 × 15.1 (8⅜ × 6) with artist's ruled margin 23.2 × 17.3
(9⅛ × 6¾) on laid paper 23.8 × 17.9 (9⅜ × 7)
T08277

Mortimer's short career, from the time he worked in the studio of the portrait painter Thomas Hudson at the age of sixteen or seventeen until his death at the age of thirty-eight, was characterised by an originality and energetic restlessness which set him apart from his contemporaries to the point where he was almost seen as dangerous company. It saw him winning prizes from the Society of Arts in 1763 and 1764 for paintings of subjects from British history, the 1764 work being a large canvas *St Paul Preaching to the Antient Druids in Britain*, which is now in the Guildhall in High Wycombe (Sunderland 1986, no.1); he was a moving spirit in the various artists' societies in London which preceded the Royal Academy; and as a draughtsman or just as a free spirit he inspired a younger generation of artists, among them Rowlandson (no.67) and Stothard (nos.64–6). Edward Dayes wrote that 'as he was a *bon vivant*, it frequently carried him into company, of which he was always the life, and at which time nothing was too extravagant for him to undertake', adding that 'Mortimer was so fascinating a companion, that [James] Barry declared he was afraid to trust himself in his company'. Blyth, Mortimer's engraver, lived so loose a life and 'so broke his constitution' that he committed suicide (Dayes 1805, pp.340–1).

An artist upon whom Mortimer certainly modelled himself was the Neopolitan Salvator Rosa (1615–1673). A painter of wild and savage landscapes, he was believed (wrongly) to have been brought up by brigands. Once Rosa had moved to Rome he dressed in great style, had a servant to carry his sword and displayed his skills as a poet and actor with great flamboyance. He was, of course, a proto-Romantic figure whose style matched the spirit of Mortimer's age. Mortimer's drawing technique was influenced by Rosa's – as *Banditti Going Out* shows – and

as a sign of his admiration of him he drew, painted and etched a portrait of Rosa in 1776–8 (Sunderland 1986, nos.140.7, a and b). But it was with his exhibition of a banditti subject in 1772 that he first acquired the sobriquet 'the English Salvator'. His source for this and his other banditti, or robber, subjects such as this drawing was Rosa's *Figurine*, a series of sixty-two small etchings depicting such figures dating from about 1656 to 1657 (Sunderland 1986, pp.54–8; Wallace 1979, pp.12–36, 135–229).

Banditti subjects were popular with artists and public alike during the eighteenth century: they were picturesque figures, brave, lawless, capable of violence and affection, working outside the bounds of society and thus conformed to a romantic ideal. Rosa's prints, and then Mortimer's, provided travellers in search of the picturesque and sublime with a stock of images with which they might people the landscapes in which they found themselves. The end effect was very real. Thomas Jones (nos.43–5) lived, along with William Pars (nos.46–8), in Rosa's old house in Rome, and when later Jones was in Naples with Francis Towne (nos.34–7) they found a gloomy spot which was 'Salvator Rosa in perfection [only wanting] Banditti to compleat the Picture' (Jones, *Memoirs*, p.104).

This drawing was etched, in reverse, by Robert Blyth (1750–1784) as the first in a series of six etchings variously employed. All six drawings were exhibited at the Society of Artists in 1773 and they were published between July and November 1779 under the general title *Six Prints Representing Banditti Variously Employed*. Other subjects were *Conversing with a Captive*, *Enjoying Domestic Happiness*, *Killing an Enemy*, *Retiring Wounded from Battle* and *Stripping the Slain* (Sunderland 1986, no.71).

RH

JAMES BARRY
1741–1806

40 *Study for* Philoctetes on the Island of Lemnos 1770

Pen and ink and grey wash on laid paper 21 × 28.6 (8¼ × 11¼)

Inscribed bottom right 'There will appear more Agony & yᵉ |
disorderd leg will be more distinctly | mark'd by having it stretched
out in air | & without any support from yᵉ rock | he sits on'
lower right and 'Jaˢ Barry invᵗ' lower left in ink

T08127

In Greek mythology Philoctetes was one of the Argonauts and the friend of Hercules (see no.14). One of Hercules' twelve labours was to kill the Hydra, a many-headed monster. Afterwards, he dipped his arrows in the poisonous gall of the Hydra so that in future any wound inflicted by them would be fatal. Hercules went on to shoot the centaur Nessus but when he donned its blood-soaked tunic he too was fatally hurt. Before his death he handed his bow and arrows to Philoctetes. Philoctetes later joined the Greeks in their war against the Trojans but because of a pungent, festering wound on his foot and his cries of pain he was abandoned on the island of Lemnos by Ulysses before they reached Troy. According to one account this wound was caused by one of Hercules' arrows falling onto his foot. When Philoctetes was eventually taken from Lemnos, his arrows were decisive in the Greek victory over Troy.

James Barry went to Italy in 1765 to pursue his studies as a history painter and he returned to London in 1771. This drawing dates from the end of his stay. It is apparently his first and only surviving study for a large oil painting which he painted for the Accademia Clementina in Bologna when he was made a member of it in the autumn of 1770. A drawing of Philoctetes in the Ashmolean Museum has an inscription by a previous owner which describes it as Barry's 'original sketch' for the painting, but it is in all likelihood Barry's record of the completed work, still in Bologna, and which he must have used later when making a print of the subject (fig.18). His treatment of the subject is related to designs on classical reliefs and cameos, but the ultimate source for the powerful and agonised figure of the injured Philoctetes is the Torso Belvedere, one of the most admired of all antique fragments in Rome (Haskell and Penny 1981, pp.311–14). Having fed 'with such divine ecstasy' on the beauties of the Torso, it was always to remain of huge importance to Barry for the way the

'perfect unison' of its parts conveyed the 'idea of corporeal force' (Barry 1809, vol.1, pp.411, 443–4). Barry had already acknowledged the importance of this work to him and his fellow artists by including a partial view of it in the background of his *Self-Portrait with Paine and Lefevre* which he had painted in Rome in about 1767. The allusion to it in *Philoctetes* adds a further autobiographical layer to one already implicit in the subject he chose for such an important picture. Barry, in Rome and thereafter, found himself an outsider and his identification with the Greek hero who symbolised the triumph of stoicism and virtue over adversity and isolation was undoubtedly deliberate.

This drawing is especially interesting for what Barry wrote on it because it highlights a dilemma which every history painter had to resolve if he was to match the ideal set by classical precedents. In a letter written to his patrons in England Barry stated that in addition to finding inspiration in Sophocles' play *Philoctetes*, an epigram by Glaucus on the painting of the same subject by the Ancient Greek painter Parrhasius had been of equal value: 'In his parched eyes the deep-sunk tears express | His endless misery, his dire distress' (quoted Pressly 1981, p.22). Barry's note on this sheet deals with the challenge which this set him: how can the artist depict great bodily pain without resorting to commonplace distortions of the face which would destroy the dignity and grandeur of a heroic figure? The right moment of the action which a painter or sculptor should depict and the need to avoid deforming expressions when depicting emotions were much discussed by artists and writers on aesthetics in Barry's time. For example, G.E. Lessing, in his 1766 essay *Laocoon* (which Barry knew), wrote that 'In the whole gamut of an emotion ... there is no moment less advantageous than its topmost note. Beyond it there is nothing further'. Here we find Barry looking for a way to increase tension while maintaining 'perfect unison'.

RH

There will appear more Agony & y
disorderd leg will be more distinctly
marked by having it stretched out in air
& without any support from y rock
he sits on.

fig. 18 James Barry
*Philoctectes in the Island
of Lemnos* 1777–1808,
etching, line-engraving
and aquatint
Tate Gallery

GEORGE DANCE
1741–1825

41 Settling the Catalogue April 1795

Graphite on laid paper 20.9 × 20.3 (8¼ × 8) laid on
a wove paper album page 35.2 × 29 (13⅞ × 11⅜)

Inscribed bottom right in pencil 'settling the
Catalogue – April 1795' and above the figures
'John Richards. R.A.' and 'Cooper, Printer'

T08159

The most complex task undertaken by Royal Academicians was arranging the works of art which were submitted for the annual exhibition at Somerset House. Responsibility for the actual display was undertaken by a hanging committee of three Academicians who in 1795 were Joseph Farington (no.50), William Tyler (d.1801) and George Dance who had to find space for 735 paintings, miniatures, drawings and sculptures by 315 artists in five rooms. Dance, who was an architect best known for the design of the rebuilt Newgate Prison, was an accomplished portraitist and witty caricaturist in both pencil and pen and ink. In 1793 he produced a series of carefully wrought pencil portraits, all true likenesses and mostly in profile, of many of the Academicians, but over the years he also made more informal sketches of colleagues and public figures either poking fun at them or, as here, showing them at work. Dance shows the moment when all the rooms had been hung and the Secretary to the Academy, John Inigo Richards (see no.26), is checking the final details of the catalogue listing artists and their works with the printer before it goes to press. Farington, to whom this album belonged, was, like Dance, deeply involved in Academy affairs, and consciously set out to record Academy life behind the scenes – most obviously in his gossipy diary: there are other sketches of RAs by Dance, including five showing Richards, pasted in the album. One of these (T08157), a back view of the portly Richards standing at a high desk like the one seen here, is dated 24 April 1795 and was probably made on the same day as *Settling the Catalogue*. In his diary entry for that day Farington wrote 'Completed the arrangement' (Farington, vol.2, p.330), and this meant that the catalogue could be finalised.

Joseph Cooper was Printer to the Academy between 1794 and 1799 when he printed the annual exhibition catalogues. He died suddenly in May 1808 having had a fit while walking from Chelsea. His obituarist in the *Gentleman's Magazine* described him as a printer 'of eminence ... who was unfortunate in business', particularly in a failed speculation to make a superior form of printing ink. Apparently, having no children, 'he acquired a tone of life a little too theatrical, and much too companionable' but 'also abounded in pleasantry and the milk of human kindness' (*Gentlemen's Magazine*, vol.78, May 1808, p.470) – exactly the sort of characteristics which appealed to Dance.

RH

John Richards R.A.

Cooper,
Printer,

settling the
Catalogue — April
1795

HENRY FUSELI

1741–1806

42 Siegfried about to Deny on Oath that Brunhild had been his Paramour 1805

Grey wash over pencil on wove paper 25.5 × 41.5 (10 × 16¼)

Inscribed in pencil top left '*4*' and in brown ink 'P.C. 11. Aug.05' over 'W.B' in grey ink bottom right;
verso the same composition in pencil inscribed in pencil 'BLAKE' partially erased centre and in pencil bottom
right 'W Blake'.

T08133

The subject of this watercolour is taken from an anony-mous thirteenth-century German epic poem, *The Nibelungenlied*, a text which Fuseli, alone among his British contemporaries, frequently illustrated. It is best known today as the source for Richard Wagner's opera cycle *The Ring*. Fuseli shows the moment outside the cathedral at Worms described in chapter 14 – 'How the Queens railed at each Other'. Siegfried, responding to a quarrel between his wife, Kriemhild, and King Gunter's wife, Brunhild, when Kriemhild accuses Brunhild of letting Siegfried and not her brother, Gunter, make love to her first after her marriage, is raising his hand to swear denial. But Gunter had in fact needed Siegfried, made invisible with his magic cloak, to subdue his new wife on their marriage bed, and he is seen here between him and Kriemhild acknowledging Siegfried's innocence. The tearful Brunhild is on the right. Fuseli has shown one of the turning-points in the whole poem: Siegfried the noble hero, having now earned the hatred of Hagen, loyal vassâl of Brunhild, and been unknowingly betrayed by Kriemheld, is later killed by Hagen (Hatto 1969).

Fuseli, which is an anglicisation of his Swiss name Füssli, was born in Zurich and went to Italy to train as a painter in 1769 before settling in London in 1779. He was a man of extraordinary intellectual energy and one of the most powerful and original of all the artists working in England at this period. One of the leading history painters of the day, he contributed to Boydell's Shakespeare Gallery from 1786; from 1791 he also embarked on his own, ultimately unsuccessful, scheme for illustrating the works of John Milton which at the time was the most ambitious art project undertaken by a single artist in Britain.

This drawing is one of a group of at least eight which can be dated to a period between May and August 1805 when the artist was staying at Purser's Cross (the 'PC' of the inscription), the villa in Fulham, west of London, which belonged to Fuseli's old friend and patron, the radical bookseller Joseph Johnson. Fuseli described the house as a 'Sweet and peaceful Little neat hut inbo-somed by a wilderness of Shrubs' (Weinglass 1982, pp.299–300, 562–3). Fuseli's first idea for *Siegfried* was drawn in pencil on the other side of this sheet and then 'traced' through with some alterations.

Fuseli continued to exhibit historical paintings, including subjects from *The Nibelungenlied* (Schiff 1973, nos.1380–96, 1490–2), at the Academy in 1807, 1814, 1817 and 1820 until the year he died. It was a sign of the times that the critics rarely noticed them, though the 'fine phrenzy' of his work was still admired (*Examiner*, 1 May 1814, p.316). With hindsight, this 1805 cycle of drawings dealing with a grand historical theme full of darkness, the mythical heroic, sexual jealousy, murder and revenge, all perfectly caught in this work, was by then a concept which had had its day: in May of the same year the young David Wilkie (see no.89) arrived in London and in 1806 captivated a new public at the Academy with his painting of a 'scene from familiar life', *The Village Politicians*. With this, in B.R. Haydon's words, Wilkie 'changed the whole system of art in the domestic style' (Haydon 1963, vol.3, p.420). Fuseli told Wilkie that it was a 'dangerous work' (Cunningham 1843, vol.1, p.116), and although he was referring to the danger of Wilkie being seduced by popular success, his words might equally have been applied to the threat it posed to his own art and that of other history painters in the grand style.

RH

THOMAS JONES

1742–1803

43 Pencerrig 1772

Oil on laid paper 31.8 × 22.2 (12½ × 8¾)

T08247

Thomas Jones was a pupil of the landscape painter and fellow Welshman Richard Wilson (see no.13). However, Jones's twentieth-century reputation does not rest with the large, ambitious canvases he painted in Wilson's manner and which are so lacking in the latter's richly evocative mood (Conisbee 1996, p.118). Even in his own day, there were probably others who would have agreed with Lord Herbert's assessment of these as 'so-so' (quoted Oppé, introduction to Jones's *Memoirs*, 1951, p.iv). Rather, Jones is remembered today for the series of astonishingly original and spontaneous oil sketches which he made in Wales in his early career and especially in Naples towards the end of a seven-year stay in Italy between 1776 and 1783. For nearly two centuries these sketches remained in the possession of Jones's descendants, itself an indication that they had been made for the artist's own instruction and pleasure rather than for sale (Stainton 1985, p.30). They only came to the attention of a twentieth-century audience in 1954, forcing many writers – including Paul Oppé himself – to revise their estimate of Jones's abilities as a painter.

Born into a large family of landowners in the Radnorshire marches, Jones was originally destined to enter the Church. However, his university education was cut short in 1761 on the death of the great uncle who had agreed to finance his studies, and by 1763 he had entered into 'Terms of Pupillage' with Richard Wilson lasting two years. It was in 1770 that he first began making oil studies on paper in the open air, but the best known of these early sketches were executed on trips home to the family estate at Pencerrig in 1772 and 1775–6. It is possible that Jones had learned the practice directly from Wilson, for in the 1750s Wilson had been acquainted in Rome with the French artist Claude-Joseph Vernet (1714–1789) whose precept, according to Sir Joshua Reynolds, was to 'paint from nature instead of drawing'. However, Wilson is not known to have made such studies himself, and it seems just as likely that Jones developed the practice independently – perhaps when planning the landscape backgrounds of his early canvases cast in the language of the historical 'Sublime' (Gowing 1985, p.17).

This sketch was made by Jones during a four-month stay at Pencerrig in the late summer of 1772. 'The fitful flashes of sunlight', wrote Lawrence Gowing, 'that pick out the corners of the harvest fields and the gaps in the clouds, which promise a break in the weather, are, I believe, how the end of summer truly is in Radnorshire' (Gowing 1985, p.20). There is another oil study of Pencerrig by Jones in the Oppé collection dating from his later visit to the family estate in 1776 (T08243).

AL

THOMAS JONES

1742–1803

44 Ariccia, Buildings on the Edge of the Town 1777

Watercolour over pencil with gum arabic on laid paper
28.3 × 42.8 (11⅛ × 16⅞)

Inscribed at top in pencil '5' and 'Larici 22d May 1777 TJ'
and 'E'; verso an unfinished sketch inscribed 'continuation
of the view marked "D"', and showing the relative positions
of 'Larici', 'Gardens of Capuchin Convt at Albano', 's',
and the 'Benedictine Convent of the Madona of the
Galoro | near Larici'

T08141

Jones is remembered today not only for his striking oil sketches but also for the important memoirs he wrote towards the end of his life. Published in full in 1951, when they were edited and introduced by Paul Oppé, the memoirs are a remarkably rich source of information about the lives of English artists (especially those who travelled to Italy) in the second half of the eighteenth century. The Italian portion of the memoirs is particularly detailed and reliable, since – as Oppé indicates – at this point Jones was clearly following (and sometimes actually incorporating) his diary.

Jones records in his *Memoirs* that between 29 April and 24 May 1777 he was staying in the town of Genzano south-east of Rome in the Alban hills, and making regular excursions in the neighbourhood of Nemi and Albano. Even before his arrival in Italy in 1776 he had become, in his own words, 'insensibly ... familiarised' with this region and with other parts of the country through the copies he had made after his 'Old Master', Richard Wilson – to the extent, indeed, that when he did finally touch Italian soil 'every scene seemed anticipated in some dream – It appeared Magick Land' (*Memoirs*, December 1776, p.55). This view is dated 22 May 1777, and Jones's memoir for that day confirms that he went to

'Larici' (Arriccia) and to the small nearby village of 'Galoro' (Galloro) with the architect Thomas Hardwick and 'Vincenzo', returning to Genzano 'by the Appian Way to dinner by 4' (*Memoirs*, p.60).

Most representations of Ariccia at this period show the famous view looking up the escarpment to Bernini's Church of Santa Maria dell'Assunzione and the Palazzo Chigi (see no.13). While still depicting the town from below, Jones shows it from the opposite side, from the south-east, a conclusion which can only be arrived at by comparing two other (more distant) views by him of Ariccia similarly seen from this direction (London, Phillips, 15 April 1985, and Hawcroft 1988, no.72; the latter is marked 'D', like the verso of this drawing, and forms a continuous panorama with it). However, so rare is this viewpoint that, although inscribed 'Larici', this watercolour has until now been misidentified as a convent at Albano (an error compounded by the misreading of the date as 11 May 1777). Jones appears to have been fascinated by the roof-lines of the variously proportioned buildings, and the patterning of window openings in the façades below (Hawcroft 1983, no.7). A few years later he was to be similarly attracted to the urban roofscape of Naples (see fig.7).

AL

THOMAS JONES
1742–1803

45 The Bay of Naples and the Mole Lighthouse 1782

Oil on laid paper 24.5 × 39.6 (9⅝ × 15⅝)

Inscribed verso in pencil 'TJ | Naples – March 1782'

T08246

During his seven-year stay in Italy Jones made two visits to Naples, one between September 1778 and January 1779 and another, more extended visit between 1780 and 1783. He was still intent on attracting commissions for large-scale oils, and on the second visit was especially hopeful of securing the patronage of the influential British envoy Sir William Hamilton (by the time Hamilton did get round to commissioning a picture in 1783 Jones had already decided to return to England; see Stainton 1996, p.183). It is from this second visit to Naples that the most celebrated of all Jones's oil studies belong, most of them painted from a window or from the flat roof of the various studios he rented.

The first set of lodgings Jones occupied, between May 1780 and 3 May 1782, is described in some detail in his *Memoirs*. He took rooms in a 'large new built house or Palace if you please' situated opposite the 'Custom house for Salt' in a noisy area near the old harbour. The ground floor was 'all appropriated to Warehouses', and the rest of the building being empty, Jones selected 'that Part of the second floor nearest the Sea, being by far the pleasantest, with the use of the Lastrica or Terras Roof' (Jones, *Memoirs*, pp.95–6). It was from this 'lastrica' that in April 1782 Jones made some of the earliest of his oil studies of roof-tops and buildings in Naples – his moving to

smaller rooms on an unspecified level of the building the previous year had clearly not prevented him access to the roof. The elevated viewpoint of this study suggests that it, too, was painted from the same spot; for from this vantage point Jones would no doubt have enjoyed views in many directions and given his proximity to the sea, presumably towards the harbour as well. Since this study is dated a month earlier than the others, it may well have been the first in this remarkable series.

The old harbour with its prominent lighthouse was a centre of great social activity in this period and offered magnificent views of Vesuvius and the Sorrentine peninsula (Hawcroft 1988, p.94). Thanks both to his elevated viewpoint and to his orientation away from the harbour, with this oil study Jones produces something very different from the more conventional representations of the scene (fig.19). He paints a simple stretch of water looking across to the Sorrentine peninsula, articulated only by the lighthouse and a sequence of rhythmically placed feluccas. The overwhelming impression is one of stillness and calm. Lawrence Gowing (1985, p.52) has described how studies like these achieve 'an enveloping unity by means quite opposite to dramatic illustration. They are gentle and precise and they illustrate nothing. They simply *are*.'

AL

fig. 19 John Robert Cozens, *Vesuvius and Somma from the Mole at Naples c.*1782–3, watercolour over pencil *Ashmolean Museum, Oxford*

WILLIAM PARS
1742–1782

46 A Bridge on the River Ticino, near Polleggio *c.*1770

Watercolour over pencil with some gum arabic on laid paper 24.3 × 33.7 (9½ × 13¼);
artist's washline border 30.8 × 40.1 (12⅛ × 15¾)
Inscribed on mount with title 'ON THE TESIN NEAR POLEGGIO.' and in
pencil 'marvellous'
T08276

'Though brought up to Portrait', commented Thomas Jones on hearing of the death of his old friend William Pars, his 'inward bias [was] in favour of Landscape … He executed his tinted Drawings after nature, with a taste peculiar to himself' (Jones, *Memoirs*, 2 November 1782 p.116). Like many of the landscape draughtsmen of his day, Pars was chiefly dependent for his livelihood on aristocratic patronage and the demand for careful records of antiquarian and topographical subjects. Although, according to Jones, Pars would 'sometimes curse his fate, in being obliged to follow such trifling an Employment; as he called it', he was never the less one of the most sophisticated and accomplished topographers of his age. He was among the first of those watercolourists in the mid-eighteenth century to find a profound inspiration in travel, and the best of his work reveals a degree of expressiveness rarely encountered in the more literal topographical drawings of his contemporaries.

The son of a London metal chaser, Pars launched his career (as Jones indicated) painting portraits, and seems at this time also to have aspired to history painting. In 1764, however, he was selected as official draughtsman on an expedition to Greece and Asia Minor with the antiquary Richard Chandler (1738–1810) and architect Nicholas Revett (1720–1804). The expedition was funded by the Society of Dilettanti, established in 1732 by a group of noblemen and gentlemen keen to further an appreciation of the arts, especially the Antique; Pars's watercolours (many of which are now in the British Museum) were engraved in the Society's own two-volume publication, *Ionian Antiquities*, which appeared between 1769 and 1797. One of those who joined the Society in the mid-1760s was Henry Temple, second Viscount Palmerston

(father of the famous nineteenth-century statesman), who in the summer of 1770 employed Pars to accompany him on a journey through Switzerland as far as Lake Maggiore, travelling back along the Rhine valley. Their travels lasted over three months, and were described in some detail in a journal kept by Palmerston.

On 15 August artist and patron crossed the St Gotthard Pass (the famous Devil's Bridge earning the briefest of mentions in Palmerston's journal), travelling as far as Airolo. When, however, they followed the river Ticino (or Tessin) down to Pollegio the next day, Palmerston was moved to comment: 'The Road lies along the Banks of the Tesin which is a beautiful River and affords a number of the most romantick scenes: particularly … a Bridge a little above Pollegio with a noble Waterfall close to it amongst vast Fragments of the Rock that have fallen from the neighbouring Mountains' (quoted Wilton 1979A, p.16). Perhaps in response to his patron's enthusiasm for this site, Pars has produced a very daring composition in which – unlike his representations of the *Bridge near Mont Grimsel* and the *Devil's Bridge* itself, both in the British Museum – he has boldly raised the arch of the stone bridge against the sky (see Wilton 1979A, pp.16, 33 and 45). Furthermore, especially when compared with other Swiss subjects Pars worked up after the tour (for example no.47), this is a remarkably vivid piece of painting, with its strong greens and yellows and vigorously applied washes. Palmerston was evidently pleased with the result, inscribing the word 'marvellous' on the mount; on another of Pars's watercolours in the Oppé collection, *The Salmon Leap on the Liffey near Leixlip* (T08190), Palmerston has similarly inscribed the comment 'Cf Fall in the Tessin (Ticino) perfectly wonderful.'

AL

ON THE TESIN, NEAR POLEGGIO.

Marcellus

106

WILLIAM PARS
1742–1782

47 Schaffhausen *c.*1770

Watercolour over pencil with pen and black ink and some gum arabic on laid paper 26.8 × 47.6 (10½ × 18¾); artist's washline border 33.5 × 54.3 (13¼ × 21⅜)

Inscribed on mount with title 'SCHAFFAUSEN.' and in upper-right corner '3'; also inscribed on verso in pencil 'Schaffousen'

T08140

On 31 August 1770, some two weeks after they had travelled along the River Ticino to Polleggio (see no.46), Pars and his patron Lord Palmerston reached Schaffhausen on the river Rhine. Here Palmerston noted in his journal the 'very considerable Bridge cover'd with a Gallery as many of the Swiss and German Bridges are' and continued: 'There is one Pier from which to either shore the Span is very great. The whole is supported by Framework consisting of vast Beams of Timber mechanically put together and which run up into the Roof of the Gallery under which one passes. I did not learn the exact length of the Bridge but from my own Computation by stepping it I am convinced it is not less than 130 Yards long. These cover'd Bridges in general have a very clumsy appearance' (quoted Wilton 1979A, p.18).

Whether it was partly in response to Palmerston's scientific curiosity about the bridge's construction and length, or whether because – unlike *A Bridge on the River Ticino* (no.46) – this subject is more purely topographical, Pars has here produced a rather drier, more conventional rendering of his subject. A faithful record of Schaffhausen's bridge and town, dominated by the fort of the Munot in the distance, it is tighter and crisper in handling than no.46, with the forms carefully outlined in pen and ink according to the traditional method of the topographer's art. However, Pars's watercolours are usually enlivened with realistically observed figures, and here he shows one seated on the river bank apparently rolling up his breeches, perhaps preparing to immerse his ankles in the river Rhine. He has extended the composition at the left by adding a 5cm strip of paper, enabling him to incorporate the bridge's stone support on the river's near side, and has then animated this section of the view by inserting a carriage moving out of the composition to the left. Some of the darkest areas in the foreground, corresponding to shadow, have been strengthened and enriched with a layer of varnish (gum arabic), which is something found in other watercolours by him made at this date (see nos.46 and 48).

When in 1771 Pars exhibited a group of his Swiss watercolours at the Royal Academy, for example, views of the Devil's Bridge in the Pass of St Gothard, of Chamonix and of Grindelwald, they were the first specifically Alpine views to be seen publicly in England (Stainton 1985, p.32). They anticipated by several years the Swiss subjects made by John Robert Cozens (for example, *A Torrent between Rocks and Trees*, *c.*1776, Oppé collection, T08773) and Francis Towne (no.35). In the early 1770s five of Pars's Swiss watercolours (mostly the exhibited subjects) were engraved by the famous print-maker William Woollett (1735–1785), and published by Pars himself, then reissued in 1783 after his death by the London publisher and printseller John Boydell.

AL

SCHAFFAUSEN.

WILLIAM PARS
1742–1782

48 Waterfall near the Lake of Killarney c.1771

Watercolour over pencil with some gum arabic on laid
paper 48.4 × 33.5 (19 × 13⅛); artist's washline border
55 × 39.8 (21⅝ × 15⅝)
Inscribed on mount with title 'A WATERFALL NEAR THE
LAKE OF KILLARNY' and in pencil 'Glengariff'
T08278

In the summer of 1771, a year after accompanying Lord
Palmerston on a journey though Switzerland (see
nos.46–7), Pars was asked to join his old patron on a tour
of Ireland and the Lake District. Their travels in Ireland
embraced all the picturesque sites, including Sligo, Lough
Key, Adare, Killarney, Lismore, Powerscourt and Leixlip
(Crookshank and the Knight of Glin 1994, p.83). The
watercolours Pars worked up after the trip, an important
group of which are in the Victoria and Albert Museum,
show his style moving in the direction anticipated by
A Bridge on the River Ticino (no.46) – that is to say towards
a softer and more atmospheric manner, with little in the
way of careful pen outlines, except perhaps to indicate
the shapes of trees. This watercolour of a waterfall near
the Lake of Killarney has been mounted by Pars himself on a washline mount for presentation to Lord
Palmerston, and inscribed with a title, just as he had done
for many of the Swiss subjects made for his patron the
previous year (see especially no.46). It may have been
Palmerston himself who added the pencil inscription
'Glengariff', perhaps remembering the more exact
location of the falls as nearer to the village of that name
in nearby county Cork off Bantry Bay. Another, more
distant view of an Irish waterfall, *The Falls of the
Powerscourt*, is in the Yale Center for British Art (repr.
Wilcox 1985, no.6), and the Oppé collection also
includes *The Salmon Leap on the Liffey near Leixlip* (see
under no.46).

In 1774 Pars received the first bursary awarded by the
Society of Dilettanti to study in Rome, initially intending
to stay three years, though in the event he remained
in Italy until his death in 1782. During these years he
painted portraits, made copies from old masters, and also
produced topographical watercolours, sometimes sketching alongside Francis Towne, Thomas Jones and John
'Warwick' Smith. Jones shared lodgings with Pars in
Rome for a few months in 1779 in a house formerly
occupied by the seventeenth-century Neapolitan painter
Salvator Rosa (1615–1673), whose craggy landscapes and
banditti subjects were popular in Britain at this date
(see no.39). Towne, a lifelong friend, later decided to
bequeath his Italian watercolours to the British Museum
out of respect for Pars, whose work for the Society of
Dilettanti's expedition to Greece and Asia Minor (see
under no.46) had been presented by the Society to the
Museum in 1799. Given Pars's penchant for waterfalls, it
is perhaps somewhat ironic that in 1782, despite being 'a
robust, hearty fellow', he should have succumbed to
'dropsy of the breast' (pleurisy) contracted from standing
too long in the water whilst sketching Neptune's grotto
under the Grand Cascade at Tivoli near Rome (Whitley
1928, vol.2, p.344).

AL

A WATERFALL NEAR THE LAKE OF KILLARNY

DAVID ALLAN
1744–1796

49 The Start of the Race in the Corso, Rome c.1767–77

Grey and brown washes over pencil with pen and brown
ink on laid paper 21.9 × 38 (8⅝ × 15)

TO8119

After studying art in Glasgow in 1767 the Scottish artist David Allan left for Italy and embarked on a career as a history painter with the encouragement of his compatriot Gavin Hamilton (1723–1798). In 1773 he became the first British artist to win an international competition at the Academy of St Luke in Rome with a heroic classical canvas, *The Departure of Hector*. However, in later years he abandoned history painting for portraiture which was to become his principal livelihood. Despite Allan's undoubted gifts as a portrait painter, nevertheless his twentieth-century reputation rests with his genre subjects, especially his representations of dances, games and public amusements, made both during his ten-year stay in Italy and on his subsequent return to Scotland.

Some of the best known of Allan's Italian genre subjects are the ten pen and wash drawings of Rome during the Carnival which were later acquired by the Prince Regent and are now in the Royal Collection (Oppé 1950, nos.21–30). Four of them, including that of *The Horse Race at Rome*, were engraved in aquatint by Paul Sandby between 1780 and 1781 (fig.20). The riderless horse-race in the Corso at Rome took place annually, as part of the Carnival festivities, from at least 1700 until well into the nineteenth century, and had its origins in a Roman custom, as a printed description accompanying Sandby's prints explains; the Romans had 'obliged' members of the Jewish community 'to run in sacks annually to divert them', but the latter 'finding it dangerous and tiresome, offered … horses to run in their stead'.

The print (and its related drawing at Windsor, Oppé 1950, no.23) shows the race in full swing. However, this drawing shows the dramatic start, a subject which was to be treated more famously a number of years later by the French Romantic artist Théodore Gericault (1791–1824). The same printed description accompanying the prints describes the start of the race thus: 'a strong rope is stretched about three feet high, at which the horses are held by men who are ready to let them all go at the signal … each horse has two men, the one to put off the bridle, the other to give a cut with the whip; on the rope falling to the ground, they all spring off at once, and run almost as fast as at Newmarket … the mortars are immediately fired to give notice to the people to keep out of their way'. The race was not without its dangers; horses could fall, and members of the crowd might become trampled underfoot.

AL

fig.20 Paul Sandby after David Allan, *The Horse Race at Rome During the Carnival* 1781, aquatint engraving *Trustees of the British Museum*

JOSEPH FARINGTON
1747–1821

50 'Original Sketches Worcester 1' c.1789

Sketchbook formerly inscribed with title as above, containing fourteen pages and bound with blue paper covers

Sketchbook size 28.4 × 38.4 (11⅛ × 15⅛)
T08446–T08460

Open at p.3, *North-East View of Worcester Cathedral*
watercolour over pencil on wove paper 27.9 × 38.1 (11 × 15)
T08449

It is for his *Diaries*, spanning the years 1793 to 1821, that the painter and Royal Academician Joseph Farington is generally remembered today. The diaries present an unrivalled account of artistic life in London at the turn of the century, as well as chronicling the day-to-day affairs, politics and rivalries at the Royal Academy itself – Farington serving on many of its influential committees as well as being on its Council at various stages of his career (Newby 1996, p.807). So powerful was his influence, indeed, that he earned the nickname 'Dictator at the Royal Academy', and the portrait painter James Northcote (1746–1831) even went so far as to claim that Farington cared infinitely more for 'the love of power' than he did for pictures themselves, at the same time dismissing Farington as being 'no painter' (quoted Hardie 1966, vol.1, p.185).

Whilst Northcote probably exaggerated Farington's appetite for power, it is true that the latter was not in fact an artist of any great imaginative powers. Although a pupil of the classical landscape painter Richard Wilson (no.13), Farington himself chose to specialise in topography. He exhibited many landscapes in oil, but few are known today – those that do survive are rather modest works which tend to reveal Wilson's influence (an example, *The Oak Tree*, is in the Tate Gallery, T00786). Farington's drawings, by contrast, are very plentiful. They range in type from carefully controlled, often rather literal topographical views generally executed in pen and ink with monochrome washes to small, bold and very spirited sketches (sometimes imaginary subjects) made either in the same media or in black and white chalks on coloured (usually blue) paper.

This example, a page from a sketchbook almost certainly used by Farington on his tour of the West Midlands in 1789, is closer in spirit to his more formal, finished views of actual places. Although the use of colour is relatively rare in Farington's work, underneath the delicate washes of pink, purple, ochre and blue he has employed the drawing style he almost always favoured for works of urban topography. This manner of draughtsmanship derives from the Venetian artist Canaletto (1697–1768), some of whose drawings Farington owned, and which became something of a 'house style' for artists working in the circle of Dr Thomas Monro in the 1790s, such as Girtin and Turner (nos.77 and 78). This drawing style is characterised by the use of short, cursive strokes (sometimes resembling dots or dashes) and of lines which vary in thickness depending on the pressure exerted by the drawing instrument (usually pencil, as here, or ink). It was particularly well suited to the description of variations in surface texture and thus ideal for recording the intricate details of architectural façades, especially highly decorated cathedral façades. This sketch is also particularly interesting in showing Farington's use of ruled pencil perspective lines, which meet at a point on the right-hand pinnacle of the cathedral's east end.

There are other views of Worcester in this sketchbook as well as studies of Malvern Abbey, Gloucester, the churches and castles at Berkeley and Thornbury, and St Mary Redcliffe, Bristol. The last image in the book is a remarkably fresh and painterly watercolour sketch made on the banks of a river (presumably the Severn), and surely coloured from nature. Another sketchbook used by Farington on this 1789 tour is in the Victoria and Albert Museum, as is a finished drawing by him in blue and grey washes of Worcester Cathedral from the river, also dated to the same year. Further drawings from the tour are in the Royal Library, Windsor, and in the City Museum and Art Gallery, Gloucester. In 1792 Farington exhibited a *View of Part of Worcester Cathedral* at the Royal Academy.

AL

JOHN 'WARWICK' SMITH
1749–1831

51 Outside Porta Pia, Rome *c.*1777–8

Watercolour over pencil on laid paper 26.5 × 47 (10⅜ × 18½)
Inscribed verso in pencil 'Distant View of the hills
of Frascati & Monte Cavo' and '25'
T08486

'Warwick' Smith enjoyed a remarkably high reputation as a watercolourist in his own day. Ackermann's *Repository of Art* for 1812 claimed he was 'the first artist who attempted to unite depth and richness of colour, with the clearness and aerial effect of Cozens [J.R. Cozens] … Indeed, it may with truth be said, that with this artist the first epoch of painting in water colours originated' (quoted in Hardie 1966, vol.1, p.116). It is now clear that Smith was not quite so much of a technical innovator as contemporary reviewers believed; indeed, to some extent Smith seems to have arrived at his painterly style through absorbing the influence of other artists' methods and styles. This is particularly true of the five years he spent in Italy between 1776 and 1781 – the period from which his finest work dates – when he was working alongside fellow artists Jones, Pars and Towne.

Born in Cumberland, the son of a gardener to the Gilpin family, Smith studied under the animal painter Sawrey Gilpin. In about 1775 his artistic gifts were spotted by the second Earl of Warwick, who funded Smith's visit to Italy – although the sobriquet 'Warwick' Smith more likely derives from the artist's settling in Warwick on his return from the Continent rather than from the source of his patronage. We know from Thomas Jones's *Memoirs* that by February 1778 Smith was living in lodgings to the north-east of Rome 'about 2 miles without the Porta Pia', the vicinity in which this watercolour was made (and close to where Towne's panorama of the Campagna was painted a few years later, see no.37).

Since Smith's view is inscribed as looking towards 'the hills of Frascati and Monte Cavo', the direction of the light indicates it must have been made at sunrise rather than sunset (and, indeed, most of the shutters on the prominent building to the left are still closed). With its pearly morning light and subtle palette of greys, greens, pinks, mauves and shades of oyster brown, it is a remarkably evocative and atmospheric watercolour which may owe something to Smith's knowledge of William Pars's work. However, it is even closer in mood and treatment to the watercolours of John Robert Cozens, who was also in Rome at this date, and who Smith would therefore presumably have known – indeed in the summer of 1777 Cozens was actually recuperating from an illness in this very vicinity, at the villa of Signor Martinelli, 'near S'a Agnese without the Porta Pia' (Jones, *Memoirs*, 1 June 1778). Indeed, before this work passed into the collection of Paul Oppé through the Coles Bequest it belonged to the famous collector Dr John Percy (1817–1889), who has inscribed on the old mount the names of Pars and J.R. Cozens as tentative attributions before finally arriving at the authorship of 'Warwick' Smith himself.

AL

JOHN 'WARWICK' SMITH
1749–1831

52 Convent of La Trinità near La Cava *c.*1778–9

Watercolour and pen and black ink over pencil, with
touches of white gouache on laid paper; 32 × 43.7 (12½ × 17¼);
artist's ruled mount 36.4 × 47.1 (14⅜ × 18½)

Inscribed in pencil in upper border 'Convent of La Trinita
19 near La Cava'

T08506

This watercolour is one of a series of twenty-four views
by 'Warwick' Smith in the Oppé collection of Naples
and the surrounding area which were once mounted in
an album; it is numbered 19 in the manuscript list of
contents which still survives, and is still mounted on its
backing sheet, although the album itself is now completely dismembered. They are a varied group, both in
size and handling. However, most of them have extensive
pencilwork which implies that they are on-the-spot
sketches, even if colour washes (and especially the small
touches of gouache in this example) were added soon
afterwards; indeed, one of them, *Near Sorento* (T08495), is
actually inscribed in places with the artist's colour notes.
It is possible that this and similar albums of Smith's work
were assembled by the artist himself (see Hardie 1966,
vol.1, p.113). If this is the case, then this one was compiled late in the artist's life, as several of its surviving pages
carry watermarks of 1825.

Thanks to Jones's *Memoirs*, we know that Smith was in
Naples between March 1778 and July 1779. During the
summers of these two years Smith took lodgings east
of Naples on the coast at Vietri, overlooking the Gulf
of Salerno; a watercolour from the album, *General View of
the Town of Vietri* (T08505), indicates with a cross 'My
Residence for two successive summers'. Indeed, most of
Smith's watercolours from the album which show views
of or near to Vietri, Amalfi, Otrano and the village of

Corpo La Cava (situated a little inland from Vietri overlooking a narrow valley) were probably sketched during
one of these summers. If so, they cannot have been drawn
in the company of Thomas Jones, who in his *Memoirs*
records frequent sketching expeditions with Smith during
his first visit to Naples between September 1778 and
January 1779. Nevertheless, many of Smith's views from
the album, including this one of the Benedictine abbey of
La Trinità near La Cava founded in 1025 by St Alferius,
do seem to show the influence of Jones's denser and
tighter watercolour technique (compare, for example,
no.44). In September 1782 (during his second trip to
Italy), John Robert Cozens was also to make a number of
sketches in and around Vietri and La Cava (see sketchbooks nos.III and IV, Sotheby's 1973).

When 'Warwick' Smith returned to England, he
travelled widely in Wales (see no.66) and the Lake
District, but he is chiefly remembered for the numerous
variants and reworkings he made of his Italian and
Swiss subjects. The latter were sometimes produced for
engraving – his *Select Views in Italy* being published in
parts between 1792 and 1799 – but they were especially
made for exhibition and sale at the Society of Painters
in Watercolour, of which Smith became a full member
in 1806, and President in 1814, 1817 and 1818. Indeed,
he exhibited a version of this subject at the Society in
1807.

AL

HENRY WILLIAM BUNBURY
1750–1811

53 'Coffee is quite ready Gentlemen' ?c.1783

Pencil and watercolour on laid paper 22.3 × 30.5 (8¾ × 12)

Inscribed in brown ink along the bottom edge
'Coffee is quite ready Gentlemen. | I hope I have not
entirely forgot you. HB' and in brown ink on the back
'To Sʳ W.W. Wynn'

T08115

Henry Bunbury was an amateur caricaturist who achieved wide fame during his lifetime for his witty and observant drawings of modern manners. Many were engraved for sale, and his friend Horace Walpole was just one of many who pasted these entertaining prints into a special album. Walpole so much admired Bunbury that he described him enthusiastically as 'the second Hogarth', and both Thomas Rowlandson (nos.67–9) and James Gillray, far greater draughtsmen and caricaturists than Bunbury, acknowledged his inventiveness by making versions of his designs (Riely 1975, pp.29–44). Bunbury's first humorous sketches date from his schooldays. In making these he was, no doubt unconsciously, drawing on a relatively new tradition, inspired by the Italian art of *caricatura* (from the Italian word *caricare* meaning 'loaded') which had been largely popularised in England in the 1750s by another amateur, George, 1st Marquess of Townshend, who satirised many of his contemporaries. These, in their turn, owed much to the Italian portrait caricaturist P.L. Ghezzi (1674–1755). But it was probably during his Grand Tour in 1769–70 that Bunbury realised that when he returned home he could profitably use his skills as a draughtsman and humorist by exploiting the Englishman's enduring love of irony. He would have seen this in Florence when he met the English artist Thomas Patch who specialised in painting caricatures of his fellow Grand Tourists, drew one of Bunbury and painted a group portrait in this style for him (Belsey 1996, no.42, p.87).

As a talented, witty and sociable gentleman (he was the son of a baronet), Bunbury was naturally welcome in the very part of society which provided the most fertile ground for humour – the houses of the rich. However, it is usually impossible to identify the origins of the humorous incidents which he depicts. Often, because he leaves so much unsaid, the pleasure is found in unravelling just what he might mean, though in the case of this drawing it is possible to be precise about some details. The inscription below the drawing rings true as a record of words, coming from the next room, overheard by the artist. The unseen speaker's gently ironic 'quite ready' and his or her's (probably the latter because a drink is being served) hope that the 'Gentlemen' have not been 'entirely forgot' say clearly that the coffee is going cold just because the men have, indeed, forgotten that it was announced – probably because they have been too preoccupied elsewhere in the house. Mildly chastened by the servant's announcement they stride purposefully towards the refreshments. There is a private joke in all this and the inscription on the back indicates that it was one shared by the artist and Sir Watkin Williams-Wynn (?1748–1789).

Bunbury was a regular visitor to the Williams-Wynn estate at Wynnstay in North Wales where during the 1780s he often participated in the family's amateur theatricals (Riely 1983, pp.4, 11, 12). Almost certainly T08115 is a product of one of these visits. A comparison between the portrait of Wynn in Sir Joshua Reynolds's group portrait *Members of the Society of Dilettanti* of 1777–9 (Penny 1986, no.109) and the central figure in a striped waistcoat shows that Bunbury has, indeed, portrayed his host. The man standing in profile in the left foreground, apparently supervising a boy poring over a book, looks every bit the tutor. From 1779 to 1783 Williams-Wynn's two boys, Watkin (1772–1840) and Charles (1775–1850), were tutored by the philologist Robert Nares (1753–1829; DNB), and a comparison between Burney's tutor and John Hoppner's portrait of Nares (photo in Witt Library) suggests that he has here shown Nares with one of his charges. The moment relished by Bunbury was Williams-Wynn, the great patrician landowner, at the mercy of a servant.

RH

142

Coffee is quite ready Gentlemen.
I hope I have not entirely forgot you HB.

JOHN DOWNMAN
1750–1824

54 View of Roof Tops, Nice 1773

Grey washes over pencil with pen and black ink on laid paper
26.5 × 36.7 (10⅜ × 14½)
Inscribed in pen and brown ink top left 'City of Nice Dec[r]. 20th. 1773'
and lower right in pencil 'View of the Tops of Buildings |
from my Bed Room Window | in the City of Nice on a bad Day |
1773. J[o] D'
T10169

Downman was born in Ruabon, North Wales, and after a period of studying drawing in Liverpool, moved to London where he worked in the studio of the American painter Benjamin West (1738–1820). In 1769 he was one of the first thirty-six students of painting to enrol at the Royal Academy Schools (Munro 1996, p.7). West specialised in history painting, the most highly regarded of all the various painting genres, and was a conscientious and sympathetic teacher. Although most of Downman's early exhibits at the Royal Academy were portraits – and he was subsequently to make his reputation as a portraitist (see no.56) – in 1773 he showed his first history painting in oils. Some years later it was to become clear that Downman's skills as a history painter left much to be desired (see Munro 1996, p.15). However, when Downman left England in late 1773 with Joseph Wright of Derby for a period of study in Italy (see no.29), he was no doubt still nurturing aspirations to become a history painter in the 'grand' style.

There is, indeed, evidence that Downman did at least make some studies on his Italian trip after the great Renaissance masters such as Raphael (see Munro 1996, pp.8–9). However, judging by the remarkable sequence of landscape studies by him in the Oppé collection, it seems to have been the Italian landscape itself which provided the greatest inspiration during his stay. Executed solely or primarily in monochrome washes and pen and ink, Downman's landscape studies are stylistically very similar to a number of landscape drawings produced by Wright of Derby on the same trip. One author interpreted this as indicating that Downman, still in his early twenties, was inclined to imitate his older sketching companion (Nicolson 1968, p.6), but if anything Downman's sketches are the more original and inventive. This is certainly true of this striking study of Nice roof-tops made during a three-week break in the city (at that date administered by the House of Savoy) *en route* to Italy. It is an astonishingly unconventional landscape for its date, made as the inscription indicates out of the artist's 'bedroom window … on a bad day'. Indeed, it has an almost photographic directness which invites comparison with similar studies of Neapolitan roof-tops made by Thomas Jones in oil almost ten years later (fig.7).

There are also three grey wash studies by Downman in the Oppé collection of the cave and shore at Nice (T09543, T10433, T10167; see Munro 1996, p.22). It seems likely that a similar grey wash study of an interior of a cave by Wright of Derby in a private collection, tentatively identified until now as having been drawn near Naples (Egerton 1990, p.150), may in fact have also been made on the shore at Nice. Certainly the two artists must sometimes have been sketching side by side at this date, as a *View near the City of Nice* by Downman in the Oppé collection (T09544) is nearly identical to Wright's view of the same scene in the Rhode Island School of Design (*Bulletin of Rhode Island School of Design*, April 1972, no.11).

AL

JOHN DOWNMAN

1750–1824

55 A Tree Trunk near Albano 1774

Watercolour with pen and black ink on laid paper
54 × 38.1 (21¼ × 15)
Inscribed lower left in pencil 'in the Wood near
Albano 1774 by J° D'
T10176

Downman and Wright of Derby remained in Rome until June 1775, and probably travelled back to England together in the late summer of the same year. The landscape drawings they made during their stay depict sites mainly in Rome or (in Downman's case) in the hill-top towns and woods outside the city, especially at Albano to the south-east. It is assumed that the two artists made an excursion together to Naples and Mount Vesuvius in the autumn of 1774, as both produced studies of the famous volcano's crater (see Munro 1996, no.7, Oppé collection, T10174; and Egerton 1990, no.86). Whilst Wright was to continue to pursue his interest in landscape after his return to England, for Downman the experience remained virtually unique – the only other occasion he is known to have made landscape sketches was on a tour to the Lake District in 1812 (Victoria and Albert Museum). All the landscapes made by Downman on his Contintental tour of 1773–4 are in the Oppé collection, with the exception of two examples in the Chicago Art Institute and in a private collection.

Downman's Italian landscapes – rather like those made by Towne a few years later (no.34) – tend to focus on the more unassuming corners of Rome and the surrounding region rather than the grand views and sweeping vistas so popular with visiting Grand Tourists. Indeed, Martin Hardie linked Downman with Towne 'as an innovator with an entirely fresh eye for form and design' (1966, vol.1, p.146), and in fact it has recently been suggested that Towne may actually have seen Downman's landscape drawings before his own departure for Italy in 1780; the two artists had made each other's acquaintance in Devon some two years before (Wilcox 1997, p.73, and

see under no.34). This study of a tree trunk, seen from such a close (and low) viewpoint, is certainly remarkable for its early date. For the intense scrutiny of natural details did not become commonplace until the Romantic generation made it part of their practice in the early nineteenth century – William Mulready (see no.90) no doubt speaking for many of his artistic colleagues when declaring that his own commitment to sketching from Nature was undertaken to 'strengthen our knowledge of the structure [of the natural world] ... to enable us to paint better views with increased truth and feeling' (Heleniak 1980, p.47). In fact, by comparison with a tree study by, say, Cornelius Varley (no.84), Downman's tree trunk, with its delicate touches of watercolour and the elegant calligraphy of its adjacent plants and ferns, has a decorative quality – even a spirit of detachment – which makes it very much a product of its own time, despite its undoubted originality.

One of Downman's drawings made in Italy in the woods near Marino, just to the north of Albano, is inscribed by him as 'done in a camera obscura' (private collection, repr. Williams 1952, fig.143). The camera obscura was an apparatus which, very much like a modern photographic camera, admitted light through a small hole or lens, projecting an image of an object or scene onto a sheet of paper, ground glass or other surface so that its outlines could be traced. This device was often used by artists at this date, as it helped in the rendering of correct perspective, as well as giving richer contrasts of light and shadow and enhanced colour. Cornelius Varley invented a similar instrument which, unlike the camera obscura, could readily be used in full daylight (see no.84).

AL

in the Wood near Coleorton 1770 by JC

JOHN DOWNMAN
1750–1824

56 Thomas Williams, a black sailor 1815

Black chalk with stump on wove paper 31.5 × 28.5 (12⅜ × 11¼)

Inscribed in pencil upper right 'Thoˢ Williams | a Sailor | Liverpool Octʳ 13ᵗʰ 1815 | Note – Burnt Umber & w... | perfectly expresses the | complexion of a Negro'

T10168

Downman was one of the most popular and fashionable portraitists of his day. He launched his career as a portraitist in oils, but from the early 1780s took up the medium of coloured chalks for his small-scale portraits which enabled him to work more quickly. By 1786 his portraits were 'universally admired & sought after by the first people of rank and taste' (*Morning Post*, 4 May), his sitters including the famous actress Mrs Siddons and members of the Royal Family. By the late 1780s, however, his popularity was flagging, and one critic commented on the 'sameness' of his portraits: 'he has but two passable faces, one face for ladies and another for gentlemen, & one or other of these prototypes all his likenesses are brought to resemble' (quoted Munro 1996, p.16). From the mid-1790s Downman therefore modified his format and style in favour of a more penetrating approach to his sitters. Nevertheless, it is Downman's original sketches of his sitters (sometimes referred to by him as 'first studies') rather than his finished portraits which tend to show his insight into personality at its best (Munro 1996, p.7).

This is a remarkably sensitive late sketch of a black sailor, Thomas Williams, made by Downman, as the inscription indicates, in Liverpool in 1815. Nothing has so far been established about Williams's identity beyond what the inscription tells us, although since he is also included in a small watercolour composition by Downman of *Mr Wilberforce abolishing the Slave Trade* (whereabouts unknown), it would seem that he was acquainted with the famous MP William Wilberforce (1759–1833) who played such a crucial part in the passing of the 1807 Act which finally made slave trading illegal. It is possible that Williams originally took his English name from his owner when still a slave. The black chalk in this drawing has been softened and smudged by Downman using a stump (a tightly rolled paper or leather cylinder with rounded points, see also no.13), enabling him to model faces and flesh tones with great subtlety. He used the same combination of media for a number of other working sketches in the Oppé collection: a study for a composition of Celadon and Amelia, characters from James Thomson's long poem, *The Seasons* (1794), and originally from the same album compiled by Downman's daughter in 1825 as the portrait of Thomas Williams; a head of Amelia herself (recently struck dead in a thunderstorm), which has been described as 'among Downman's most virtuoso performances' in this technique; and an enchanting study of a kitten (T10171, T10173, T10166; see Munro 1996, nos.46–8).

Although it was chiefly as a portraitist that Downman earned his living, he regularly exhibited paintings on religious, literary and historical themes at the Royal Academy and elsewhere. His 1819 exhibit at the Academy, an allegorical subject entitled *A late Princess personifying Peace crowning the Glory of England reflected on Europe, 1815*, was bought by Sir Watkin Williams-Wynn, who is depicted at his estate at Wynnstay in North Wales in a drawing in the Oppé collection by Henry Bunbury (no.53). The Tate Gallery also has a small oval portrait in oils by Downman of Miss Jackson (T01885), the daughter of the organist and composer William Jackson of Exeter Cathedral, whom Downman married when she was in her forties, and who was described by Farington in 1810 as 'the ugliest & most forbidding woman in the world' (*Diary*, 2 November, vol.10, p.3783).

AL

HENRY TRESHAM
1750 or 1751–1814

57 The Devastation of the Earthquake at Messina, Sicily: The Palazzata *c.*1783–88

Brown ink and ink and watercolour wash over pencil
on laid paper 26.5 × 41.1 (10⅜ × 16⅛) mounted on laid
paper support 37.4 × 52.2 (14¾ × 20½) with artist's
washline border

Inscribed in ink below the border 'Devastation of the |
EARTHQUAKE | at | MESSINA'

T08265

Tresham was born in Dublin where, from 1765, he studied at the Dublin Society's drawing school. In 1775 he passed through London on the way to Rome where he had arrived by September 1775. His patron on this Italian trip which lasted until about March 1788 (Allen 1996, no.32) appears to have been the MP John Campbell, later Lord Cawdor (*c.*1753–1821); this drawing and two others in the Oppé collection which also show Messina after the earthquake (T08263–4) came from his collection.

After he returned to London, Tresham distinguished himself as a history painter, and it was undoubtedly with such a career in mind that he, like so many of his contemporaries, went to study in Rome. So the chief object of his study during the Italian years was inevitably the Antique – just as it had been with, for example, Richard Dalton (no.14). However, this by no means precluded seeking out and relishing landscape, particularly landscapes rich in historical associations, and Tresham's earthquake drawings are a good example of how such a sensibility could be dramatically stimulated by actual events: Tresham accompanied Thomas Jones (nos.43–5) and William Pars (nos.46–7) on their sketching trips around Rome including the volcanic landscape of Lake Albano and its vicinity which had prompted Jones to muse not only on its classical associations but also on its 'Awful marks of the most tremendous Convulsions of nature in the remotest Ages' (Jones, *Memoirs*, pp.55,58–9).

Just as the continually smoking Vesuvius (nos.21, 92) was a constant reminder of the destruction of Pompeii in AD 79, so the great earthquake which shook southern Italy on 5 February 1783 and devastated parts of Calabria and Sicily uniquely brought modern spectators into direct contact with a similarly apocalyptic moment. In reporting immediately back to London from Naples Sir William Hamilton wrote of boiling seas and shifting mountains, and that in Messina 'the superb building, called the Palazzata, which gave the port a more magnificent appearance than any port in Europe can boast of, had been entirely ruined', concluding that 'in short ... Messina was no more' (*Annual Register* for 1785, pp.50–1). Members of the Naples Academy, together with some draughtsmen, went to collect and record the facts of the disaster (*Annual Register*, p.56). Hoping to be a witness to these great events, Thomas Jones offered his services as a draughtsman free to Hamilton when in April 1783 he set off to look at the earthquake damage in Calabria, but Hamilton declined the offer (Jones, *Memoirs*, p.122).

Tresham appears to have been the only British artist to travel to Sicily and make a true record of the devastation. His views inevitably recall, for example, some of the engravings of the ruins of the ancient city of Palmyra which appeared in Wood and Dawkins's *The Ruins of Palmyra* (1753), or those of Greek ruins published by Le Roy (see under no.63) and it seems quite reasonable to assume that, along with his awareness of Pompeii, a parallel between the fates of ancient and modern civilisations was very much in Tresham's mind when he sat among the ruins sketching. In this drawing, just visible in the distance on the quayside and an intact survivor, is one of Messina's most famous monuments, the Fountain of Neptune of 1557 by the sculptor G.A. Montorsoli. When the German writer J.W. Goethe visited Messina in May 1787 he described it as an 'accursed city' and commented that 'there can be no more dreary sight in the world than the so-called Palazzata ... which now looks revoltingly gap-toothed and pierced with holes' (J.W. Goethe, London 1962, p.289)

RH

Devastation of the
EARTHQUAKE
at
MESSINA.

HENEAGE FINCH, FOURTH EARL OF AYLESFORD
1751–1812

58 Tenby ?1803

Pencil, pen and brown ink, and pink, grey and brown washes on laid paper
21 × 24.8 (8¼ × 9¾); artist's washline border 26.2 × 30. 3 (10¼ × 11⅞)
Inscribed in pen and brown ink in artist's washline border lower left 'Tenby'
T08126

According to the diarist Joseph Farington, the pupils of whom the drawing master John 'Baptist' Malchair was most proud were Sir George Beaumont (1753–1827) and Heneage Finch, later Fourth Earl of Aylesford. Indeed, Aylesford is usually recognised as the single most talented member of the 'Oxford School', his work being 'infinitely more accomplished' (Oppé 1943, p.197) than that of his teacher.

It was whilst an undergraduate at Oxford between 1767 and 1771 that Aylesford received tuition from Malchair, years when the Oxford School was in its heyday. 'Natural objects have, strictly speaking, no outline', Malchair was later to write in his *Observations on Landskipp drawing with Many and Various Examples Intended for the use of beginners*, 1791 (Ashmolean Museum, Oxford); and, indeed, Aylesford's early drawings are exercises in the sort of tonal sketching from nature that Malchair is known to have recommended to his pupils. However, under the influence of other artists such as Piranesi and especially of Rembrandt, Aylesford later developed a more personal language of drawing, in which grey, brown, pink or, perhaps, red-brick washes would be applied over slight pencil underdrawing, and then outlines added in ink to highlight and particularise form. In 1809 Farington recorded in his diary that Beaumont had seen some of Aylesford's recent drawings, describing them as 'studies from nature but executed in the stile of Rembrant' (*Diary*, 13 June 1809, vol.9, p.3486) – a description one could apply to the large majority of Aylesford's mature drawings.

Aylesford had succeeded to the title in 1777, and despite obtaining a series of Appointments which required his regular attendance at Court, remained a keen amateur artist throughout his life, even exhibiting at the Royal Academy (in an honorary capacity) in the 1780s. His drawings are rarely dated, but like this view of Tenby many are inscribed with their titles, often in the artist's own pale pink washline border. Three other views of Tenby by Aylesford are in the British Museum, and there is a fourth in a private collection. The British Museum also has a study by Aylesford of a bathing woman at Tenby, Margaret Davies, aged seventy-five, dated 1803, which may provide a clue to the dating of all these Tenby drawings, although he is known to have made frequent tours to Wales. Aylesford's drawing style was closely imitated by other members of his family, with the result that his work can be difficult to distinguish from theirs.

As well as a talented draughtsman, Aylesford was also an accomplished amateur architect and a keen collector, forming what is reputed to have been an unequalled collection of Rembrandt's prints. Rembrandt's influence is particularly pronounced in Aylesford's own etchings, a full catalogue of which was published by Paul Oppé in 1924.

AL

Tenby.

JOHN ROBERT COZENS
1752–1797

59 Satan Summoning his Legions c.1776

Brown washes with touches of yellow and red, with pen and black ink on
laid paper; diameter 27 (10⅝), sheet size 28.8 × 33.4 (11⅜ × 13⅛)
T08231

'The greatest genius that ever touched landscape' – so wrote John Constable in 1835 of John Robert Cozens, when preparing for one of his Hampstead lectures on art (Beckett 1966, p.147). Son of Alexander (nos.15–20), John Robert Cozens was one of the first artists to use watercolour consistently for its own sake as a purely expressive medium, and is remembered for his lyrical, evocative landscapes which are usually inspired by actual places (see no.60). However, his early work generally resembles that of his father, by whom he was taught, both in its imaginary content and in the use of monochrome washes.

This drawing, for example, is one of a group of imaginary scenes made by John Robert c.1776 (the others are mostly roundels as well) set in subterranean caverns or in landscapes with fantastic rock formations recalling Alexander's (see no.20). One of the other roundels shows Hannibal, the famous Carthaginian general, with his army on a crag above the plains of Italy (repr. Sloan 1986, p.101), and is thought to relate to an important oil (now lost) which John Robert exhibited at the Royal Academy in 1776, *Landscape with Hannibal in his March over the Alps, showing to his Army the Fertile Plains of Italy*. This oil, which was greatly admired at the time of its exhibition (and later had a powerful influence on J.M.W. Turner, no.78) seems to have been based on the sort of 'blot' drawing (see fig.14) which Alexander had recommended for the composing of imaginary landscapes (see nos.18–20). It is conceivable that these early roundels by John Robert were evolved from blots as well, though, thanks to the recent discovery of an album of his early drawings in the National Library of Wales, we now know that his convincing rendering of rock forms, crevices and caves owes much to the scenery he had seen and sketched on a trip to Matlock in Derbyshire in 1772 (Sloan 1986, p.103). The drawings anticipate some of the striking Alpine subjects he was to produce after his first tour to the Continent between 1776 and 1779, such as

Chiavenna or Via Mala in the Grisons, as well as his extraordinary watercolours of caverns in the Roman Campagna (Sloan 1986, pp.123–4, 133–6).

Some of the roundels in this group have only recently been identified as showing scenes from John Milton's epic poem *Paradise Lost*. This one represents the moment in Book I (ll.283–350) when Satan moves to the edge of the sea of fire, and stands with shield and upheld spear calling forth his fallen angels. Oppé (1952, p.126) suggested that the figure of Satan itself may have been drawn by another artist such as G.B. Cipriani (see no.22); another roundel in the Oppé collection (T08232) may show a scene from Book II where Satan passes through the Gulf between Heaven and Hell (Sloan 1986, pp.103–4). Until about 1776 Satan was generally depicted in British art as evil and despicable – Cozens's roundel is one of the very earliest to show him in heroic guise, thus anticipating some of the better-known representations of him in this role by later romantic artists such as James Barry (no.40). Milton was a republican and regarded as a model by those wishing to see Europe freed from tyranny, whilst *Paradise Lost* is itself a work concerned with rebellion (Pointon 1970, p.95).

For four years between c.1772 and 1776 John Robert Cozens lived in Bath with or near his uncle, the artist Robert Edge Pine (1730–1788), and may have come to share the latter's republican, and pro-American, sympathies. If so, then Cozens's casting of Satan as hero could, perhaps, be read as a symbol of his own support for the cause of the rebellious American colonies (who were, of course, to achieve their independence from Britain in 1776). In a similar way his oil painting of Hannibal shown at the Academy in 1776 might be read as a criticism of a monarchy's unrestrained exercise of power, Britain in this case equated with Carthage and the disasters which were to befall her on Hannibal's march to conquer Rome (Sloan 1986, p.112).

AL

JOHN ROBERT COZENS
1752–1797

60 View from Isola Borromea, Lago Maggiore c.1783

Watercolour over pencil on laid paper 26.4 × 38.3 (10⅜ × 15⅛)
Inscribed verso in pen and brown ink 'Lago Maggiore, Lombardy'
T08130

It is John Robert Cozens who is usually credited with achieving the vital transition from topographical view-making to romantic watercolour painting in Britain in the late eighteenth century. From his father's highly expressive but imaginary views John Robert absorbed a special understanding of the emotive powers of landscape. He harnessed this to actual views observed from nature, producing watercolours of an evocative power which elicited from John Constable another of his famous remarks about Cozens, that he was 'all poetry' (letter to John Fisher, 1821, Beckett 1968, p.72). Henry Fuseli called Cozens's watercolours 'creations of an enchanted eye', drawn with an 'enchanted hand' (quoted Sloan 1996, p.99).

Cozens's early drawings are usually executed in mono-chrome washes, influenced no doubt by his father's work (see no.59). Even the sequence of fifty-seven Alpine views John Robert made for the connoisseur and collector Richard Payne Knight (1751–1824), with whom he travelled through Switzerland to Italy in 1776, are essentially 'tinted' drawings with emphatic pen outlines (an example is in the Oppé collection, T08773). It was only towards the end of Cozens's first stay in Italy (he remained there until 1779) that he began to use colour, though his palette usually remains restricted to a range of soft blues, greens and grey; and he also began to define form using small touches of the brush, thus painting rather than drawing in watercolour. He developed a sure understanding of tone, and became a master of atmospheric recession.

This watercolour is one of a large series of drawings commissioned from Cozens by William Beckford, the temperamental young author and millionaire who was a friend and patron of his father, Alexander. John Robert had started making watercolours of Italian subjects for Beckford as early as 1780, and two years later he accompanied him on a journey to Italy, travelling through Germany and the Alps to Rome and Naples, and then returning to England in 1783 via the Italian Lakes and the Grande Chartreuse. During this, his second trip to the Continent, Cozens filled seven sketchbooks (Whitworth Art Gallery, Manchester) with small pencil and grey wash studies of sites observed during his travels, all carefully annotated with details of the locations and often dates as well, and it was from these that he later worked up more elaborate versions in colour. For example, this water-colour of Lake Maggiore seen from 'Isola Borromea' (Isola Bella), is based on a study he made on the second page of the seventh sketchbook (Sotheby's 1973, p.61 and repr.). The study, like many of the others in the sketch-books, is squared for transfer onto a second sheet.

Beckford eventually came to own an important collec-tion of ninety-four Italian subjects by Cozens, though in 1805, some years after the artist's death, he sold all of them at auction, probably because by that date he found them old-fashioned (Stainton 1985, p.37). His collection included some of the most colourful (and thus least characteristic) of all Cozens's work (Wilton 1980, p.12). This one, with its sun setting in an orange and red haze behind rich blue hills reflected in the lake, reminded Paul Oppé of the famous watercolour of the *Blue Rigi* which J.M.W. Turner was to paint nearly sixty years later (1952, p.145; Turner's watercolour is reproduced in Wilton 1979B, p.237). In fact, a copy of this composition was made in the 1790s by an artist – probably Turner himself – working in the circle of Dr Thomas Monro (see under no.61), although the copy was probably made from Cozens's original sketchbook page or from a tracing rather than from the watercolour itself (Wilton 1980, p.62). There is also a slight pencil copy made after this subject by Cozens's father, Alexander, in the Oppé collection (T08812). John Robert's original watercolour was owned at one stage by the writer on art Samuel Redgrave (1802–1876).

AL

JOHN ROBERT COZENS
1752–1797

61 The Cloud ?*c*.1785

Watercolour over pencil on laid paper 35 × 39 (13¾ × 15⅜)
Inscribed verso in pen and brown ink 'Cozens'
and in pencil 'Cozens sky'
T08144

Most of John Robert Cozens's mature watercolours take topography as their starting-point, that is to say, they usually depict views of actual places, especially sites sketched on travels abroad (see no.60). His preferred subject is the broad vista or sweeping plain where topographical features tend to be relegated to the far distance or subsumed within the overall design – vehicles for the expression of light and atmosphere which are in fact the true theme of his landscapes. As Laurence Binyon pointed out, skies always play an integral part in the design of Cozens's watercolours, as well as contributing to their mood, at one moment perhaps 'infinitely luminous', at another 'charged with menace and oppressive cloud' (1944, p.47).

This watercolour is unusual for Cozens in being almost purely a sky study, divorced from any identifiable topographical context. Paul Oppé wrote how the presentation of a long low hillside with its line broken by a single tower was reminiscent of his father's coast scenes as well as the latter's 'drawing of the great cloud [no.17] which perhaps he had actually in mind' (1952, p.154). It is, indeed, possible that Cozens was thinking of one of Alexander's sky studies when he made this watercolour, for it is clear that he took an active interest in his father's work well into his mature career. In 1776, for example, having found a batch of Alexander's Italian drawings in Florence (which the latter had lost on his return journey to England in 1748), John Robert then used one or two of them, including Alexander's original sketch for no.15, as the basis for watercolours of his own. A possible model

in the case of this sky study may, as Oppé pointed out, have been *The Cloud* itself (no.17), or one of the oil studies Alexander made in connection with *The Various Species of Composition of Landscape, in Nature* (see no.16). It might even have been adapted from one of the sky studies Alexander engraved for his treatise, *A New Method of Assisting the Invention in Drawing Original Compositions of Landscape* (1786), such as pl. no.20 which it broadly resembles (repr. Wilton 1980, pl.21). Whatever the exact source, John Robert's approach is subtler and less schematic than his father's, and his skies in general are more concerned with atmosphere, space and light.

By 1794 Cozens was suffering from an incurable mental illness, and his final years were spent in the care of the physician and amateur artist Thomas Monro (1759–1833). In 1795 Sir George Beaumont and others organised a fund to support Cozens's family, to which the artist's former patron Payne Knight contributed, though Beckford did not – soon afterwards he was to dismiss Cozens as 'an ungrateful scoundrel' (Farington, *Diary*, 17 June 1797, vol.3, p.855). Shortly before Cozens's death, Monro established an informal 'academy' at his house in Adelphi Terrace in the Strand in London, inviting promising young artists to come and sketch in the evenings, and especially to make copies of watercolours by Cozens (chiefly the Italian and Alpine subjects; see no.60). In this way Cozens's evocative and expressive approach to landscape painting was absorbed by artists of the next generation, in particular by the young Thomas Girtin and J.M.W. Turner (nos.77–8).

AL

JOHN FLAXMAN
1755–1826

62 Alcestis and Admetus 1789

Pen and black ink and grey wash over some pencil approx. 22.3 × 40.7 (8¾ × 16)
on off-white laid paper 23.8 × 41.7 (9⅜ × 16⅜)
Inscribed in grey ink bottom right 'John Flaxman 1789.' and beneath the figures
from left in ink beneath the bottom edge of the design 'son & daughter |
of Alceste & Admetus' 'Admetus' 'Alceste' 'Hercules' and in a different hand
in pencil on the back 'm u'

T08234

Flaxman was the son of a sculptor and maker of plaster casts and models. He learnt to model and draw in his father's London shop before enrolling as a student in the Royal Academy Schools in 1769. Through Stothard (nos.64–6) Flaxman met William Blake (1757–1827), and during the early 1780s they had a patron in common. This was the bluestocking Harriet Mathew under whose guidance he probably started learning Latin and Greek. When, in autumn 1787, Flaxman and his wife set off on the obligatory visit to Italy to pursue his studies his luggage included 'some classical books' (Meteyard 1865–6, vol.1, p.506).

The subject of this drawing comes from the tragedy *Alcestis*, by the Greek playwright Euripedes, which dates from 438 BC. It was based on the legend of Admetus and his wife Alcestis. Apollo, the friend of Admetus, has persuaded the Parcae to let Admetus escape death if someone else can be found to die in his place. Only Alcestis is prepared to do this. In her long, intensely moving farewell to her husband, son and daughter Alcestis emerges as a woman of great nobility; she imposes one obligation upon Admetus for the sacrifice she is making for him – that for the sake of their children he must not re-marry. Admetus promises not to. Hercules, visiting Ademetus, sees his grief and resolves to bring back Alcestis from the dead. This he does, though he shows Admetus a veiled woman whom he says he has won in a competition. Urged by Hercules to lift her veil – the moment Flaxman depicts here – Admetus discovers that she is his wife. Hercules enjoins Admetus henceforth to treat his wife justly. The story, which is one of faithfulness on trial and the glorification of true love, dealt with a popular neo-classical theme. It gained a European-wide audience through C.W. Gluck's opera *Alceste* of 1767 (with a second 1775 version) which is perhaps the saddest opera ever written.

In this design in particular but also in Flaxman's consistent interest in the subject we find epitomised one of the principal aspirations of the neoclassical artist. This is summed up in the words of the German art historian J.J. Winckelmann (1717–1768): 'there is but one way for the moderns to become great, and perhaps unequalled; I mean, by imitating the ancients' (Winckelmann 1765, p.1ff). With Flaxman the unaffected simplicity of the finished design shows the process to be more instinctive than self-conscious – the product of a sculptor's eye practised in gauging the exact significance of line and contour. Flaxman had already worked on this subject before he left for Italy when he made a large drawing of *Hercules Rescuing Alcestis from Death* (British Museum 1888.5.3.143). Once in Rome, some time between August 1788 and January 1790, clearly under the influence of what in 1793 he was to describe as 'the ancient sarcophogi [which] present a magnificent collection of compositions from the great poets of antiquity' (quoted in Bindman 1979, p.86), he was at work on 'a large bas-relief the figures 4 feet high of Hercules delivering Alcestis from Orcus [that is, the god of Hell]' (BM Add. MS 39780, f.45v.). But this drawing took its inspiration from another classical source – the Greek red figure vases of about 500–300 BC on which figures were drawn in outline and the background painted in black. Flaxman seems to have adopted this style by May 1788 when he referred to the fact that 'my drawings have surprised some of the best English artists here, who thought they were copied from the stories on Greek vases' (quoted in Constable 1927, p.31). This work represents a stage in Flaxman's development of an even purer linear style which he had developed by 1792 when he drew the designs for *The Odyssey* and Dante's *Divine Comedy* (engraved by Thomas Piroli in 1793), which made Flaxman famous throughout Europe.

RH

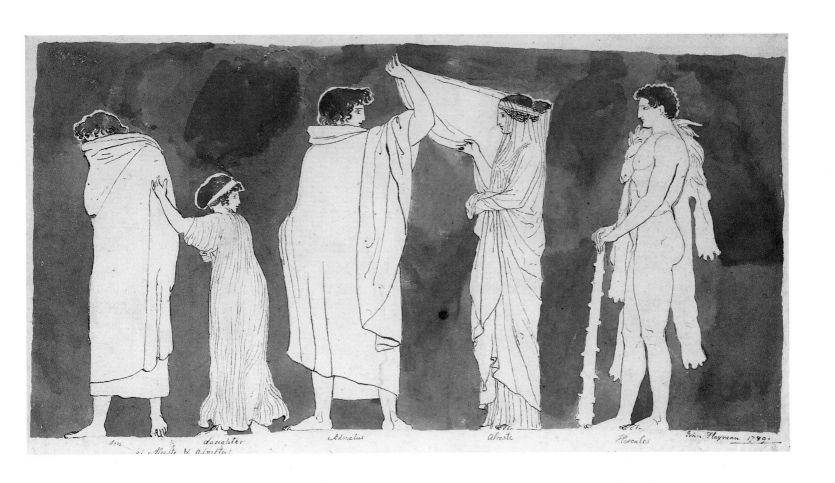

Son | Daughter | Admetus | Alceste | Hercules
of Alceste & Admetus

John Flaxman 1789.

JOHN FLAXMAN after LE MOINE and MICHELINOT
1755–1826

63 The Evolution of Religious Architecture ?c.1810

Pen and brown ink on lightweight laid paper trimmed irregularly at top
38.7 × 27 (15¼ × 10⅝)

Inscribed in ink in three columns from left, with numbers relating to drawings on the same sheet, [a] 'No | 1 simple Caban - Egypt^n | 2 Caban surrounded with a wall | 3 Egypt^n Temple | 4 ruins of a Temple at Esnay | 5 ruins of a temple at Etfou | 6 ruins at Luxor | Call'd the tomb of Osymandue | AAA different Perystiles | b a vestibule | c the statue of the God | d a vestibule | 7 Temple of Bubastis | 8 Temple of serpent Knupis | 9 Elevation of D^o | 10 plan of a Tabernacle | 11 its facade | 12 Temple of Solomon | 13 Phenician Temple | Egyptian, Hebrew, | and Phenician | Temples' ; [b] 'Greek & Roman Temples | 14 a Caban sustain'd | roof sustain'd by trunks | of trees - perhaps gave | the first Idea of Columns | 16 Temple at Anteo | 18 Greek Prostyle | without the hind Columns | and amphiprostyle with | 20 Greek Perystere | 22 Greek Dyptere | 23 Greek temple | resembles that near Bazar at Athens | 24 Tower of the winds | 25 Temple of Jupiter | Olympus at Athens | 28 plan of the Pantheon | 29 Temple at Balbec' ; [c] 'Christian Temples | N^o | 31 Catacombs of early | Christians − | 32 ancient Basilique | 33 ancient Basilique | of St Peter − Rome | 34 St Sophia at Constantinople | 36 St Mark's at Venice | 39 St Augustine − Rome | 41 St Peters − ' and, below a plan lower centre, 'Royal Chapel | at Versailles −'

T10193

This is a tracing with some omissions from plate 1 in volume I of the second edition of *Les Ruines des plus beaux monuments de la Grèce, considerées du côte de L'Histoire et du Côte de L'Architecture* by J.D. Le Roy which was published in Paris in 1770. The plate, engraved by Michelinot after Le Moine, illustrates an introductory essay (p.vii–xxiv) on the history of architecture which did not appear in the first edition of 1758. The latter edition with its plans, elevations, studies of the architectural orders and views of ancient Greek buildings in their settings, particularly the Acropolis, was highly influential in spreading the taste for the neo-classical style in the eighteenth century – a movement in which Flaxman as a sculptor and designer was a central figure. As the sale of Flaxman's library at Christie's in June 1828 reveals, not only was he widely read and erudite but, specifically, he owned a number of important modern books on Egyptian, classical and Christian architecture, though he seems not to have possessed a copy of Le Roy. In this sketch Flaxman copied Le Roy's numbering system and his brief descriptive notes are taken from the French explanation of the plans on the page opposite the plate; because of lack of space on the sheet Flaxman could not adopt the severe, almost abstract, three-column arrangement of plans on Le Roy's plate (repr. Serra 1986, p.78, pl.25).

Although the very thin paper on which Flaxman made his tracing is Italian and would not have been available in England, and although he could well have seen Le Roy's book when he was in Italy, it is most likely that this work dates from some time after 1810 when he was appointed the first Professor of Sculpture at the Royal Academy and formed part of his background research for the lectures which he delivered annually from 1811. In his lectures, some of which were published posthumously in 1829, it is possible to discern the overarching theme that, as the sculptor explained to the art critic Ludwig Schorn in 1826, 'art in Christianity can rise higher than in paganism, since Christian ideas are more sublime than pagan ones, and the best that the art of Greece and Rome has produced is … also contained in Christian ideas' (quoted in Bindman 1979, p.31). Flaxman was equally concerned with the place of sculpture in buildings – as the reference in no.6c of this drawing clearly implies. In his lecture on Egyptian sculpture he refers to Bubastis (7) (Flaxman 1906, p.63) and illustrates a statue of her (pl.x) while his lecture on modern sculpture refers to the plan of St Mark's (36) (1906, p.244) and the Catacombs (31) and St Sophia (34) (1906, p.246).

RH

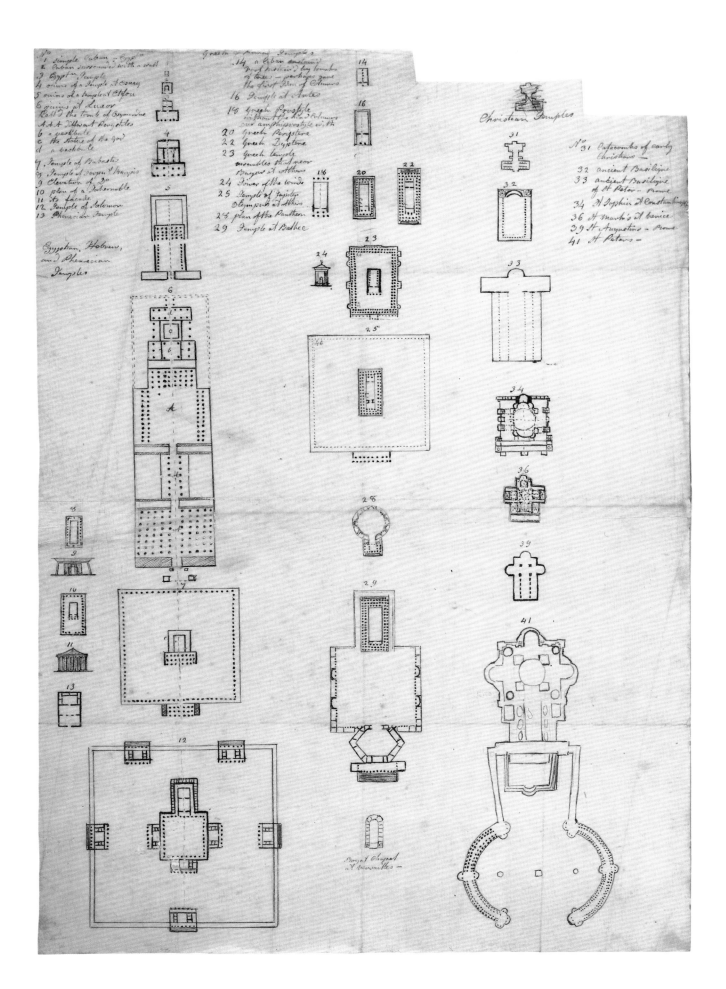

N.° 1. simple Cabin — Egypt
2. Cabin surrounded with a wall
3. Egyptian Temple
4. ruins of a Temple A Esnay
5. ruins of a temple at Etfou
6 ruins at Luxor
call'd the tomb of Ozymandias
A.A different Peristyles
b a vestibule
c the statue of the god
d a vestibule
7. Temple of Babaste
8. Temple of Serapis & Isis
9. Elevation of 30
10 plan of a Tabernacle
11. its facade
12. Temple of Salomon
13. Phenician Temple

Egyptian, Hebrew,
and Phenecian
Temples

Greek & Roman Temples
14. a Cabin enclosing
good mothers big tombs
of trees — perhaps gave
the first idea of Columns
16. Temple at Antes
18. Greek Prostyle
in them & his his 3 Columns
our amphisprostyle with
20. Greek Peristyle
22. Greek Dipstone
23. Greek temple
resembles that near
Bagos at Athens
24. Tower of the Winds
25. Temple of Jupiter
Olympus at Athens
28. plan of the Pantheon
29. Temple at Balbec

Christian Temples

N.° 31 Catacombs of early
Christians —
32. ancient Basilique
33. ancient Basilique
of St Peter — Rome
34. St Sophia at Constantinople
36. St Mark's at Venice
39. St Augustino — Rome
41. St Peters —

Royal Chapel
at Versailles —

THOMAS STOTHARD
1755–1834

64 A Group of Five Maidens *c.*1790–5

Pencil, pen and brown ink with grey wash and pen
work on laid paper 25.3 × 14.3 (10 × 5⅝)
Inscribed in black ink bottom centre 'T. Stothard'
T10067

Stothard was born in London, the son of a publican. After
his father died in 1770 his mother apprenticed him for
seven years to a silk weaver and designer in Spitalfields.
In 1777 he became a student in the Royal Academy. Like
his close friend Flaxman during the 1780s he produced
designs for Josiah Wedgwood, the china manufacturer.
From 1778 he made his greatest and most enduring
contribution to the art of his day with his designs
for engraved book illustrations. During the 1780s many
of these designs were engraved by William Blake
(1757–1827) whom Stothard had met in 1779, and
Stothard's effective transposing of the current linear neo-
classical style, with all its overtones of grandeur, into a

lower key but still highly effective means of elegantly
illustrating a text on a small scale undoubtedly influenced
Blake's early illuminated books such as *Songs of Innocence*
of 1789.

As has been pointed out by Shelley Bennett, this
drawing relates to another Stothard drawing in the
Huntington Art Collections (no.000.92, fig.21). This
latter drawing has been associated with a design for John
Bunyan's *The Pilgrim's Progress* engraved in 1788, though
there is no incident in the book which can be associated
with such a group of female figures. The Oppé drawing
has been usually titled *The Wise Virgins* after the New
Testament parable of the ten wise and foolish virgins.
However, since they can be identified as originally part
of a composition of seven figures there is no reason
to believe that this is the subject of T10067. The frieze-
like grouping of female figures does, in fact, occur in a
number of Stothard's designs of the 1780s and 1790s
including *The Pilgrim's Progress* plate, the painting *A
Confirmation* exhibited at the Academy in 1792 and *Alfred
in the Danish Camp* of about the same period (repr. Bray
1851, pp.51, 27 and xxiv respectively). Of these a figure
in the latter bears the closest resemblance to one of the
figures, that on the left, in this drawing. The back of this
sheet is rubbed with graphite suggesting that Stothard
transferred, or intended transferring, the design onto
another piece of paper or even a canvas.

The spontaneity and vigour of this drawing, with its
dynamic outlines in pen and ink with its grey washes used
to define light and shade as well as background added
later, are typical of a style found among artists who
moved in the circle of Flaxman (see no.62), Fuseli (no.42)
and Blake during the 1780s and 1790s and which has
roots in a study of the Antique.

RH

fig. 21 Thomas Stothard *A Group of Seven Maidens* ?*c.*1790–5,
pen and ink on paper
*Henry E. Huntington Library and Art Gallery, San Marino,
California*

THOMAS STOTHARD
1755–1834

65a An Illustration to *Sohrab* ?1800–5

Pen and brown and grey ink and watercolour
with some gum arabic on lightweight white wove paper
9.1 × 6.1 (3⅝ × 2⅜)
Inscribed in ?brown ink bottom right 'T. Stothard.'
T10073

65b An Illustration to Shakespeare's *King John*: Constance and Arthur ?*c.*1802

Pen and grey ink and watercolour with some gum arabic
on lightweight white wove paper 6.5 × 8.3 (2½ × 3¼)
Inscribed in grey ink bottom left 'T. Stothard.'
T10074

In their scale and handling these two watercolours are typical of the sort of works which can be associated with Stothard's projects for book illustrations in the early 1800s, although no prints after them have been found. The text which Stothard illustrated in the first work has not been identified, but Shelley Bennett has identified the second, formerly called *A Mediaeval Subject*, as an illustration to Act III, scene i of Shakespeare's play *King John*.

Lady Constance, mother of Arthur, nephew of King John, has learnt that Philip, King of France, who had promised to defeat John in battle so that Arthur could ascend to the throne that was rightly his, has instead formed an alliance with John. She is in the French king's tent when she hears the news. Arthur attempts to calm her but she is inconsolable: '... my grief's so great | That no supporter but the huge firm earth | Can hold it up. Here I and sorrows sit; | Here is my throne; bid kings come bow to it.' King John and King Philip, who stand immediately behind Constance and Arthur, have arrived together with others of their family; among them are Lady Blanch and the Dauphin, Lewis, fourth and fifth from the left, whose arranged marriage has resolved the Kings' conflict.

Stothard painted at least two other versions of the same scene and these suggest a date for this work: an oil painting (no. FA 205; oval, 28.6 × 31.8 cm) which is in the Victoria and Albert Museum and which was engraved by James Heath in 1802 for an edition of Shakespeare containing twenty-two illustrations by Stothard, published as a part-work by Heath and Robinson between 1802 and 1804; and there is a small engraving of about 1804 by James Parker (d.1805), after Stothard, which shows almost the same composition as the Victoria and Albert and Oppé works but with Arthur standing behind Constance (Balmanno, no.1477).

After his death Stothard was described by one obituarist as one who 'could have no enemy. His character was simplicity itself' (quoted in Bennett 1988, p.5). This mildness of temper can be seen in his art, and in these two small pictures, both in the restrained sentimentality of his portrayal of emotions and in the sweetness of his palette. Despite his good nature, however, Stothard did earn the scorn of William Blake after Blake quarrelled with him in 1806–7 over what he thought was Stothard's piracy of his idea to paint the subject of Chaucer's Canterbury Pilgrims. (Stothard's oil painting of the subject is in the Tate Gallery, NO1163.) In an entry in his notebook Blake attacked Stothard for the 'blundering blurs' of his drawings which he had engraved and claimed, with some slight truth, that it was through the prints by him after his work that Stothard had 'got his reputation as a Draughtsman'. (Erdman and Moore 1977, p.N52).

RH

THOMAS STOTHARD
1755–1834

66 Hafod c.1810

Pencil with stump work on thin wove paper
20.9 × 16.4 (8¼ × 6½)
Inscribed in pencil bottom right 'Hafod'
T10075

The inscription on this drawing identifies the view as a scene at Hafod, the estate of Thomas Johnes MP on the banks of the river Ystwyth not far from Aberystwyth in Wales. From 1780 when he inherited Hafod until his death Johnes dramatically improved the valley and the hills which surrounded his house according to the latest picturesque principles. The Picturesque, as the word suggests, invited the viewer to look at the landscape as a picture: Johnes, with his Gothick house, the winding paths, bridges over rushing torrents, hewn-out caves and, as one writer put it, the 'mighty and magnificent theatre of varied forests ascending majestically from the river' which he planted (Cumberland 1796, p.30), very consciously created a series of views which did just this. Johnes was also a scholar, patron of art and had a fine library, so Hafod soon became a magnet for educated travellers who wished to experience a terrain in which 'the Painter's Eye, the Poet's Mind' (Cumberland 1796, p.1) came together. Artists who responded to Hafod included Thomas Jones (see nos.43–5) in 1786 (Hallett 1992), J.C. Ibbetson and John 'Warwick' Smith (nos. 51–2; Clay 1948, pp.37–8) in 1793 who produced a series of views of the estate, and probably J.M.W. Turner in 1798.

Stothard was not among these first visitors. Although two of his very first exhibits in 1777 were of Welsh landscapes, his livelihood and reputation thereafter rested almost exclusively on the numerous designs he produced for engraved book illustrations. In fact he was not an artist who, in looking at landscape, would be swayed by the rules of picturesque theory. Rather, his sketchbooks were filled with sketches of 'whatever his leisure permitted, and chance presented to him' (C.R. Leslie quoted in Fleming-Williams 1994, p.66). He was not one, then, to look at landscape selectively and even critically, as Turner

did in 1798 when he saw Snowdon as 'green and un-picturesque' on a clear day (Farington, vol.3, p.1060) or as Johnes himself did when he wrote that 'the first green of spring is enchanting, though it may not be picturesque' (Moore-Colyer 1992, p.196).

Stothard's first known visit to Hafod was in September 1805 when he was there as drawing master to Johnes's twenty-one-year-old daughter Mariamne. (Moore-Colyer 1992, pp.198–9). The house at Hafod burnt down in 1807, and Stothard's next known visit was in 1810 when he painted eight murals in oil for Johnes's new library. Stothard wrote at this time to his wife of how 'I have no exercise but what the pencil [i.e. paint-brush] affords me.... Sometimes I get an hour out of doors, to get a little air. The small room I paint in affords me none' (Moore-Colyer 1992, p.262; Bray 1851, p.55). This drawing is on paper watermarked 1807 and it there-fore seems most likely that it dates from this 1810 stay, as probably do a number of other similar sketches done as a relief from mural painting (Bennett 1979, pp.273–7).

This sketch, drawn with a soft pencil and using a short-hand of looped lines and squiggles which catch the motif but also indicate an artist used to working in a hurry, speaks plainly of 'the crisped heads of Hafods woods' (Cumberland 1796, p.10), perhaps above one of the trib-utaries of the Ystwyth.

Stothard's modest output of mature landscape drawings tends to be rather overlooked because of his work as an illustrator and his early links with a much greater figure, William Blake. However, from about 1811, when they became friendly, it is conceivable that the directness of Stothard's way of looking at landscape influenced Constable and they are recorded as going on walks when they both sketched (Bennett 1979, p.275; Fleming-Williams 1994, p.65).

RH

168

Hafod

THOMAS ROWLANDSON
1756–1827

67 A Bench of Artists 1776

Pen and grey and black ink over pencil on handmade laid paper
27.2 × 54.8 (10¾ × 21⅝)
Inscribed, left to right in ink beneath the figures 'Mr Burgess'
'Mr Scarodornoff.' 'Mr Negri' 'Mr Beechy' 'Mr Riley' 'Mr Grignion.'
'Mr Hayes.' and in ink along the bottom edge 'A Bench of Artists.
Sketched at the Royal Academy in the Year 1776 –'

T08142

Rowlandson was born in London and he was admitted as a student to the Royal Academy on 6 November 1772, at the age of sixteen.

Rowlandson's drawing is a rare eighteenth-century view of Royal Academy students at work. If Zoffany's famous group portrait of the Academicians of 1771–2 shows the new artistic establishment at its most confident (Bignamini and Postle 1991, no.5), Rowlandson's view of his rather crumpled colleagues reminds us of the workaday side of the student artist's life with all its drudgery as well as its attendant hopes and fears. The solidity of the curved bench on which they are sitting suggests that they are in the Academy for the Living Model rather than in the Plaister Academy, where casts of classical statues were drawn and where seating arrangements had to be movable. Each student is using a *porte-crayon* – a wooden or metal holder which gripped the lead or chalk. The lampshades were designed to stop the light by which the students drew spilling over onto the model who, placed in front of the bench, would have been posed by the Keeper under a light bright enough to emphasise outline and light and shade. It would have been unusual for a student to take pen and ink into the life class, so Rowlandson first drew his colleagues in pencil (visible under the ink), and then finished the drawing later. To make this sketch he presumably stopped doing what he was there for – which was to study the model. Indeed, Rowlandson is reported as having an agreeably mischievous attitude to the life class: on one occasion he fired a pea from his peashooter at the model and the ensuing disturbance almost resulted in his expulsion from the Academy (Hayes 1972, p.14).

Nothing is known about Mr Negri, but the other students can be identified: on the far left is Thomas Burgess who was admitted as a student on 30 January 1769. He is the oldest person present and is therefore probably the same Thomas Burgess who had been a member of the Incorporated Society of Artists in 1766 (Pye 1845, p.119) and associated with William Shipley's drawing school in the 1750s and 1760s (Allan 1979, pp.82, 88, 152; Wood 1913, p.168); Gavril Ivanovich Skorodumov (1755–1792) who, having won a gold medal at the Imperial Academy in St Petersburg in 1772, travelled to London to study. He was admitted to the Academy on 9 November 1773, went to Paris for two months in 1774, possibly with Rowlandson, and having been a pupil of Francis Bartolozzi and worked mainly as an engraver from 1775 onwards, returned to Russia in 1782 (Cross 1980, pp.211–17); William Beechey (1753–1839) was admitted a student in October 1774, made his debut as a portraitist in the 1776 Royal Academy exhibition and was later knighted; Henry Riley (b.1749) who was admitted in June 1773; Charles Grignion (1754–1804) was admitted as a painting student in August 1769 and won the RA Gold Medal for History Painting in 1776; Joseph Hayes (b.1753), perhaps the son of the ornithological artist William Hayes (1729–1799), was admitted as a painting student in November 1772 (Hutchison 1962).

Among his comments which Skorodumov sent back home in 1777, he listed the best artists in London as Joshua Reynolds, Benjamin West, John Hamilton Mortimer, Nathanial Dance and J.B. Cipriani. At this time Mortimer, physically a powerful man and an equally energetic and inventive painter and draughtsman, exercised a considerable influence over the younger generation of artists, including Rowlandson. In this drawing the bold technique of hatching and dotting in ink is very much in Mortimer's manner (see no.39) and could only have been done with an informed knowledge of his drawings and prints.

RH

170

A Bench of Artists Sketched at the Royal Academy in the Year 1776

THOMAS ROWLANDSON
1756–1827

68 Sir Joseph Banks about to Eat an Alligator (also known as *The Fish Supper*) 1788

Pen and black ink and grey wash on laid paper 16 × 21.2 (6¼ × 8⅜) on laid paper support 16.1 × 21.3 (6⅜ × 8⅜)
T08469

69 Two Women Sewing by Candlelight

Pencil, pen and ink and watercolour line and wash on cream wove paper 15.2 × 23.8 (6 × 9⅜)
Inscribed bottom right in pencil 'R'
T08273

From his time as a student in the Royal Academy right up until his death Rowlandson was admired as a draughtsman of uncommon powers. Such were his abilities that it was inevitable he would be marked out from the very beginning as a genius who would add lustre to the British School. Rowlandson equally clearly set out, in his easy-going way, to be seen as one. His lifelong friend Henry Angelo later commented on the fact that 'his studies from the human figure at the Royal Academy, were made in so masterly a style, that he was set up as a rival to [John Hamilton] Mortimer' (no.39) though, of course, in looking to Mortimer Rowlandson was inviting such a comparison. Angelo went on to describe Rowlandson's powers as 'so very versatile, and his fancy so rich, that every species of composition flowed from his pen with equal facility' (Angelo 1828, vol.1, p.233). These two drawings show two extremes of Rowlandson's style and subject matter.

Sir Joseph Banks illustrates lines from a satirical poem by Rowlandson's friend Dr John Wolcot whose pen-name was Peter Pindar. The poem, *Peter's Prophecy; or, The President and Poet; or, An Important Epistle to Sir J. Banks* was published some time before November 1788 with Rowlandson's drawing as a frontispiece etched the same size in reverse by the artist and without a title. Pindar's target was the President of the Royal Society, Sir Joseph Banks (1743–1820), who was about to face the annual re-election for the Presidential chair. Banks, who had accompanied Captain Cook on the *Endeavour*, was criticised by some for his snobbery, his flattering ways and his excessive interest in natural history rather than the great philosophical issues which had concerned eminent predecessors in the Society like Isaac Newton. In his poem

Pindar warns Banks that the members of the Society want more than a continuing diet of dragonflies, snails and frogs (all visible in the etching but not the drawing) and snakes. He has Banks rising to the challenge, and incidentally demonstrating his stupidity, by showing his fellow members that he is prepared to eat something more substantial: 'Tell, then, each pretty PRESIDENT CREATOR, G—d d–mn him, that I'll eat an *Alligator*.' Banks, looking very like his official portraits, lifts up his knife in anticipation of the feast.

The vigour and inventiveness with which Rowlandson used a reed pen, as seen here, is unique and was admirably suited for translation into the rapid, fluid lines created by the etching needle. Both the conception and the execution of the design are in complete harmony with the verve and wit of Pindar's attack. By contrast, in the later (though Rowlandson's work is very difficult to date) *Women Sewing* we see Rowlandson responding in a completely different way to another world. Angelo noted that Rowlandson 'always carried his sketchbook with him', and this work may well have started as a slight pencil drawing in a sketchbook which he then worked up with pen and ink and watercolour washes with the outlines strengthened using a fine brush dipped in dark red watercolour. With an unerring eye for detail Rowlandson has captured the two very different expressions on the faces of the women as they reach two different stages of using the needle and thread – similar in spirit, in fact, to a drawing of the same subject by his contemporary John Flaxman (repr. Irwin 1979, p.76). Unlike the two other Rowlandsons illustrated this is more characteristic of most of his output in its use of delicate watercolour washes.

RH

GEORGE GARRARD

1760–1826

70 Mr Taylor's Barn, Marlow ? c.1795

Oil on ?laid paper, 19.5 × 23.5 (7⅝ × 9¼)

Inscribed on verso in pencil 'Mr Taylors Barn at | Marlow' and, alongside unfinished oil sketch of a long-horned cow, 'Lancaster'. Also inscribed on attached sheet 'Mr Taylors Barn at Marlow. | the original study for the background of | the Picture of Taylor's Fat Cow – from wh | a large print was engraved.'

T08131

'He practises in various ways & makes no prominent figure in any one branch' (Farington, *Diary*, quoted Croft-Murray 1961, p.3). It was probably Garrard's unwillingness to specialise in any one field of art which was the cause of his failure ever to gain full membership of the Royal Academy. Garrard had launched his career as an animal painter, training under the sporting artist Sawrey Gilpin (1783–1807) who was later to become his father-in-law. However, under the guidance of his most important patron, Samuel Whitbread II (1764–1815), Whig MP and son of the founder of the famous brewery, Garrard began to expand his repertoire to include industrial and urban landscapes as well as rustic genre. By about 1800 he was attempting to gain additional recognition as a sculptor, producing a wide range of animal subjects in plaster or bronze, as well as a substantial number of portrait busts in marble. Thanks in part to Whitbread's support, in 1798 Garrard also secured the passing of an important Copyright Act for sculptors – the counterpart

to Hogarth's act of 1735 protecting printmakers.

Numerous oil sketches by Garrard of animals and landscape bound in albums were included in the last of the three sales of the artist's effects after his death (Croft-Murray 1961, p.4). His landscape sketches seem mostly to have been executed for his own pleasure in and around London in the 1790s, though this one was used for the background of his painting *The Holderness Cow* which he exhibited at the Royal Academy in 1797, and which was engraved by William Ward in mezzotint the following year (fig.22). The lettering on the print tells us that this pedigree cow was bred near Malton in Yorkshire (Holderness being a district in the former East Riding) by one T. Taylor, and subsequently purchased at two years old by his brother living in Great Marlow, Buckinghamshire. The print was published by Garrard himself and dedicated 'to the Right Honble Lord Somerville President of the Board of Agriculture'. This tribute presumably reflects the fact that it was about this time that the recently established Board of Agriculture commissioned Garrard to produce exact scale-models of various 'Improved breeds of cattle', for which the artist later wrote his own explanatory illustrated text (see Deuchar 1984, pp.86–7).

A L

fig. 22 William Ward after George Garrard, *Holderness Cow* 1798, mezzotint engraving *British Museum*

GEORGE BARRET JUNIOR
1767–1842

71 Composition: Sunset *c.*1825–30

Watercolour, gouache and gum arabic with sponging
and stopping-out on laminated wove paper
22.2 × 18.3 (8¾ × 7¼)

T08128

Born the son of a prolific and successful landscape painter of the same name, George Barret the younger was a founder member of the Society of Painters in Watercolour. Like most of the early members of the Society, he was primarily a landscape painter, his early exhibits chiefly scenes along the Thames in the vicinity of London. However, from the 1820s his exhibition staple became the idealised Claudian landscape, and indeed it is this side of his work for which he is best known today. Exhibited under such generalised titles as 'Twilight', 'Evening' or 'Sunset', these compositions were invariably executed in a range of warm, especially brownish colours, 'as though he were trying to paint not merely a Claude but the golden varnish that covers a Claude' (Hardie 1967, vol.2, p.129). Some years later he was to publish his palette of predominantly warm colours – Raw Sienna, Indian Red, Brown Madder, Gamboge and Vandyke Brown, for example – in his *Letters on the Theory and Practice of Water-Colour Painting* (1840).

The Society of Painters in Watercolour (today the Royal Watercolour Society) was founded in 1804 and held its first exhibition in April 1805. Attempting to emulate the effect of oils, the watercolourists now began to produce work which was both stronger in tone and richer and deeper in colour. However, the increased density of colouring resulted in a greater proportion of the paper's white surface being obscured (and a corre-

sponding loss of reflected light), so the watercolourists then had to invent methods to bring the white of the paper back. One way was by sponging or scraping, both of which Barret uses here: it is sponging which contributes to the noticeable woolliness of texture; whilst scraping brings into prominence the bright ball of the setting sun. (Barret originally intended the sun to appear lower and towards the centre, but scraped back too far and made a hole in the paper, which he subseqently disguised by laminating the sheet, and then painting over the hole in a darker tone.) Another way of achieving lights was to mask a selected area of the white paper with a 'stopping-out' agent to prevent it being obscured by subsequent wash layers, a technique associated especially with Barret's work and that of Francis Oliver Finch (1802–1862), a member of the Society as well as a peripheral member of 'The Ancients' (see under no.97). Both artists used wax as a stopping-out agent, especially for lights in foliage (Bayard 1981, p.20).

Barret gained a firm contemporary reputation but died in poverty. Samuel Palmer, the most famous of 'The Ancients', commented in his 1824 notebook: 'Carefully avoid getting into that style which is elegant and beautiful but too light and superficial; not learned enough – like Barret. He has a beautiful sentiment and it is derived from Nature, but Nature has properties which lie still deeper' (quoted Bayard 1981, p.44).

AL

REVD WILLIAM HENRY BARNARD
1767/9–1818

72 The Back of a House in Oxford ?c.1790–95

Grey washes over pencil no laid paper 26.9 × 19.3 (10⅝ × 7⅝)
Inscribed verso in pencil '9' and 'Oxford'
T08129

A pupil of John Baptist Malchair (see no.24) when an undergraduate at Oxford, William Henry Barnard is usually identified as the man of that name who matriculated at Pembroke College on 22 June 1790 at the age of twenty-three (Williams 1952, p.93). The son of an Irish parson (and grandson of the Bishop of Derry), Barnard himself took orders in 1793. Of all Malchair's pupils it is perhaps Barnard whose work is most readily confused with that of the master.

Malchair's pupils were encouraged to work in monochrome (pencil, chalks and grey washes) rather than watercolour and taught to describe form using tone and mass rather than outline (see under no.58). In fact, Malchair's students did sometimes use colour, but when they did it was generally only added over substantial preliminary underdrawing in pencil or chalk, this being the method favoured by William Crotch, for example (see no.76). Barnard, like Malchair, however, generally used colour more sparingly, and frequently not at all.

Barnard also tended to favour the same sort of humble, inconsequential subject that Malchair had found in the alleyways and back streets of Oxford. This unidentified (and, perhaps, unidentifiable) view by Barnard of a hidden corner somewhere in Oxford, for example, can be compared with Malchair's *Merton Stable Yarde* 1775 (Ashmolean Museum, Oxford), which is similarly executed in grey washes over pencil and which features at the heart of its composition a drainage hole and a stack of logs. Most of Barnard's drawings of Oxford would seem to date from the 1790s.

The fact that various members of the 'Oxford School' often made copies from each other's drawings only adds to the potential for confusion over attribution. For example, another drawing by Barnard in the Oppé collection, *Castellated Mill on a Waterfall* (T09426), was copied from a drawing by Malchair (also in the Oppé collection, T09427); Malchair's version had in turn been copied from an original by Sir George Beaumont.

AL

JOSHUA CRISTALL
1767/8–1847

73 Fields at Sunset ?*c*.1810–20

Watercolour on wove paper 8.7 × 15.3 (3⅜ × 6)
Inscribed lower left in pen and brown ink 'J.C'
T08468

Cristall, like Barret (no.71), was a founder member of the Society of Painters in Watercolour, but was unusual in being primarily a figure painter. He had strong literary interests (the poet George Dyer and the writer Mary Wollstonecraft were early friends) and a great enthusiasm for the classics. This, and his training at the Royal Academy Schools in the 1790s under the history painter James Barry (no.40), may have influenced his decision to concentrate on subject paintings rather than landscape. His exhibits at the Society in its early years were large elaborate compositions on a pastoral or arcadian theme with monumental figures in a complex design. From 1808 he supplemented them with more modern pastoral subjects featuring figures observed from the life – Hastings fishermen or Scottish peasant girls – but still presented with a classical air. Cristall served as President of the Society in 1816 and 1819, and again from 1821 to 1831, though he ceased to take an active role in its affairs on moving to Herefordshire in 1822. He resigned as President in 1831 on discovering that fellow member G.F. Robson (1788–1833) had been cutting out the figures from two of his watercolours (both subjects from Shakespeare's *A Midsummer Night's Dream*), pasting them onto new sheets of paper and persuading Barret (no.71) to paint in new backgrounds – and then exhibiting them at the Society under Cristall and Barret's joint names (Roget 1891, vol.1, p.440).

This is one of a series of vivid *plein-air* sketches by Cristall in the Oppé collection. Others in the immediate group include a view of Hastings dated 1807 and of Hampstead dated 1816; there are in addition two coloured sketches made by Cristall near Paddington Fields in 1817 (close to where he lived, and still rural at this date) and of Dolgelly in 1820. Such pure landscapes provide a refreshing contrast to the artist's more ambitious exhibition watercolours, but they are rare – to the extent, indeed, that one writer believed that other examples must exist masquerading under other artist's names (Davies 1927, p.2). In fact this watercolour was once attributed to John Constable, an error suggested partly by the inscription 'J.C.' lower left. Paul Oppé himself provided the correct attribution. Cristall may have learned to use washes with such confidence and freedom during the tour he made in Wales in 1803 with Cornelius Varley (no.84); certainly some of his most striking landscape sketches date from that trip.

AL

HENRY EDRIDGE

1769–1821

74 Farm Buildings *c.*1810–15

Watercolour over pencil on wove paper
13.1 × 16.6 (5⅛ × 6½)
T10101

Henry Edridge was apprenticed at an early age to the miniature painter and mezzotint engraver, William Pether (*c.*1738–1821), and it was as a miniaturist working on ivory that he launched his career. He later evolved his own successful formula for making small-scale portrait drawings on paper, where the sitter (or sitters) would be presented full-length in a landscape, and drawn chiefly in pencil, with slight touches of colour reserved mainly for the faces and landscape. From 1802 he was frequently in demand as a portraitist at Winsdor Castle – and many years later Paul Oppé himself was to catalogue the drawings by Edridge of royal sitters in the Royal Collection (see Oppé 1950, pp.45–8). It was as a portrait draughtsman that Edridge earned both his contemporary reputation and his living, by 1806 being able to increase the price he charged for a full-length drawing from 15 to 20 guineas (Farington, *Diary*, 30 March 1806, vol.7, p.2706).

Edridge's watercolour landscapes are less well known and relatively rare. They seem mostly to date from the early years of the nineteenth century when he was to be found sketching in the vicinity of Fetcham in Surrey and especially at Bushey in Hertfordshire – these being the two country retreats of the physician, collector and amateur draughtsman Dr Monro whom Edridge had come to know through his friendship with the topographer Thomas Hearne (1744–1806). Depicting cottages, farms or country lanes, and executed in a palette of russets, browns and yellow-greens, these watercolours (especially the more finished examples) are often confused with the early landscapes of William Henry Hunt (1790–1864), who was also a member of the Monro circle. Edridge's broader sketches like this one are especially delicate and free.

Edridge also produced an impressive range of pencil drawings, both landscapes and architectural subjects. Here he used the short, cursive pencil strokes which so typify the drawing style of the 'Monro School' (see no.50). This style is used by him especially effectively for the remarkable sequence of drawings made on two tours of northern France in 1817 and 1819, examples of which are in the the British Museum.

AL

JULIA BENNET (LADY WILLOUGHBY GORDON)
1775–1867

75 Cottage at Wigmore, Kent 1803

Watercolour over pencil on laid paper 24.5 × 31.6 (9⅝ × 12⅜);
artist's mount 28.7 × 35.3 (11¼ × 13⅞)

Inscribed on artist's mount 'Sketch from Nature at Wigmore |
1B.1803' and on verso 'Sketch from Nature | at Wigmore |
by Julia Isabella Levina Bennet | (afterwᵈˢ Lady Gordon) | 1803.'

T08138

Towards the end of 1798 J.M.W. Turner told Farington that he was 'determined not to give any more lessons in drawing. He has only ... five shillings a lesson' (*Diary*, 28 November, vol.3, p.1098). Julia Bennet and the Revd Robert Nixon of Foot's Cray, Kent, are the two best documented of Turner's few known pupils, the former receiving instruction in 1797. Indeed, it is as a pupil and also as a patron of Turner that Julia Bennet is usually remembered, for in the 1820s she commissioned from him an oil painting of her seaside villa at Niton on the Isle of Wight which Turner is known to have based on her sketches (Gage 1987, p.157).

Judging by the stylistic evidence presented by a group of her sketches made at her home near Beckenham in Kent between 1802 and 1805, it was Paul Oppé who first speculated that Julia Bennet may also have taken lessons from Thomas Girtin (Oppé 1939, p.20). This was confirmed many years later by the appearance of a copy made by her from one of Girtin's watercolours, and which she had inscribed 'after Girtin, a very good drawing master' (private collection). For this watercolour of a cottage at Wigmore near Maidstone she has selected Girtin's favourite paper, a coarse laid cartridge of a warmish tint containing slight flecks which give a subtle variety to the surface (Hardie 1967, vol.2, p.15). In handling and subject-matter it is reminiscent not only of Girtin's own work but also that of his favourite pupil, Amelia Long of Bromley Hill Place, afterwards Lady

Farnborough (1772–1837), and who as a neighbour of Julia Bennet's may, indeed, have originally recommended Girtin as a drawing master. It is twice inscribed by her as a 'Sketch from Nature', a practice no doubt instilled in her by Girtin himself (see no.77).

In 1805 Julia Bennet married General Sir James Willoughby Gordon (1772–1851), who in 1812 as Quartermaster-General accompanied the Duke of Wellington's army to Spain during the Peninsular Wars, incurring the latter's wrath for misdirecting a supply column and contributing to the loss of some 3,000 men (Miles 1981). In subsequent years he continued as Quartermaster-General based at Horse Guards in Whitehall. Around 1818 to 1820, Lady Julia Gordon made seven prints after her own drawings using the new printmaking technique of lithography, invented in 1798 in Munich by Alois Senefelder, and employing the latter's lithographic press which had been bought by the Quartermaster-General's department for the reproduction of maps and circulars for the civil service (Miles 1981). The Gordons were important patrons of David Wilkie (no.89). In 1834, Wilkie wrote to Sir Willoughby asking leave to propose marriage to their daughter, Julia Emily Gordon (1810–1896), but his request was refused (Miles 1981). Julia Emily was a talented amateur artist like her mother, and is represented in the Oppé collection by four watercolours depicting views in northern France (T08897–08900).

AL

Sketch from Nature, at Wigmore

AB. 1803

DR WILLIAM CROTCH
1775–1847

76 View from Hurley Bottom 1806

Watercolour over pencil on laid paper 22 × 43.2 (8⅝ × 17)

Inscribed on verso in pencil '19–1806 | Aug 30– 5pm Wm Crotch | View of Hurley Bottom' and also in pen and brown ink on a label formerly attached to back of sheet 'Hurley | Bottom | WC | Aug 30 | 1806 | 5pm. | From the | Marlow | Road to | Maidenhead'

T08123

Like John 'Baptist' Malchair (no.24), William Crotch was both musician and artist, and being resident in Oxford for seventeen years came under Malchair's influence for much longer than most of his pupils and protégés, the majority of whom were undergraduates. Malchair's unpublished *Observations on Landskipp drawing* of 1791 (see under no.58) describes the preliminary instruction which his pupils received indoors, but the chief aim of his teaching was to get them drawing from nature. It is known, for example, that Malchair would take his pupils into the Oxford countryside for whole days of sketching, and he himself made a number of drawings in the vicinity of the city – views of Headington Hill or Shotover Hill, for example – which are remarkable for the directness of their presentation. By the time Crotch came to know Malchair in 1797 the latter's eyesight was failing rapidly, and expeditions such as these would presumably have no longer been feasible. Yet it is Crotch who, amongst all the artists of the 'Oxford School', one most closely associates with a type of open, panoramic landscape favoured by Malchair, and which also finds precedents in the work of William Taverner (no.8).

As he had developed an interest in transient effects in nature, Malchair had started to inscribe his drawings with the precise hour when they were made, and this is a habit which was also adopted by William Crotch. This view of Hurley Bottom, for example, is inscribed on the reverse as having been made at 5 p.m. Shortly after moving to London towards the end of 1805 Crotch became acquainted with John Constable who around this time began to inscribe his drawings in a similar fashion, presumably under Crotch's influence and thus an interesting (and unusual) example of the amateur contribution to mainstream landscape painting in this period. Indeed, Crotch's view from Hurley Bottom, dated August 1806, makes a fascinating comparison with Constable's watercolour which, if correctly identified as a view of Epsom, is datable to the very same month (no.81). Crotch's watercolours, especially those painted on a smaller scale, have occasionally been wrongly attributed to Constable. However, Crotch's work usually reveals the tell-tale diagonal shading, sloping backwards, which is the unmistakable sign of a left-handed artist.

Besides his connection with Constable, Crotch is also remembered today as one of the most precocious musical infant prodigies of all time (Fleming-Williams 1994, p.62). He composed an oratorio, *Palestine*, and in 1822 became the first Principal of the Royal Academy of Music.

AL

THOMAS GIRTIN
1775–1802

77 Trees in a Park c.1798–1800

Grey and coloured washes over pencil on
laid paper 24.3 × 43.8 (9½ × 17¼)
Inscribed in pencil lower right 'Girtin'

T08112

'If Tom Girtin had lived, I should have starved'. Turner's famous verdict on the premature death of Thomas Girtin of consumption at the age of twenty-seven is revealing on two accounts. It tells us something about the spirit of friendly rivalry between the two artists at the turn of the century, but it also reflects Turner's profound respect for Girtin's extraordinary talents as a watercolourist.

In fact, not only did the two artists share similar backgrounds (Girtin was the son of a London brushmaker, Turner of a Covent Garden barber), but their careers followed very similar paths in the 1790s. Both artists evolved their early drawing styles and copied watercolours by J.R. Cozens at Dr Monro's 'Academy' in the Strand. Both embarked on tours throughout the country in search of picturesque subjects suitable for translation into exhibition watercolours or – especially in Turner's case (see no. 78) – reproductive engravings destined to grace the pages of the many antiquarian publications appearing on the market at this date. They both enjoyed the patronage of the nobility, and in particular that of Edward Lascelles of Harewood House in Yorkshire, although Lascelles was inclined to rate Girtin's talents above Turner's, the latter he felt 'effect[ing] his purpose by industry – the former more genius' (Farington, *Diary*, 9 February 1799, vol.4, p.1154). Most importantly, however, in the late 1790s Girtin and Turner were the prime leaders in the revolution of watercolour technique,

evolving a bolder and more expressive use of the medium in response to the more dramatic and evocative scenery they encountered in Yorkshire and North Wales.

Girtin has been credited by one writer as being 'the first to see the tree as a mass ... and to render its general tone, its lights and shadows, rather than its leaves' (Hardie 1967, vol.2, p.18). Nevertheless, individual studies of trees are rare in the artist's work. Indeed, given his fondness for sweeping vistas, Girtin tended to favour broad stretches of open countryside – moorland, estuaries and hills – rather than individual motifs. Even this view is scenic in its bias; the inclusion of sheep and deer (one can be seen emerging from behind the central clump of trees) indicates that Girtin made his study in a park. The scene has not been identified and, indeed, could have been made on any number of estates belonging to the gentry which Girtin might have visited; one possibility is that it shows a view in Cassiobury Park, Hertfordshire, the Earl of Essex being one of the artist's patrons (Girtin and Loshak 1954, p.25). Girtin enjoyed a reputation for making sketches in the open air, one of his early biographers recording that 'when he had made a sketch at any place, he never wished to quit until he had given it all the proper tints' (*Gentleman's Magazine*, quoted Roget 1891, vol.1, p.95). However, the large scale of this study would suggest that Girtin may on this occasion have added colour in the studio.

AL

JOSEPH MALLORD WILLIAM TURNER
1775–1851

78 High Wycombe from the Marlow Road c.1802

Watercolour over pencil on wove paper 15.3 × 22.1 (6 × 8¾)
T08245

During the 1790s and for most of the following decade the Continent was effectively closed to travellers owing to the French Revolutionary and Napoleonic Wars. Turner, therefore, like many other landscape artists at this date, spent much of his early career travelling round Britain in search of suitable material which could be worked up into finished watercolours for exhibition or engraved for publication – antiquarian and picturesque subject-matter being especially popular at this time. It was on the basis of such comparatively modest work that the prolific and remarkably talented young Turner established his reputation, as well as earning a substantial income. In 1798 he reported to Farington that he had 'more commissions at present than He could execute & got more money than He expended' (*Diary*, 24 October 1798, vol.3, p.1075).

This watercolour of High Wycombe was one of seven subjects Turner was commissioned to make shortly after the turn of the century for William Byrne's *Britannia Depicta*, a publication which, it is clear from an advertisement in the copy in the British Museum, was originally intended to be part of a much larger work by the Revd Daniel Lysons and his father Samuel entitled *Magna Britannia: or a Concise Topographical Account of the Several Counties of Great Britain*. As it was, only engravings illustrating Bedfordshire, Berkshire and Buckinghamshire, and some for Cambridgeshire, Cheshire, Cornwall and Cumberland were published; topographical volumes like these were normally issued in parts to subscribers and often ran aground before completion if the publishers failed to retain the subscribers' interest, or if (as was often the case) the series were over-ambitious in the first place. Turner's seven designs are generally superior to those provided by the other topographical draughtsmen

for this publication, such as Thomas Hearne (1744–1806), William Alexander (1767–1816), Farington and 'Warwick' Smith (see nos.50 and 51–2). However, William Byrne's engravings, including the one he made after this watercolour, are rather hard and scratchy and fail to do justice to Turner's original designs. In later years Turner was to help train and supervise a whole team of engravers capable of translating his preliminary watercolours with much greater sensitivity and skill.

Of the seven watercolours Turner supplied for this project High Wycombe was the first to be engraved, in 1803, and the lettering on the print acknowledges Turner's elevation to the status of Royal Academician the previous year (at the remarkably young age of twenty-six). It has the subdued palette characteristic of much of Turner's work in watercolour at this date, the strong tonal contrasts no doubt intended to aid the engraver in translating the design into black and white. The accompanying text to the plate explains that the building in the foreground of the view is the former manor house of Loakes, renamed Wycombe Abbey after it was sold in 1795 by the Marquis of Lansdowne to Lord Carrington and 'wholly rebuilt in the Gothic style' by James Wyatt (1747–1813), the architect who also designed the fantastic Abbey at Fonthill for William Beckford. Wycombe Abbey is now an independent school for girls.

The first recorded owner of this watercolour was W.G. Rawlinson (1840–1928) who formed an important collection of prints by and after Turner (now mainly at the Yale Center for British Art, New Haven) and who published the standard catalogue *The Engraved Work of J.M.W. Turner* (2 vols., 1908–13). The engraving by William Byrne after Turner's watercolour of High Wycombe is number sixty-five in Rawlinson's catalogue.

AL

JOHN CONSTABLE
1776-1837

79a Shipping in the Thames or Medway 1803

Grey wash over pencil on laid paper 9.7 × 16.8 (3⅞ × 6⅝)
T08120

79b Shipping in the Thames or Medway 1803

Grey wash over pencil on laid paper 9.8 × 16.7 (3⅞ × 6⅝);
verso: another sketch of shipping, pencil, inscribed '5'
T08121

'Had I accepted the situation offered it would have been a death blow to all my prospects of perfection in the Art I love.' In a letter of 29 May 1802 (Beckett 1964, pp.31–2), Constable expressed his relief at having recently turned down the post of drawing master at the Royal Military Academy in Great Marlow. The decision seems to have prompted him, as he wrote in the same letter, to think 'more seriously on my profession than at any time of my life'. He had now become convinced 'of the truth of Sir Joshua Reynolds's observation that "there is no easy way of becoming a good painter" … only … by long contemplation and incessant labour'. It remained a cherished conviction. In 1830 he wrote of the precocious landscape painter R.P. Bonington (no.93), who had died two years before, that 'it is not right in a young man to assume great dash … without study, or pains' (Beckett 1966, p.141).

Unlike Bonington, Constable was a slow developer. The son of a wealthy corn merchant from East Bergholt in Suffolk, he was already in his early twenties when he finally obtained his father's permission to leave the family business, moving to London where he entered the Royal Academy Schools. In 1802, realising that he had been 'running after pictures and seeking the truth at second hand', he made a series of careful oil studies from nature of his native scenery near East Bergholt, in and around the Stour valley. It was a promising start, but Constable's subsequent progress as a landscape painter in oils was slow and intermittent, and during these early years of his career he was also painting portraits (see no.80) and altarpieces, though most of all he concentrated on drawing and watercolour (see no.81).

These drawings were made in the late spring of 1803, when Constable spent nearly a month on board the *Coutts*, an East Indiaman captained by his father's friend Robert Torin; the ship was sailing to China, and Constable joined it between London and Deal. He is said by his first biographer, C.R. Leslie (1794–1859), to have made as many as 130 drawings on the voyage, but fewer than fifty are known today (Reynolds 1996, 03.5–51), seven of which are in the Oppé collection. They are rapid sketches of the shipping he saw on the Thames, the Medway and along the coast, for the most part executed in pencil alone, though a few – like these two – have tonal washes of grey. During these 'experimental years of self-discovery', as they have been called (Fleming-Williams 1994, p.88), Constable was highly susceptible to the influences of other artists, and these early shipping studies have often been likened in style to the drawings of the marine artist Willem Van de Velde the younger (1633–1707), whose work Constable was certainly aware of about this time (Reynolds 1973, p.51). In fact, in their use of free-flowing, even wriggly lines, with affirmative pressure applied at either end of the pencil strokes (see especially no.79a), these shipping studies are even closer to some of Richard Wilson's chalk drawings which Joseph Farington, a former pupil of Wilson's, may perhaps have lent Constable to copy, just as he also lent him an example of one of Wilson's oils (Fleming-Williams 1994, pp.96–8).

When in 1837 Constable's son, Charles Golding Constable (1821–1879), heard of his father's death, he wrote to express his concern about the fate of the sketches Constable had made aboard the *Coutts* so many years before: being a sailor, Charles Golding took an especial interest in them (Fleming-Williams and Parris 1984, p.12). He was also anxious about the safekeeping of two of Constable's Brighton sketchbooks, no doubt thinking of the shipping studies his father had made there in the 1820s.

AL

JOHN CONSTABLE
1776–1837

80 Mary Ann Bridges at the harpsichord with two of her sisters c.1804

Pencil on laid paper with traces of a discoloured fixative 23.7 × 18.8 (9¼ × 7⅜)
T08148

On 1 June 1804 Farington wrote in his *Diary* that Constable had called, informing him that he had 'of late been much employed painting portraits large as the life for which He has *with a hand* 3 guineas, – without 2 guineas. – This low price affords the farmers &cto indulge their wishes and to have their Children and relatives painted' (vol.6, p.2340).

This pencil study, and a second one in a private collection (Reynolds 1996, 04.3), are studies for the portrait of *The Bridges Family* (Tate Gallery, fig.23) which Constable also painted that year. George Bridges (1764–1835) of Lawford Place, Essex, was a banker and merchant of some standing in Essex and Suffolk (Parris 1981, p.29), and no doubt could comfortably have afforded the higher price Constable would presumably have charged for this, his largest known group portrait. Bridges is shown with his wife, Mary, and their eight children in what was probably the drawing-room of Lawford Place; Lawford church can be seen through the window. The girl at the harpsichord is the eldest daughter, Mary Ann (b.1790), seen in this preliminary drawing with two of her sisters (or, possibly, a sister and brother). Constable has used a fixative on the drawing – a substance to fix or hold the graphite

onto the surface of the paper – which had badly discoloured, though thanks to recent conservation work this is now less visible. In later years Constable was to use a fixative known as isinglass, a high-grade glue made from the swimming bladders of fish, which does not darken with age (McAusland 1994, p.17).

In 1800 Bridges and his merchant father, also George, had formed a partnership with a local entrepreneur, George Elmer, and eleven years later they took out a twenty-one-year lease on Mistley, the port on the Stour estuary from which Constable's father, Golding, shipped his cargoes of corn and coal to and from London, and where he rented granaries and a coalyard; indeed, as a 'tenant at will', Golding Constable was taken over in this transaction (Parris 1981, p.26). As fellow merchants at Mistley, Golding Constable and the younger George Bridges would have been in frequent contact with each other, but their families do not appear to have moved in the same social circles. In a letter of 31 January 1813 Constable's mother told him that Mr and Mrs Bridges and their son had recently made a call on his uncle, David Pike Watts, in London: she described how they had drawn up in their carriage, announced themselves with 'loud raps' and on leaving had each deposited their cards which, she informed Constable, his uncle had 'returned in the same *"fashionably"* friendly way', but adding that 'these are – customs & usages – unpractised – in Humble villages' (Beckett 1962, p.89; quoted Parris 1981, p.29).

It is said that at the time that Constable was painting *The Bridges Family* portrait, the young artist 'showed an admiration' for Mary Ann, and that his 'visits were in consequence discouraged' (MacColl 1912, p.268). Perhaps he was perceived as an inappropriate suitor. When, five years later, Constable transferred his affections to Maria Bicknell, daughter of the solicitor to the Regent and the Admiralty, he was to come up against similar objections from her grandfather, East Bergholt's rector, Dr Rhudde.

fig.23 John Constable, *The Bridges Family* 1804, oil on canvas
Tate Gallery

AL

JOHN CONSTABLE
1776–1837

81 View over a Valley, probably Epsom Downs *c.*1806

Watercolour over pencil on wove paper 9.5 × 12.4 (3¾ × 4⅞)
T08249

When Constable called on Farington in the summer of 1804 and told him he was busy painting portraits of the local farming community near East Bergholt in Suffolk (see no.80), he also mentioned that he had a 'House of His own near his Fathers where He works hard and has time in the afternoons to cultivate Landscape painting' (Farington, *Diary*, 1 June 1804, vol.6, p.2340). Very little, however, has survived of Constable's landscape work in oils for the period *c.*1804–6. Indeed, during these years he seems especially to have concentrated on landscape watercolour painting and drawing, learning how to describe forms more convincingly in depth as well as how better to represent light and atmosphere in nature.

Before 1805 Constable had used watercolour only occasionally, and then rather timidly: there are a few finished watercolours which date from the turn of the century – controlled and precise works which follow the conventions of the 'tinted drawing' – and also a number of sketches made, for example, in Derbyshire in 1801 and Windsor in 1802, which, though looser in execution, are still very restricted in palette. During the years 1805 and 1806, however, Constable produced a substantial number of more colourful, painterly and expressive watercolours. These resemble the work of Thomas Girtin (see no.77) in their attention to atmospheric effects and in their presentation of stretches of broad, open countryside with a strong horizontal emphasis, though extending gradually into depth to a distant horizon (Kitson 1957, p.348).

According to C.R. Leslie, Sir George Beaumont – an early patron of Constable's – owned some thirty examples of Girtin's work in watercolour, and advised Constable to study them for their 'great breadth and truth' (Leslie 1951, p.5). Nevertheless, by 1805 Beaumont and Constable appear to have been rather out of touch (see no.82, and Parris, Shields and Fleming-Williams 1975, p.145). It seems, then, more than likely that the immediate impetus for Constable's enthusiastic adoption of watercolour in 1805 was the first, highly successful, exhibition of the Society of Painters in Watercolour held in London in April that year (Fleming-Williams 1991, p.396). Indeed, that exhibition featured a number of watercolourists, Cornelius Varley (no.84), for instance, and his brother, John, whose work was also strongly influenced by Girtin at this date.

This watercolour has until now been identifed as a view near Dedham in Suffolk. However, it is now clear that it is almost certainly a detached, trimmed page from the sketchbook (now completely dismembered) which Constable used on a visit to his relations, the Gubbinses, at Epsom in August 1806; it is particularly close, for example, to another watercolour made that year (Reynolds 1996, 06.106) recently identified by Ian Fleming-Williams as from the same 'Epsom book'. In September Constable set off on a tour of the Lake District, and filled the remaining pages of this sketchbook with views in, or *en route* for, Cumbria (another watercolour by Constable in the Oppé collection, T08228, of almost identical dimensions to this one is a Lakeland subject presumably from the same dismembered Epsom book). Constable's tour in the Lake District, funded by his uncle, David Pike Watts (see no.80), lasted seven weeks and was extraordinarily productive. However, it was the last time he travelled anywhere with the specific purpose of gathering material for paintings. Thenceforward, he drew and painted only wherever his friendships, family ties or professional commitments happened to take him (Parris, Shields and Fleming-Williams 1976, p.64).

AL

JOHN CONSTABLE

1776–1837

82 Album of fifteen drawings after Alexander Cozens (1717–1786)

'A Series of Sketches by John Constable R.A. Illustrating the Various Species
of Composition of Landscape in Nature' c.1823

Album size 32.1 × 43.1 (12⅝ × 17)

T08095–T08109

Open at no.3, pen and brown ink over pencil with grey washes on wove paper 11.3 × 18.6 (4½ × 7⅜)

Inscribed in pen and brown ink 'A Varied Landscape on one side. And a flat country or Water on the other'

T08097

In October 1823 Constable was invited to stay at the house of Sir George Beaumont (1753–1827), Coleorton Hall in Leicestershire. Beaumont was an important connoisseur, collector and amateur artist, and in the late 1790s had offered Constable valuable encouragement in his chosen career as a painter, allowing him access to his collection of paintings in London. However, after about 1802 their acquaintance had lapsed, and patron and artist were not in contact again until about 1819, Constable's six-week stay at Coleorton in 1823 marking the high point of their renewed assocation (Parris, Fleming-Williams and Shields 1976, p.134). Shortly after he arrived at Coleorton Constable wrote excitedly to his wife, Maria, informing her he was 'in a room full of Claudes … real Claudes and Wilsons and Poussins &c. almost at the summit of my earthly ambitions'. Soon afterwards he was to tell her that he was making copies after two of Beaumont's Claudes. Indeed, so absorbed did Constable apparently become in studying his patron's fine collection that he was invited to stay over Christmas, an offer which Maria admitted was 'complimentary' of Sir George, 'but he forgot at the time that you had a wife' (Beckett 1964, p.302).

Another of the attractions for Constable in staying at Coleorton was hearing Beaumont's 'delightfull stories about painting' and about the artists the latter had known in his youth, one of whom was Alexander Cozens (nos.15–20), the inventor of the famous 'blot' technique of composing landscapes who had taught Beaumont drawing at Eton. It was almost certainly during his stay at Coleorton in 1823 that Constable recorded various anecdotes about painters, including some remarks about Cozens, and also made lists of the 16 'Compositions', 14 'Objects' and 26 of the 27 'Circumstances' (omitting 'fire') which together make up Cozens's *Various Species*

of Composition of Landscape, in Nature (for Constable's transcripts see Wilton 1980, p.26). Cozens had been working on this treatise in the late 1760s and early 1770s, and although it remained largely unpublished (see no.17), some of its chief ideas seem to have been transmitted to Beaumont by his tutor, the Revd Charles Davy (it was Davy's notes, and his metrical version of the 16 'Compositions' which Constable apparently copied).

It was presumably also at Coleorton in 1823 that Constable made his copies after the etchings of the 16 'Compositions' from Cozens's *Various Species* (fig.24), fifteen of which are in this album (on paper watermarked 1822), while the sixteenth is in the Fogg Art Museum, Cambridge, Mass. (all sixteen are repr. in Reynolds 1984, pls.425–40). Constable's copies differ from the set of outline etchings in the British Museum in showing the addition of tonal areas of grey wash. However, there is a washed set of the etchings in an album by the minor animal painter George Gregory in the Tate Gallery – which, among other things, includes Gregory's recipes and notes for 'photographic papers', 'puff paste', 'camomile pills', 'spruce beer' and a 'Room to breed canarys'. Gregory was also connected with Beaumont (he died at Coleorton in 1852), and his washed set of etchings, like Constable's copies, may have been made from a similar set which Beaumont owned. Some of Cozens's original pen and ink drawings for the 'Compositions', in reverse direction to the etchings themselves, are in the Oppé collection, including that for 'Composition' no.3 (T08853).

Constable also knew of Cozens's 'blot' technique, making 'blot-like' drawings himself as early as 1798, and some especially expressive examples in the 1830s (Fleming-Williams 1990, pp.276–309).

AL

3. A Varied Landscape on one side. And a flat country or Water on the other

The Various Species of Composition of Landscape, in Nature.

fig. 24
Alexander Cozens,
*The Various Species
of Composition of
Landscape in Nature*
*c.*1765–75, four
etchings on one
sheet
*Trustees of the
British Museum*

SIR ROBERT KER PORTER
1777–1842

83 An Ancient Castle *c.*1799–1800

Grey wash over some pencil on laid paper 20.9 × 29.6 (8¼ × 11⅝)
T08532

This work, with its air of fantasy and its grey watercolour washes is immediately recognisable as a product of what is usually known as either Girtin's Sketching Club or the Sketching Society. We know a little about the club's origins and its membership from an inscription on the back of a drawing made by one of its members, Louis Francia (1772–1839), at its first meeting (Pointon 1985, pp.89–95). According to the rules of the Society, it was to meet weekly with each member taking it in turn to be the host. The host would chose a literary quotation which was to be illustrated and then after the drawings had been completed the group would have supper (Guillemard 1922 pp.189–95; Oppé 1923B, pp.189–98; Hamilton 1971). It first met in Ker Porter's studio at 16 Great Newport Street, Leicester Square, on 20 May 1799 – a venue which was highly symbolic and may even have been a catalyst in shaping the idea of such an artists' club: Porter's studio was the studio that Sir Joshua Reynolds, first President of the Royal Academy and most clubbable of artists, had occupied from 1753 until 1760, and the aims of this 'select society of Young Painters' calling themselves 'the Brothers' who came together in 1799 were clearly inspired by Reynolds's oft-stated ambitions for British landscape painting. They met with 'the purpose of establishing by practice a school of Historical Landscape, the subjects being original designs from poetical passages'. As a forum in which the imagination was exercised and reigned supreme, the Sketching Society is a perfect example of the Romantic sensibility at work; the essence of the same process for an individual artist can be seen in the thinking behind Cozens's 'blot.' (no.18). W.T. Thornbury has Thomas Girtin (no.77) as the founder (Thornbury 1862, vol.1, p.108), but it is most likely that the moving spirit behind the club was the energetic Ker Porter: not only did he host its inaugural meeting but not long before in 1797 he had formed a literary club with his sisters (one of whom was an author) and the writer T.F. Dibdin with the essays produced by

its members being published in a short-lived periodical. As a group endeavour the Sketching Society had its roots in the competitive and emulative spirit which Porter knew from his time in the Academy schools and in the collegiate spirit in which three of the members, Francia, Girtin and T.R. Underwood had once worked, together with the young Turner, for Dr Monro.

However social the event, the intention behind these evening sessions was, initially anyway, deeply serious and undoubtedly seen by the participants as 'national' in its purpose. They obviously took inspiration from what Reynolds had to say about landscape in his annual *Discourses* to his students. By choosing to render their designs in dark monochrome washes the artists were following the advice to achieve 'grandeur of effect ... by reducing ... colours to little more than chiaro oscuro' (4th Discourse, 1771; Wark 1975, p.61). Like Reynolds they sought an elevated style of landscape painting based on 'the influence of a poetical mind' rather than an exact representation of nature (13th Discourse, 1786; Wark 1975, p.238); following Edmund Burke they looked to achieve effects of 'striking sublimity' by the use of 'sad and fuscous colours' (Burke 1756, p.82)

Porter's work, along with others of the same subject by six members of the Sketching Society, came from a famous collection owned by John Percy (see under no.51). J.L. Roget (1891, vol.1, p.100) suggested that they were products of the same session though this is unlikely (Oppé 1923B). All seven works were sold at Percy's sale in April 1890 and three of them, T08532, a Cotman (T08122), and a Girtin (T08919), are in the Oppé collection. Porter's drawing can be approximately dated to the period between May 1799 and January 1800 after which the Society regrouped with a different membership among whom were Cotman (nos.85–6) and later Cristall (no.73). The Sketching Society lasted until 1851 and included Clarkson Stanfield (no.92) and John Constable's biographer C.R. Leslie among its members.

RH

CORNELIUS VARLEY
1781–1873

84 Study of a Tree 1803

Watercolour over pencil on wove paper 37.6 × 27.2 (14¾ × 10¾)
Inscribed lower left in pen and brown ink 'C Varley 1803'
T08470

Cornelius Varley's better-known elder brother John (1778–1842) was a famous teacher of watercolour and is remembered for the pithy aphorisms he coined for his pupils (and put to good effect in his own work), such as 'Nature wants cooking' (Redgrave 1866, vol.1, p.498). Cornelius Varley's approach to art could hardly have been more different. Brought up from the age of twelve by his uncle Samuel Varley, a watch and instrument maker as well as an amateur scientist, Cornelius gradually came to appreciate that, in his own words, 'knoledge is no burden but lightens all other burdens' (Pidgley 1973, introduction). For many years his interest in science and art ran in tandem, as his enquiring mind came to scrutinise all aspects of the natural world. A sketchbook used by him in Wales in 1802, for example, containing views of Dolbardern, Barmouth, Harlech and elsewhere, is also inscribed with recipes for curing poisonous animal bites and cancer of the lips (Fitzwilliam Museum, Cambridge; see Munro 1994, p.97).

Varley seems to have been strongly influenced by Thomas Girtin's practice of sketching from nature in all weathers, having apparently seen him 'sitting out for hours in the rain to observe the effect of storms and clouds upon the atmosphere' (Pidgley 1972, p.781). Indeed, Varley made many cloud studies of his own in the early years of the century, in pencil or in watercolour, some on loose sheets such as the example on the back of this tree study, and others in a sketchbook he used in Wales in 1803 (New York, Pierpont Morgan Library; see

Ryskamp 1990). Generally the sketches he made at this date are left unfinished, which suggests that the impulse behind them is as much scientific curiosity as artistic feeling (Wilcox 1985, no.40); and some of them, like this tree study, show him using the edge of his paper as if it were a palette, dabbing the brush, perhaps testing the saturation of his washes. Nevertheless, Varley's watercolours are aesthetically compelling works, combining careful observation with intensity of feeling in a manner which anticipates Constable and the emerging strain of naturalism in early nineteenth-century Britain. Indeed, Constable may have seen Varley's work at the first exhibition of the Society of Painters in Watercolour in 1805 (of which Cornelius and his brother John were founder members); two of his twelve exhibits that year were listed by him as sketches made 'on the spot'.

Varley resigned from the Society of Painters in Watercolour in 1820, his interests turning increasingly towards the invention and manufacture of scientific instruments. The most famous of these was a type of camera lucida which he patented in 1811 and which enabled the user to project a reduced image onto paper which could then be traced by hand; his own drawings made with this device are inscribed 'PGT' ('Patent Graphic Telescope'). In 1814 he became a fellow of the Society of Arts and in 1851 mounted a display of optical instruments at the Great Exhibition for which he won a prize medal. He also invented the first soda-water apparatus.

AL

C Varley 1803

1603

JOHN SELL COTMAN
1782–1842

85 Doorway of the Refectory, Rievaulx Abbey 1803

Watercolour over pencil on laid paper 31.9 × 25.5 (12½ × 10)

Inscribed twice in pencil on along top edge 'Ivy' and lower right
'Rivaulx Abbey Augt 8 1803', and numbered in pen and brown
ink lower right '6'

T08248

Cotman was one of the most original landscape water-colourists of his generation. His twentieth-century reputation rests on the work he produced in the earlier part of his career which, rather like that of Francis Towne – and in his own day as little appreciated – reveals an interest in structure and pictorial pattern, expressed through carefully ordered areas of flat colour. Towne's best work, as for so many of his eighteenth-century con-temporaries, had been inspired by scenery encountered abroad. Cotman, on the other hand, like Girtin and Turner, found a powerful imaginative stimulus closer to home in the landscape of the north of England. Indeed, when the famous nineteenth-century critic John Ruskin wrote that of all Turner's drawings it was 'those of ... Yorkshire ...[that] have the most heart in them', he might just as well have been referring to Cotman – except, as it happens, Ruskin seems never to have commented on Cotman's work at all (Kitson 1937, pp.332–3).

Born in Norwich, like Turner the son of a barber, Cotman had little formal training before his move to London in 1798. The following year, like Turner and Girtin before him, he joined Dr Monro's 'Academy' in the Strand, and also became a member of the Sketching Society, succeeding Girtin as its leading spirit (see under no.83). His watercolours of c.1800–2 are greatly influenced by Girtin, with strong tonal contrasts and an essentially sombre palette (two examples, *Houses at Epsom*, 1800 (T08765) and *Llangollen* (T08237), are in the Oppé collection). Cotman's distinctive watercolour style began to emerge in about 1803 in drawings made at meetings of the Sketching Society and on the first of his visits to Yorkshire to stay with the Cholmeley family at

Brandsby Hall some fifteen miles north of York. Indeed, this drawing of Rievaulx, as well as being one of the first of Cotman's drawings to show his single-minded con-centration on isolated motifs (Stainton 1985, p.57), is also regarded as one of the earliest to show the emergence of his new watercolour style – though pencilwork (with its small dots and dashes, so characteristic of the Monro School house style) still plays a substantial role (Kitson 1937, p.54). However, one writer has made the important observation that drawings made at almost exactly the same date by John Varley (1778–1842) – fellow member of the Sketching Society and brother to Cornelius (no.84) – show a very similar move towards the adoption of clean, flat washes; he suggests that Varley, as the older of the two artists, was probably the dominant influence, even if it was Cotman who was to apply the new style in such a singular manner (Hardie 1967, vol.2, p.75).

Cotman drew the famous ruined Cistercian abbey at Rievaulx near Helmsley several times on his trip to North Yorkshire in 1803, firstly in July when sketching in company with Paul Sandby Munn (1773–1845), then between 7 and 9 August on his own (when this water-colour was made). His various representations of the abbey are in a number of collections (see Rajnai 1982, p.48), a striking pencil drawing looking into the transept being in the Tate Gallery (T00973). This watercolour of the Refectory doorway was etched by Cotman for his *Miscellaneous Etchings* of 1811 (Popham 1922, no.12). One of the subscribers to this series was the third Viscount Palmerston – son of Pars's most important patron (see no.46) and the future Prime Minister – whom Cotman met in 1803 when staying with the Cholmeleys at Brandsby (Kitson 1937, p.57).

AL

6

JOHN SELL COTMAN
1782–1842

86 On the Greta c.1805

Watercolour over pencil with very slight traces of gouache on laid paper 22.8 × 33.3 (9 × 13⅛)

Inscribed on verso in pencil 'On the Greta' and numbered in pen and brown ink '20'

T08145

Cotman's stay with the Cholmeley family at Brandsby Hall in North Yorkshire in 1803 (see no. 85) was the first of three very happy visits there made during consecutive summers. It was the third of these visits, in 1805, which was to be the most productive, for it was during this year that, in addition to studies near Brandsby, Cotman also made the famous sequence of striking watercolour studies on the river Greta near Rokeby on the Yorkshire-Durham border. Altogether he spent about five weeks in and around Rokeby, staying some of the time with the Morritts at Rokeby Hall itself (John Morritt was a classical scholar who had been on the Grand Tour, collecting the famous *Rokeby Venus* by the seventeenth-century Spanish painter Velàzquez now in the National Gallery) and the rest of the time at a nearby inn. The wooded slopes and winding paths close to the river Greta in Rokeby Park inspired what Laurence Binyon described as 'the most perfect examples of pure watercolour ever made in Europe' (1931, p.132).

On the banks of the river Greta Cotman absorbed himself in the task of translating nature into art, and Lindsay Stainton (1985, p.58) has tellingly analysed his method. Pure, translucent wash layers are applied by him without monochrome underpainting and with minimum shadow, defining shape with their crisp edges rather than (like Towne) by means of outline – his procedure has been likened to that of the Japanese woodcut artist printing flat colours from superimposed woodblocks (Hardie 1967, vol.2, pp.80–1). There is an avoidance of any effect of movement; and, in denial of traditional methods of creating depth in a picture, natural forms are reduced to simple, flat shapes and presented in planes very close to the picture surface. The resulting images, with their tendency towards abstract design, can be difficult to 'read' but are always compelling in their combination of shape and pattern. Despite their pictorial resolution,

however, it seems likely that at least some of Cotman's Greta studies were coloured on the spot. In 1805 Cotman specifically wrote to a patron that his 'chief Study' that summer had been 'colouring from Nature', his sketches 'close copies of that ficle Dame' (Kitson 1937, pp.79–80). In an important early article on Cotman written in the 1920s Paul Oppé pointed out that close-up studies of bank, water, tree trunks and rock were an especially convenient choice of subject for the artist when attempting to colour from nature, being comparatively independent of atmospheric change (1923A, p.ix).

However, these watercolours failed to find favour with the public. Attempting to sell Cotman's *Miscellaneous Etchings* of 1811 (see no.85), a York bookseller pointed out that 'two thirds of mankind, you know, mind more about what is represented than how it is done'. In 1806, 'blackballed' from joining the Society of Painters in Watercolour in London, Cotman returned to Norwich, becoming a leading member of the Norwich Society of Artists, and depending on his faithful patron, the Yarmouth banker Dawson Turner, for commissions of antiquarian and architectural subjects, many of which he worked up as etchings. The most important of these were the *Architectural Antiquities of Norfolk*, 1812–18, and the *Architectural Antiquities of Normandy*, 1822, the latter based on drawings gathered on three separate trips to Normandy, some of them made with the Graphic Telescope invented by Cornelius Varley (see no.84 and Pidgley 1972, pp.785–6). Although there was an element of drudgery to this work and Cotman was sometimes short of money, as Oppé pointed out (as a corrective to previous accounts), Cotman's later career was spent 'neither in misery nor without recognition' (1942, p.163). Indeed, in 1833 Cotman was appointed drawing master at King's College, London, a prestigious post he retained until his death in 1842.

AL

WILLIAM HAVELL
1782–1837

87 Grange Bridge, Cumberland *c*.1807–8

Watercolour over pencil on blue wove paper with
touches of white gouache 21.4 × 27.3 (8¾ × 10¾)
Inscribed in pencil upper left 'Grange Bridge' and
lower right '18'
T08172

The son of a Reading drawing master, Havell was the youngest of the sixteen founder members of the Society of Painters in Watercolour, and one of the most talented. His compositions 'were much admired even in the first year's exhibition' in 1805, although 'he was yet a very young man' (W.H. Pyne, quoted Roget 1891, vol.1, p.295). Most of Havell's early exhibits at the Society were Welsh views, based on material gathered on sketching tours in 1802 and 1803. However, when his fellow Society member John Glover (1767–1849) proved so successful at selling watercolours of Lakeland scenery at the very same exhibitions, in 1807 Havell set off for Cumberland with R.R. Reinagle (1775–1862) 'to store themselves with subjects for drawings' (Farington, *Diary*, 15 August 1807, vol.8, p.3106). He settled for a year or more in a cottage at Ambleside, and was in regular contact with the Hardens of Brathay Hall, influential patrons of the arts in the area who had met Constable on his tour of the Lakes the previous year.

This study, and another one of comparable size made by Havell about the same time, *Skelwith Force and Langdale Pikes* (Abbot Hall Art Gallery, Kendal), are executed in the unusual combination of coloured washes and white bodycolour on a paper of mid-tone. Compared with the more traditional sketching medium of pencil and white paper, this combination offered a richer range of tones and a greater subtlety in the description of light and shade – as did the more popular sketching medium

of black and white chalks on coloured papers. The latter technique was one which had often been favoured by oil painters (see no.13), and it may be no coincidence that Havell was at this date also developing his skills as a painter in oils. In 1813 he was one of those members of the Society most in favour of allowing members to exhibit oils as well as watercolours, a decision which led to its reconstitution for seven years as the Society of Painters in Oil and Watercolours. From about 1830 Havell worked exclusively in oil.

In 1815 Havell had painted one of his largest and most ambitious oils, *Walnut Gathering at Petersham*, a picture he believed surpassed even J.M.W. Turner in its merits – the connoisseur and collector Sir George Beaumont had once warned the poet William Wordsworth about Havell's lack of humility. When the picture was rejected for exhibition by the directors of the British Insitution (of which Beaumont was one), an embittered Havell left the country on an embassy to China. He subsequently supported himself for eight years in India painting portraits in watercolour. On his return to England he became increasingly reliant on venues outside London for the sale of his work, exhibiting an oil of *Grange Bridge* based on this study, for example, at the Liverpool Academy in 1844 (Owen and Stanford 1981, p.24). The sketch itself was later owned by J.L. Roget, who in 1891 wrote what has now become the standard history of the Society of Painters in Watercolour.

AL

Grange Bridge

THOMAS UWINS
1782–1857

88 A Study of Hops *c.*1811

Watercolour over pencil on laid paper
34.5 × 22.2 (13⅝ × 8¾)
T08268

'This place is all in a bustle with the hop-picking', wrote Thomas Uwins in September 1811 to his brother Zechariah from Farnham in Surrey. 'I have made a great many sketches, and propose doing more; that it has never been made more use of by artists is altogether a mystery to me, it is so much superior to any other harvest that we in England have to boast' (Uwins 1858, vol.1, p.35).

Uwins had first started exhibiting at the Society of Painters in Watercolours in 1809, becoming a member in 1810, and by 1811 his studies of gleaners, lacemakers and furze cutters had already hung on its walls. The idea of adding hop-pickers to his range of rustic genre was probably inspired by the example of Joshua Cristall (no.73), who sent a large watercolour depicting a hop harvest to the Society in 1807. Certainly, hop-picking had never been as popular a subject for British artists as the wheat harvest, lacking its religious connotations, and perhaps also because the end product, beer, unlike bread, was a luxury (Payne 1993, p.142). On the other hand, it was the sort of 'national' subject which British artists sought out during the war with France (Hamlyn 1993, p.62). Hops were grown in Kent and Surrey and harvested by temporary workers, usually women and children from the East End of London (Payne 1993, p.19). In addition to this remarkably sensitive and detailed watercolour (and a smaller study) of individual hops, there are sketches by Uwins in the Oppé collection of workers picking and stripping hops.

Observing the hop-pickers in Farnham in 1811, Uwins had contemplated what the 'gathering [of] the vintage on the continent' might be like. In 1817, with peace restored in Europe, he travelled to France to observe the process at first hand. His sketches of the Burgundian grape harvest were used many years later for an elaborate oil, the *Vintage in the Claret Vineyards of the South of France, on the Banks of the Gironde*, which he exhibited at the Royal Academy in 1848 (Tate Gallery, N00387). In the early 1820s he fell back on his skills as an illustrator and painter of watercolour portraits to pay off a bad debt, and between 1824 and 1831 settled in Italy. His extensive correspondence dating from the years in Italy is an important document for the period, and was substantially incorporated into his wife's *Memoir of Thomas Uwins RA*, 1858. It includes an amusing profile of William Havell (no.87) in Naples, preferring 'a beefsteak with … gravy … and a mutton chop that will burn the mouth' to 'figs for his breakfast, and maccaroni … for his dinner' (Uwins 1858, vol.2, p.124). In 1838 Uwins was elected a Royal Academician, having by this date established a repuation for his Italian genre subjects in oil. In 1845 he was appointed Surveyor of the Queen's Pictures and in 1847 Keeper of the National Gallery.

AL

SIR DAVID WILKIE
1785–1841

89 Interior of a Cottage: Study for 'The Irish Whiskey Still' 1835

Pencil, brown pen and ink and watercolour on wove paper 17.7 × 25.8 (7 × 10⅛)

Inscribed in brown ink bottom right 'D W' and in pencil in another hand 'WILKIE' bottom
left and on the back in brown ink 'Given to Mr Nasmyth by Miss Wilkie'

T08599

Competitiveness has always been at the heart of the art
world and this was particularly true of the nineteenth-
century British art world. Painters were constantly in
search of new subject-matter as the annual exhibitions at
the Royal Academy, the British Institution and the
Society of British Artists grew larger, and with it the need
for artists to establish a reputation, outshine their rivals or
bolster their existing fame by catching the eyes of critics
and patrons by virtue of the novelty of what they had
done. For the greatest artists, such as Wilkie or Turner, it
was an original technique as much as subject-matter
which brought them pre-eminence but for most sustaining a reputation had to rest principally on the skill with
which they mined new veins of subject-matter. In the
inevitable restlessness of this search, certainly, lay some of
the dangers of which Fuseli spoke to Wilkie (see no.42)
when he first took London by storm with his scenes from
familiar life which looked back to seventeenth-century
Dutch old masters while nonetheless being modern.

Travel abroad was an essential part of this search.
Wilkie travelled extensively in Europe and it was, of
course, his death on the way back from Palestine in 1841
which inspired Turner's *Peace. Burial at Sea* (N00528). In
August and September 1835 Wilkie visited Ireland for the
first time. The poetic picturesqueness of the 'primeval
simplicity' of the life of the peasants and the colours of
their clothes provided him with a wealth of 'perfectly
new and untouched' material. He was nervously aware
that it might be soon discovered by others and wrote
back home that he felt 'quite afraid that other artists will
soon be coming the same way' (Errington 1975, p.21).

Wilkie made a number of sketches for possible pictures
while he was in Ireland, although in the end only
three finished oil paintings resulted: *The Peep-o'Day-Boys'
Cabin*, shown at the Royal Academy in 1836 (Tate
Gallery N00332; Hamlyn 1993, no.74) and *The Irish
Whiskey Still* (Rega Museum) which he first painted in
1839, and then another, exhibited, version in 1840
(National Gallery of Scotland). This characteristically vigorous pen and ink and wash drawing in a style which
some contemporaries compared with Rembrandt's, made
on the spot in Ireland, was used by Wilkie for the interior
in which he placed the whisky still and its owners in
the 1839 picture. In constructing his finished paintings
Wilkie produced careful studies of individual parts of
the composition, particularly groups of figures, before
bringing them together on canvas. Sketches for the
figures on the left of the 1839 picture are in the National
Gallery of Scotland and the Victoria and Albert Museum,
and a sketch for the whisky still is also in the National
Gallery of Scotland (Errington 1975). Although there
were many Irish sketches included in Wilkie's studio sale
in 1842, T08599 was clearly kept by the artist's sister
Helen who at some point gave it to a Mr Nasmyth.

RH

WILLIAM MULREADY

1786–1863

90 James Leckie and Little Mary ?c.1828

Pen and brown ink and some pencil on thin wove paper
16.5 × 11.4 (6½ × 4½)
Inscribed in ink 'James Leckie and little Bet [deleted] Mary'
and in a later hand in pencil on the back 'W. Mulready'
T08233

The two impromptu studies on this sheet are the first ideas for a small oil painting dated 1828 which is listed in Mulready's Account Book under 25 June 1830 as 'Father & Child' (Heleniak 1980, no.117, pl.113; Pointon 1986 no.109, pl.xiv). It is essentially a private work, catching as it does a slight incident involving Mulready's ward (perhaps even his daughter) Mary, daughter of the 'wretch' Mrs Leckie, married to James, who replaced Mulready's wife in his affections (Pointon 1986, pp.68–9). The deletion in the inscription implies that when Mulready gave his sketch a title the name of Mrs Leckie's other daughter, Elizabeth (d.1844), who went on to marry Albert Fleetwood Varley (1804–1876), first came to mind. Mulready frequently explored the motif of the child in his paintings, usually with a serious, moralising intention. In the finished oil painting based on these sketches Mulready kept the pose of the two figures but placed them in a cottage interior and showed the child pointing to an illustration in what looks like a family Bible. Behind them, with her back to the viewer, the mother is talking to a baker at the door.

While Mulready was famous as a painter of genre pictures or 'scenes from familiar life' and was one of the most sensitive colourists of his day whose brilliant palette prepared the way for the Pre-Raphaelites' use of colour, he also had a considerable reputation within his profession as a superb draughtsman. Writing in November 1857, the artist Richard Redgrave commented on how Mulready, at the age of seventy-three, was not only still drawing in the life class 'like any young student' but also attending another life class for three days a week.

Mulready showed Redgrave 'some pen-and-ink studies which he was making at the rate of one per night' and told another friend '" I used to draw rapidly in pen-and-ink; but I find I have lost some of my power. I used to be able to draw half a dozen hands carefully and correctly in an hour. Now I find I can't do that. I must restore that power; I must get it up again!"' (Redgrave 1891, p.178). The compulsiveness of this activity comes over both in the power behind his pen work and also in the great quantity of drawings which have survived: preparatory studies for pictures and sketches amounting to, as one critic wrote, 'a method of study which, instead of relaxing as age increases, delights in the solution of the difficulties of the art' (*Art-Union* 1848, p.208).

In June 1848 the Society of Arts organised, with Mulready, an exhibition of his paintings which was the first such show intended to promote the formation of a National Gallery of British Art. It is a measure of the importance which Mulready attached to intense preparatory work with the pencil and pen in the making of paintings – and thus to the ultimate success of the British School – that he included a great number of drawings in the exhibition. The critic of the *Athenaeum* immediately recognised this, thereby acknowledging the habitual neglect of drawing in the Royal Academy in particular, by urging students to 'look at them earnestly … and learn the success of that series of finished works on which you have been gazing with such delight' (*Athenaeum*, 10 June 1848, p.584). The Pre-Raphaelite Brotherhood, founded in 1848, in the emphasis they placed on drawing owed a debt to Mulready.

RH

FRANCIS DANBY
1793–1861

91 Romantic Woodland c.1824–5

Watercolour with touches of gum arabic and scratching-out
on wove paper 19.4 × 26 (7⅝ × 10¼)

T08139

The first half of the nineteenth century saw the establishment of a number of important regional artistic schools in Britain. The first of these, and perhaps the best known, was the Norwich School founded in 1803, which included such leading names as John Sell Cotman (see nos.85–6) and John Crome (1768–1821) and was the first provincial institution to maintain regular exhibitions. Another important local school of artists, albeit less cohesive than that at Norwich, was that set up in Bristol in the 1820s, of which the most important figure was Francis Danby.

Members recruited to these schools tended to have local connections, but Danby was a Bristolian purely by adoption. Born in Wexford, and brought up mainly in Dublin, he was passing though Bristol in 1813 *en route* from London to Ireland when he decided to take up residence there – either because he had insufficient money to continue his journey or because he saw pictorial possibilities in the local scenery (Greenacre 1973, p.34). He remained in the city for over ten years, practising as a drawing master and producing paintings for a local clientele – watercolours, especially views of the Avon Gorge and St Vincent's Rocks, and small, intense landscape oils of scenes in and around Bristol with remarkable natural detail and often including children playing with innocent concentration. On moving to London in 1824 he abandoned these for large, aspiring biblical canvases painted in a spirit of rivalry with his contemporary John Martin (1789–1854), and for 'poetic landscapes', as he termed them, intensely elegiac in mood and reminiscent of the paintings of Claude Lorraine. In 1829, having failed to become a Royal Academician (Constable won by a single vote), and by now embarrassed by financial and marital problems, he fled to the Continent.

In 1837 he returned to London and ten years later settled in Exmouth where he died.

This watercolour was first published with a tentative attribution to Danby in 1942 by the twentieth-century British 'Neo-Romantic' painter John Piper (1903–1992). Four years later it was illustrated in a pioneeering article on Danby by the eminent poet and critic Geoffrey Grigson. The attribution has since been questioned (by Greenacre 1973, p.84), but is retained here on the strength of the watercolour's compositional and stylistic similarities with other examples of Danby's work. The watercolour has been associated, probably incorrectly, with Danby's trip to Norway in 1825, but in date it does, nevertheless, seem to stand at the point of transition between Danby's Bristol and London periods: with its intimate mood, inclusion of young children and intensely observed natural details (in particular the small clusters of white flowers) it seems to hark back to the early Bristol oils, but with its air of fantasy it seems to look forward to the later, more elegiac works. One author has interpreted the children as looking both 'at home and vaguely lost', suggesting an element of folktale explicable to him only by reference to a literary source, and he cites as a possibility one of the illustrations to Blake's *Songs of Innocence and Experience* (Adams 1973, p.59).

Before entering the Oppé collection, this watercolour was owned by the prominent Oldham industrialist and collector Charles E. Lees (1840–1894). In 1888 Lees gave eighty British watercolours to Oldham Art Gallery (Coombs 1993, p.4), and in 1894 thirteen more to the Whitworth Art Gallery in Manchester, of which he was one of the original governors (Nugent 1993, p.5).

AL

CLARKSON STANFIELD
1793–1867

92 An Eruption of Mount Vesuvius 1839

Watercolour and gouache on blue wove paper
12.8 × 17.7 (5 × 7)
T08222

Clarkson Stanfield was widely viewed as the leading marine artist of his time with J.M.W. Turner being seen as the greatest. Stanfield's fame rested very much on the particularly realistic way in which he depicted dramas at sea, and his success here owed much to the fact that he had been both a mariner and then a theatrical scene-painter. Like Turner but also like many of his colleagues (see, for example, J.F. Lewis, nos.94–6) Stanfield was a seasoned traveller and between 1823 and 1851 made eight sketching tours on the Continent. The longest of all of them, lasting from August 1838 until March 1839, took him via France and Switzerland to Italy, down to Ischia, and back to London along the French Riviera and the river Rhône.

Having been delayed by storms, Stanfield arrived in Naples from Ischia on 29 December 1839. Two days later he and some friends together with some guides climbed up to the edge of the crater of Mount Vesuvius. In a letter to his wife, Rebecca, which he wrote on 16 January Stanfield described how he and three others of the party stayed until about eight o'clock at night to watch the fire in the crater before returning to Naples. At five o'clock the following morning, New Year's Day, in Stanfield's words, 'one of the most magnificent eruptions took place that has been seen for many years'. This drawing and three others in the Oppé collection (T08221, T08223, T08224) depict distant views of Vesuvius at various stages of its eruption, presumably later that day, with T08223 showing the scene towards sunset. Like Tresham, for example (no.57), and many artists before, Stanfield made the most of a rare opportunity of watching and recording the terrible forces of Nature at work. Some idea of his excitement can be gained from the fact that in all there are eight known sketches of the event, all on blue paper, with one of them (T08224) a particularly successful

experiment in catching the effects of sulphurous smoke with yellow-brown chalks: this drawing and the others in the Oppé collection; two sketches in black chalk in the National Library of Scotland; one in the Victoria and Albert Museum in black and coloured chalks like T08824; and another, the same size and medium as T08221–3 in a private collection (van der Merwe 1979, no.218). Two slight sketches in black chalk on the backs of T08223 and T08224 also seem to relate to the same subject.

The distant view, with the silhouette of Castello del'Ovo to the right, the carefully finished smoke and ash plumes and the fact that none of them is made over a rapid preliminary pencil or chalk drawing suggests that Stanfield made these watercolours from a comfortable vantage point to the north of Naples. By contrast the large (26.3 × 36.3; $10^{3/8}$ × $14^{5/16}$) chalk drawing in the Victoria and Albert Museum taken from a point much nearer the cone seems to date from a trip on 2 January 1840 when Stanfield and a companion got up to the lava field – a sight which he told his wife 'was the most wonderful and sublime you can conceive'. On the following day he got even closer to the crater and spent the night on the mountain. Stanfield was, not surprisingly, overawed by all that he had seen, telling his wife that 'it was a most glorious sight and I ought and am most grateful for that ill-wind that detained me at Ischia'. Before Stanfield moved on to Rome he dined with the Duke of Buccleuch and not long after he returned to England he was reported to be working on an oil painting of the subject for him (van der Merwe 1979, no.218). All three of the Vesuvius scenes in the Oppé collection were once attributed to Turner (Wilton 1979, nos.1039–41) but were given to Stanfield by Eric Shanes (Shanes 1981, p.47).

RH

RICHARD PARKES BONINGTON
1802–1828

93 Verona, Piazza dell'Erbe c.1826–7

Watercolour over pencil with touches of gouache
on wove paper 20.6 × 26.5 (8⅛ × 10⅜)
T08146

Born near Nottingham in 1802, Bonington spent most of his short life in France. His father – a gaoler turned drawing master and painter – moved the family to Calais in 1817 where he set up a lace-manufacturing business using private looms smuggled into France following the mechanisation of Nottingham's own lace industry. His young son, Richard Parkes, decided to become an artist rather than follow his father in the lace business, but after a dazzling and highly productive career lasting little more than a decade, died of tuberculosis in London a month before his twenty-sixth birthday. He was one of the most influential painters of his generation.

Although Bonington was an accomplished painter in oils, it was chiefly for his astonishing skill in the use of watercolour – a medium rarely employed by French painters at this date – that he earned his contemporary reputation and the admiration of his colleagues. He had initially been taught watercolour in Calais by Louis Francia (1772–1839), a French artist who had spent many years in England (see under no.83), and, indeed, Bonington's early work in the medium resembles that of Francia and Girtin in its breadth and use of low tones. It was Bonington's mature watercolours, however, like this one, with their stronger colour and sparkling luminosity, which so impressed his fellow artists. The celebrated romantic painter Eugène Delacroix, with whom Bonington shared a studio in the mid-1820s, wrote tellingly of the latter's 'lightness of touch which, particularly in watercolour, makes his pictures like diamonds that flatter and seduce the eye, quite independently of their subjects' (letter to T. Thoré, 30 November 1861).

Some of Bonington's finest watercolours are those which relate to his tour to northern Italy in 1826 with his patron Baron Charles Rivet. This one is closely modelled on an elaborate pencil drawing made on the tour (fig.25),

and was presumably worked up on his return to Paris soon afterwards. It shows Verona's famous Piazza dell'Erbe (the site of a Roman forum) with its lively market stalls and, in the far distance, the baroque façade of the Palazzo Maffei and the adjacent medieval Gardello tower. There is evidence of substantial scraping away of colour in the area of the tower, but this may represent an attempt by Bonington to suggest the tower's rough surface rather than – as one author believes – a correction with which he was then dissatisfied, apparently leaving the rest of the watercolour unfinished (Noon 1991, p.251). It is true that this watercolour, especially areas of the foreground, is not worked out in detail (rather less so, indeed, than the original sketch). Nevertheless, as Paul Oppé himelf pointed out, the range of technical devices which Bonington employed in his watercolours – vivacious pencil underdrawing, rich contrasts of colour, fine strokes made with the point of the brush for structure and accent sometimes known as his *touche coquette*, and occasional broken, granular wash layers of dry colour – all these are contrived by Bonington 'to give to the finished drawing the life and brilliance of a spontaneous sketch' (1937, p.13). This watercolour, then, may well be 'complete' in the sense that the artist was content to take it no further.

In 1824 Bonington won a gold medal at the Paris Salon when he sent four oils (three of them marines), a watercolour and a lithograph – John Constable being awarded the same prize that year on exhibiting his famous canvas *The Hay Wain* (National Gallery, London). In later life Bonington added so-called 'troubadour' subjects to his range of work, that is small-scale figure subjects set in rich, historic interiors or on balconies, inspired by the example of Venetian painting (see fig.26).

AL

fig. 25
Richard Parkes Bonington,
Piazza dell'Erbe, Verona 1826,
pencil and gouache
*The Trustees of the Bowood
Collection*

JOHN FREDERICK LEWIS
1805–1876

94 The Escorial ? 1833

Watercolour, touches of gouache over pencil on
buff-coloured wove paper 26 × 36.3 (10¼ × 14¼)
laid on support of the same size
Inscribed in pencil bottom left 'J F Lewis'
T08166

Taking his lead from his friend David Wilkie (see no.89) who had been in Spain in 1827–8, Lewis set off in the summer of 1832 on what his patron Richard Ford described as 'a sort of picturesque tour of Spain, having orders for young ladies' albums and from divers book sellers'. He was in Madrid by late August and travelled on to Granada, Seville, Gibraltar, then over the straits to Morocco and Tangier before returning to Madrid on 21 September 1833 where he spent the autumn and when he probably visited the Escorial (Lewis 1978, pp.15–20, 44–5). He was back in London by January 1834 (Ford 1942, pp.124–9).

The Escorial, a vast structure containing a mausoleum, a church, a monastery, a palace and a library was built by King Philip II between 1563 and 1584 and is about twenty-eight miles north-west of Madrid. While certainly one of the sights of Spain, because of its severe grandeur it appears rarely to have inspired visitors. Ford, who wrote the first guidebook to Spain, was highly critical, saying that 'the clean granite, blue slates, and leaden roofs, look new and as if built yesterday for an overgrown commonplace barrack, lunatic asylum, or manufactory' and that it was 'cold as the grey eye and granite heart of its founder' (Ford 1855, vol.2, p.752). Lewis's view shows the south terrace and façade with the twin spires and large dome of the Basilica beyond. With its bright palette, particularly in the blue of the sky, and its rapid pencil under-drawing and the exuberant use of water-colour and gouache, Lewis's response to this severe building is very different from that of Ford and other travellers. While he has suggested a sense of the immensity of the Escorial by giving the façade more windows than it has, and so lengthening it, the touches of red and blue indicating window blinds together with the free use of wash have enlivened what, was for Ford at least, an 'ashy pile'.

After Europe became accessible to travellers again after Wellington's victory at Waterloo in 1815, Spain gradually became a popular destination for artists who were constantly in search of new subject-matter: the exotic costumes of the peasantry and the Moorish architecture of the south were particular attractions, as was the prospect of painting in a southern climate with all that meant for working with or even discovering a bright palette. David Roberts, another of Lewis's friends, left London for Madrid in October 1832 and stayed in Seville for five months before coming back in October 1833. When Lewis himself returned he showed more than three hundred of his Spanish sketches at a conversazione of art-lovers at The Graphic Society on 8 January (*Athenaeum*, 11 January 1834, p.34). It seems very likely that T08166 was among these. Some idea of the impact Lewis's work then made on the art world can be seen in a letter which the artist J.S. Cotman (see nos.85–6) wrote to a patron: 'words cannot convey to you their splendour. My poor *Reds, Blues* and *Yellows* … are *faded fades* to what I saw there' (Kitson 1937, p.306).

RH

JOHN FREDERICK LEWIS
1805–1876

95 An Interior ?c.1834

Watercolour, gouache, gum arabic with some scraping out
on wove paper 30.2 × 37.5 (11⅞ × 14¾) mounted on thin card
30.9 × 38.1 (12⅛ × 15)

T08173

The artificiality of this scene is obvious. With her pretty
features and in the carefully posed act of stitching lace
onto a piece of linen, the woman conforms to a type seen
in the sweet, fancy portraits illustrated in the fashionable
drawing-room annuals of the 1830s which had names like
The Keepsake or *Forget-me-Not*. She and all the studio
props around her have been brought together by the artist
so he can show his virtuosity in rendering different
textures and effects of brilliant colour. Lewis's artistic and
technical aims in *An Interior* could not be more different
from those seen in the utterly spontaneous *The Escorial*
(no.94), and here, as well as in one important detail
discussed below, the work tells us a lot about how watercolour art in Britain had developed by the early 1830s
and how British artists saw their own and some of their
colleagues' achievements.

Lewis became a full member of the Society of Painters
in Watercolours in June 1829. The competitiveness of the
annual exhibitions of this Society, in rivalry with the
Royal Academy, stimulated watercolour artists to raise
their art to new heights by matching the substance of oil
painting and, in the brilliance of their palette, equal the
effects of oil pigments. Lewis, who had started as an oil
painter, soon became one of the most successful watercolourists. In *An Interior* the use of gouache or bodycolour and gum arabic gives the pigments weight and, as
can be seen in the way lines have been scratched with
the end of a brush handle in the shield on the cupboard,
the capacity to be worked while wet. Highlights have
been realised by scraping the dried pigment away with
a sharp penknife until the surface of the white paper
beneath has been lifted. Particularly interesting, however,
is Lewis's inclusion, in the left foreground, of a picture by
R.P. Bonington (see no.93), an artist he seems not to have
known but clearly admired for he copied one of his
pictures in 1835 (Lewis 1978, p.38). The painting appears
to be a lost oil, a watercolour version of which is in
Glasgow (fig.26; Noon 1991, no.124). Bonington's reputation after his death in 1828 and throughout the 1830s

was enormous and here we see Lewis paying tribute to
the genius who died young. The composition recalls
some of Bonington's own interior scenes, and the fact
that the woman is stitching lace might even be read as a
reference to Bonington's father's trade as a lace manufacturer. Not only has Lewis shown an oil in his watercolour, and thus implied that work in the two mediums
deserved equal recognition; but he has also placed the
Bonington next to a seventeenth-century Dutch old
master in a way that juxtaposes high-life and low-life
subjects as well as proclaiming that Bonington's and,
indeed, his own scenes from familiar life are worthy of
being judged alongside the old masters.

This picture has been called *In the Studio*, but a more
correct title would seem to be *An Interior* since Lewis
exhibited two works with this title at the SPW in 1833
and 1834: the former showed 'massive and lumbering
furniture of the old world' (*Literary Gazette*, 4 May 1833,
p.283), a description which perhaps matches another
similar watercolour by Lewis in the Victoria and Albert
Museum (no.620–1870) rather than T08173.

RH

fig.26
R.P. Bonington
Venetian Balcony
c.1826–7,
watercolour and
bodycolour on paper
*Glasgow Museums:
Art Gallery and
Museums, Kelvingrove*

JOHN FREDERICK LEWIS
1805–1876

96 The Bazaar of the Ghûriyah from the steps of the Mosque of El-Ghûri, Cairo 1841–51

Pencil, watercolour and gouache on beige tinted wove paper
54 × 38 (21¼ × 14) on laid paper 69 × 51 (27⅛ × 20⅛)
Inscribed top right '254' and bottom left in pencil 'Mosque & Street of the Gowrieh | Cairo.'
T08183

This drawing shows the bazaar in the street of the Ghuriyah on the east side of the Mosque of El-Ghûri in Cairo. Lewis's viewpoint is from the top of the steps leading up to the mosque looking north down a narrow street towards the Sûk (that is, bazaar) el-Attarin, where attar of roses and other perfumes could be bought, and then beyond that, to the Sûk en Nahhâsin where coppersmiths sold their wares. The Ghûriyah bazaar specialised in cotton and silk, and bolts of these fabrics can be seen stacked up in the stalls on the far side of the street. Another drawing, horizontal in format though the same size and in the same medium as this one and made at about the same time, in the Witt collection shows the view in the opposite direction, the artist's viewpoint in this instance being near the half-concealed archway visible to the right in T08183 (Staley 1975, repr. p.96).

In 1837 Lewis left England and travelled to Italy, Greece, the Levant and Egypt where he arrived in about November 1841. He remained there for ten years, spending most of his time in Cairo where he lived in considerable style. William Makepeace Thackeray, in his *Notes of a Journey from Cornhill to Cairo*, remembered Lewis in London as a dandy with faultless boots and cravats and brilliant waistcoats and kid gloves. He visited him in Cairo in 1844 and found Lewis, with his servants, his splendid residence and 'coolness and langour', completely adapted to the Egyptian way of life and altogether like an 'oriental nobleman' (Thackeray 1846, pp.142–4). The house in which he lived was later depicted by Lewis in an oil painting of 1864, a study for which is in the Tate Gallery (N01688).

This extravagant lifestyle obviously appealed to Lewis and the opportunity for such escapism (or lotus eating) may have been behind the wanderlust which is such a characteristic of his career. But at least one aspect of it –

dressing like a native – was a very practical matter for any European artist who hoped to capture fully the colour and excitement of a Muslim country, especially its places of worship. When the artist David Roberts had visited Egypt earlier and, in January 1839, drew both the bazaar of El-Ghûri and the interior of the mosque, the Pasha Mohammad Ali gave him permission to go inside the mosque only on condition that he did not look or behave like a Christian.

One of the primary purposes behind Lewis's persistent sketching of these Eastern sights was to lay up a store of subjects which could be made into finished pictures for sale after he had returned to England. For their sheer novelty and brilliance Lewis's Eastern studies certainly had the desired effect on his home public, for when he exhibited his watercolour *The Hareem* in London in 1850 it caused a sensation, the *Art Journal* describing it as 'the most extraordinary production that has ever been executed in water-colour' (p.179).

There is a finished watercolour version of T08183 (Fine Art Society 1980, no.23) and also a version in oil. The latter was apparently left unfinished and exhibited at the Royal Academy in 1877 when it was described by one critic as possessing 'a strong effect of light and colour' and 'elaborately drawn' (*Athenaeum*, 26 May 1877, p.676). The view shown in the drawing in the Witt collection – very close to the same view taken by David Roberts in 1839 and reproduced as a lithograph by Louis Haghe in Roberts's *Egypt and Nubia* of 1842–9 (repr. Bourbon 1996, p.219) – was painted in watercolour and oil (repr. Staley 1975, no.40.). However, much of the spontaneity of sketches made on the spot like this one, with its fine pencil work, animated touches of colour and the sense of the weatherbeaten roofing, is lost in these more carefully considered products of a cold northern studio.

RH

GEORGE RICHMOND
1809–1896

97 Portrait of Henry Walter 1829

Pencil heightened with white tempera on wove paper prepared with
gypsum and clay-based filler with glue medium, 17.8 × 12.4 (7 × 4⅞)
Inscribed 'Dec.ʳ 2ⁿᵈ 1829. GR' in pencil (added later) bottom right
'H Walter' and in pencil bottom left 'died May 23.1849 |
at Torquay.' and on the back in ink 'drawn from Henry Walter |
by Geo Richmond | decʳ. 2. 1829.' and 'He died & was buried
at Torquay | died Monday 5 [deleted]23ᵈ of May 1849. I was present, |
at his funeral on Sunday the 29ᵗʰ | His age I never knew exactly'
T08721

George Richmond and Henry Walter belonged to the group of seven young men, five of them artists, known as 'The Ancients', who, with Samuel Palmer at their head, gathered around the artist and poet William Blake soon after Palmer first met him in October 1824. The rough, almost experimental nature of the gesso-like ground on which this portrait is drawn owes a clear debt to Blake and his 'fresco' painting technique with which Richmond had already experimented – notably in his *The Creation of Light* of 1826 which is in the Tate Gallery (T04164).

Along with Edward Calvert (1799–1883), another of 'The Ancients', Walter was one of Palmer's earliest friends. He was clearly highly regarded by both Palmer and Richmond. In his correspondence with members of his circle Palmer frequently asks them to send his love to Walter and in 1839 wrote that Walter 'is a most excellent person … his principles are most excellent' (Lister 1974A, vol.1, p.269). Richmond noted on an 1835 portrait of Palmer by Walter (British Museum) that Walters's few works 'are all marked by high artistic qualities and fine sentiment'. None the less, Walter was an unlikely member of 'The Ancients': he was older than the others (he was probably born about 1786) and as a drawing master who had produced a number of lithographic drawing manuals in the 1820s his artistic background and his art were conventional. However, the evidence from these manuals and from the titles of some of the works he exhibited in the 1820s indicates a close study of the pastoral which approached 'The Ancients'' response to the landscape of Shoreham in Kent where they produced their best work, and which in its keenness of observation at least had something in common with Palmer's and his colleagues' intensely spiritual way of viewing of landscape.

Richmond, who was a brilliant draughtsman, went on to become one of the finest portrait painters of his day, and during the late 1820s when 'The Ancients' were closest he seems quite naturally to have become unofficial portraitist to the group. Apart from this drawing there is another likeness by Richmond of Walter – a half-length of him seated, dated 28 December 1827 (Lister 1974B, pl.12); in July 1827 he had begun a miniature of Welby Sherman (Lister 1981, p.171) and in February 1828, he drew Samuel Palmer (repr. G. Grigson, *Horizon,* vol.13, 1946, p.312) and then also in 1828 Palmer 'assuming a character' (Grigson 1947, pl.3); in May 1828 Sherman again, sleeping 'as he may be seen after dinner' (Cleveland Museum; repr. Lister 1981, pl. 7); in March 1829 Frederick Tatham (Commander 1957, no.131); and the same year a miniature of Palmer (National Portrait Gallery). On the back of T08721 there is a slight pencil drawing of a woman wearing a hat in half-length profile.

RH

228

Died May 23. 1849
at Torquay.

H. Walter

Dec. 2ᵈ 1829

GEORGE RICHMOND
1809–1896

98 A Field near Margate 1850

Watercolour and gouache on cream wove paper
18 × 26.4 (7⅛ × 10⅜)
T08272

Although Richmond became an important and successful portraitist, he continued to draw and paint landscape throughout his career. These works remained private, and Oppé records on the back of this watercolour that it was bought from the artist's granddaughter, Mrs Davey. As the name 'The Ancients' (see no.97) implies, their art involved looking back to an earlier Golden Age as a way of both informing their own work and also reviving the art of their time. Their debt to Blake for this was enormous, specifically his wood engravings illustrating Robert Thornton's 'Imitation' of Virgil's *Pastorals* which Samuel Palmer described as 'visions of little dells, and nooks, and corners of Paradise; models of the exquisitest pitch of intense poetry' (quoted in Butlin 1990, p.177). The memorable lines near the beginning of Blake's poem *Milton* (dated 1804) suggest how sought after was a return to this Ancient mode by the poet himself, but they also suggest something of the intense spirituality of the mood of 'The Ancients' – Samuel Palmer certainly but also his colleagues – which led to the importance they attached to landscape: 'And did those feet in ancient time. | Walk upon England's mountains Green: | And was the Holy Lamb of God. | On England's pleasant pastures seen!' In 1838 Richmond described these early years as 'a dream of sentiment' (quoted in Lister 1981, p.46).

This much later work is undated, but stylistically and in its subject-matter is so close to a watercolour which is inscribed and dated 'Margate Septr 1850' (Colnaghi 1976, no.69, repr.) that it can be definitely associated with it. Richmond travelled down to Margate in Kent at the end of August 1850 where he joined his wife, Julia, and their children who were staying along with the painter C.W. Cope and his family (Lister 1981, p.76). Cope was an old friend with whom Richmond had made a sketching tour of the north of England in 1849 (Lister 1981, p.72). Cope recorded that 'Richmond and I usually sketched from Nature out-of-doors in the morning, and played bowls in the afternoon…'. (Cope 1891, p.190). During this holiday, but after Cope had left, the Richmonds' three-month-old daughter died from whooping cough. In sending his condolences Cope also attempted to persuade Richmond to join him and draw some landscapes: 'You must come, and I really believe that you ought, as a duty. Nothing is so wholesome, after over-anxiety and suspense, as the quiet induced by the beauty of Nature' (Cope 1891, p.191).

The style of Richmond's later landscape art is very much his own, painted, as Cope implies, for the opportunity which it gave for contemplation. So while this picture was painted when Pre-Raphaelitism, with its strict adherence to nature, was new (and which Richmond approved of as having 'hit a mark' (Stirling 1926, p.136)), it acknowledges no debt to it; but it does possess the directness of vision, arrived at on his own, which conforms to what John Ruskin had set out in the first volume of *Modern Painters* in 1843, and which had influenced the Pre-Raphaelites as 'rejecting nothing, selecting nothing, and scorning nothing'. However, if Richmond's 1838 comment suggests an abandonment of youthful fervency, it is still possible to detect in this work a spiritual intensity, albeit sombre, which might be attributable to his child's illness or death: the bare earth and the corn stooks which are in the foreground show that the harvest has been gathered in and the trees are bent by a strengthening wind. The corn stooks, placed as they are as a framing device, take on a symbolic importance which harks back to the ecstatic vision of The Ancients' years in Shoreham, though now tempered by a bleakness which comes with age.

RH

JOHN WILLIAM INCHBOLD
1830–1888

99 Peat Burning c.1864–6

Oil on cream wove paper 17.9 × 25.6 (7 × 10⅛)
Inscribed in the paint when it was still wet 'LET EVIL'
and 'Gilh …' [?] bottom right and verso in pencil
'J.W. Inchbold'

T08136

This extraordinarily compelling oil sketch was in a portfolio of thirty-four works by Inchbold which Paul Oppé bought at auction in November 1913. Oppé appears to have given the work its title. Because the idea of burning peat in the open air at first sight seems unlikely, it has been suggested that the subject shows heather being burnt off, as it commonly was on heath and moorland (Newall 1993, no.29, p.60), though to do this there would seem to be no reason for stacking the heather in ordered piles such as those seen in the foreground. However, with these mounds being so prominent, with the recurring flashes of fire, plumes of smoke and a tower-like structure with a fire at its base in the distance this picture conveys a sense of some industry at work. In fact, peat was sometimes burnt in the open moorland where it was dug in order to make peat charcoal: mounds of peat were ignited and then covered with turf and mud to make a blue-grey charcoal which was rather like coke. What Inchbold has depicted tallies with such a process. This charcoal, certainly made during the 1800s on Dartmoor, which Inchbold visited in the 1850s and 1860s (Newall 1993, nos.4 and 11), was used in metal smelting during the nineteenth century (although until when is uncertain), and most often in tin smelting (Woolner 1967, pp.118–20; Rackham 1989, p.316). This suggests that perhaps a Cornish landscape is shown here, and Piers Townshend has pointed out that the shape of the tower is reminiscent of a tin mine engine house and its chimney. A connection between this painting and Inchbold's visit in the late summer of 1864 to Tintagel, Cornwall with his friend the poet Algernon Swinburne (Newall 1993, p.17), therefore seems possible. Equally, however, it might show a moorland scene in or around Inchbold's native Yorkshire where peat was undoubtedly also used in local industries. There are two small oil sketches in the Oppé collection, both of them described by Inchbold as 'Recollections', of the landscape around Barden Tower

near Bolton Abbey and dated 1865–6 (T09024, T09025), both the same size as *Peat Burning*; although, unlike these, *Peat Burning* is clearly a *plein-air* work, T09024 contains clouds of a similar type and colour to those seen in this picture and therefore suggests another possible date and location for the subject. Ultimately the clue to the precise whereabouts of the view almost certainly lies in the largely indecipherable word inscribed in the bottom right-hand corner of the picture.

Inchbold, having enjoyed some success in the 1850s as a Pre-Raphaelite artist, in later years was dogged by lack of recognition. Two of the most striking features of *Peat Burning* are the strange formation of pink clouds and, less obviously, a second inscription which reads 'LET EVIL'. Writing of his painting *Stonehenge*, dated 1866–9 and thus roughly contemporaneous with *Peat Burning* (Newall 1993, no.31), Inchbold referred to the way in which 'the clouds are meant to suggest what is at once fiery and spiritual' in his view of a religious site. At the same time he also referred to the difficulty of reconciling painting from nature 'with another and entirely distinct vision before the imagination, and perhaps with a heart somewhat maimed and broken by that deadly and relentless opposition I seem to inspire most innocently in some quarters'. Swinburne described Inchbold as 'a very religious man and a strong Churchman' (quoted in Newall 1993, p.8). In *Peat Burning* the simple biblical intensity of a sentence left unfinished in the paint (perhaps harking back to 'Let … evil speaking be put away from you, with all malice' from Ephesians), the portentous dream-like clouds, the flames, smoke and steam of fires, and the blackness beyond at dusk combine to suggest that in Inchbold's troubled mind the landscape before him actually shifted from the certainties of realism to a 'distinct vision' of a kind of Hell, its inevitability for him removed only by a final redemptional thought.

RH

FREDERIC, LORD LEIGHTON
1830–1896

100 Fanny Kemble: A Study for *Jezebel and Ahab* c.1862

Black and white chalk, approx. 14.5 × 13 (5¾ × 5⅛) on blue wove paper
22.5 × 28.5 (8⅞ × 11¼)
Inscribed in a later hand bottom right in pencil 'Study of Head: for the Dante'
T08208

Frederic Leighton was the most eminent of all native artists working during Queen Victoria's reign, but though he was English he was very much a product of a Continental training. For most of his contemporaries his large figure paintings, often of classical subjects, represented Academic art at its very best. Born in Scarborough, between 1839–40 and 1859, when he finally settled in London, he studied art in Rome, Florence, Berlin, Frankfurt and Paris and travelled extensively throughout Europe. Leighton's training, his cosmopolitan outlook and his intellectual range were unique among his English contemporaries, and although there was some hostility in the London art world at his early, glittering success because it was not founded on a Royal Academy training, he eventually became President of the Royal Academy in 1878. One result of Leighton's rigorous training on the Continent was the importance he attached to the making of preliminary drawings to settle a composition in all its details before he began painting it in oil.

This drawing was originally mounted with a label which named the subject as the actress Fanny Kemble (1809–1893) and as having been bought in 1897 by the artist H.B. Brabazon (1821–1906) at the exhibition and sale of 241 of Leighton's sketches which opened in December 1896 at the Fine Art Society. The catalogue for this show noted that exhibits were stamped with the monogram 'LLC' ('Lord Leighton's Collection') to certify that they were drawings left by Leighton; this sheet has such a stamp and it can therefore be identified with no.62 in the catalogue, 'Study of Head of Miss Fanny Kemble'. Despite looking like a study of a male face, this characteristically sensitive chalk drawing does, indeed, portray the actress Fanny Kemble whom Leighton had met in 1854 (Ormond 1996, p.71), and it is confirmed by comparison with a photograph of her in middle age (Ransome 1978, pl.7).

Christopher Newall has pointed out that this drawing is a study for the head of Elijah in Leighton's RA picture of 1863 *Jezebel and Ahab* which is now in Scarborough (Newall 1996, no.28). That Leighton should use a woman to model for a male figure is at first surprising though earlier he used a study of a boy for the head of the girl in his *Lieder ohne Worte* of 1860–1 (T03053; Tate Gallery 1981, pp.32–3; Ormond 1996, no.21). However, as Fanny Kemble herself reported, she modelled for *Jezebel and Ahab*, though initially only for the figure of Jezebel: Leighton 'despairing of finding a model to assume a sufficiently dramatic expression of wickedness … was deploring his difficulty one day when Henry Greville … said to him, "Why don't you ask her" – pointing to me'. She went to Leighton's studio and was 'duly placed in the attitude required, and instructed on what precise point on the wall opposite me to fix my eyes … endeavouring, after my old stage fashion, to assume as thoroughly as possible the character which I was representing'. After a short time the strain of the pose caused Fanny nearly to faint but she recovered, continued to model for Jezebel and then concluded the session by 'lending another aspect of my face to my friend for his Elijah' (Kemble 1882, vol.2, pp.92–3), the result, presumably, being this drawing.

Although the use of a woman to pose for a male figure seems unusual, this drawing would none the less have been used to help set a male model when Leighton started painting. S.P. Cockerell wrote of how the artist would pin such a drawing 'on a standard close to his canvas [and] painted from nature and corrected the form from the drawing as he went along' (Cockerell 1896, p.12). The pin holes at the corners of this sheet confirm this usage.

RH

Study of Head, ? for the Baudle

Bibliography

Place of publication is London unless otherwise stated.

Adams 1973: Eric Adams, *Francis Danby: Varieties of Poetic Landscape*, 1973.

Alexander 1996: David Alexander, 'J.B.C. Chatelain' in Jane Turner (ed.), *The Dictionary of Art*, 1996, vol.6, p.153.

Allan 1979: D.G.C. Allan, *William Shipley, Founder of the Royal Society of Arts: A Biography with Documents*, 1979.

Allen 1987: Brian Allen, *Francis Hayman*, exh. cat., Yale Center for British Art, New Haven and Kenwood 1987.

Allen 1996: Brian Allen in Andrew Wilton and Ilaria Bignamini (eds.), *Grand Tour: The Lure of Italy in the Eighteenth Century*, exh. cat., Tate Gallery 1996.

Angelo 1828: Henry Angelo, *Reminiscences of Henry Angelo*, 2 vols., 1828.

Anon 1788: *The Complete Art of Boxing*, including *The General History of Boxing*, 1788 (containing extracts from Captain Godfrey's *Treatise upon the Useful Science of Self-Defence*, 1747).

Balmanno 1797–1818: Robert Balmanno, *Collection of Prints after Thomas Stothard*, vol.3, 1797–1818.

Barry 1809: *The Works of James Barry, Esq.*, vol.1, 1809.

Bayard 1981: Jane Bayard, *Works of Splendor and Imagination: The Exhibition Watercolor 1770–1870*, exh. cat., Yale Center for British Art 1981.

Beckett 1962: R.B. Beckett (ed.), *John Constable's Correspondence* vol.1: *The Family at East Bergholt 1807–1837*, London and Ipswich 1962.

Beckett 1964: R.B. Beckett (ed.), *John Constable's Correspondence* vol.2: *Early Friends and Maria Bicknell (Mrs Constable)*, Ipswich 1964.

Beckett 1966: R.B. Beckett (ed.), *John Constable's Correspondence* vol.4: *Patrons, Dealers and Fellow Artists*, Ipswich 1966.

Beckett 1968: R.B. Beckett (ed.), *John Constable's Correspondence* vol.6: *The Fishers*, Ipswich 1968.

Belsey 1996: Hugh Belsey in Andrew Wilton and Ilaria Bignamini (eds.), *Grand Tour: The Lure of Italy in the Eighteenth Century*, exh. cat., Tate Gallery 1996 (42).

Bennett 1979: Shelley M. Bennett, 'Some Unpublished Landscapes by Thomas Stothard and their Influence on John Constable', *Master Drawings*, Autumn 1979, no.17, pp.273–77.

Bennett 1988: Shelley M. Bennett, *Thomas Stothard: The Mechanisms of Art Patronage in England c.1800*, Columbia, Missouri 1988.

Bignamini 1988: Ilaria Bignamini, 'Art Institutions in London 1689–1768: A Study of Clubs and Academies', *Walpole Society*, vol.54, 1988, pp.19–148.

Bignamini and Postle 1991: Ilaria Bignamini and Martin Postle, *The Artist's Model: Its Role in British Art from Lely to Etty*, exh. cat., University Art Gallery, Nottingham and Kenwood 1991.

Bindman 1979: David Bindman (ed.), *John Flaxman*, exh. cat., Royal Academy 1979.

Binyon 1931: Laurence Binyon, *Landscape in English Art and Poetry*, 1931.

Binyon 1944: Laurence Binyon, *English Water-Colours*, 1933, 2nd ed. New York 1944.

Bourbon 1996: Fabio Bourbon, *Egypt Yesterday and Today: Lithographs by David Roberts, RA*, Shrewsbury 1996.

Bower 1997: Peter Bower, *Report on the Papers found in One Hundred Works from the Oppé Collection*, 1997 (copy available in the Clore Gallery Study Room, Tate Gallery).

Bray 1851: Anna Eliza Bray, *The Life of Thomas Stothard, RA, with Personal Reminiscences*, 1851.

Bulletin of Rhode Island School of Design 1972: Museum Notes, Section II: 'British Watercolors and Drawings from the Museum's Collection', *Bulletin of Rhode Island School of Design*, 1972.

Burke 1756: Edmund Burke, *A Philosophical Enquiry into the Origins of our Ideas of the Sublime and the Beautiful* (1756), ed. J.T. Boulton, 1958.

Butlin 1990: Martin Butlin, 'William Blake 1757–1827', Tate Gallery Catalogue of the Permanent Collections, vol.5, 1990.

Clay 1941: Rotha Mary Clay, *Samuel Hieronymus Grimm of Bergdorf in Switzerland*, 1941.

Clay 1948: Rotha Mary Clay, *Julius Caesar Ibbetson 1759–1817*, 1948.

Cockerell 1896: S. Pepys Cockerell, *Catalogue of a Collection of Studies for Pictures ... by the late Lord Leighton PRA*, Fine Art Society, Dec. 1896, p.12.

Colnaghi 1976: *English Drawings and Watercolours*, P. & D. Colnaghi & Co. Ltd, 1976.

Commander 1957: John Commander, *Samuel Palmer and his Circle*, exh. cat., Arts Council of Great Britain 1957.

Conisbee 1996: P. Conisbee in P. Conisbee, S. Faunce and J. Strick, *In the Light of Italy: Corot and Early Open-Air Painting*, exh. cat., National Gallery of Art, Washington 1996.

Constable 1927: W.G. Constable, *John Flaxman 1755–1826*, 1927.

Coombs 1993: Trevor Coombs, *Watercolours: The Charles Lees Collection*, Oldham Art Gallery 1993.

Cope 1891: C.H. Cope, *Reminiscences of Charles West Cope RA*, 1891.

Cordingly 1974: David Cordingly, *Marine Painting in England 1700–1900*, 1974.

Croft-Murray 1961: E. Croft-Murray, *George Garrard*, exh. cat., Cecil Higgins Art Gallery, Bedford 1961.

Croft-Murray 1962 & 1970: E. Croft-Murray, *Decorative Painting in England 1537–1837*, vol.1, 1962, vol.2, 1970.

Croft-Murray MS: E. Croft-Murray, *Catalogue of British Drawings in the British Museum*, vol.2, unpublished manuscript.

Crookshank and the Knight of Glin 1994: Anne Crookshank and the Knight of Glin, *The Watercolours of Ireland: Works on Paper in Pencil, Pastel and Paint c.1600–1914*, 1994.

Cross 1980: A.G. Cross, 'By the Banks of the Thames': Russians in Eighteenth-Century Britain, Newtonville, Mass. 1980.

Cumberland 1796: George Cumberland, *An Attempt to Describe Hafod ...*, 1796.

Cunningham 1843: Allan Cunningham, *The Life of Sir David Wilkie; with his Journals, Tours and Critical Remarks on Works of Art; and a Selection of his Correspondence*, 3 vols., 1843.

Davies 1926–7: R. Davies, 'Joshua Cristall (1767–1847)', *The Old Water-Colour Society's Club Journal*, 1926–7, vol.4, pp.1–20.

Dayes 1805: *The Works of the Late Edward Dayes*, 1805.

Dennistoun 1855: James Dennistoun, *Memoirs of Sir Robert Strange, Knt*, 2 vols., 1855.

Deuchar 1984: Stephen Deuchar, *Paintings, Politics and Porter: Samuel Whitbread and British Art*, exh. cat., Museum of London 1984.

Deuchar 1996: Stephen Deuchar, 'Dominic Serres' in Jane Turner (ed.), *The Dictionary of Art*, vol.28, 1996, pp.481–2.

Dunlop 1949: Ian Dunlop, 'Cannons, Middlesex: A Conjectural Reconstruction', *Country Life*, 30 Dec. 1949, pp.1950–4.

Edwards 1808: Edward Edwards, *Anecdotes of Painters who have resided or been born in England ...*, 1808.

Egan 1812: 'One of the Fancy' [Pierce Egan], *Boxiana, or Sketches of Ancient and Modern Pugilism*, 1812.

Egerton 1984: Judy Egerton, *George Stubbs 1724–1806*, exh. cat., Tate Gallery and Yale Center for British Art 1984.

Egerton 1990: Judy Egerton, *Wright of Derby*, exh. cat., Tate Gallery 1990.

Einberg 1970: Elizabeth Einberg, *George Lambert 1700–1765*, exh. cat., Kenwood 1970.

Einberg 1987: Elizabeth Einberg, *Manners and Morals*, exh. cat., Tate Gallery 1987.

Einberg and Egerton 1988: Elizabeth Einberg and Judy Egerton, *The Age of Hogarth: British Painters Born 1675–1709*, Tate Gallery Catalogue of the Permanent Collections, vol.2, 1988.

Erdmann and Moore 1977: David Erdmann and Donald K. Moore (eds.), *The Notebook of William Blake*, Oxford 1977.

Errington 1975: Lindsay Errington, *Work in Progress: Sir David Wilkie: Drawings into Paintings*, exh. cat., National Gallery of Scotland, 1975.

Farington, *Diary*: Kenneth Garlick, Angus Macintyre and Kathryn Cave (eds.), *The Diary of Joseph Farington*, 16 vols., New Haven and London, 1978–84.

Fine Art Society 1980: *Travellers Beyond the Grand Tour*, exh. cat., Fine Art Society 1980.

Finsten 1981: Jill Finsten, *Isaac Oliver: Art at t he Courts of Elizabeth I and James I*, published PhD thesis, 2 vols., New York and London 1981.

Flaxman 1906: John Flaxman, *Lectures on Sculpture* (1829), 1906.

Fleming-Williams 1990: Ian Fleming-Williams, *Constable and his Drawings*, 1990.

Fleming-Williams 1991: Ian Fleming-Williams in Leslie Parris and Ian Fleming-Williams, *Constable*, exh. cat., Tate Gallery 1991.

Fleming-Williams 1994: Ian Fleming-Williams in *Constable, a Master Draughtsman*, exh. cat., Dulwich Picture Gallery and Art Gallery of Ontario, Canada 1994.

Fleming-Williams and Parris 1984: Ian Fleming-Williams and Leslie Parris, *The Discovery of Constable*, 1984.

Ford 1942: Brinsley Ford, 'J.F. Lewis and Richard Ford in Seville 1832–3', *Burlington Magazine*, vol.80, 1942, pp.124–9.

Ford 1951: Brinsley Ford, *The Drawings of Richard Wilson*, 1951.

Ford 1960: Brinsley Ford (ed.), 'The Letters of Jonathan Skelton written from Rome and Tivoli in 1758, together with correspondence relating to his Death ...', *Walpole Society*, vol.36, 1960, pp.23–82.

Ford 1855: Richard Ford, *A Handbook for Travellers in Spain*, 3rd edition, 2 vols., 1855.

French 1980: Anne French, *Gaspard Dughet called Gaspar Poussin 1615–75 ...*, exh. cat., Kenwood 1980.

Gage 1987: John Gage, *J.M.W. Turner: 'A Wonderful Range of Mind'*, New Haven and London 1987.

Girtin and Loshak 1954: T. Girtin and D. Loshak, *The Art of Thomas Girtin*, 1954.

Godfrey 1984: Richard Godfrey, *English Caricature: 1620 to the Present*, exh. cat., Victoria and Albert Museum 1984.

Goethe 1962: J.W. Goethe, *Italian Journey*, transl. W.H. Auden and Elizabeth Mayer 1962.

Goodreau 1977: David Goodreau, *Nathaniel Dance 1735–1811*, exh. cat., Kenwood 1977.

Gowing 1985: Lawrence Gowing, *The Originality of Thomas Jones*, 1985.

Greenacre 1973: Francis Greenacre, *The Bristol School of Artists: Francis Danby and Painting in Bristol 1810–1840*, exh.cat., Bristol City Art Gallery 1973.

Grigson 1947: Geoffrey Grigson, *Samuel Palmer: The Visionary Years*, 1947.

Guillemard 1922: Dr Guillemard, 'Girtin's Sketching Club', *Connoisseur*, vol.63, no.252, August 1922, pp.189–195.

Hallett 1992: Roger Hallett, 'The "Hafod" Sketchbook of Thomas Jones', *Welsh Historic Gardens Trust Newsletter*, no.6, August 1992, pp.7–14.

Hamilton 1971: Jean Hamilton, *The Sketching Society 1799–1851*, exh. cat., Victoria and Albert Museum 1971.

Hamlyn 1993: Robin Hamlyn, *Robert Vernon's Gift: British Art for the Nation*, exh. cat., Tate Gallery 1993.

Hammelmann 1968: Hanns Hammelmann, 'John Vanderbank 1694–1739', *The Book Collector*, Autumn 1968, pp.285–99 (reprinted in Hammelmann 1975).

Hammelmann 1975: Hanns Hammelmann and T.S.R. Boase (ed.), *Book Illustrators in Eighteenth Century England*, 1975.

Hardie 1966–8: Martin Hardie, *Water-colour Painting in Britain*, 3 vols., 1966–8.

Haskell and Penny 1981: Francis Haskell and Nicholas Penny, *Taste and the Antique: The Lure of Classical Sculpture 1500–1900*, New Haven and London 1981.

Hatto 1969: A.T. Hatto, *The Nibelungenlied: A New Translation*, 1969.

Hawcroft 1983: Francis Hawcroft, *The Most Beautiful Art of England: Fifty Watercolours 1750–1850*, exh. cat., Whitworth Art Gallery, Manchester 1983.

Hawcroft 1988: Francis Hawcroft, *Travels in Italy 1776–1783: based on the 'Memoirs' of Thomas Jones*, exh. cat., Whitworth Art Gallery, Manchester 1988.

Haydon 1963: W.B. Pope (ed.), *The Diary of Benjamin Robert Haydon*, 5 vols., Cambridge, Mass. 1960–3.

Hayes 1970: John Hayes, *The Drawings of Thomas Gainsborough*, 2 vols., 1970.

Hayes 1972: John Hayes, *Rowlandson: Watercolours and Drawings*, 1972.

Hayes 1980: John Hayes, *Thomas Gainsborough*, exh. cat., Tate Gallery 1980.

Heleniak 1980: Kathryn Moore Heleniak, *William Mulready*, New Haven and London 1980.

Herrmann 1986: Luke Herrmann, *Paul and Thomas Sandby*, 1986.

Hertford 1805: *Correspondence between Frances, Countess of Hartford … and Henrietta Louisa, Countess of Pomfret, between the years 1738 and 1741*, 3 vols., 1805.

Hodnett 1978: Edward Hodnett, *Francis Barlow: First Master of English Book Illustration*, 1978.

Howgego 1956: J.L. Howgego (ed.), *William Marlow*, exh. cat., Guildhall Art Gallery 1956.

Hutchison 1962: Sidney C. Hutchison, 'The Royal Academy Schools, 1768–1830', *Walpole Society*, vol.38, 1960–2, pp.123–191.

Hutchison 1986: Sidney C. Hutchison, *The History of the Royal Academy 1768–1986*, 1968, 2nd ed., 1986.

Irwin 1979: David Irwin, *John Flaxman 1755–1826: Sculptor Illustrator Designer*, 1979.

Johnson 1994: Lewis Johnson, *Prospects, Thresholds, Interiors: Watercolours from the National Collection at the Victoria and Albert Museum*, 1994.

Jones, *Memoirs*: A.P. Oppé (ed.), 'Memoirs of Thomas Jones', *Walpole Society*, vol.32, 1946–8, published 1951.

Kemble 1882: Frances Anne Kemble, *Records of Later Life*, 3 vols., 1882.

Kerslake 1977: John Kerslake, *Early Georgian Portraits*, National Portrait Gallery, 2 vols., 1977.

Kingzett 1982: Richard Kingzett, 'A Catalogue of the Works of Samuel Scott', *Walpole Society*, vol.48, 1980–2, pp.1–134.

Kitson 1937: Sydney D. Kitson, *The Life of John Sell Cotman*, 1937.

Kitson 1957: Michael Kitson, 'John Constable, 1810–1816: A Chronological Study', *Journal of the Warburg and Courtauld Institutes*, vol.20, 1957, pp.338–57.

Leger 1995: *British Paintings, Watercolours and Drawings*, Leger Galleries Ltd, 1995.

Leger 1996: *British Paintings, Watercolours and Drawings*, Leger Galleries Ltd, 1996.

Leslie 1951: C.R. Leslie, *Memoirs of the Life of John Constable*, 1951 (published in form of 2nd ed., 1845).

Lewis 1978: Michael F. Lewis, *John Frederick Lewis 1805–1876*, Leigh-on-Sea 1978.

Lister 1974A: Raymond Lister (ed.), *The Letters of Samuel Palmer*, 2 vols., Oxford 1974.

Lister 1974B: Raymond Lister, *Samuel Palmer: A Biography*, 1974.

Lister 1981: Raymond Lister, *George Richmond: A Critical Biography*, 1981.

Liversidge 1980: Michael J.H. Liversidge, 'Six Etchings by William Marlow', *Burlington Magazine*, vol.122, 1980, pp.549–53.

Lugt 1921: Frits Lugt, *Les Marques de Collections de Dessins et d'Estampes*, Amsterdam 1921.

Lugt 1956: Frits Lugt, *Les Marques de Collections de Dessins et d'Estampes: Supplément*, The Hague 1956.

MacGregor 1989: Arthur MacGregor (ed.), *The Late King's Goods*, London and Oxford 1989.

MacColl 1912: D.S. MacColl, 'Constable as a Portrait-Painter', *Burlington Magazine*, vol.20, 1912, pp.267–73.

Mayhew 1967: Edgar de N. Mayhew, *Sketches by Thornhill in the Victoria and Albert Museum*, 1967

McAusland 1994: Jane McAusland in *Constable, a Master Draughtsman*, exh. cat., Dulwich Picture Gallery and Art Gallery of Ontario, Canada 1994.

Merwe 1979: Pieter van der Merwe, *The Spectacular Career of Clarkson Stanfield 1793–1867*, exh. cat., Tyne and Wear Council Museums 1979.

Meteyard 1865: Eliza Meteyard, *The Life of Josiah Wedgwood*, 1865–6, vol.1.

Miles 1981: Hamish Miles, *Fourteen Small Pictures by Wilkie*, exh. cat., Fine Art Society 1981.

Miles 1880: Henry Downes Miles, *Pugilistica: Being one Hundred and Forty-Four Years of the History of British Boxing*, 3 vols., 1880.

Miles and Simon 1979: Ellen G. Miles and Jacob Simon, *Thomas Hudson 1701–1779: Portrait Painter and Collector*, exh. cat., Kenwood 1979.

Moore-Colyer 1992: Richard Moore-Colyer (ed.), *A Land of Pure Delight: Selections from the Letters of Thomas Johnes of Hafod, Cardiganshire (1748–1816)*, Llandysul, Dyfed 1992.

Munro 1994: Jane Munro, *British Landscape Watercolours 1750–1850*, exh. cat., Fitzwilliam Museum, Cambridge 1994.

Munro 1996: Jane Munro, *John Downman 1750–1824*, exh. cat., Fitzwilliam Museum, Cambridge 1996.

Murdoch 1985: Tessa Murdoch: *The Quiet Conquest: The Huguenots 1685 to 1985*, exh. cat., Museum of London 1985.

Newall 1993: Christopher Newall, *John William Inchbold: Pre-Raphaelite Artist*, exh. cat., Leeds City Art Galleries 1993.

Newall 1996: Christopher Newall in Richard Ormond, Stephen Jones et al., *Frederic, Lord Leighton: Eminent Victorian Artist*, exh. cat., Royal Academy 1996.

Newby 1996: Evelyn Newby, 'Joseph Farington' in Jane Turner (ed.), *The Dictionary of Art*, 1996, vol.10, pp.806–7.

Nicolson 1968: Benedict Nicolson, *Joseph Wright of Derby: Painter of Light*, 2 vols., 1968.

Noon 1991: Patrick Noon, *Richard Parkes Bonington; 'On the Pleasure of Painting'*, exh. cat., Yale Center for British Art, New Haven, and Petit Palais, Paris 1991.

Nugent 1993: Charles Nugent, *From View to Vision: British Watercolours from Sandby to Turner in the Whitworth Art Gallery*, exh. cat., Whitworth Art Gallery, Manchester 1993.

O'Connell 1997: Sheila O'Connell, 'J.B.C. Chatelain' in *Allegmeines Künstler-Lexicon*, vol.16, revised ed., Munich and Leipzig 1997 (forthcoming).

Oppé 1919: A.P. Oppé, 'The Parentage of Alexander Cozens', *Burlington Magazine*, vol.35, 1919, pp.40–1.

Oppé 1920: A.P. Oppé, 'Francis Towne, Landscape Painter', *Walpole Society*, vol.8, 1919–20, published 1920, pp.95–126.

Oppé 1923A: A.P. Oppé, 'The Watercolour Drawings of John Sell Cotman', *The Studio*, special number, ed. Geoffrey Holmes, 1923.

Oppé 1923B: A.P. Oppé, 'Cotman and the Sketching Society', *Connoisseur*, vol.67, no.268, December 1923, pp.189–98.

Oppé 1924: A.P. Oppé, 'The Fourth Earl of Aylesford', *Print Collector's Quarterly*, vol.2, October 1924, pp.262–92.

Oppé 1928: A.P. Oppé, 'A Roman Sketchbook by Alexander Cozens', *Walpole Society*, vol.16, 1927–8.

Oppé 1937: A.P. Oppé, Introduction to *Catalogue of an Exhibition of Pictures and Drawings by Richard Parkes Bonington and his Circle*, Burlington Fine Arts Club 1937.

Oppé 1939: A.P. Oppé, 'Talented Amateurs: Julia Gordon and her Circle', *Country Life*, 8 July 1989, pp.20–1.

Oppé 1942: A.P. Oppé, 'Cotman and his Public', *Burlington Magazine*, Cotman number, July 1942.

Oppé 1943: A.P. Oppé, 'John Baptist Malchair of Oxford', *Burlington Magazine*, August 1943, pp.191–7.

Oppé 1946: A.P. Oppé, *Catalogue of an Exhibition of Drawings and Paintings by Alexander Cozens*, exh. cat., Graves Art Gallery, Sheffield 1946.

Oppé 1948: A.P. Oppé, *The Drawings of William Hogarth*, 1948.

Oppé 1950: A.P. Oppé, *English Drawings: Stuart and Georgian Period in the Collection of His Majesty the King*, 1950.

Oppé 1952: A.P. Oppé, *Alexander and John Robert Cozens*, 1952.

Ormond 1996: Leonée Ormond in Richard Ormond, Stephen Jones et al., *Frederic, Lord Leighton: Eminent Victorian Artist*, exh. cat., Royal Academy 1996.

Owen and Stanford 1981: Felicity Owen and Eric Stanford, *William Havell 1782–1857*, exh.cat., Reading Museum and Art Gallery 1981.

Parris 1981: Leslie Parris, *The Tate Gallery Constable Collection*, Tate Gallery 1981.

Parris, Fleming-Williams and Shields 1976: Leslie Parris, Ian Fleming-Williams and Conal Shields, *Constable: Paintings, Watercolours and Drawings*, exh. cat., Tate Gallery 1976.

Parris, Shields and Fleming-Williams 1975: Leslie Parris, Conal Sheilds and Ian Fleming-Williams, *John Constable: Further Documents and Correspondence*, London and Ipswich 1975.

Pasquin 1796: Anthony Pasquin (Anthony Williams), *Memoirs of the Royal Academicians and An Authentic History of the Professors of Painting ... who have practised in Ireland*, 1796.

Paulson 1970: Ronald Paulson, *Hogarth's Graphic Works*, 2 vols., New Haven and London, revised ed., 1970.

Payne 1993: Christiana Payne, *Toil and Plenty: Images of the Agricultural Landscape in England 1780–1890*, New Haven and London 1993.

Penny 1986: Nicholas Penny (ed.), *Reynolds*, exh. cat., Royal Academy of Arts 1986.

Pidgley 1973: Introduction to *Exhibition of Drawings and Watercolours by Cornelius Varley*, Colnaghi 1973.

Pierce 1960: S.R. Pierce, 'Jonathan Skelton and his Watercolours – A Checklist', *Walpole Society*, vol.36, 1960, pp.10–22.

Pointon 1970: Marcia Pointon, *Milton and English Art*, Manchester 1970.

Pointon 1985: Marcia Pointon, *Bonington, Francia and Wyld*, 1985.

Pointon 1986: Marcia Pointon, *Mulready*, 1986.

Popham 1922: A.E. Popham, 'The Etchings of John Sell Cotman', *The Print Collector's Quarterly*, October 1922.

Pressly 1981: William L. Pressly, *The Life and Art of James Barry*, New Haven and London 1981.

Pressly 1983: William L. Pressly, *James Barry: The Artist as Hero*, exh. cat., Tate Gallery 1983.

Pye 1845: John Pye, *Patronage of British Art: An Historical Sketch*, 1845.

Quarm and Wilcox 1987: Roger Quarm and Scott Wilcox, *Masters of the Sea: British Marine Watercolours*, 1987.

Rackham 1989: Oliver Rackham, *History of the Countryside*, 1989.

Raines 1966: Robert Raines, *Marcellus Laroon*, 1966.

Rajnai 1982: Miklos Rajnai (ed.), *John Sell Cotman 1782–1842*, exh. cat., Victoria and Albert Museum and other venues, Arts Council of Great Britain 1982.

Ransome 1978, Eleanor Ransome (ed.), *The Terrific Kemble*, 1978.

Redgrave 1866: R. and S. Redgrave, *A Century of Painters of the English School*, 2 vols., 1866.

Redgrave 1891: F.M. Redgrave, *Richard Redgrave, CB, RA: A Memoir, Compiled from his Diary*, 1891.

Reynolds 1973: Graham Reynolds, *Victoria and Albert Museum: Catalogue of the Constable Collection*, 2nd edition 1973.

Reynolds 1984: Graham Reynolds, *The Later Paintings and Drawings of John Constable*, 2 vols., New Haven and London 1984.

Reynolds 1996: Graham Reynolds, *The Early Paintings and Drawings of John Constable*, 2 vols., New Haven and London 1996.

Riely 1975: John Riely, 'Horace Walpole and "the Second Hogarth"', *Eighteenth-Century Studies*, vol.9, 1975–6.

Riely 1983: John Riely, *Henry William Bunbury 1750–1811*, exh. cat., Gainsborough's House, Sudbury 1983.

Roberts 1986: Jane Roberts, *Master Drawings in the Royal Collection*, exh. cat., Queen's Gallery 1986.

Roberts 1995: Jane Roberts, *Views of Windsor: Watercolours by Thomas and Paul Sandby from the Collection of Her Majesty Queen Elizabeth II*, 1995.

Robertson 1985: Bruce Robertson, *The Art of Paul Sandby*, exh. cat., Yale Center for British Art 1985.

Roget 1891: J.L. Roget, *A History of the 'Old Water-Colour' Society*, 2 vols., 1891.

Ryskamp 1990: C. Ryskamp, 'A Cornelius Varley Sketchbook in the Morgan Library', *Master Drawings*, vol.28, no.3, Autumn 1990, pp.344–59.

Sandby 1892: William Sandby, *Thomas and Paul Sandby: Royal Adademicians ...*, 1892.

Schiff 1973: Gert Schiff, *Johann Heinrich Füssli 1741–1825*, 2 vols., Zurich and Munich 1973.

Serra 1986: Joselita Raspi Serra (ed.), *Paestum and the Doric Revival 1750–1830*, exh. cat., National Academy of Design, New York 1986.

Shanes 1981: Eric Shanes, review of Wilton 1979, *Turner Studies*, vol.1, no.1, Summer 1981, p.47.

Sheppard 1966: F.H.W. Sheppard (ed.), *Survey of London: The Parish of St Anne Soho*, vol.33, 1966.

Simon 1974: Jacob Simon, *English Baroque Sketches*, exh. cat., Marble Hill House, Twickenham, 1974.

Sloan 1985: Kim Sloan, 'A New Chronology for Alexander Cozens; Part I: 1717–59', *Burlington Magazine*, vol.127, 1985, pp.70–5.

Sloan 1986: Kim Sloan, *Alexander and John Robert Cozens: The Poetry of Landscape*, London and New Haven 1986.

Sloan 1996: Kim Sloan, 'J.R. Cozens' in Jane Turner (ed.), *The Dictionary of Art*, vol.8, 1996, pp.96–9.

Smith 1828: J.T. Smith, *Nollekens and his Times*, first published 1828, new edition Wilfred Whitten (ed.), 2 vols., 1920.

Solkin 1982: David H. Solkin, *Richard Wilson: The Landscape of Reaction*, exh. cat., Tate Gallery 1982.

Sotheby's 1973: *Catalogue of Seven Sketch-Books by John Robert Cozens*, Sotheby's, 29 November 1973, with an introduction by Anthony Blunt.

Sotheby's 1979: *An Exhibition of Old Master and English Drawings ... from the Collection of Charles Rogers 1711–1784*, Sotheby's 5–9 September 1979.

Stainton 1985: Lindsay Stainton, *British Landscape Watercolours 1600–1860*, exh. cat., British Museum 1985.

Stainton 1996: Lindsay Stainton in Andrew Wilton and Ilaria Bignamini (eds.), *Grand Tour: The Lure of Italy in the Eighteenth Century*, exh. cat., Tate Gallery 1996.

Stainton and White 1987: Lindsay Stainton and Christopher White, *Drawing in England from Hilliard to Hogarth*, exh. cat., British Museum 1987.

Staley 1975: Allen Staley in Christopher Forbes, *The Royal Academy (1837–1901) Revisited*, exh. cat., Metropolitan Museum, New York and Princeton University Art Museum 1975.

Stephens 1996: Richard Stephens, 'New Material for Francis Towne's Biography', *Burlington Magazine*, vol.138, August 1996, pp.500–5.

Stirling 1926: A.M.W. Stirling, *The Richmond Papers*, 1926.

Stroud 1971: Dorothy Stroud, *George Dance Architect, 1741–1825*, 1971.

Sunderland 1988: John Sunderland, 'John Hamilton Mortimer: His Life and Works', *Walpole Society*, vol.52, 1988.

Tate Gallery 1978: *The Tate Gallery 1974–6: Illustrated Catalogue of Acquisitions*, 1978.

Tate Gallery 1981: *The Tate Gallery 1978–80: Illustrated Catalogue of Acquisitions*, 1981.

Tavener 1994: John P. Tavener, 'William Taverner Jr.: Artist 1700–1772', vol.4, unpublished notes and documentation on the life of William Taverner 1994, (copy deposited in Witt Library, Courtauld Institute, University of London).

Thackeray 1846: William Makepeace Thackeray, *Notes on a Journey from Cornhill to Cairo* (1846) ed. Sarah Searight, Heathfield 1991.

Thornbury 1862: W. Thornbury, *The Life of J.M.W. Turner, RA*, 2 vols., 1862.

Tyler 1971: Richard Tyler, *Francis Place*, exh. cat., York City Art Gallery and Kenwood 1971.

Uwins 1858: Sarah Uwins, *A Memoir of Thomas Uwins, RA*, 2 vols., 1858.

Vertue vols.1–6: The Notebooks of George Vertue, *Walpole Society*, vols.18, 20, 22, 24, 26, 30, 1930–55.

Wallace 1979: Richard W. Wallace, *The Etchings of Salvator Rosa*, Princeton 1979.

Walpole 1937–83: W.S. Lewis and others (eds.), *Horace Walpole's Correspondence*, 48 vols., Oxford and New Haven 1937–83.

Walpole 1888: Horace Walpole, *Anecdotes of Painting in England ...*, 3 vols., new ed., 1888.

Wark 1969: Robert Wark, *Early British Drawings in the Huntington Collection 1600–1750*, Huntington Library, California 1969.

Wark 1975: Robert Wark (ed.), Sir Joshua Reynolds, *Discourses on Art*, New Haven and London, 1975.

Weinglass 1982: David Weinglass, *The Collected English Letters of Henry Fuseli*, New York and London 1982.

Whitley 1928: W.T. Whitley, *Artists and their Friends in England 1700–1799*, 2 vols., 1928.

Wilcox 1985: Scott Wilcox, *British Watercolours: Drawings of the Eighteenth and Nineteenth Centuries from the Yale Center for British Art*, exh. cat., Yale Center for British Art 1985.

Wilcox 1997: Timothy Wilcox, *Francis Towne*, exh. cat., Tate Gallery 1997.

Williams 1952: Iolo Williams, *Early English Watercolours*, 1952.

Wilton 1979A: Andrew Wilton, *William Pars: Journey through the Alps*, Zurich 1979.

Wilton 1979B: Andrew Wilton, *The Life and Work of J.M.W. Turner*, Fribourg 1979.

Wilton 1980: Andrew Wilton, *The Art of Alexander and John Robert Cozens*, exh. cat., Yale Center for British Art, New Haven 1980.

Wilton and Lyles: Andrew Wilton and Anne Lyles, *The Great Age of British Watercolours 1750–1880*, exh. cat., Royal Academy and National Gallery of Art, Washington 1993.

Winckelmann 1765: J.J. Winckelmann, *Reflections on the Painting and Sculpture of the Greeks*, transl. into English by H. Fuseli, 1765.

Wood 1913: H.T. Wood, *A History of the Royal Society of Arts*, 1913.

Woolner 1967: David Woolner, 'Peat Charcoal', *Devon and Cornwall Notes and Queries*, vol.30, 1965–7, pp.118–20.

Zerner 1969: Henri Zerner, *The School of Fontainebleau: Etchings and Engravings*, 1969.

A Checklist of Artists in the Oppé Collection

This checklist is based on the unpublished catalogue of the Oppé collection compiled by Miss Aydua Scott-Elliott in the 1960s. Some of the works included in Miss Scott-Elliott's volume were later disposed of, while other items, not listed originally, have been identified in the course of the accessioning of the collection by the Tate Gallery.

Some recent reattributions have been incorporated here, although until the Oppé collection has been fully catalogued, the checklist must to some extent remain provisional. Drawings by artists catalogued under headings such as 'attributable to' or 'in the style of' artists already listed have not been given separate entries. Approximately one hundred works in the collection are categorised as British School from the seventeenth, eighteenth and nineteenth centuries. An additional one hundred-or-so anonymous items await further identification. The checklist does not include names of the artists or engravers of approximately seven hundred prints which are part of the Oppé collection.

Access to the Oppé collection

The works can be viewed by appointment, and subject to availability, in the Clore Gallery Study Room. Users can have supervised access to an electronic catalogue of works in the Oppé collection, which will be produced in the form of World Wide Web pages: it is intended that every work will be illustrated with a colour digital image. An edition of the web pages will be published on the Internet in the near future.

An asterisk next to an artist's name indicates that work by the artist is included in this book.

DP

ADAM, Robert 1728–1792
ALEXANDER, William 1767–1816
ALKEN, Henry Thomas 1785–1851
attributed to ALKEN, Samuel, Senior 1756–1815
*ALLAN, David 1744–1796 no.49
AMICONI, Giacomo 1682–1752
ARTAUD, William 1763–1823
ATKINSON, John Augustus 1775–c.1833
*AYLESFORD, Heneage Finch, Fourth Earl of 1751–1812 no.58
AYLESFORD, Heneage Finch, Fifth Earl of 1786–1859

*BARLOW, Francis ?1626–1704 no.2
*BARNARD, Rev. William Henry 1767 or 1769–1818 no.72
*BARRET, George, Junior 1767–1842 no.71
BARROW, Joseph Charles active 1789–1802
*BARRY, James 1741–1806 no.40
attributed to BARTOLOZZI, Francesco 1727–1815
BAXTER, Thomas Tennant born 1894
BEAUMONT, Sir George Howland, Bt 1753–1827
BECKER, Ferdinand? active 1793–1825
BELLOGUET, A. Nineteenth century
BENAZECH, Peter Paul c.1744–c.1783
attributed to BERKELEY, Rev. C.J.R. Nineteenth century
BIRCH, Samuel John Lamorna 1869–1955
*BONINGTON, Richard Parkes 1802–1828 no.93
attributed to BOURNE, James 1773–1854 or DELAMOTTE, William Alfred 1775–1863
attributed to BOYCE, George Price 1826–1897
attributed to BOYNE, John c.1750–1810
BRABAZON, Hercules Brabazon 1821–1906
BRANDARD, Robert 1805–1862

attributed to BRIGGS, Henry Perronet 1791–1844
BRIGHT, Henry 1810 or 1814–1873
BROWNE, Hablot Knight ('Phiz') 1815–1882
manner of BUCK, Adam? 1759–1833
attributed to BUNBURY, Charles Eighteenth century
*BUNBURY, Henry William 1750–1811 no.53
BURNET, James 1788–1816
BURNET, John 1784–1868
BURNEY, Edward Francis 1760–1848

CALLCOTT, Sir Augustus Wall 1779–1844
CALVERT, Charles 1785–1852
CALVERT, Edward 1799–1883
*CARWITHAM, Thomas active 1713–1733 no.4
CHANTREY, Sir Francis Legatt 1781–1841
*CHATELAIN, Jean Baptiste Claude c.1710–c.1758 no.11
CHINNERY, George 1774–1852
*CIPRIANI, Giovanni Battista 1727–1785 no.22
COLE, George Vicat 1833–1893
COLLET, John c.1725–1780
COLLINGS, Samuel exhibited 1784–1789
COLLINS, William 1788–1847
*CONSTABLE, John 1776–1837 nos.79–82
attributed to COOK, William, of Plymouth exhibited 1877–1879
attributed to COOPER, George exhibited 1792–1830
COOPER, Richard, Junior c.1740–c.1814
attributed to CORBOULD, Richard 1757–1831
COTMAN, John Joseph 1814–1878, or COTMAN, Miles Edmund 1810–1858
*COTMAN, John Sell 1782–1842 nos.85–6
COX, David 1783–1859
*COZENS, Alexander 1717–1786 nos.15–20
*COZENS, John Robert 1752–1797 nos.59–61
*CRISTALL, Joshua 1767 or 1768–1847 no.73
attributed to CROME, John 1768–1821
*CROTCH, Dr William 1775–1847 no.76
CROWE, Eyre 1824–1910
CUITT, George, Junior 1779–1854

DALL, Nicholas Thomas active 1748–1776
*DALTON, Richard 1715 or 1720–1791 no.14
attributed to DAMER, Anne Seymour 1748–1828
*DANBY, Francis 1793–1861 no.91
*DANCE, George 1741–1825 no.41
*DANCE-HOLLAND, Sir Nathaniel 1735–1811 nos.30–1
DANIELL, Thomas 1749–1840
DAVIS, Edward Thompson, of Worcester 1833–1867
DAVIS, John Scarlett 1804–1845
*DEACON, James c.1710–1750 no.12
attributed to DE LOUTHERBOURG, Philip James 1740–1812
DENHAM, John Charles exhibited 1796–1858
DEVIS, Anthony 1729–1816
DEVOTO, John active 1708–?1752
DE WINT, Peter 1784–1849
*DOWNMAN, John 1750–1824 nos.54–6
DOYLE, Richard 1824–1883
DUNKER, Balthazar Anton 1746–1807
DYCE, William 1806–1864

*EDRIDGE, Henry 1769–1821 no.74
ETTY, William 1787–1849

*FARINGTON, Joseph 1747–1821 no.50
FINCH, Francis Oliver 1802–1862

*FLAXMAN, John 1755–1826 nos.62–3
FOSTER, William active 1772–1812
FRANCIA, François Louis Thomas 1772–1839
FRIPP, Alfred Downing 1822–1895
FRIPP, George Arthur 1813–1896
*FUSELI, Henry 1741–1825 no.42

*GAINSBOROUGH, Thomas 1727–1788 no.23
*GARRARD, George 1760–1826 no.70
GEIKIE, Walter 1795–1837
GENT, G.W. exhibited 1804–1822
attributed to GILLRAY, James 1757–1815
GILPIN, Rev. William 1724–1804
*GIRTIN, Thomas 1775–1802 no.77
GLOVER, John 1767–1849
GOODALL, Edward Angelo 1819–1908
*GORDON, Lady (née Julia Isabella Levina Bennet) 1775–1867 no.75
GORDON, Julia Emily c.1810–1896
attributed to GORDON, Sir Harry Percy, 2nd Bt died c.1860
attributed to GORE, Charles 1729–1807
GOTCH, Thomas Cooper 1854–1931
GRAVELOT, Hubert François 1699–1773
*GRIMM, Samuel Hieronymous 1733–1794 no.27
GYLES, Henry c.1640–1709

HACKERT, Jacob Philippe 1737–1807
HADEN, Sir Francis Seymour 1818–1910
HAMILTON, William 1751–1801
HARDIE, Martin 1875–1952
HARDING, The Hon. Charles Stewart, Viscount 1822–1894
HARDING, James Duffield 1797 or 1798–1863
attributed to HARRIS, John active 1686–1740
attributed to HASSELL, John ?1767–1825
HAUGHTON, Matthew Eighteenth century
attributed to HAUGHTON, Moses, the Elder 1734–1804
*HAVELL, William 1782–1857 no.87
*HAYMAN, Francis 1708–1776 no.10
HAYTER, Sir George 1792–1871
attributed to HAYTER, John 1800–1891
HEAPHY, Thomas 1775–1835
HEARNE, Thomas 1744–1817
attributed to HEATH, Henry Nineteenth century
attributed to HENDERSON, John 1764–1843
HILLS, Robert 1769–1844
HOARE, Prince 1755–1834
attributed to HOARE, Sir Richard Colt 1758–1838
*HOGARTH, William 1697–1764 no.6
HOLLAND, James 1799 or 1800–1870
attributed to HOOK, Dr Richard 1635–1703
HOPPNER, John 1758–1810
HOWITT, Samuel 1756–1822
HUNT, William Henry 1790–1864
HUSSEY, Giles 1710–1788

style of IBBETSON, Julius Caesar 1759–1817
INCE, Joseph Murray 1806–1859
*INCHBOLD, John William 1830–1888 no.99
JACKSON, John 1778–1831
attributed to JACKSON, Samuel Phillips 1830–1904
JEFFERYS, James c.1751–1784
JONES, George 1786–1869
*JONES, Thomas 1742–1803 nos.43–5

KAISERMANN, Franz 1765–1833
KEENE, Charles Samuel 1823–1891

KINNARD, W. active 1807–1828
KNIGHT, John Baverstock 1788–1859

LABRUZZI, Carlo 1748–1817
LAING, J.S. active 1847
LAMBERT Eighteenth century
LANDSEER, Sir Edwin Henry 1803–1873
LAPORTE, John 1761–1839
LAROON, Marcellus, the Younger 1679–1772
LAURENCE, Samuel 1812–1884
LAW, Alfred Nineteenth century
LAWRENCE, Sir Thomas 1769–1830
LEECH, John 1817–1864
*LEIGHTON, Frederic, Lord 1830–1896 no.100
LENNOX, Lord William Pitt 1799–1881
LESLIE, Charles Robert 1794–1859
LEWIS, George Robert 1782–1871
*LEWIS, John Frederick 1805–1876 nos.94–5
LINNELL, John 1792–1882
LIVERSEEGE, Henry 1803–1832
LOCK, William, of Norbury, Junior 1767–1847
LOCKER, Edward Hawke 1777–1849
LONG, Amelia (Lady Farnborough) 1772–1837
LONG, Charles (Baron Farnborough) 1760 or 1761–1838
LOUDOUN, Edith Maud Rawdon-Hastings, Countess of 1833–1874

MACARTNEY, Carlile Henry Hayes 1842–1924
attributed to MACKENZIE, Frederick 1787–1854
MACLISE, Daniel 1806–1870
*MALCHAIR, John Baptist 1729–1812 no.24
MARKS, Henry Stacy 1829–1898
*MARLOW, William 1740–1813 no.38
MARSINGALL, A. Nineteenth century
MARTIN, Charles 1812 or 1820–1906
MARTIN, Elias 1739–1818
MARTIN, J., of Canterbury Nineteenth century
MARTIN, John 1789–1854
MASTERS, E. Nineteenth century
MAY, Phil 1864–1903
attributed to MERIVALE, Frances Nineteenth century
METHUEN, Lord 1886–1974
after MILLAIS, Sir John Everett, Bt 1829–1896
attributed to MILLER, James exhibited 1773–1791
MILLINGTON, Professor Eighteenth century
MONRO, Dr Thomas 1759–1833
MOORE, T. Eighteenth century
MORE, Jacob c.1740–1793
*MORTIMER, John Hamilton 1740–1779 no.39
*MULREADY, William 1786–1863 no.90
attributed to MUNN, Paul Sandby 1773–1845
MURRAY, Charles Fairfax 1849–1919
MUSGRAVE, George active 1872

NASH, Frederick 1782–1856
NASMYTH, Patrick 1787–1831
NATTES, John Claude c.1765–1822
attributed to NEALE, John Preston 1780–1847
NEWTON, Ann Mary (née Severn) 1832–1866
NEWTON, Sir William 1785–1869
NICHOLSON, Francis 1753–1844
NICHOLSON, Thomas Henry died 1870
NICHOLSON, Sir William 1872–1949

attributed to O'CONNOR, James Arthur 1792–1841
*OLIVER, Isaac c.1560 or 1565–1617 no.1
OLIVER, William c.1804–1853

OPPENHEIMER, J. Twentieth century
attributed to ORAM, W. active 1745–1777
ORPEN, Sir William 1878–1931
OTTLEY, William Young 1771–1836

attributed to PALMER, Samuel 1805–1881
PARROTT, William 1813–1869
*PARS, William 1742–1782 nos.46–8
PAYNE, William c.1776–c.1830
PERCY, Lady Susan Elizabeth ?1782–1847
PHILLIP, John 1817–1867
PICKERSGILL, Henry Hall 1812–1861
PLACE, Francis 1647–1728
POCOCK, Isaac 1782–1835
POCOCK, Nicholas 1741–1821
attributed to POLLARD, Robert, 1755–1838
*PORTER, Sir Robert Ker 1777–1842 no.83
attributed to POWELL, Joseph c.1780–1834
POYNTER, Sir Edward 1836–1919
PROUT, Samuel 1783–1852
PRYDE, James 1866–1941
PYNE, William Henry 1769–1843

attributed to RALPH, Benjamin active 1763–1770
attributed to RALSTON, John 1789–1833
REBECCA, Biagio c.1735–1808
REINAGLE, Ramsay Richard 1775–1862
attributed to REYNOLDS, Samuel William, Junior 1794–1872
RICH, Alfred William 1856–1921
*RICHARDS, John Inigo 1731–1810 no.26
RICHARDSON, Jonathan 1664 or 1665–1745
RICHARDSON, Thomas Miles, Junior 1813–1890
*RICHMOND, George 1809–1896 nos.97–8
RIGBY, Elizabeth (Lady Eastlake) 1809–1893
RILEY, John 1646–1691
ROBERTS, David 1796–1864
ROBSON, George Fennel 1788–1833
ROMNEY, George 1734–1802
*ROWLANDSON, Thomas 1756–1827 nos.67–9
RYLEY, Charles Reuben c.1752–1798

SAILMAKER, Isaac 1633 or 1634–1721
SALA, George Augustus Henry 1828–1896
*SANDBY, Paul c.1730–1809 no.25
SANDBY, Thomas 1721–1798
SANDERS, Ann active 1778
SCOTT, Frances (Lady Douglas) 1750–1817
*SCOTT, Samuel c.1702–1772 no.9
SEABROOKE, Elliott 1886–1950
SEBA, Albertus 1665–1736
*SERRES, Dominic 1722–1793 no.21
SERRES, John Thomas 1759–1825
SEYMOUR, James ?1702–1752
SHARPE, Charles Kirkpatrick 1781–1851
SHELLEY, Samuel 1750–?1808
SHERINGHAM, George 1884–1937
SHERLOCK, William P. c.1780–c.1821
SINGLETON, Henry 1766–1839
SKEAF, D. active 1803–1819
*SKELTON, Jonathan c.1735–1759 nos.32–3
SKIPPE, John 1741–1811 or 12
attributed to SMALLWOOD, William Frome 1806–1834
SMETHAM, James 1821–1889
attributed to SMIRKE, Robert 1752–1845
SMITH, John Raphael 1752–1812
SMITH, John Thomas 1766–1833
*SMITH, John 'Warwick' 1749–1831 nos.51–2

SOLOMON, Simeon 1840–1905
SPENCER, Lady Eighteenth century
*STANFIELD, Clarkson Frederick 1793–1867 no.92
STARK, James 1794–1859
STEVENS, Alfred 1817–1875
*STOTHARD, Thomas 1755–1834 nos.64–6
attributed to STRUTT, Arthur John 1819–1888
SUNDERLAND, Thomas 1744–1828
SUTHERLAND, Elizabeth Leveson-Gower, Duchess-Countess of 1765–1839

TASSAERT, Philippe Joseph 1732–1803
*TAVERNER, William 1700–1772 nos.7–8
attributed to TAYLOR, Richard exhibited 1775–1791
THOMSON, Rev. John, of Duddingston 1778–1840
THOMSON, W. active 1826
*THORNHILL, Sir James 1675 or 1676–1734 no.3
TILLEMANS, Peter c.1684–1734
TOLLEMACHE Nineteenth century
TOMKINS, William c.1730–1792
TONKS, Henry 1862–1937
*TOWNE, Francis 1739–1816 nos.34–7
*TRESHAM, Henry 1750 or 1751–1814 no.57
TROWER, Walter John, Bishop of Gibraltar c.1804–1877
attributed to TURNER, Daniel active 1782–1801
*TURNER, Joseph Mallord William 1775–1851 no.78
TURNER, W. Nineteenth century
TURNER, William, of Oxford 1789–1862
TURTON, M. Nineteenth century?

UNDERWOOD, Thomas Richard c.1772–1836
*UWINS, Thomas 1782–1857 no.88

attributed to VAN ASSEN, Benedict Anthony 1767–c.1817
*VANDERBANK, John 1694–1739 no.5
*VARLEY, Cornelius 1781–1873 no.84
VARLEY, John 1778–1842
VARLEY, William Fleetwood 1785–1856

WALE, Samuel ?1721–1786
WALKER, Anthony 1726–1765
WARD, James 1769–1859
WATSON, John Dawson 1832–1892
WEST, Benjamin 1738–1820
WESTALL, Richard 1765–1836
WHARNCLIFFE, Lady (née Caroline Mary Elizabeth Creighton) c.1776–1853
WHEATLEY, Clara c.1750–1838
WHEATLEY, Francis 1747–1801
*WILKIE, Sir David 1785–1841 no.89
WILLIAMS, Hugh William 1773–1829
WILSON, Andrew 1780–1848
*WILSON, Richard 1713–1782 no.13
attributed to WILSON, William A. exhibited 1801–1836
WINTOUR, John Crawford 1825–1882
WITHERINGTON, William Frederick 1785–1865
attributed to WOODWARD, George Montard c.1760–1809
WORLIDGE, Thomas 1700–1766
*WRIGHT, Joseph, of Derby 1734–1797 nos.28–9
attributed to WYCK, Jan 1652–1700
WYKEHAM ARCHER, J. 1808–1864